WILLIAM CALLOW R.W.S.

WILLIAM CALLOW
R.W.S.

Jan Reynolds

B T BATSFORD LTD, LONDON

Also by the Author:

The Williams Family of Painters

First published 1980

Printed in Great Britain by
Butler & Tanner Ltd, Frome and London,
for the publishers B T Batsford Ltd,
4 Fitzhardinge Street, London W1H 0AH
ISBN 0 7134 1438 3

Contents

The Illustrations

The Author and Publishers wish to express their gratitude to the owners of the original works for their permission to produce them as illustrations in this book and their names are given in the captions to the plates.

Illustrations nos. 8, 39, 40, 80, 98 are reproduced by gracious permission of Her Majesty the Queen.

Acknowledgments

MUCH of the information contained in this book is the product of original research, although it is necessary to acknowledge an important source of biographical material in *William Callow, R.W.S., F.R.G.S.*, an autobiography, edited by H. M. Cundall, published by A. and C. Black in 1908. Unless otherwise stated, first-person quotations by Callow are from this source.

Many art galleries, museums, libraries and individuals have answered my requests for information, but a particular acknowledgment is due to the following: The staff of the Central Library, Sheffield, for patient assistance with a wide range of queries and the County Library, Bakewell, for the loan of many specially obtained reference books, also J. Harris of the County Reference Library, Aylesbury, for most helpful provision of information relating to Buckinghamshire. I would also like to acknowledge assistance from John Sunderland, Witt Librarian, Courtauld Institute of Art; Lionel Lambourne, Victoria and Albert Museum; Royal Archives, Windsor Castle; J. Watson, Local History Librarian, Greenwich; K. K. Yung and Sarah Wimbush, National Portrait Gallery; Mary Haworth, British Library; Marylebone, St Pancras and City of Westminster Central Libraries; Central Library, Lowestoft; City Library, Liverpool; Castle Museum, Norwich; Bibliothèque d'Art et d'Archéologie, Paris; Goethe Institut, London; James Roundell; Cynthia Brown; Joyce Sims; Malcolm Fry; Donald Hoy; J. L. Naimaster; Elizabeth Gray; F. Gordon Roe; Maurice Callow; Nancy Arnott; C. R. Taylor; G. Schurer; John Munday, H. D. W. Lees; Janice Carpenter; Isobel Mordy; Andrea Rose; Clovis Whitfield; R. H. Wood; Stuart Leger; S. Loveridge; J. L. Wybrew; C. J. Baker; C. Staines.

A special appreciation is due to Paul Rich for his knowledgeable interest in my research and most kind and helpful assistance.

Acknowledgment is accorded to the Editor of *The Connoisseur* for permission to reproduce some references which first appeared in my article on William Callow, published in February 1978. As a result of this article, I was contacted by Constance K. Callow, widow of Leonard Callow, the great-great nephew of William Callow. I am most grateful to Constance Callow and her son, Simon Callow, for their invaluable help in allowing me access to family items and for giving permission for the illustration of the pencil sketches, water-colour drawings and photographs, which are acknowledged in this book to the possession of the Callow family.

Affectionate gratitude to my Mother for sharing the stress and frustrations in the life of a writer, as well as the joys and achievements.

Baslow, 1979 Jan Reynolds

Abbreviations used in the text:

A.W.S. – Associate of the Royal Water-colour Society

R.W.S. – Royal Water-colour Society

Cundall in italics in the text and catalogue refers to H. M. Cundall's book *William Callow, R.W.S., F.R.G.S.*, published by A. and C. Black, 1908.

CHAPTER I

Family Background, Childhood and the Early Years in France, 1812–1836

WILLIAM CALLOW, son of Robert and Elizabeth Callow, was born in Greenwich on 28 July 1812.

In 1380, a William Calewe or Calo was Lord of the Manor of Great Deane, now Mitcheldean, in Gloucestershire. Over three hundred years later his descendants were still living in the area, among them Benjamin Callowe, Vicar of Netherswell and Rector of Stow-on-the-Wold. An East Anglian branch of this family became established in Norfolk and Suffolk in the early eighteenth century. Adam Callow had a son, Daniel, who was agent to various landowners in Suffolk. Adam was a brother of John Callow (1730–1786) who lived in Lowestoft and was the grandfather of William Callow. There is no reason to disbelieve the family tradition that John Callow was a decorator at the Lowestoft porcelain factory, although evidence for this is not well documented in contemporary records.[1] Parish registers and family references show that the children of John and Sarah Callow included John (date of birth unknown), James, baptised in 1776, William in 1779 and Ann in 1781, but it was their youngest child, Robert, born in 1786, who was to be the father of William Callow. Mary Callow, daughter of Daniel Callow, lived in Greenwich after her marriage.

James Callow became a carpenter and builder with premises at the rear of what is now known as 13 St Margaret's Place, Lowestoft. In 1950–4, during restoration work on St Margaret's Church, Lowestoft, one of the old tie-beams was found to have the inscription 'J. Callow 1829'.[2] It was from this sturdy background of rural craftsmen that William Callow was to inherit his creative ability. John Callow, builder, who was the porcelain decorator's son, appears in a London directory at 13 St Mary Hill in 1811 and from 1811 to 1819 in Morden Street, Greenwich – a borough about five miles south-east of London, where family links had been established through the marriage of Mary Callow.

On 8 November 1812, William Callow was baptised at St Alfege's Church,

[1] a. From unpublished notes on the Callow family (1906) by James Callow, in possession of C. K. Callow.
b. *The Connoisseur*, September 1937, illustrated a jug, decorated with the name of 'Willm Callow, Ludham 1773', who was no doubt one of the Norfolk connections. The jug was not decorated by John Callow, although the article mentions that he was a painter at the Lowestoft factory.

[2] Information from an unpublished supplement to *The Chronicles of a Suffolk Parish Church, St Margaret's, Lowestoft* (1949) by permission of Hugh D. W. Lees. Entries from parish records supplied by the Central Library, Lowestoft. Note: Robert Callow was only six months old when his father died on 24 September 1786.

Greenwich, the occupation of his father being given as 'carpenter', although Robert Callow was later generally described as a builder or even 'gentleman'. John and Robert Callow appear to have been their own masters and occupied in a fairly substantial manner in their trade. In 1813, Robert Callow was contracted to superintend some alterations to the Norman Cross Barracks, near Shilton, in Huntingdonshire. One of the earliest recorded details of the childhood of William Callow relates to the French prisoners of war who were then being held in the barracks. These lonely exiles were much taken with the infant William, never realising how closely his future life was to be associated with their native France.

A daughter, Ann, had been born to Robert and Elizabeth Callow in 1811, but would seem to have died in infancy. They returned to Greenwich in 1814, where another daughter, Mary, was born in 1815 and baptised at St Alfege's Church on her first birthday, 27 September 1816. It was shortly afterwards that the Callows moved to London, where they lived in Camden Town (i.e. the St Pancras district). Their daughter, Sarah, was born in 1820.[3]

William Callow was a gentle, rather quiet child, who showed his potential talent at an early age, when he developed an exceptional enthusiasm for drawing. Robert Callow appears as a kind and sensible man, who wisely encouraged this gift in his son. He bought prints for him to copy and was responsible for placing him with the engraver, Theodore Fielding, who had advertised for a boy to assist with colouring prints and aquatint engraving. Theodore Henry Adolphus Fielding (1781–1851) was a son of T. N. Fielding (*see* Copley Fielding). He first exhibited in 1799, mostly water-colours, landscapes and architectural studies. He was later to be known almost exclusively for his work as an engraver, e.g. *A Picturesque Tour of the English Lakes*, published in 1821, *British Castles* in 1825, etc. Theodore Fielding wrote a number of instruction books, of which the most important was *The Art of Engraving* (1841).

William Callow was only eleven years old when he commenced with Fielding at 26 Newman Street, where he worked from 8 a.m. until 6 p.m. In the early days, he found the work and the hours tedious and tiring, but this first position was to have a formative influence on the entire pattern of his career. The Fielding studio was in the London artists' quarter, which had become centred on the St Marylebone district, after the founding of the Royal Academy in 1768. This expanded into Newman Street, which was purpose-built and had been a prestigious area for painters, sculptors and architects, but was now less fashionable and included the premises of gilders, wood-carvers, paper-stainers and other craftsmen. It was a densely populated district, but this lively maze of narrow streets was still not far from the fields and commons that stretched out beyond the city to the heathlands of Highgate and Hampstead.

Callow was to work at 26 Newman Street for the next two years, but he also continued to receive lessons in the evenings from a schoolmaster near his home, which can now be definitely identified as one of the houses in Tottenham Place, near Tottenham Court Road (approximately on the present site of Beaumont Place).

[3] Local and genealogical information from J. Watson, Local History Librarian (London Borough of Greenwich), Blackheath; Isobel Mordy, Association of Genealogists and Record Agents; and Rev. P. Malins, M.A.

During this period he was noticed by Anthony Vandyke Copley Fielding (1787–1855), an eminent name in English landscape water-colour painting. He was the second son of Theodore Nathan Fielding, a portrait and landscape painter, who practised chiefly in Lancashire and Yorkshire. Copley Fielding studied under John Varley, whose sister-in-law he married in 1806. He became an Associate of the Society of Painters in Water-colours (1810), a full member in 1813, Treasurer from 1817, Secretary in 1818, and he succeeded Joshua Cristall as President in 1831, holding that office for the rest of his life. Copley Fielding was a prolific contributor to the Society (e.g. in 1820, he sent 43 frames, presenting 56 works). Many of these were probably originally executed as demonstration pieces for his pupils. Copley Fielding lived for many years in Brighton and is thought to have made a considerable fortune from his work. He was best known for his coastal pieces, which were frequently noticed in the *Art Journal* (e.g. Society of Painters in Water-colours – No. 31 '... a coast view treated with an effect which this artist always paints with much success – that of a rolling sea, responding to a stormy sky....' – No. 22 '... the distance is airy and transparent ... the flat and edgeless tones of these drawings have very much the appearance of having been produced by watercolour over crayon....' – *Art Journal*, p. 201, 1847).

The benign influence of Copley Fielding was to be a constant factor in the career of William Callow. In 1824, a gift from this painter of a ticket for the exhibition of the Society of Painters in Water-colours made a vital impression on the young Callow. The sight of the work of Copley Fielding exhibited with that of such artists as John Varley (1778–1842) and David Cox (1783–1859) was a revelation and an inspiration.

In 1825, Callow was willingly articled to Theodore Fielding for eight years' instruction in water-colour drawing and aquatint engraving. The latter had now moved to Kentish Town and it was there that Callow worked with his fellow pupils, Charles Bentley and John William Edge, with whom he was to form lasting friendships. It seems likely that in some directions he gained more from their help than from the instruction of Theodore Fielding. The water-colourist Charles Bentley (1806–1854), son of a master carpenter and builder, was born in Tottenham Court Road, London. He not only had a similar family background to Callow, but had also started his career with Theodore Fielding, colouring prints, followed by an apprenticeship. Charles Bentley encouraged William to paint and was to have an influence on his work which can be recognised in some of the coastal pieces of the established Callow.

Theodore Fielding moved out to Croydon in 1827, in order to be nearer his appointment as Professor of Drawing at the Royal Military College, Addiscombe; Bentley and Edge had now completed their articles, but Callow returned to Newman Street where he continued under Thales Fielding (1793–1837). This engraver and water-colourist was the third son of T. N. Fielding. He exhibited with the Society of Painters in Water-colours from 1816 and was elected an Associate member in 1829. Thales Fielding exhibited 'Macbeth and the Witches' at the Paris Salon in 1824, where, with Constable, Bonington and Copley Fielding, he was amongst a group of English water-colourists whose work had attracted considerable attention.

Thales Fielding was later Professor of Drawing at the Royal Military Academy, Woolwich.

William was chiefly employed on engraving work, but all his spare moments, early and late, were still occupied with his own attempts at water-colour painting, as they had been for the past two years.

'Hampstead Heath – my first sketch in colours – W. Callow – about 1825' is illustrated (*no. 1*). It is fortunate that this later inscription (in the adult handwriting of Callow) has authenticated a uniquely vivid glimpse of the unformed style of William Callow, at the age of 13 or 14. He has seen the water-colours of John Varley, David Cox and Copley Fielding, and the manner of the trees and the treatment of the sky show that he has some conception of method, an awareness of the effect for which he is aiming, but the joy of this sketch is in the sense of immediacy and enthusiasm that it communicates. There is more genuine creativity in this small water-colour drawing than in many of the finished works of the established Callow. A general reference for this early experiment in colours is as follows: sky – blue grey, rather heavy; trees and grass – dirty yellow-green; tree trunks – dark reddish brown; foreground – light sand; path – mauve; buildings – muted brick red.[4] He wrote:

> I used to show my drawings to Copley Fielding, who gave me great encouragement and kind advice. At last when I had seven drawings I determined to try and sell them. I set off to a dealer's at the bottom of Holborn Hill, considering all the way how much I should ask for them and thinking how rich I should be on my return. I felt rather nervous on entering the shop, but on showing the drawings to the dealer, he agreed to my price viz. one guinea the lot. He would not, however, give me any money, but offered painting materials in exchange, which I took, being delighted at having, as I thought, made such a good bargain.

It is customary to refer to a work painted in water-colours as a water-colour drawing, owing to the fact that, previous to the nineteenth century, this classic English method was regarded very much as a branch of drawing. The term painting was reserved for work executed in oils. Water-colours accepted by the Royal Academy were considered of comparatively little importance – 'tinted' drawings to be hung with architectural studies or even consigned to the sculpture rooms. Many artists, knowing that their work was of originality and quality, greatly resented such an attitude and this led directly to the foundation of separate water-colour societies in the early nineteenth century. The Society of Painters in Water-colours was founded in 1804 and their first exhibition was held in 1805. Attendances and sales were so good that others were prompted to found the New Society of Painters in Miniature and Water-colours in 1807. This rival (and less exclusive) Society never attained the same status as the 'Old' Water-colour Society – the inevitable term by which this association was most often known.

It is an obvious misnomer to describe the work of certain water-colourists as drawings, but with reference to the water-colours of William Callow, the term can

[4] Colour notes: Henry E. Huntington Library and Art Gallery, San Marino, California.

be apposite. He was an artist whose talent was expressed in a constant fascination with the use of line. A study of his work gives an impression that he was someone who had special pleasure in the actual physical manipulation of pencil on paper and the deft movement of a brush. All his life Callow was never to lose his enthusiasm for the act of drawing and it is this inclination that strongly motivates his established style. Robert Callow could not have encouraged William in a more suitable direction when he placed him in Newman Street.

His early training under Theodore Fielding would include constant academic exercises in pencil drawing and perspective. As Martin Hardie[5] points out, even the mechanical work of tinting prints must have provided valuable experience in brush manipulation and control of wash. In conforming to a prepared outline he was also absorbing lessons in composition. The aquatint process on which Callow was employed was basically a form of etching, i.e. an intaglio process, the opposite of a relief method, such as a wood-cut. The effect is produced by covering a metal plate with a waxy substance and incising the required lines into the wax. The design is then eaten into the metal by immersion in an acid bath, repeating the process in some parts and 'stopping out' (with varnish) other areas. The finished plate is inked, wiped off, covered with damp paper and both are passed through a press, which forces the paper into the ink in the grooves. In the mezzotint process, the surface of the plate is first worked with a rocker, an instrument which produces a mass of small blurred dots. The design is effected by scraping off varying degrees of burr. Aquatints are a combination of the two methods, with diverse treatments being worked on a resinous ground, aiming to give the effect of a water-colour, often with the addition of hand colouring. It will be realised that the plates have to be worked in reverse, which means that any fault in the drawing of the engraving will be very obvious in a finished print, particularly in respect of vertical lines and the general balance of the composition. The same test of accuracy can be produced by looking at a drawing in a mirror (or even turning it upside-down). If the illustrations in this book are subjected to such a test, it will be observed just how confident and accurate a draughtsman Callow was to become – a capability which must have owed much to the demands of his work with the Fieldings.

In 1829, Robert Callow was superintending some building work at Windsor Castle. He would appear to have been employed in a rather senior capacity as he was freely able to show William all over the castle ('I was delighted with everything I saw and made some sketches there'). Between 1824 and 1840, the architect Sir Jeffrey Wyatville (1766–1840) was in charge of extensive alterations to the Upper Ward and Round Tower, Windsor, which might explain a subsequent link between Wyatville and the son of Robert Callow (*see* list of exhibits with the Norfolk and Norwich Fine Arts Association, page 236). Early in the same year, William spent some time with Theodore Fielding at his home in Coombe Lane, Croydon, assisting him with some work. 'I vividly remember my strolls along the quiet lanes where the nightingales sang, the lovely walks across the fields to Coombe Hurst, not then enclosed, and sitting on the hill to watch the sun go down, sometimes sketching but always with a feeling of peaceful enjoyment.'

[5] Martin Hardie, *Water-Colour Painting in Britain*, Vol. III (The Victorian Period), Batsford, 1968.

The Newman Street studio was closely associated with another Fielding studio in the Rue St Georges, Paris. This was run by Newton Smith Fielding (1799–1856), the youngest of the Fielding brothers, who had established a wide reputation in France as an engraver. He was also a water-colourist and had first been known in France as an animal painter. Subsequently, his original engravings included *Animals drawn on Stone* (Paris, 1829) and also landscape and marine pieces, e.g. *Subjects after Nature* (London, 1836).

Shortly after his return to London, William was surprised to be asked by Thales Fielding if he would be willing to go to France to assist with the engraving of a work on Switzerland for Jean-Frédéric d'Ostervald (1773–1850). Ostervald had come originally from Neuchâtel, Switzerland, to Paris, where he succeeded his brother as an art editor and publisher. He had published prints and other work engraved by both Thales and Newton Fielding (e.g. 'Entrance to the Port of Dunkirk' – an aquatint by Thales Fielding, after the work of R. P. Bonington). J.-F. d'Ostervald was obviously an important contact to whom it might be very worth while for the Fieldings to lend the services of one of their apprentices.

William Callow, not yet 17, with no experience of travel beyond Croydon, accepted the idea of Paris with an enthusiasm that was typical of the man he was to become, always fascinated with new places and people. All the known facts of the childhood and early life of Callow suggest a loving family background, which must have contributed to his obvious stability as an adult. Robert and Elizabeth Callow, whose children now included John (aged six), were surprised at the turn of events and anxious, but William had promised to be ready within a week and his family did all they could to prepare him for the new venture.

'On 16 July 1829, I left home alone for a foreign country. I scarcely knew a word of French and all I had to assist me were a few questions written on a sheet of paper, without answers.' William was seen off by his father and one of his sisters, from Charing Cross, and travelled all night by mail coach to Dover, where he had his first glimpse of the sea. Callow continued the long journey by steamer, coach and diligence. This last form of transport was to be frequently mentioned by Callow. A diligence was the Continental version of a stage coach, drawn by five horses, with a postillion, and only used for long distances. Callow finally reached Paris on 19 July, only to discover that Ostervald was away from home. He had now been travelling continuously for 72 hours, but with the aid of the French phrases, Callow made his own way to an hotel. Ostervald seems to have shown a rather casual attitude to his young assistant, but Callow was a person who rarely complained even when events went badly against him, as happened when he had only been in Paris for three days – and was still waiting for the return of Ostervald.

'I was asked if I would lend some money for a short time. I only possessed a five-pound note, which my father had given me; this I lent, but never saw it again. Consequently, I can truly say that I started life in Paris penniless. . . .' On 2 June 1829, the pound was worth 25 francs, 65 centimes – *Lutyen's Course of Exchange* (Paris quotations). Thus, one franc was approximately the equivalent of nine old pence and one farthing. Callow mentions 25 sous (about one shilling and a penny-halfpenny) as the price of a dinner and the very high cost of postage on a letter to England (one franc), which gives some idea of the amount involved in losing five pounds. It made a colourful reminiscence in later years, but there was never any real danger of Callow starving in the traditional artist's garret, because he was still apprenticed to the Fieldings, who would hardly have allowed this to happen. In fact, the living quarters arranged by Ostervald proved too far from his work and Callow was almost immediately offered accommodation with Newton Fielding in the Rue St Georges studio.

'As we lived near Montmartre we frequently walked there to enjoy the extensive view of the country near St Denis.' The first pencil drawing ($4\frac{3}{8} \times 6\frac{1}{2}$ in. – 110 × 165 mm) in the volume of sketches in the Victoria and Albert Museum is of Montmartre, inscribed 'August 2nd, 1829'. Callow had been in Paris for a fortnight.

It would be during the time that Callow was working for J.-F. d'Ostervald that he first met the Swiss engraver and water-colourist Sigismund Himely (1801–1872), whom he later mentions as a friend. Himely had worked in Neuchâtel and had been brought to Paris by Ostervald. Engravings by Himely appeared in *Voyage pittoresque dans la vallée de Chamouni et autour de Mont Blanc*, published by J. F. d'Ostervald, Quai des Augustins, Paris, in 1826. As this date is too early for Callow to have been involved with the project, it must be deduced that the work with Swiss connotations for which he was employed would be M. Sauvan, *Le Rhône*, published by Ostervald in 1829. Illustrations by both Himely and Callow were included in this publication.

By the end of 1829, his chief occupation appears to have been with Newton Fielding, whom he assisted with engraving and lithographic work, while still being endlessly fascinated with water-colours. Callow considered that his first real progress in water-colours had been as a result of watching the methods of Newton Fielding, but it is the work of Thomas Shotter Boys and Richard Parkes Bonington (1802–1828) that predominates as the most important of the influences on his general style. Bonington, born in Nottingham, was a pupil and protégé of Louis Francia (1772–1839), a French water-colourist who had worked in England and been influenced by Girtin. Bonington went to Paris in 1816, where Francia introduced him to Eugène Delacroix (1798–1863), who was of course a major figure of the Romantic movement in France. Delacroix and Bonington were friends, with a mutual enthusiasm for the possibilities of water-colour painting, but it was the remarkable talent of Bonington in this medium that was to have a vital influence in the French and British Schools of Painting. Thales Fielding had been in Paris (1823–4) and was also a friend of Delacroix, sharing an atelier with him in the Place de la Sorbonne. Thales and Newton Fielding had engraved aquatint plates for publication in *Excursion sur les Côtes et dans les Ports de Normandie* (Paris, 1823–5). Five of these plates were after the work of Bonington. It has sometimes been thought that Callow was a pupil of Bonington, but as the latter had died from tuberculosis in 1828, this is clearly impossible, although Callow would acquire some initial knowledge of the style of Bonington in the Fielding studios.

William Callow assimilated life in France with enthusiasm and was soon inscribing some of his sketches with the French names of days and months. He was determined to learn the language and decided that the best method would be to visit the theatre as often as possible. Callow was to acquire a fluent command of French and later translated one of the novels of Sir Walter Scott.

By early 1830, Fielding and Callow had moved to the Rue St Honoré. Paris was then the acknowledged centre of the art world, even though the city was frequently disrupted by political disturbance. The throne was occupied by Charles X, brother of Louis XVIII, who had become King when the monarchy was restored after the defeat of Napoleon in 1814. In the summer of 1830, Callow made two small pencil drawings of a group of buildings amongst trees inscribed 'Près le Bois de Boulogne. Jeudi. Juillet 22me' (Victoria and Albert Museum, E 856–857 – 1937). William Callow narrowly escaped death, only a few days after sketching this peaceful scene. His own description of events has a quiet immediacy:

> On the evening of 26 July we were suddenly startled by an uproar in Place Vendôme and on Fielding and myself rushing into the street to ascertain the cause, we found an excited mob crying out 'À bas Charles X!' The mob proceeded down Rue St Honoré, breaking all the lamps which were hung by cords across the street and also many of those in front of the shops and cafés, at which the shutters had not been closed in time. The streets were quickly deserted by the respectable part of the population and the entire city was in the hands of the revolutionists....

Barricades were erected by the mob and soldiers began firing indiscriminately. On 28 July, his eighteenth birthday, Callow was sent out by Newton Fielding to try to obtain some money that was owing from a picture dealer, living in the Rue de Roule. Callow never forgot the experience:

> ... after climbing over several barricades I could proceed no further and was compelled to return, having run a considerable risk for nothing....

After several days of living on bread, butter and currants, Callow and Fielding decided to chance going out in search of provisions. Both of them were obliged to don tricolour cockades, i.e. a badge worn on the hat. The tricolour had been the symbol of the French Republic since 1789.

> We were about to cross a street to get to the river Seine, when we were suddenly stopped by a bystander, which act doubtless saved our lives, for in the next moment a volley was fired down the street by a detachment of soldiers and the roadway was strewn with killed and wounded persons, lying in all directions. On arriving at the Quai we had quickly to dip behind a wall to avoid the bullets which were flying about. It was most unpleasant and I should never have ventured out had not Newton Fielding been so anxious that I should accompany him.

On 31 July, they again went in search of food and found the situation much changed. Charles X had fled, the troops had been driven out and the tricolour cockades were more than ever necessary.

> The weather was extremely hot, but the streets were still barricaded and not a vehicle was to be seen; the mob, which had returned from pursuing the

> soldiers, were dressed in uniforms, helmets, etc., taken from the killed and wounded – a sight it would be impossible ever to forget....

The 1830 Revolution was probably the most dramatic event of Callow's entire life, but it seems that he did not relish the excitement and detested the violence. Louis Philippe, Duc d'Orléans, accepted the Governor-Generalship of the Kingdom and Callow watched him addressing the people from the balcony of the Palais Royale. Printed leaflets were showered down into the crowd. Callow collected one of these and, with the tricolour cockade, kept it for the rest of his life.

France continued in turmoil. Louis Philippe was the son of the Duc d'Orléans who had been the younger brother of Louis XIV. Charles X had abdicated in favour of his nine-year-old grandson, the Duke of Bordeaux, but the liberal element refused to accept the child as King. Their choice was Louis Philippe, who agreed to take the throne shortly after the end of the 1830 revolution.

Because of this unsettled political situation, Fielding and Callow had returned to England, where arrangements were made for Callow to stay in Croydon with Theodore Fielding and assist with the colouring of prints, although such an occupation was now below his level of attainment. After six months, Callow was eager to return to France and started his journey on 2 February 1831. The sea at Dover was extremely rough and passengers had to be rowed out to the steamer in small boats (for an exorbitant charge of five shillings),

> On reaching the steamer we were hauled on board by the sailors; my shins were severely bruised, my Inverness cape flew over my head and a packet of sandwiches, with which my mother had thoughtfully provided me, dropped into the sea.

– a description that somehow conveys the impression of a rather precise young man.

Callow rejoined Newton Fielding in their old quarters in the Rue St Honoré. They were to move to several other addresses before settling once again in the Rue St Georges in 1832 (*see* list of works in the Henry E. Huntington Library, San Marino, California, page 201).

In 1831, William was still only 19 and very poor, sometimes reduced to hawking a drawing round the dealers in an attempt to obtain the price of a meal. Newton Fielding was unwell and unable to do much work. In consequence, Callow used to make drawings for Fielding which this artist would then touch up with 'a duck or some object'. Of necessity, Fielding was virtually selling drawings by Callow as his own work, although these were eventually to become known for what they were and be termed Callow–Fielding drawings.

It was in 1831 that William Callow first met the painter Thomas Shotter Boys (1803–1874), who was to have a most important influence on his style. Boys was an artist whose talent should have placed him in the forefront of English water-colourists, but he has only recently been given his due recognition (e.g. Centenary Exhibition, Nottingham University Art Gallery and Thos. Agnew and Sons, 1974; also *Thomas Shotter Boys* by James Roundell, published 1974).

The careers of Callow and Boys had a similar start, but a very different ending.

Thomas Shotter Boys had been born in the Pentonville district of London, the son of James Boys, who was rather less well placed than some of the other members of the Boys family. In 1817, Boys was apprenticed to George Cooke, the engraver, with whose son, E. W. Cooke, he was to form a firm friendship. Boys was first employed in France as an engraver and knew the Fieldings, which is probably how he came to meet Callow. He later devoted himself to water-colour painting and lithography. Boys was a topographical artist, who is best known for his picturesque and colourful city scenes, in which the buildings often have the appearance of a theatrical back-cloth, against which his lively figures and inimitable touches of detail provide a fascinating glimpse of the period. His water-colours combine a beautiful freedom of pure and luminous wash, with a crisp definition of line. His was a genuinely innovative talent, which he also used to make important advances in the technique of lithography, of which he was an outstanding master. The style of Boys was influenced by Girtin, Samuel Prout and his friend R. P. Bonington. T. S. Boys had been described as a pupil of Bonington, but as the two men were almost exact contemporaries, a more likely supposition is that Boys acquired his water-colour technique very much in the company of Bonington during a period when they lived in adjacent Paris studios. In later years, Callow did not appear to accept that T. S. Boys had been a friend of Bonington, as if this were somehow detrimental to the name of both artists. Not only did he refute a pupil/teacher relationship, but he also stated that there was only a mere acquaintanceship between them. This has puzzled art historians, because the known facts point to a real friendship and exchange of ideas between Thomas Shotter Boys and R. P. Bonington. A possible theory might be that Callow was rather strait-laced, while Bonington had lived more in the manner of *la vie de Bohème*. T. S. Boys may have felt that the subject of Bonington was better not discussed.

Boys had been very disturbed by the death of Bonington and it seems possible that his subsequent association with Callow filled a void in his life at that period.

> Boys used to ramble about the ancient part of the cité of Paris in search of old buildings to sketch. I often accompanied him and was encouraged by him to make sketches. In fact, I learnt a great deal of the theory and practise of art from Boys and it was from him I first acquired my taste for making water-colour drawings of picturesque old houses and churches, for which subjects I have a partiality ever since.

Callow was seeing Paris very much as it had been for centuries. 'The streets which were lighted with oil lanterns suspended down the middle by cords, were laid with cobblestones with gutters running down the centre and without any side pavements, there was no sanitation and whenever there was a storm the streets were flooded.' An extensive scheme of reconstruction was soon to be inaugurated by Louis Philippe, which radically altered the entire architectural character of Paris.

William Callow had arrived in Paris at a time when the climate of French art had been very much influenced by Bonington, whose name was already assuming the romantic aura so often associated with an artist who dies young. Water-colour had been almost abandoned in France at the end of the eighteenth century. A revival of interest in the medium must have been inevitable, but it was Bonington who had given it a fresh impetus which had an additional impact when introduced into the prevailing vacuum in French water-colour style.

The most direct influence from R. P. Bonington is to be found in the river scenes of Callow. 'Rouen' (*illustration no. 24*) is such an example. Bonington discarded most of the classical traditions of Claude and Poussin and was concerned with a more realistic treatment of landscape, which he portrayed with a unique brilliance of effect, a sparkling vigour and luminosity of tone. One of the marks of the style of Bonington is the 'broken wash', a sweep of firm colour deliberately placed to allow the texture of the paper and the ground tint to be revealed. In the work of some artists this would be mere accidentalism. In Bonington it was a display of calculated dexterity. He also developed an exceptional mastery of the technique of using paint on a very fine brush, pointing up details with lines as subtle as those of a pen or pencil. The technique was later used by J. D. Harding, T. S. Boys and others, but has often come to be particularly associated with William Callow. This calligraphic method would have an appeal for an artist who was so much concerned with exploring the intricacies of line, but in discussing characteristics from the style of Bonington, it should be emphasized that these were received very much as part of an influence which had already been assimilated into the style of T. S. Boys.

The style of Boys shows an elegant precision of treatment. Some of his lines were even ruled and James Roundell suggests that he may also have used the Graphic Telescope as an aid to accurate reproduction of topographical detail. This was invented by Cornelius Varley and produced the reflection of a view onto paper. It is possible that Callow may have experimented with the Graphic Telescope, if Boys was using the device, but his natural control of line was so accurate that there is no presumption of mechanical aids in the work of Callow. Boys, like Bonington, produced a sense of grandeur by means of careful effects of scale, which require skilful judgment of the angle of representation. But, within these disciplines, Boys displayed a creative flair for composition, using shadow to dramatic effect and paying great attention to small details. In the work of this artist the exact position of one of his crisp figures is more than a mere grace note; it is of vital significance in establishing the essential character of a drawing. All these aspects of style were emulated by Callow.

T. S. Boys and R. P. Bonington had been in the habit of exchanging ideas and each was known sometimes to have executed finished work from the sketches of the other. Callow partly continued this procedure, making a series of sketches from the bridges of Paris, and other views, as working references for Boys, who often paid him in books. Bonington had frequently not signed his work, which he considered should speak for itself. Some opinion has it that many drawings, emanating from France and attributed to Bonington, were actually by Callow. In the opinion of the writer, this theory has been overstated, in view of the fact that a study of the work of Callow shows him as a most enthusiastic inscriber and one who more often than not signed exhibited works. Certainly, the possibility of confusion does arise in the period when Callow was executing work for Boys and we can accept that some mis-attributions probably resulted, but not on the scale that is often believed. C. E. Hughes noticed a drawing, attributed to Bonington, but with a clearly impossible 1835 watermark – this work he thought to be by Callow. Attributions of early water-colours by Callow to Boys are inevitable, as Callow would not be expected to sign studies worked in conjunction with Boys and for his purposes. (*See* Castle Museum, Nottingham, page 188.)

'Paris from the Tuileries (L'Institut' (*illustration no. 2*) is a preliminary study which Callow executed for Boys in 1831. The scene has a similarity to a Bonington water-colour of the same subject – 1828. There is a tracing in the British Museum by T. S. Boys of this sketch by Callow, in almost exact detail. Boys retained the colour notes and even the same figures on the parapet, but slightly revised the architecture on the left, because Callow made a note that it was not steep enough. In 1833, Boys executed a finished water-colour of this subject, based on the general outlines of the Callow sketch. This drawing and *illustration no. 3* are full of minute observations, which make a rewarding study with the use of a magnifying glass, revealing the exact angle of the head on a statute, or the position of a chimney on the skyline, while more transient features are also suggested and noted, such as 'wood floating' and other pencilled information referring to the figures in which Callow would know that Boys would be interested (e.g. 'a great number of people looking at the Honoré people', referring to the figures on the parapet). In making such studies, Callow would be consciously attempting to interpret a scene in a manner suitable to the style of Boys. This had the effect of introducing some of these characteristics into his own work. 'Rue de Rivoli, Paris' (*illustration no. 6*) relates to this period. The buildings to the left of the drawing are represented from a typical Boys angle, as is the perspective of the open foreground, leading the eye into the composition. The foreground also has a suggestion of the water-colour method of Bonington, but the general influence is directly from Boys. This influence, however, is wholly absorbed into a strong impression of individual confidence, which is displayed in the fluent yet beautifully controlled brush-work, so deftly pointed up with touches of keenly observed detail. The natural talent of Callow was now very evident.

In sketching 'Church of St Eustache', 4 September 1831 (*illustration no. 4*), Callow was exploring his new interest in such buildings, which had been fostered by his aquaintance with Boys. He was to use this sketch 18 years later, as the basis of a water-colour with the title 'A Street Market in Paris with the Church of St Eustache beyond', signed and dated 1849 (*Sotheby's catalogue*, plate X, 20 April 1972). The topographical details and composition closely followed the illustrated sketch, although the area of blank wall end was raised and narrowed and the centre foreground filled with a bustle of figures. The vague figure (right) disappeared, but his broom remained propped against the wall. Although 'Notre Dame' (*illustration no. 5 fig. A*), a preparatory drawing on tissue, has been conveniently placed with similar subjects in Paris, dated 1831, the handling of the figures points to this being executed at a rather later date. Callow was now making other friendships and contacts which were to provide a stimulating influence on his career. It was probably towards the end of 1831 that he met Baron Henri Joseph François de Triqueti (1804–1874), the distinguished French sculptor, painter and writer on art, who had a studio in one of the houses where Callow lived. Triqueti exhibited at the Paris Salon from 1831 to

1861, where he was to be awarded a First Class Medal for Sculpture in 1842. In 1841, Ferdinand, Duc d'Orléans, the eldest son of Louis Philippe, was thrown from a phaeton and killed. Triqueti was the sculptor for his tomb in the Chapelle St Ferdinand. Queen Victoria's later admiration for this work led to her commissioning Triqueti as sculptor and mural decorator for the Albert Memorial Chapel at Windsor.

Triqueti had married the youngest daughter of the Reverend Edward Forster, who had been Chaplain to the British Embassy from 1818 to 1828. Forster was a somewhat unusual cleric who published several books of engravings, including *The British Gallery of Engravings* (1807–13). After the death of the Reverend Forster his widow, who was a daughter of Thomas Banks, R.A., remained in Paris, where she was a well-known figure in the art world, giving weekly receptions that were attended by many French and English artists. Callow became friendly with Triqueti and as a result was asked to the home of Mrs Forster, where he was soon a frequent visitor. A pencil sketch, inscribed 'Day before Mrs. F. Boulevard Pigalle, Paris, Mercredi, 19, 1832' (Victoria and Albert Museum, E 888 – 1937), must be a reference to the date of a visit to Mrs Forster. One might speculate on the notable figures that Callow may have encountered at these receptions: almost certainly Delacroix and probably Fréderic Chopin, who was a friend of Delacroix. This was the Paris of the painters Ingres and Eugène Isabey, of the novelists Alexandre Dumas and George Sand, of the composer Hector Berlioz and his English wife, the actress Harriet Smithson.

In 1833, Newton Fielding married and returned to England. During that year, Callow had officially completed his apprenticeship, although the contract never seems to have been given a very formal interpretation. William Callow was now on his own in Paris, but his association with the Fieldings continued to have an important background influence in establishing him as an independent name. The friendships with Charles Bentley and Thomas Shotter Boys, the introduction to the work of Bonington, with overtones from Girtin, Francia and the world of Delacroix, had all resulted from his life with the Fieldings.

Callow lived with Sigismund Himely for some months, assisting him with copperplate engraving, but in May 1833, he and Boys took an atelier at 19 Rue de Bouloi, an address in Paris not far from the Louvre Museum. Callow was obviously working extremely hard and soon accumulated enough money for a trip to England. While on this visit he not only made a sketch of Pall Mall and some views of Richmond for Boys, but also carried out a slightly more unusual commission. For some reason, Boys wanted to give John Constable the present of a Turkish scimitar. Callow was asked to deliver this somewhat unlikely gift and was much gratified at having an opportunity to meet the most revered name in English landscape painting. There is no record of this incident in the literature on Constable, but the theory has been put forward that the sword could have been one of the studio properties of Bonington.[6] As such, it would have value in the eyes of Boys, which he may not

[6] A Turkish sword appears in sketches by Bonington and Delacroix of the Count of Palatiano in the costume of a Palikar (Professor Alastair Smart, catalogue of the Thomas Shotter Boys Centenary Exhibition, Nottingham University).

have realised would not be so apparent to others. While he was in London (in order to deliver another Boys gift) Callow called on George Cooke (1781–1834), the engraver, who was then living at Albion House, Barnes Terrace, Barnes. On this occasion, he also met Edward William Cooke (1811–1880), who wrote in his diary for 4 July 1833: 'Callow and W. J. Cooke came to dinner at 4 . . .'[7] W. J. Cooke (1797–1865) was a nephew of George Cooke and had married Mary Boys, sister of T. S. Boys. Callow appears to have been made very welcome by the Cookes. He and E. W. Cooke exchanged some drawings and Callow was exceptionally pleased with a gift from George Cooke of several proofs from his Turner plates. These would be from *Picturesque Views on the Southern Coast of England* from drawings principally after Turner, engraved by W. B. Cooke (elder brother of George), G. Cooke and several other prominent engravers – published by John and Arthur Arch, London, 1826.

Callow greatly admired the work of Turner, whose style he had first encountered in the form of engravings. During the early life of Callow, literally thousands of mezzotints and line engravings were published, after the work of Turner, either as separate prints or illustrations in books and also in popular annuals such as *The Keepsake*. Some of the prints which Robert Callow provided for William to copy would almost certainly be after the work of Turner. By the time that George Cooke gave Callow the Turner 'pulls' he had developed an enthusiastic reverence for the work of this artist. About 1836, Callow acquired his own copies of *Picturesque Views on the Southern Coast of England* and also *Picturesque Views in England and Wales*, which he appears to have used as teaching manuals ('I was always studying them in those days and they were a great help to me in every way'). In studying *Picturesque Views* he was extending his knowledge in a familiar field. Callow understood the technique which had been required to produce these engravings. The subtle delicacy of line and organisation of masses in the Picturesque series must have frequently influenced Callow to see the subject possibilities of a landscape, in terms which might have been visualised by Turner. He was also to follow in the early Turner tradition of travelling and sketching from nature, collecting large quantities of detailed topographical material from which he worked up his finished water-colours.

'Cloisters at Royaumont', dated 21 August 1833 (*illustration no. 9*), is one of a series of water-colour sketches executed while Callow was visiting that area (about 20 miles from Paris) with a friend who is described in the autobiography as a 'Mr. Sweiter'. Later references to Baron Schweiter (also spelt by Cundall as Schweitzer) suggest that his companion at Royaumont was probably the painter Baron Ludwig Auguste Schwiter (1805–1899), who was a friend of Delacroix (in whose will he was left a painting by Watteau and also an unfinished work by Theodore Fielding). Callow undoubtedly came to know Baron Schwiter (see later references in text). In 1833, Callow and friend walked part of the way to Royaumont, where they were to stay with some people called Vandermere. 'Royaumont Park', included in works by Callow in the Eton College collection,[8] relates to this visit (photograph ref. number 632/14/3, Witt Library, Courtauld Institute of Art), as do ten pencil sketches in the

[7] Unpublished diaries of E. W. Cooke (Cooke Collection). Information from John Munday.

[8] Eton College has a collection of 10 water-colours by Callow, from the collection of the late Alan D. Pilkington, donated between 1957 and 1967 and by bequest in 1973. (Nos. 47–56, Courtauld Institute of Art handlist.)

Victoria and Albert Museum. 'The Refectory of the Abbey, Royaumont' is dated 31 August 1833 (ref. E926–1937). Callow was obviously fascinated with the picturesque quality of these ruins. He was also charmed with the company of the Vandermeres and the Marquis de Bellisin, who lived nearby. They were 'invited to make day excursions with him in the neighbourhood and to dinner in the evenings with music and dancing afterwards. Altogether this was a most enjoyable visit.' Callow had a natural ease of manner that made him readily accepted in any society. People were said to have liked him at sight and chance acquaintances frequently became life-long friends. It is therefore somewhat puzzling that his relationship with Boys does not appear to have continued into later years.

T. S. Boys left the Rue de Bouloi atelier in 1834, for reasons that are not known, although the date of his marriage is thought to have been about this time. It is possible that the two men were not very compatible studio companions. Boys was now entering a phase of intensely innovative lithography, which is a cumbersome craft requiring space for stones, presses, acid pans, etc., and often producing a decidedly stained and untidy appearance in the artist. This was not the style of Callow. Once he was established, there is no evidence that he ever again touched an engraving plate or lithographic stone. His immediate ambition was to teach, an occupation which Boys always disliked.

Callow now assumed sole responsibility for the atelier and started a drawing class, which was at once a success. His lessons soon attracted members of the French nobility to the studio of the handsome young English artist, whose manner they must have been pleasantly surprised to find so entirely without any element of the 'farouche'. His pupils were to include the Comte de Faucigny, Viscomte de Rouget and his cousin, Comte de Nicholai, and many others. The fees charged by Callow were quite moderate, as most of the cultured French families were now much less wealthy than before the Revolution – but Callow would realise that the very fact of their patronage was an important asset. A form of barter in lieu of fees for lessons and drawings was also sometimes used. Callow exchanged several of his drawings and sketches with Comte de Faucigny for an elegant Louis XIV clock and with a Mademoiselle Naudet for old pistols, swords and various antiques, with which to decorate his atelier. In five years in France, William Callow had progressed from an apprentice engraver to a fashionable drawing master, with his own establishment.

Thomas Shotter Boys was indirectly responsible for a water-colour drawing by Callow, which was to prove a turning point in his career. A sketch that he had done in England in 1833, while making topographical studies for Boys, was later the basis of a highly successful work which Callow exhibited as No. 267 'Vue de pont de Richmond en Angleterre' at the Paris Salon in 1834.

The award of gold medals to Copley Fielding, Constable and Bonington at the Paris Salon in 1824 had stimulated a new French interest in English water-colourists. It was fortunate for the young Callow that such a trend should have occurred at the start of his own career. *Lettres sur le Salon de 1834* (published Paris, Delaunay, 1834, p. 401) commented:

Un autre Anglais (son nom du moins nous le fait croire) M. Calow [sic], dans une,

> 'Vue prise de la terrasse de Saint-Germain', *et une autre du* 'Pont de Richemont', *se montre coloriste vrai et dessinateur exact; il y a de l'air et beaucoup d'effet dans ces deux morceaux.*

The critic may not have been familiar with the name of Callow, but it is obvious that he had registered the character of his work very perceptively. It should be noted that it was for a water-colour with a similar title ('Vue du Richmond') that Callow was to be awarded a Gold Medal from the Paris Salon in 1840 – not for the 1834 exhibit as is sometimes stated. The 1840 medal (Third Class) was awarded in the section for pastels, water-colours and miniatures and was included in the general catalogue no. 215 'Vues diverses' (*see* list of exhibits at the Paris Salon, page 229). The Paris Salon exhibitions brought Callow into close contact with the work of Delacroix, Ingres, Horace Vernet, De la Roche, Descamps, Gudin and Eugène Isabey. It is possible to discern a feeling from the latter in some of the sea-pieces of Callow, particularly those on the coast of Normandy, a favourite subject of Isabey, in the tradition of Bonington.

Shortly after the opening of the 1834 exhibition, Callow was visited by an equerry of King Louis Philippe, who enquired if he would be willing to give lessons in water-colour painting to the second son of the King, who was known as the Duc de Nemours (1814–1896). Callow attributed the opportunity to the success of his Salon exhibits, which no doubt provided the initial impetus, but it appears to have been subsequently overlooked by Callow and others that Newton Fielding during some of the time that he was in France is also recorded as having been drawing master to the family of Louis Philippe (Thieme and Becker, *Allgemeines Künsterlexicon*, 1968). If this is so, his connection with the Fieldings would again recommend Callow, as would the fact that he was English. The Orléans family had many links with England and the British throne, including a cousinship between Queen Victoria and Louis Philippe, through their mutual ancestor, Frederic V, Elector Palatine of Bohemia, In 1832, Princess Louise (1812–1850), the eldest daughter of Louis Philippe, had married King Leopold of the Belgians, the maternal uncle of Queen Victoria. She was exceptionally fond of Leopold and Aunt Louise. The Duc de Nemours, whom Callow was engaged to teach, was later to marry Princess Victoria of Saxe Coburg-Gotha, first cousin to both Queen Victoria and Prince Albert.

The first lesson took place on 12 March 1834, at the Tuileries Palace, in a room overlooking the gardens. Callow was then 21 and his pupil was 20. In spite of being nervous (and afraid that his French was still imperfect) the lesson went well. Louis Philippe was known as 'The Citizen King' and was often ridiculed for his homely ways, but an equally unassuming manner in his family was welcomed by Callow, who soon felt at ease. After Callow had given only a few of these lessons, he was informed by the Duc de Nemours that his sister, Princess Clémentine d'Orléans, also wished to receive instruction in water-colour painting. The Princess usually took her lessons in a room in the Tuileries Palace, with a view of the Place de Carrousel. A lady-in-waiting was always present.

William Callow was to give lessons to Princess Clémentine, twice a week, nearly all the year round, for the next seven years. If one considers that the total number of lessons probably approached 600 (allowing for '*vacances*') it becomes evident that the personality of Callow must have been as vital a factor as the quality of his tuition. Callow accorded a careful priority to the demands of these lessons, which always took place at the somewhat surprising hour of 8 a.m. If the Princess was staying outside Paris, in one of the royal residences at St Cloud or Neuilly, then Callow had to get up at 6 a.m. in order to walk to the latter place in time for a lesson. He did this on one cup of tea, English-fashion, summer and winter, breakfasting on his return. After each lesson, Callow was given an order for twenty francs by the lady-in-waiting. In the period 1829–34, the sterling equivalent of one franc had varied very little, but remained approximately ninepence farthing (*Tables of Exchange*, James Laurie, 1845). The average fee received by Callow for each lesson would be equal to fifteen shillings and sixpence.

> And when the orders reached twenty, I presented them at the Bank and received the money owing, five hundred francs, in five-franc pieces, which I carried away in a bag.

Only three years before, Callow had considered himself fortunate to find a ten-sous piece in the street (above five old pennies) to make up the price of a meal.

Callow also gave some lessons to Prince Francis Ferdinand, Duc de Joinville, third son of Louis Philippe. In later life he was to recall his association with the French royal family as one of his happiest memories. 'I cannot speak too highly in praise of this charming family; they were always amiable, kind and anxious to do whatever they thought would give me pleasure.' The Orléans may not have been a very typical royal household, but neither was Callow an ordinary drawing master.

His work was now selling well and was in demand by the French dealers. In the 1908 autobiography, Callow states that he received 40 francs for a water-colour drawing in 1834 and considered it a good price at that time, but as this was only the equivalent of one pound, ten shillings and ten pence, it must be taken as a misprint for 400 francs (just under 15 guineas).

It was in 1834 that the painter John Frederick Lewis (1805–1876) called at the atelier in order to see Boys, not realising that the latter was no longer there. Lewis, who had been living in Spain, was a prominent but controversial figure in the Society of Painters in Water-colours. He was immediately impressed with the quality of Callow's drawings and strongly advised him to submit some work to the Society, with an application to become an Associate. But, in spite of his growing reputation in France, Callow still regarded the 'Old' Water-colour Society as the revered province of Copley Fielding and similar artists and quite beyond his sphere. Consequently he did not take the advice of J. F. Lewis. The latter remained in France for some time and Callow posed for him on several occasions – once for a drawing of his ear and also wearing a cap of Zumalcarrequi, a Spanish grandee.

'View of the River, Rouen', a pencil sketch inscribed 'Mai 30/35' (Victoria and Albert Museum, E 978 – 1937) relates to the start of a walking tour, on which

Callow was accompanied by John Edge and an engraver named Larbarlestier. Edge was now established as a topographical and marine painter. Callow wrote:

> From thence we walked by the Seine to Jumièges, where there is a most interesting ruin of an old abbey situated beside the river. The next day we followed the right bank of the river to Quillebœuf [*illustration no. 10*]. We proceeded to Honfleur, where we made some sketches and the next day crossed to Havre [3 June 1835]. Larbarlestier left us and Edge and myself took the steamer to Southampton. After touring round the foot of the Isle of Wight, we went to Portsmouth [*illustration no. 11*] and walked to Winchester, making a large number of sketches on the way and finally took the coach to London. This tour proved to be a very pleasant one and in this manner I was able to make sketches of many interesting places unfrequented by travellers.

Sketches in possession of the Callow family show that Callow was in Yarmouth on 8 July 1835. 'I afterwards went on a visit to some relatives in Lowestoft, my father's birthplace.' One of these connections would be his uncle James Callow, the carpenter and builder, and probably also his uncle John Callow (formerly of Greenwich), who appeared in the Lowestoft parish census for 1831. Callow sketched the lighthouse and Rotterdam House, Lowestoft, on 9 July 1835. The date on 'Stern View of Two Fishing Boats on the Beach at Lowestoft' (*illustration no. 26*) should not be taken as having been altered from 1835. Callow was again in Lowestoft with his brother John, in 1839. Maurice Callow, whose grandfather was a cousin of William Callow, is in possession of 'Lowestoft Fishing Boat), signed and dated 1839. (Exhibited Victoria, Australia, 1976. *See* Chapter IV, note 4.)

In 1835, when he returned to France, Callow took with him his younger brother, who was then 13 years old and had no inclination towards art, but wanted to be a sailor. William Callow had different ideas and was determined to make an artist of his brother. Immediately following the Lowestoft sketches is one of a jetty, inscribed 13 July, Calais, 1835, on which there is also an enlarged detail of the fixing of a rope pulley. Callow was probably trying to interest the eye of young John in this nautical detail. John Callow was soon established as part of the ménage in the Rue de Bouloi. (*See* pages 93–4 for a summary of the career of John Callow, A.W.S.)

Callow now had so much work on hand that he refused the offer of an appointment as artist to a scientific expedition round the world. One of his many commissions at this time was for a series of drawings of deep sea-fishing for his friend, the engraver, Sigismund Himely. (*See* sepia engravings of 'Whale Fishing', etc., in the British Museum – listed on page 169.)

But, in 1836, William Callow did make time to undertake his most ambitious walking tour, leaving John Edge in charge of the atelier. As a child, Callow had never even played a game of cricket, but he was to prove a man of exceptional physical stamina. Extracts from his diary vividly describe the events of the tour and also bring into revealing focus the personality of William Callow.

CHAPTER II

Diary of a Walking Tour, 1836

I CANNOT do better at this point than quote verbatim the diary which Callow kept of his walking tour in 1836:

June 6:
We, i.e. myself, a German friend named Soherr, and his dog, left Paris by diligence at eight o'clock in the evening for Chartes (*colour plate*) and the weather being fine, we had a pleasant journey.

June 7:
A fine view of the town with the cathedral on a hill as we approached Chartres at six o'clock in the morning. A man on the diligence recommended us to some lodgings, which turned out to be a shoemaker's. We could not see the interior of the cathedral as the roof had unfortunately been burnt three days previously, so visited the churches of St Pierre and St André, where we found a great many curious monuments.

June 8:
At eleven o'clock we started off with our knapsacks and walked to Bonneval, a distance of seven leagues,[1] arriving there in the evening, very tired and weary, as we were not accustomed to long walks. After dinner we visited the fourteenth-century church; we were obliged to go there in our slippers as we were so footsore.

June 9:
After breakfast I made some sketches whilst Soherr, who was an architect, took some measurements of the church. We then started for Châteaudun, reaching that place at five o'clock. We visited the old château, surmounted by a fine tower of the sixteenth century. In the evening we started off again, and slept in an auberge on the roadside.

June 10:
After starting at half-past seven in the morning we reached a village, where we had breakfast, and, as the weather was so warm, we rested here till the evening, when we continued our walk to Orléans, where we arrived in the dark. We tried to put up at the Hôtel de la Boule d'Or, but because we were wearing blouses, on account

[1] One league = 2 miles 743 yards (3.9 km)

of the dust, they refused to admit us, so we went to the Hôtel de France, where we fortunately ran across an English friend, named Talbot, who had previously arranged to meet us at Orléans and accompany us on the tour.

June 11:
Visited the Cathederal, built by Henry IV, and made some sketches of the river Loire, which with its fine bridge and boats with large white sails, was very picturesque.

June 12:
Quitted Orléans at 7.30 a.m. and walked beside the Loire to the village of Meung, where we breakfasted; afterwards Talbot and I smoked and rested outside the auberge, whilst Soherr made some measurements of the church. I had placed a wine-glass on the ground, and an old woman accidentally broke it. The daughter of the house thereupon roundly abused her and made her cry, all because of a trifling damage of two sous, which I paid. Afterwards we visited the church, and found it to be nothing remarkable; but this was the way with Soherr all the time we were together; he made drawings of the worst and left the best. In the afternoon we continued beside the Loire to Beaugency [*illustration no. 13*]. Passing through a village we saw a procession carrying the Host, it being a fête day; the villagers had hung up sheets against the walls for the want of tapestry. I did not expect to see so much religious devotion so near Paris. The pretty town of Beaugency was also en fête; we arrived too late to see the procession, but the sides of the houses were still covered with 'toile' and the streets strewn with flowers. In the evening we went on the fine old bridge, with twenty-five arches over the river and saw a beautiful sunset effect, but it was too dark to sketch it.

June 13:
Arose at 6 a.m. to make a sketch from the river; afterwards set off along a road beside the Loire, which is here very beautiful, to St Laurent, where we breakfasted, and then we went on to the Château de Chambord, belonging to the Duc de Bordeaux.

June 14:
Got up early and visited the Château, examining every part of it, even going on the roof for the sake of the view; the house contains a very curious double spiral staircase. After early breakfast we walked to Blois[2] (four leagues) where we arrived about midday and put up at the Hôtel de la Tête Noire. Visited the curious old château, which is now the barracks, also the churches of St Nicholas and St Louis, and afterwards made two sketches of the picturesque town from the river. On returning to our hotel we were accosted by a gendarme, who demanded our passports in a very insolent manner. I informed him that if he would come to the hotel we would produce them. He then became very abusive, and said that foreigners ought to have

[2] 'Blois' – pencil sketch ($4\frac{1}{4} \times 10\frac{5}{8}$ in. – 107×269 mm) dated Juin 14.36. (Victoria and Albert Museum, E 991 – 1937)

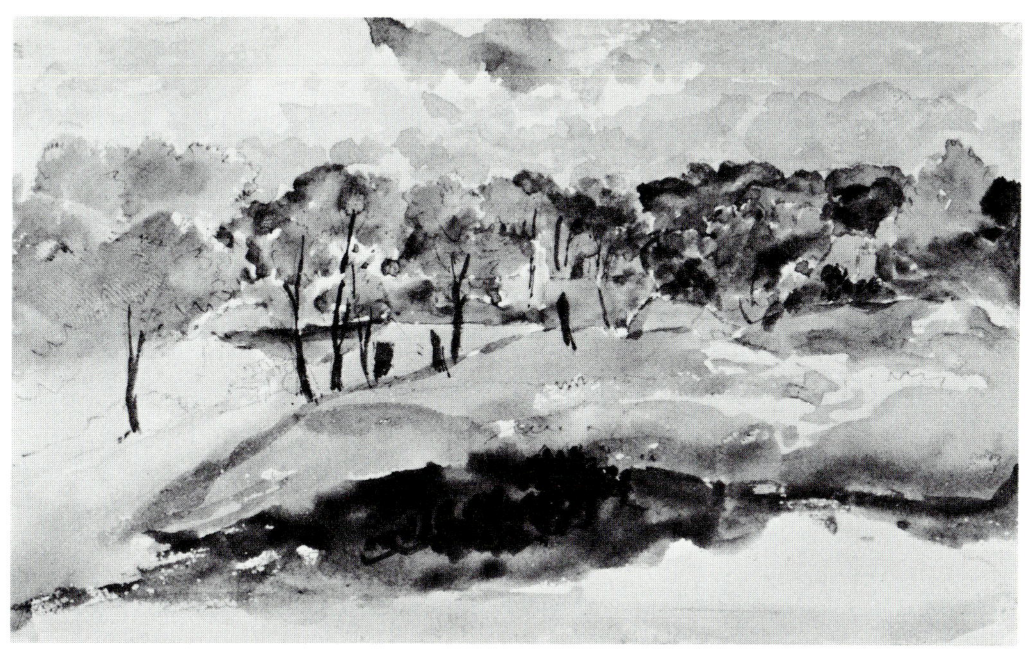

1. 'Hampstead Heath' Water-colour ($5\frac{1}{2} \times 3\frac{1}{2}$ in. – 140×89 mm)
Inscribed below the drawing in the artist's adult hand: *Hampstead Heath my first sketch in colours – W. Callow about 1825*
Collection: Henry E. Huntington Library and Art Gallery, San Marino, California, USA

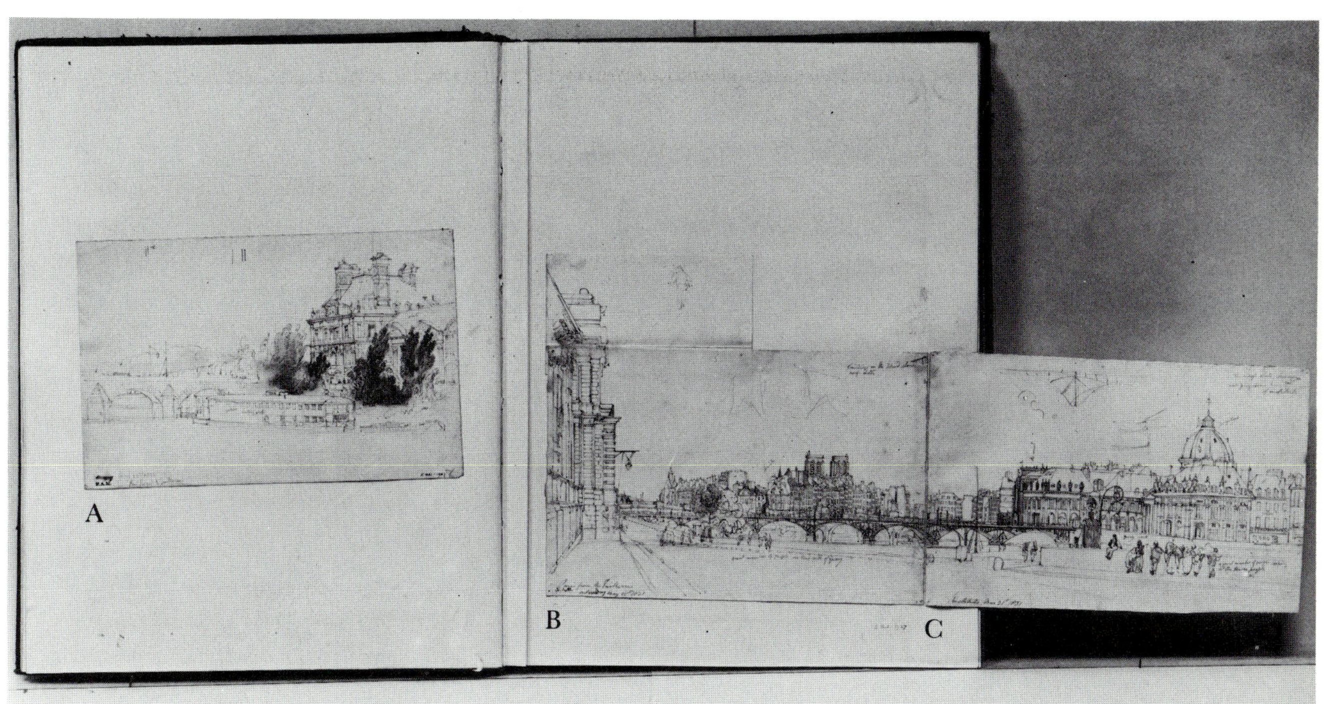

2. Figure A 'Pont Royale and the Tuileries' Pencil 22 May 1831 (left) ($6\frac{1}{2} \times 9\frac{3}{4}$ in. – 165×248 mm)
Figure B 'Paris from the Tuileries' Pencil 28 May 1831 (centre)
Figure C 'L'Institut' 31 May 1831 (right)
Inscribed with colour notes. Size (over two sheets of sketchbook) ($9\frac{1}{8} \times 19\frac{1}{2}$ in. – 232×496 mm)
Collection: Victoria and Albert Museum, Crown Copyright

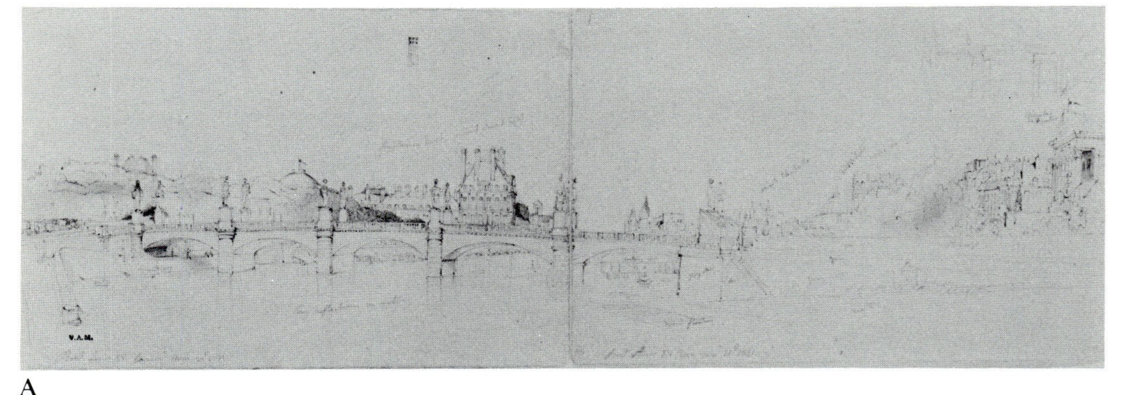

A

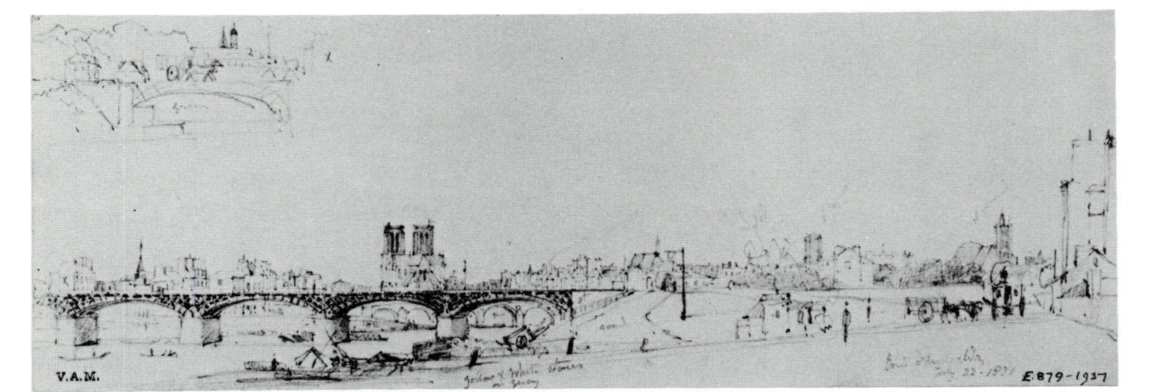

B

3. Figure A 'Pont de la Concorde, Paris' Pencil ($6\frac{1}{8} \times 18\frac{3}{4}$ in. – 156 × 476 mm)
Inscribed: *Pont Louis XV Samedi Mai 21. 1831*
Figure B 'Pont d'Austerlitz, Paris' Pencil ($3\frac{1}{2} \times 10\frac{1}{8}$ in. – 89 × 257 mm)
Inscribed: *July 22 1831*
Collection: Victoria and Albert Museum, Crown Copyright

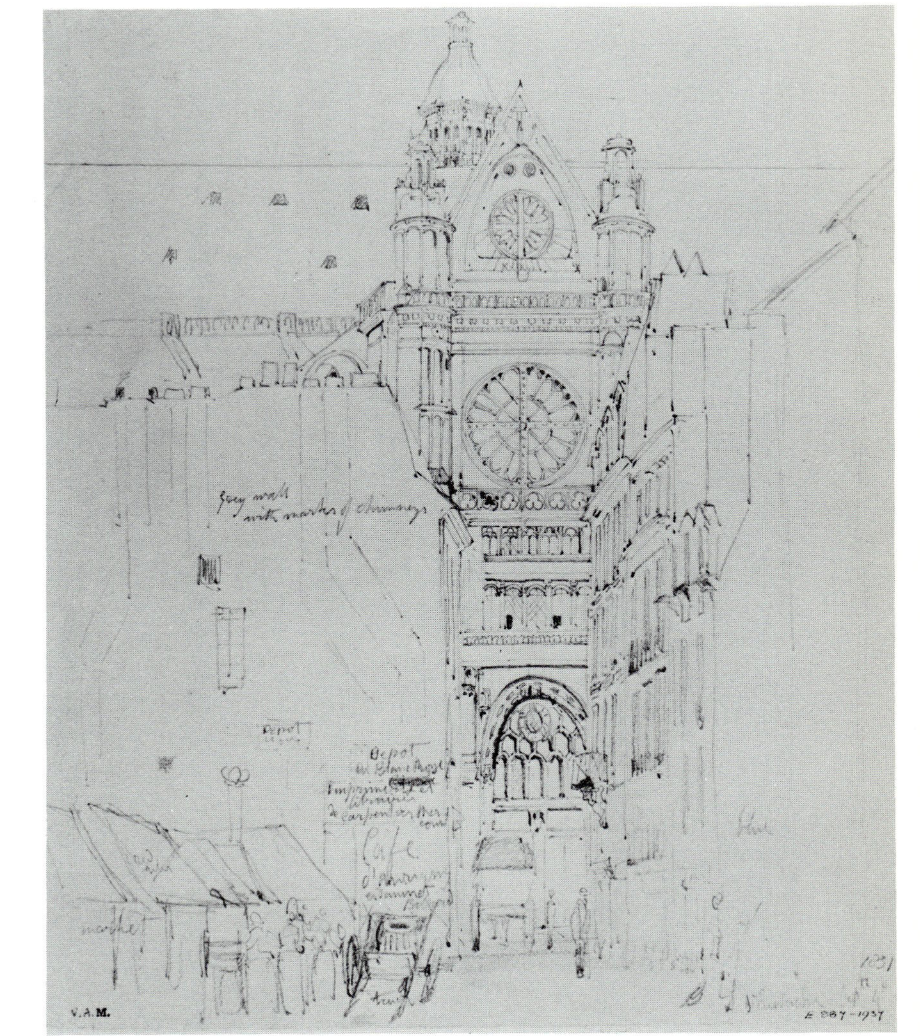

4. 'Church of St Eustache, Paris' Pencil ($10\frac{1}{4} \times 8\frac{5}{8}$ in. – 260 × 219 mm)
Inscribed: *Septr. 4th. 1831*, with colour notes
Collection: Victoria and Albert Museum, Crown Copyright

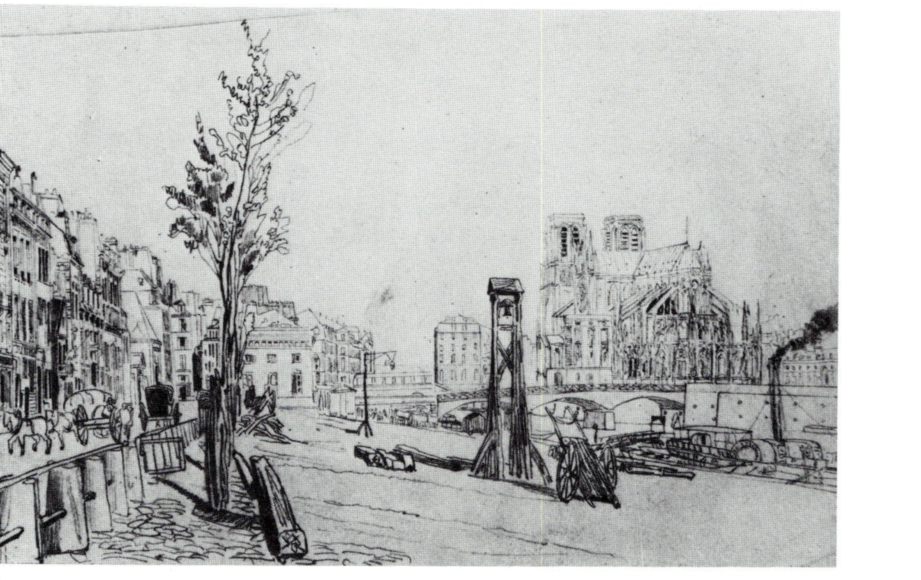

A

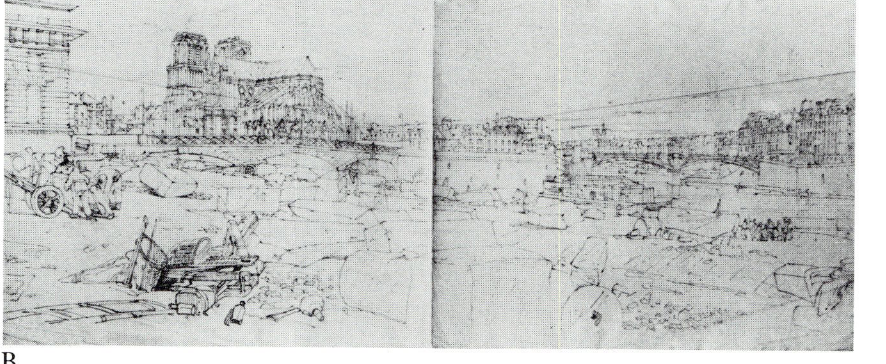

B

5. Figure A 'Notre Dame, Paris' (11 × 7 in. – 279 × 178 mm) Carbon pencil on tracing paper
Figure B (24 × 10 in. – 610 × 254 mm) Lead pencil on tracing paper
In possession of the Callow family

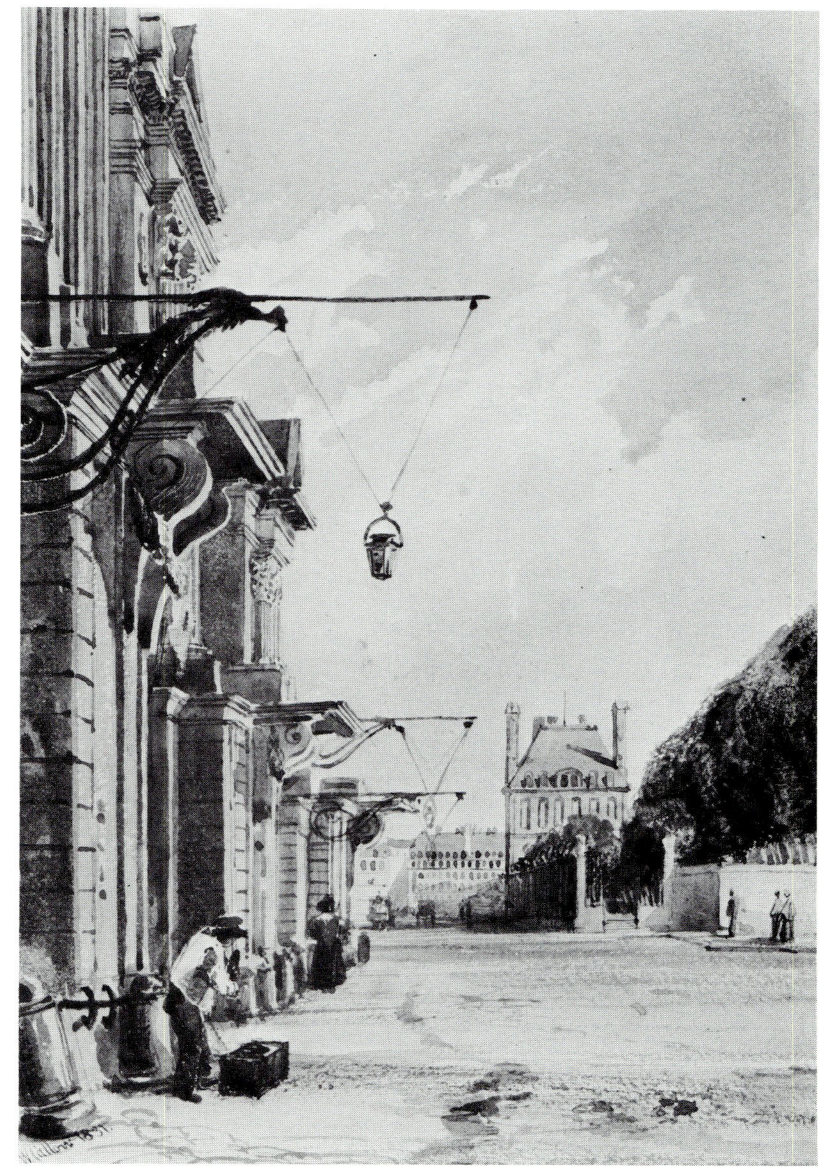

6. 'Rue de Rivoli, near the Tuileries, Paris' Water-colour ($8\frac{7}{8} \times 6\frac{1}{4}$ in. – 225 × 169 mm)
Signed and dated: W. Callow 1831
Exhibited: Carnavalet Museum, Paris ('Paris Romantique', 1957)
Collection: Victoria and Albert Museum, Crown Copyright

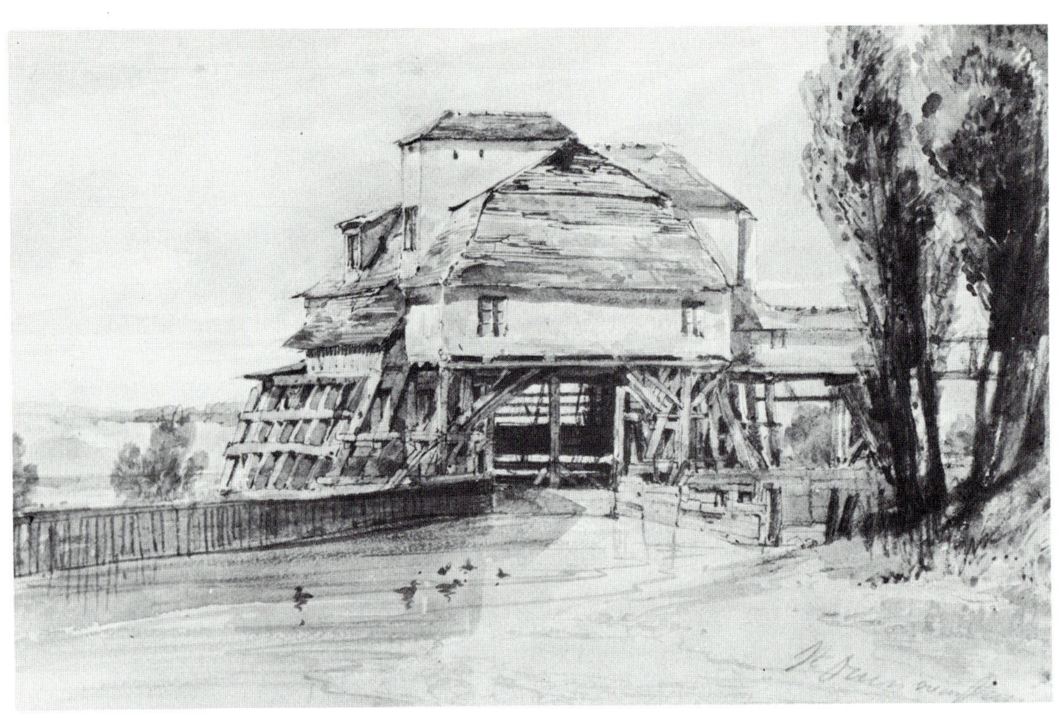

7. 'Watermill at St Ouen, 1831' Water-colour and Indian ink over pencil ($6\frac{5}{16} \times 9\frac{7}{10}$ in. – 160×240 mm) *See* Catalogue section for full inscription.
Collection: Rhode Island School of Design, Providence, Rhode Island, USA

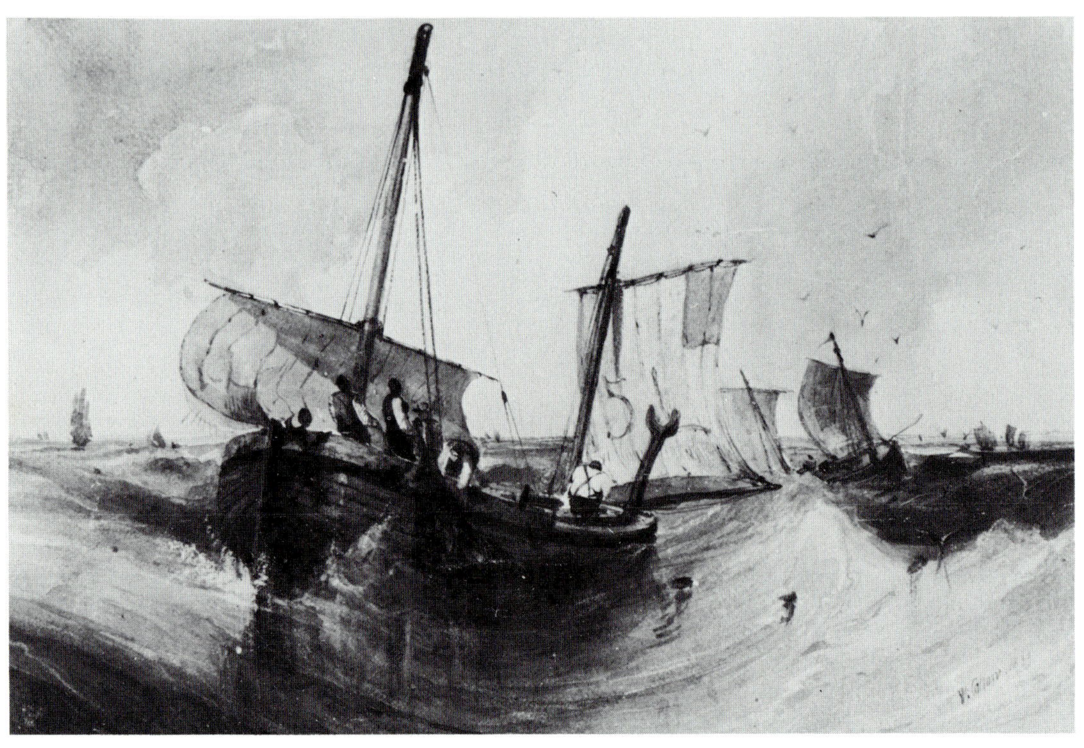

8. 'Fishing Boats at Sea' Water-colour ($7 \times 10\frac{1}{4}$ in. – 178×260 mm)
Signed and dated: W. Callow 1833 (right)
Reproduced by gracious permission of Her Majesty the Queen

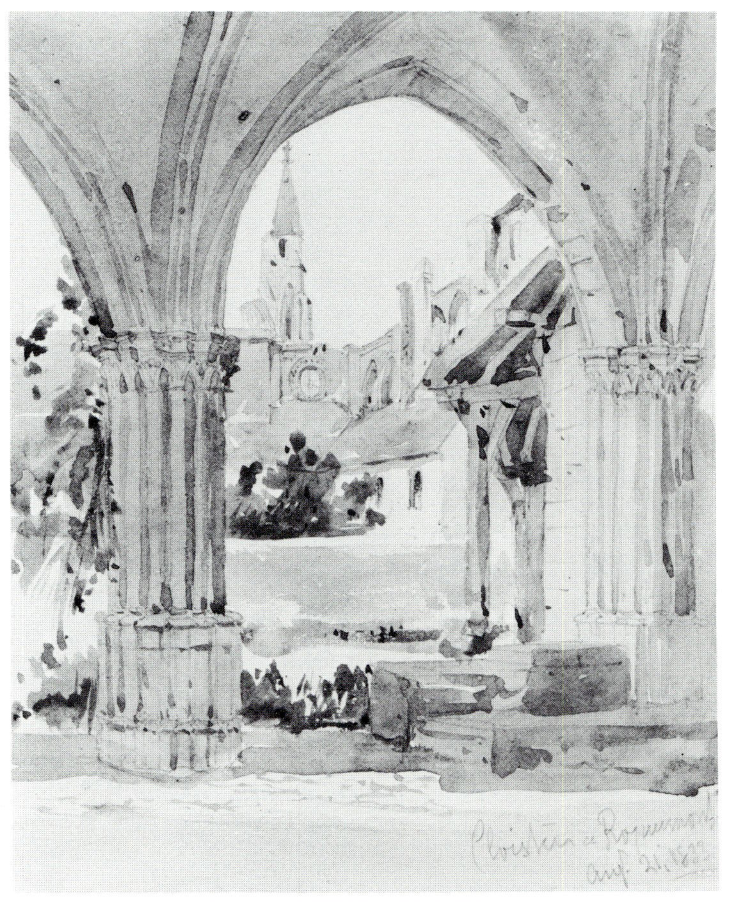
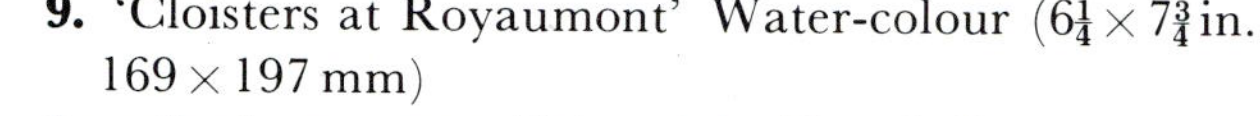

9. 'Cloisters at Royaumont' Water-colour ($6\frac{1}{4} \times 7\frac{3}{4}$ in. – 169 × 197 mm)
Inscribed on verso: *Cloîtres à la Tour de Royaumont Août 21 1833*
Collection: Henry E. Huntington Library and Art Gallery, San Marino, California, USA

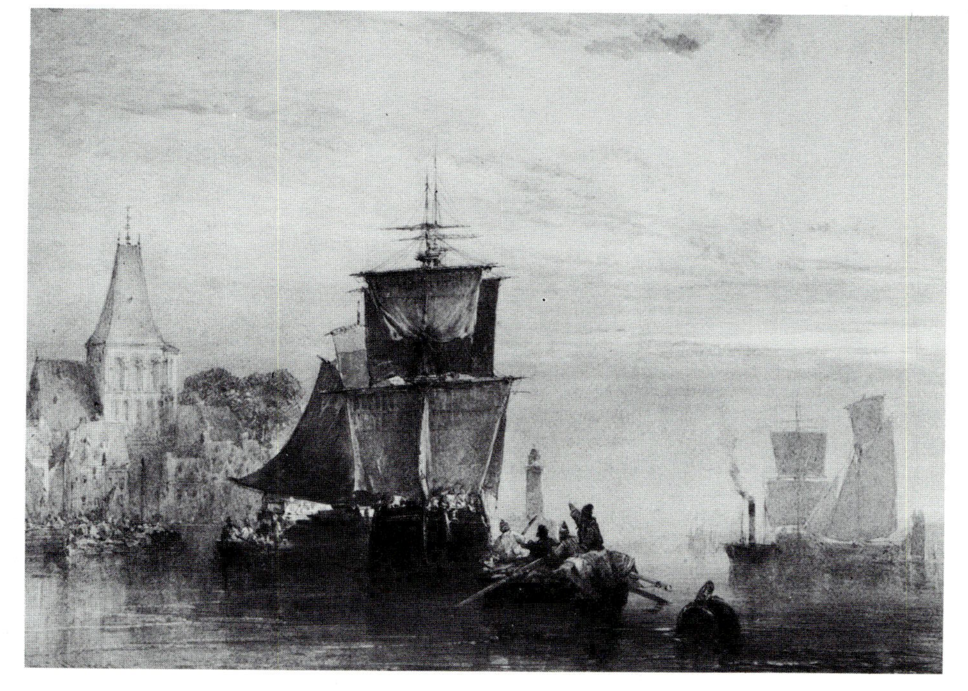

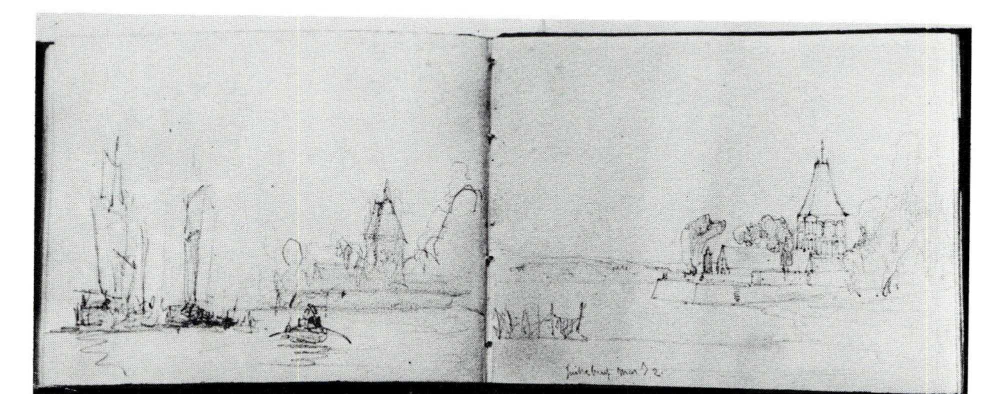

10. 'Quillebœuf on the Seine' Water-colour (14 × 20 in. – 356 × 508 mm)
Signed: Wm Callow (left)
Collection: City Art Gallery, Manchester
Sketch below: 'Quillebœuf', inscribed: *Mardi 2* from a series made in June 1835
Callow collection

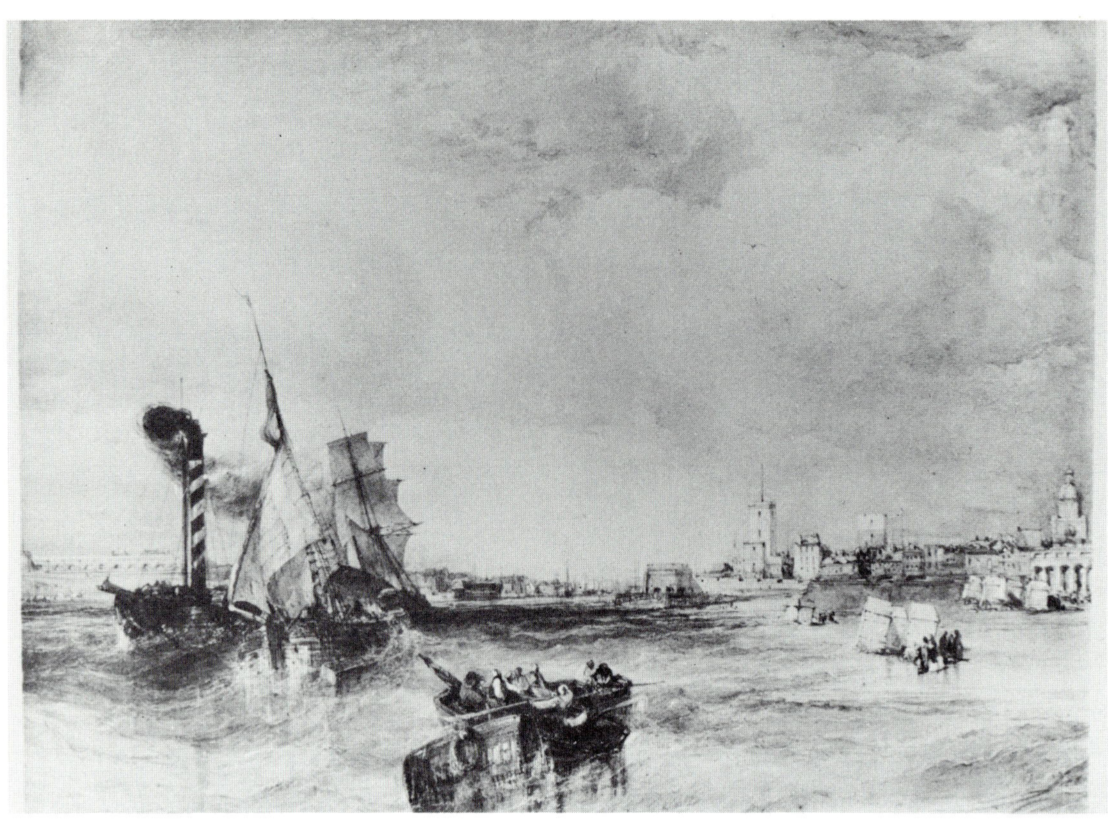

11. 'Portsmouth' Water-colour ($16\frac{1}{8} \times 22$ in. – 410×559 mm)
Signed: W. Callow
By courtesy of Birmingham Museums and Art Gallery

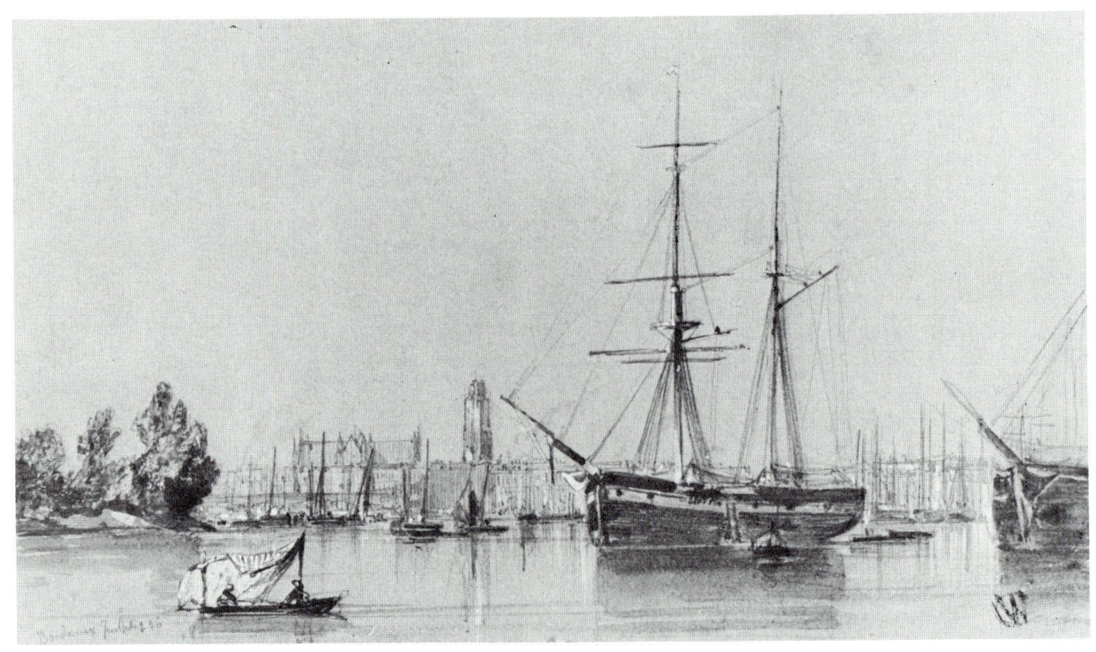

12. 'Bordeaux' Water-colour on grey paper ($5\frac{3}{8} \times 9\frac{1}{8}$ in. – 137×232 mm)
Signed with monogram (right). Inscribed: *Bordeaux Juillet/36* (left)
Exhibited: 'Masters of British Water-colour' – Royal Academy, 1949
By courtesy of Birmingham Museums and Art Gallery
Photograph: Courtauld Institute of Art

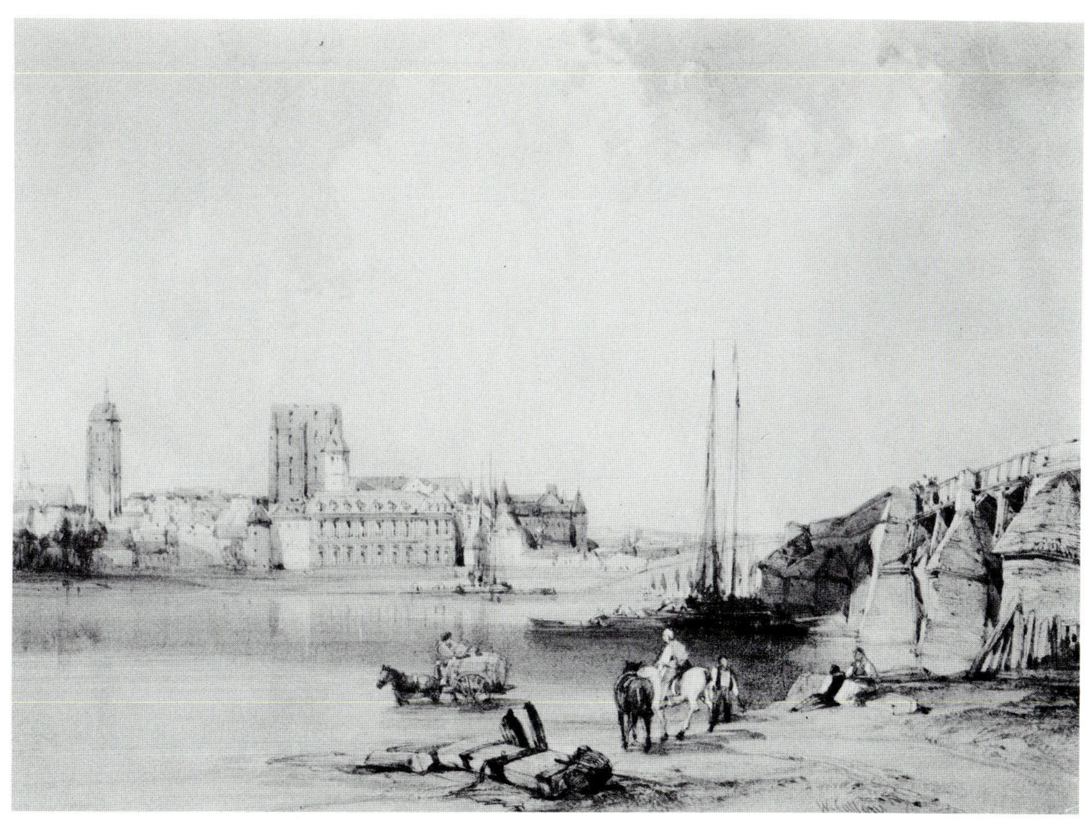

13. 'Beaugency-sur-Loire' Water-colour (10×13 in. – 254×330 mm)
Signed: W. Callow (right)
Collection: R. W. Mills

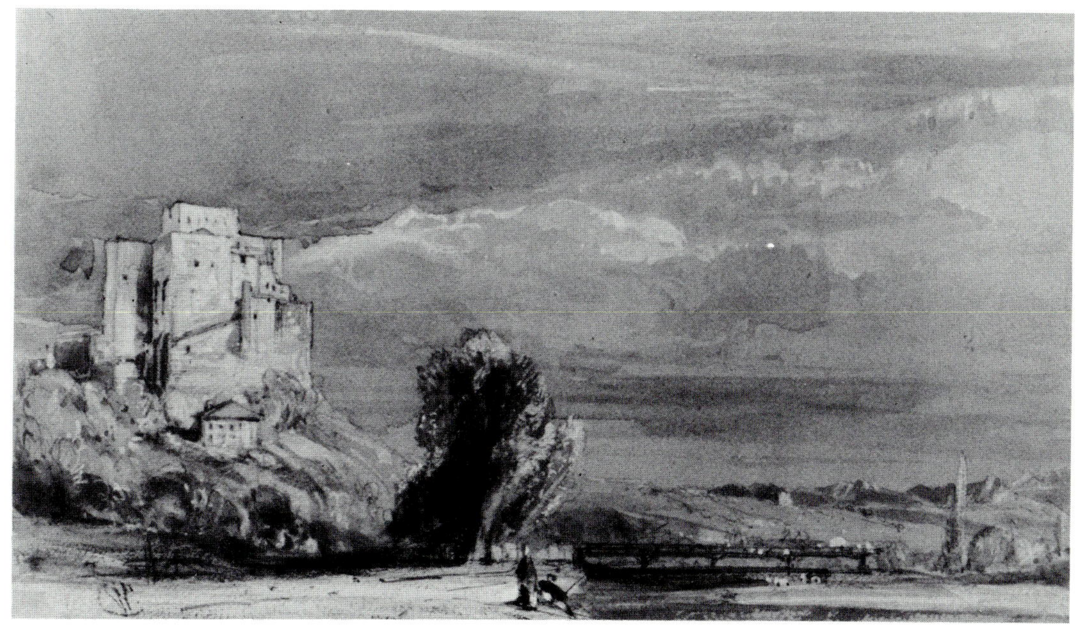

14. 'Château de Montélimar' Water-colour ($5\frac{1}{4} \times 9\frac{1}{4}$ in. – 133×235 mm)
Signed with monogram which reads 'CW' (left). Inscribed on verso: *Château de Montélimort* (sic) *Août 2/36*
Collection: Cecil Higgins Art Gallery, Bedford

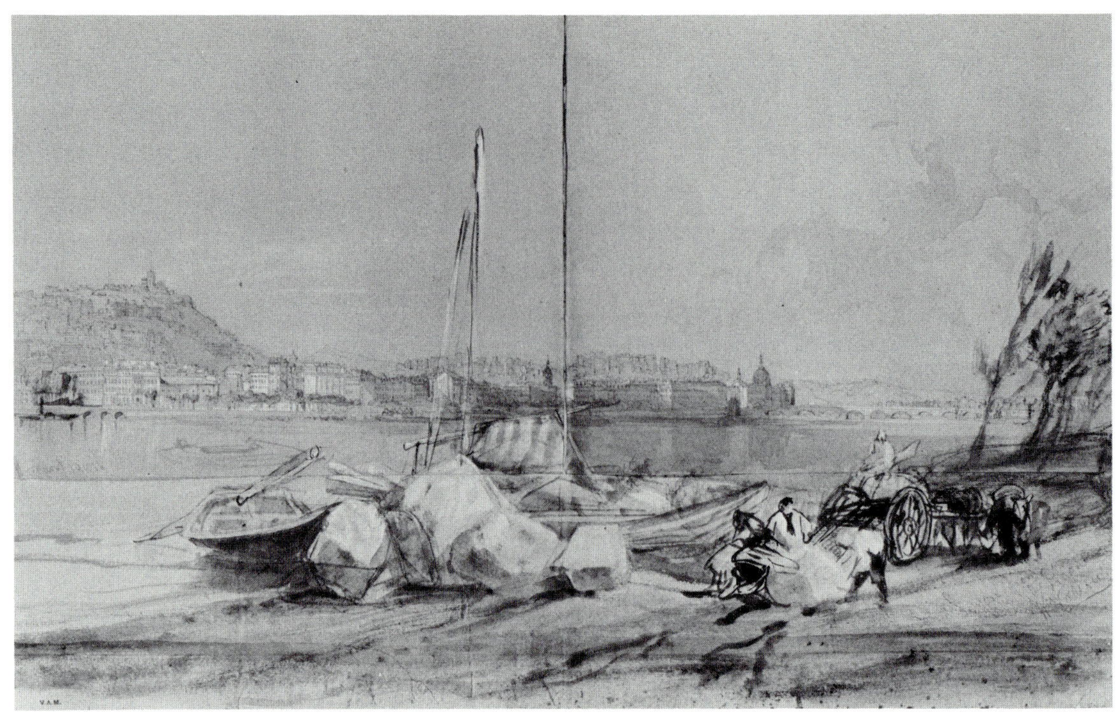

15. 'Drawing of Lyons' on three sheets of paper. Pencil and sepia, heightened with white (13 × 21 in. – 330 × 533 mm)
Inscribed: *Lyon [sic] Août 10 1836* (left) and signed Wm. Callow, with the inscription: *Lyon from the Rhône* (right)
Collection: Victoria and Albert Museum, Crown Copyright

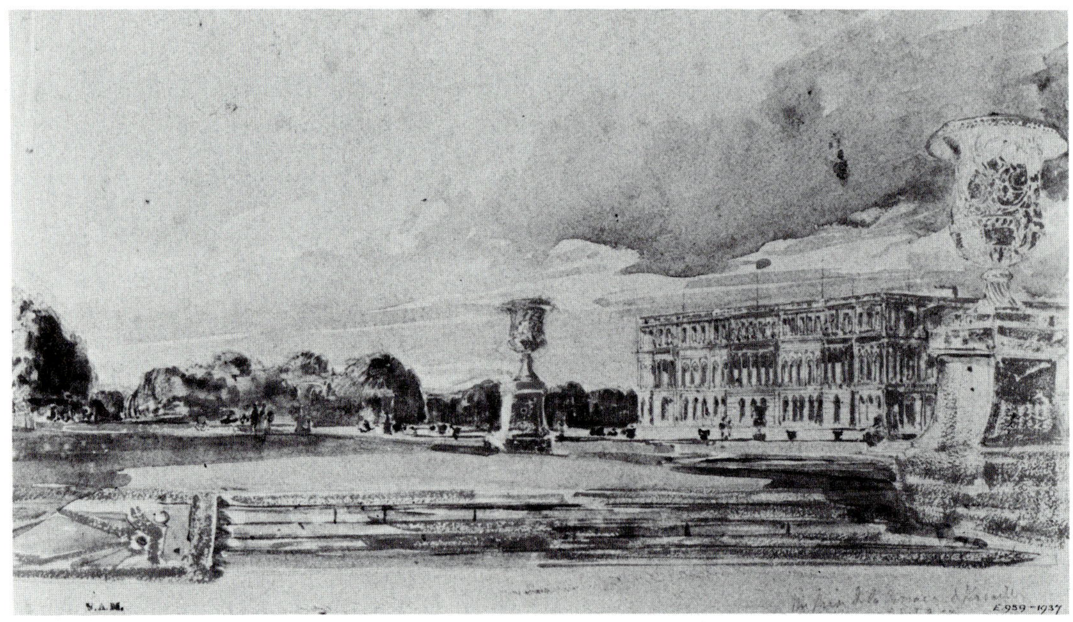

16. 'Vue prise de la terrasse de Versailles' Pencil and water-colour (6⅝ × 11⅝ in. – 168 × 295 mm)
Preliminary study for 'Versailles' – National Gallery of Canada, Ottawa
Collection: Victoria and Albert Museum

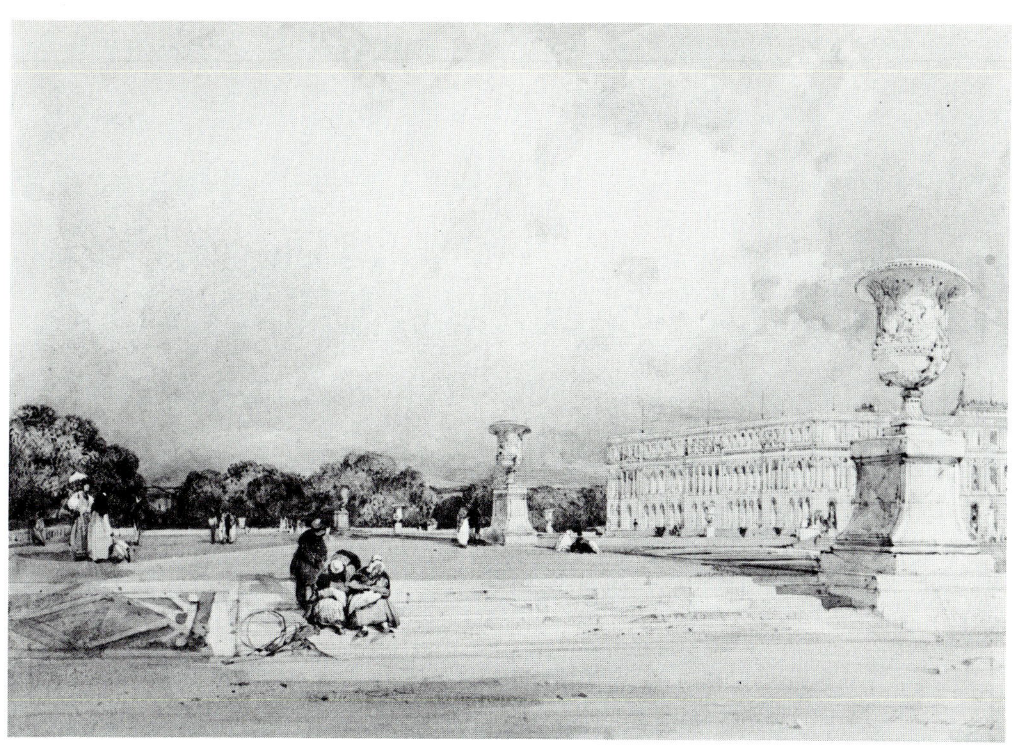

17. 'Versailles' Water-colour on Whatman paper ($9\frac{1}{5} \times 12\frac{7}{10}$ in. – 232×322 mm)
Signed and dated: W. Callow 1837 (lower right)
Collection: The National Gallery of Canada, Ottawa

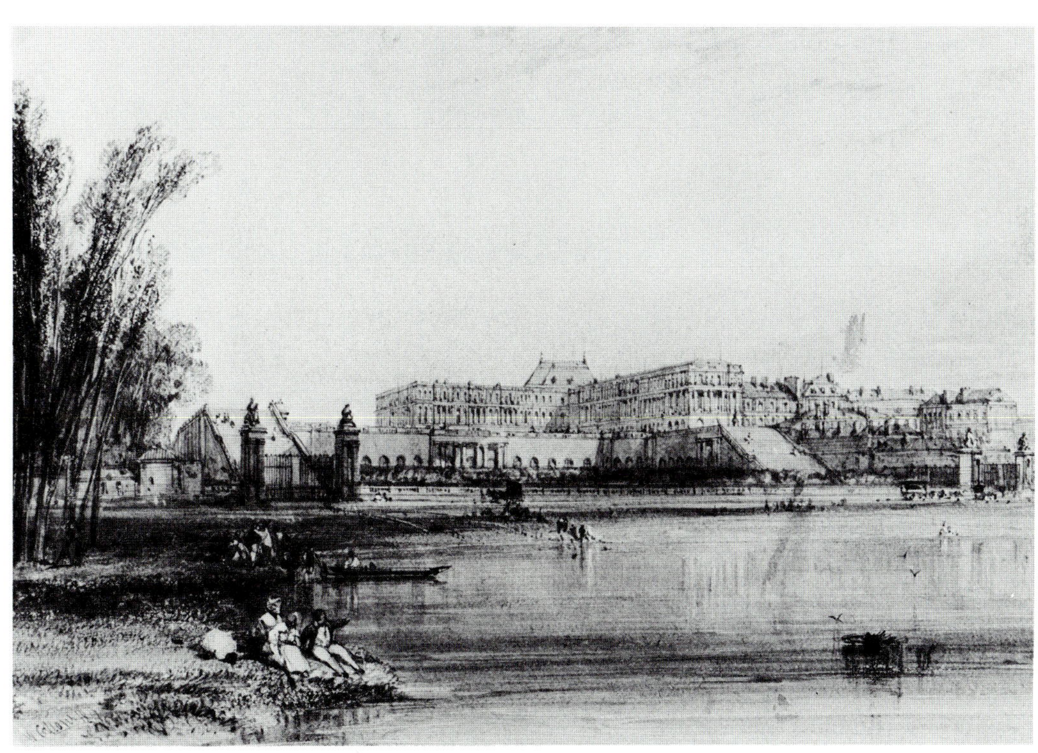

18. 'Le Château de Versailles et l'Orangerie vus de la pièce d'eau des Suisses' Pen and wash.
Signed and dated: W. Callow 1837
Collection: Musée National du Château de Versailles, France

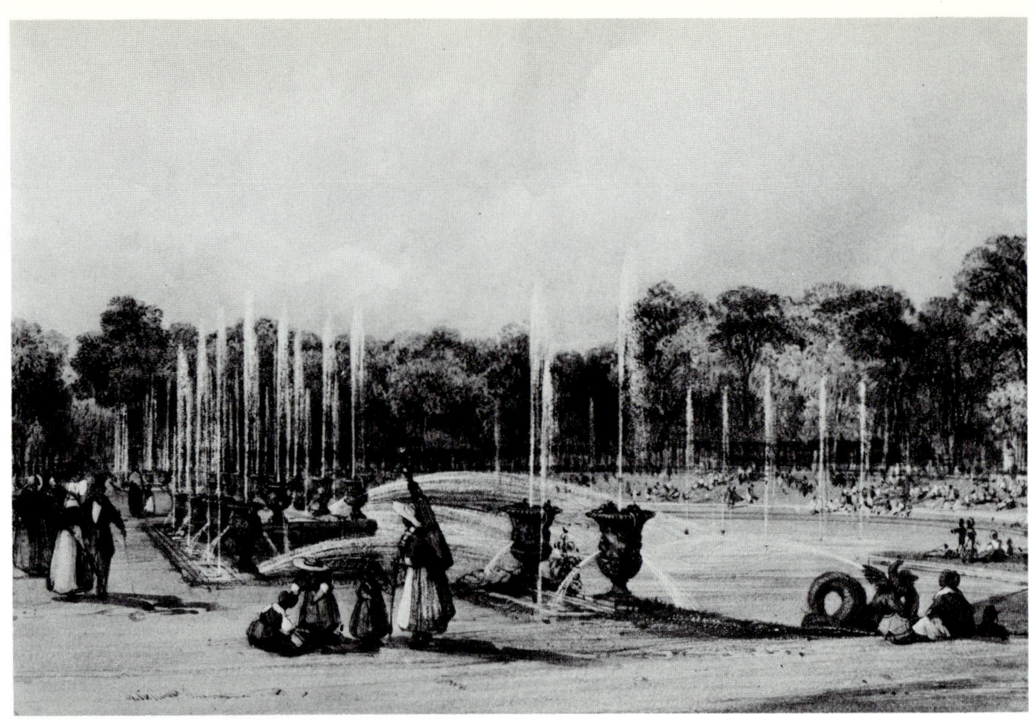

19. 'The Gardens of Versailles' Water-colour, heightened with white ($8 \times 11\frac{1}{2}$ in. – 203×292 mm)
Signed and dated: W. Callow 1837
Photograph: The Fine Art Society Ltd

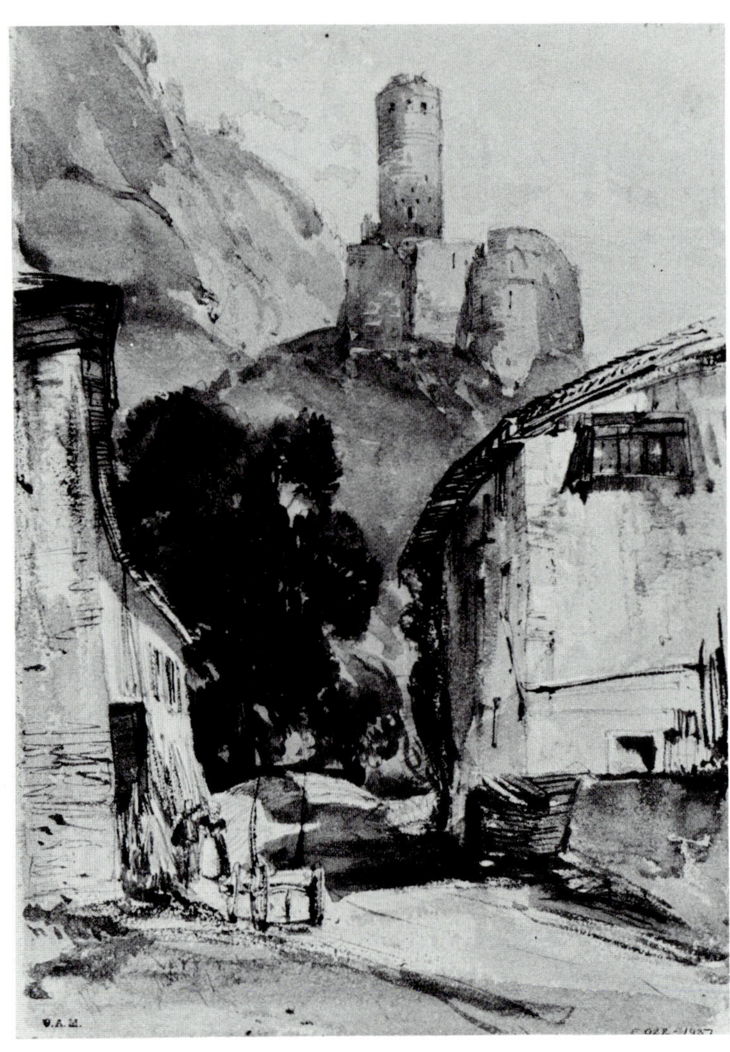

20. 'Castle of La Batiaz, Martigny, Switzerland' Pencil and water-colour ($10\frac{1}{4} \times 7\frac{1}{4}$ in. – 260×184 mm)
Signed with monogram and inscribed: *Martigny, Augt. 22/38*
Collection: Victoria and Albert Museum, Crown Copyright

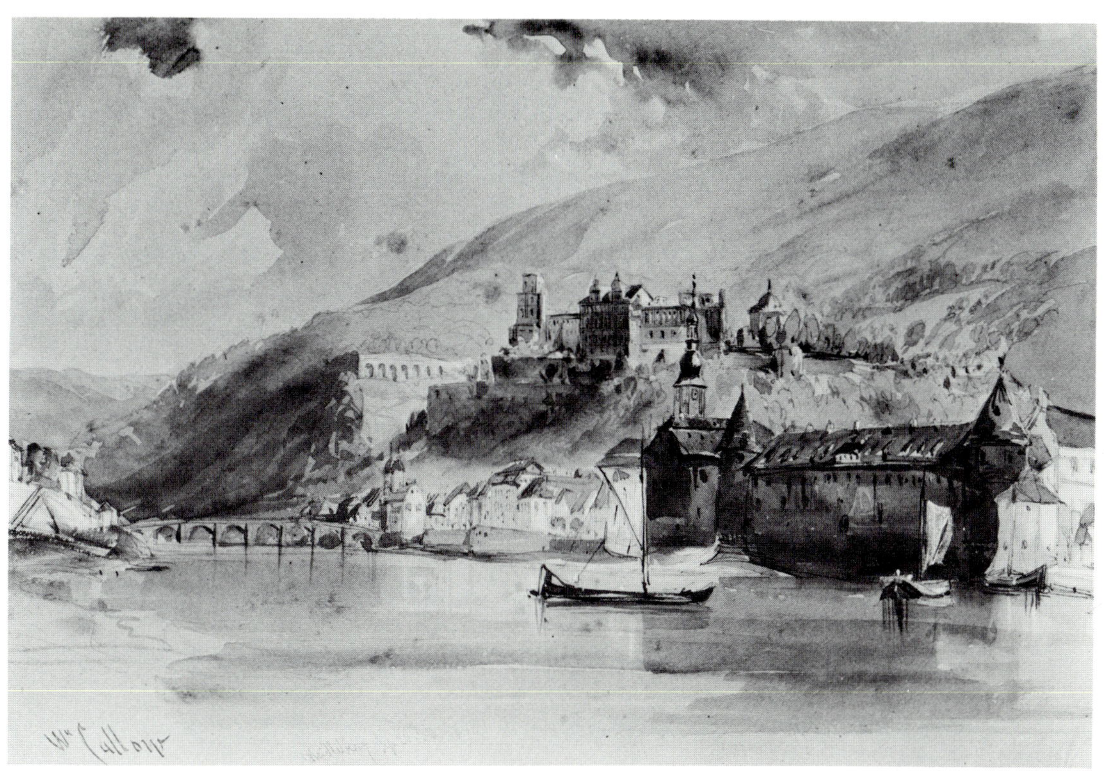

21. 'Heidelberg' Water-colour ($9\frac{3}{5} \times 13\frac{3}{10}$ in. – 244×337 mm)
Signed: Wm. Callow (left). Inscribed: *Heidelberg Sept 20/38* (reads *30*, but this figure is impossible)
Collection: City of Southampton Art Gallery

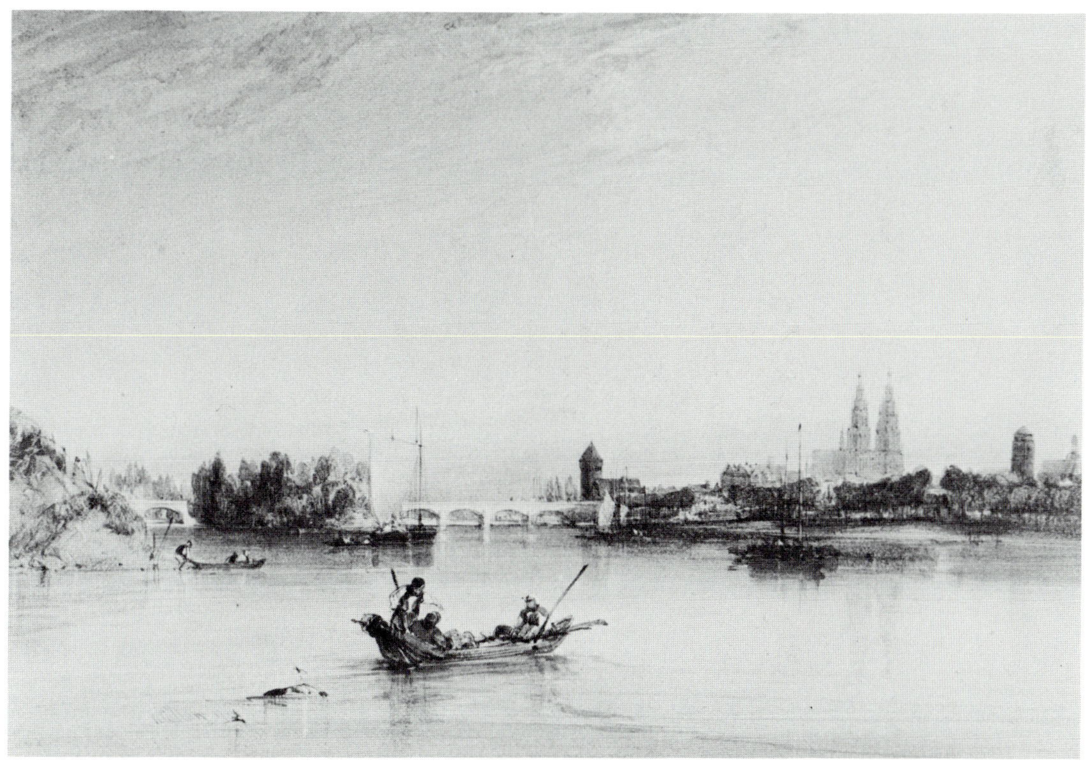

22. 'Tours' Water-colour ($9\frac{1}{4} \times 13$ in. – 235×330 mm)
Signed: W. Callow and dated 1839
Collection: Castle Museum, Nottingham

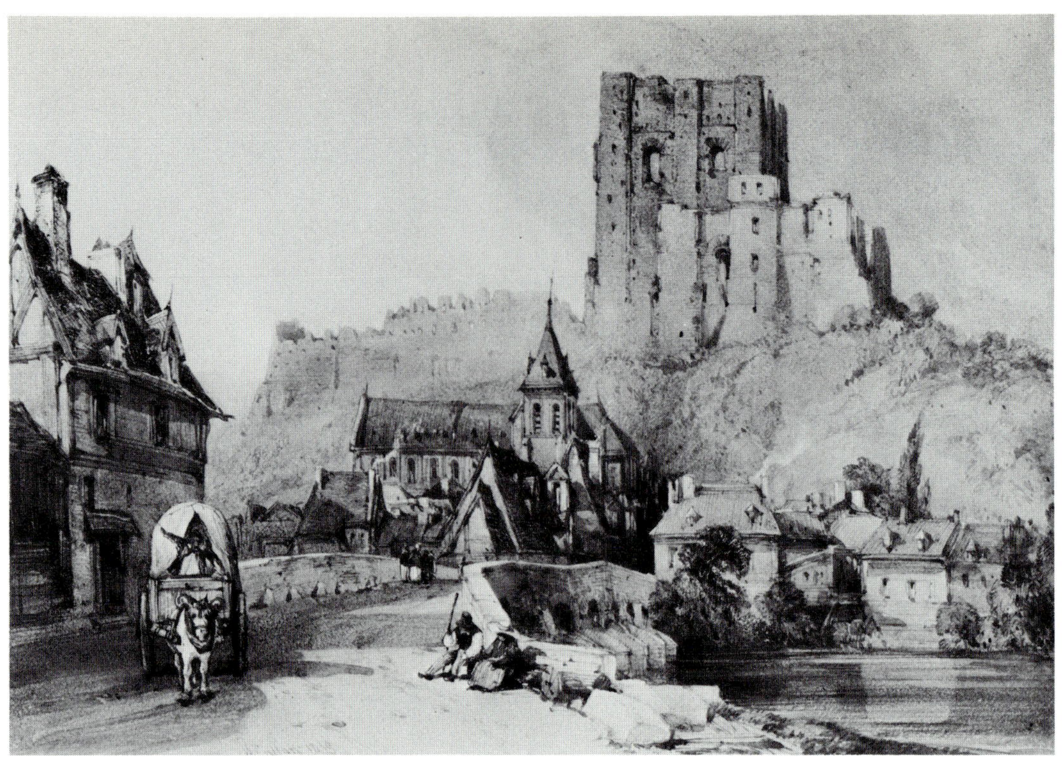

23. 'Montrichard on the Cher' (Loir-et-Cher) Water-colour ($9\frac{1}{8} \times 12\frac{1}{2}$ in. – 232 × 317 mm)
Signed and dated: W. Callow 1839
Exhibited: 'British Water-colours from the Victoria and Albert Museum' – International Exhibitions Foundation, USA, 1966/7, no. 9
Collection: Victoria and Albert Museum, Crown Copyright

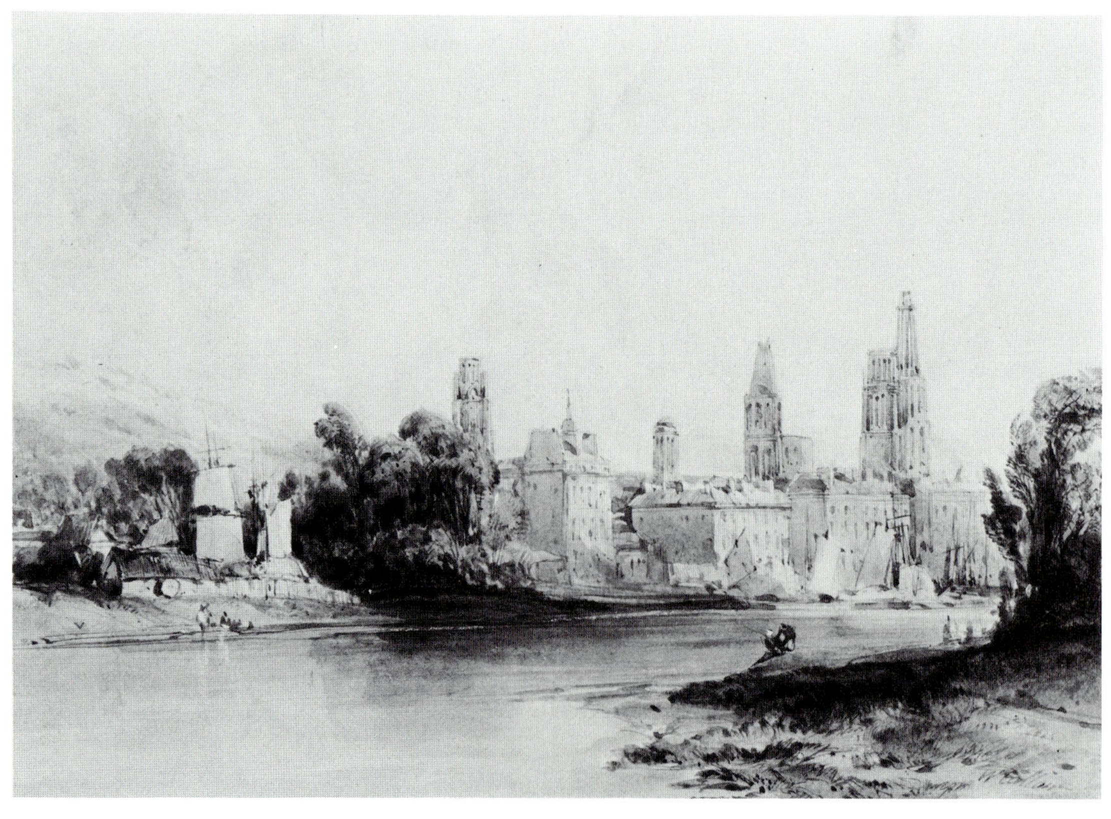

24. 'Rouen' Water-colour (7 × 9 in. – 177 × 228 mm)
Signed in water-colour: W. Callow (right)
Reproduced by permission of the Syndics of the Fitzwilliam Museum, Cambridge

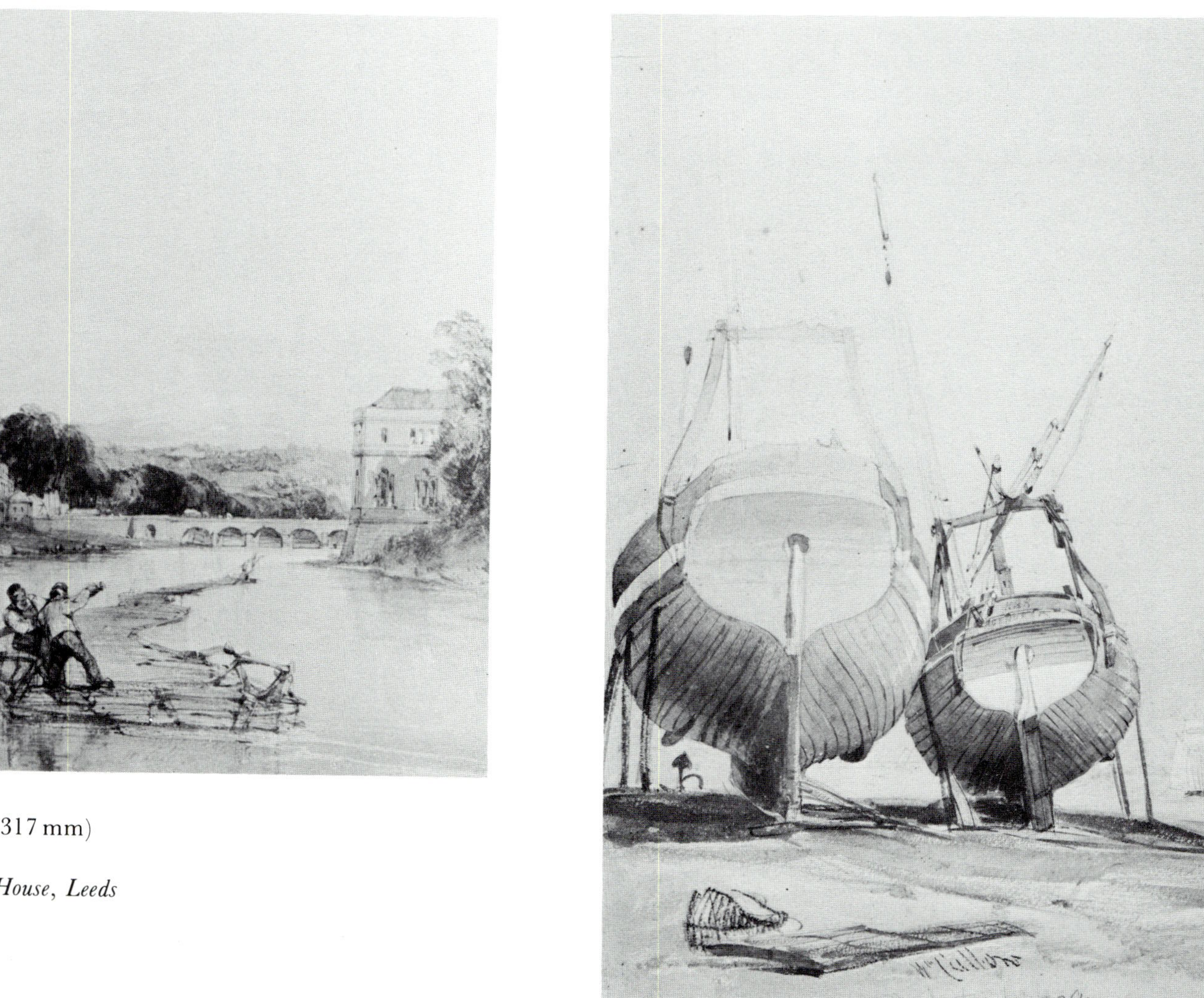

25. 'Sèvres' Water-colour ($9\frac{2}{5} \times 12\frac{1}{2}$ in. – 237×317 mm)
Signed' W. Callow (off centre right)
Collection: City Art Gallery and Temple Newsam House, Leeds
Photograph: Courtauld Institute of Art

26. 'Stern View of Two Fishing Boats on the Beach at Lowestoft'
Water-colour ($14\frac{1}{8} \times 10\frac{1}{8}$ in. – 359×257 mm)
Signed. Wm Callow. Inscribed: *On the beach/Lowestoft Sept. 17.39.*
Collection: National Maritime Museum, London

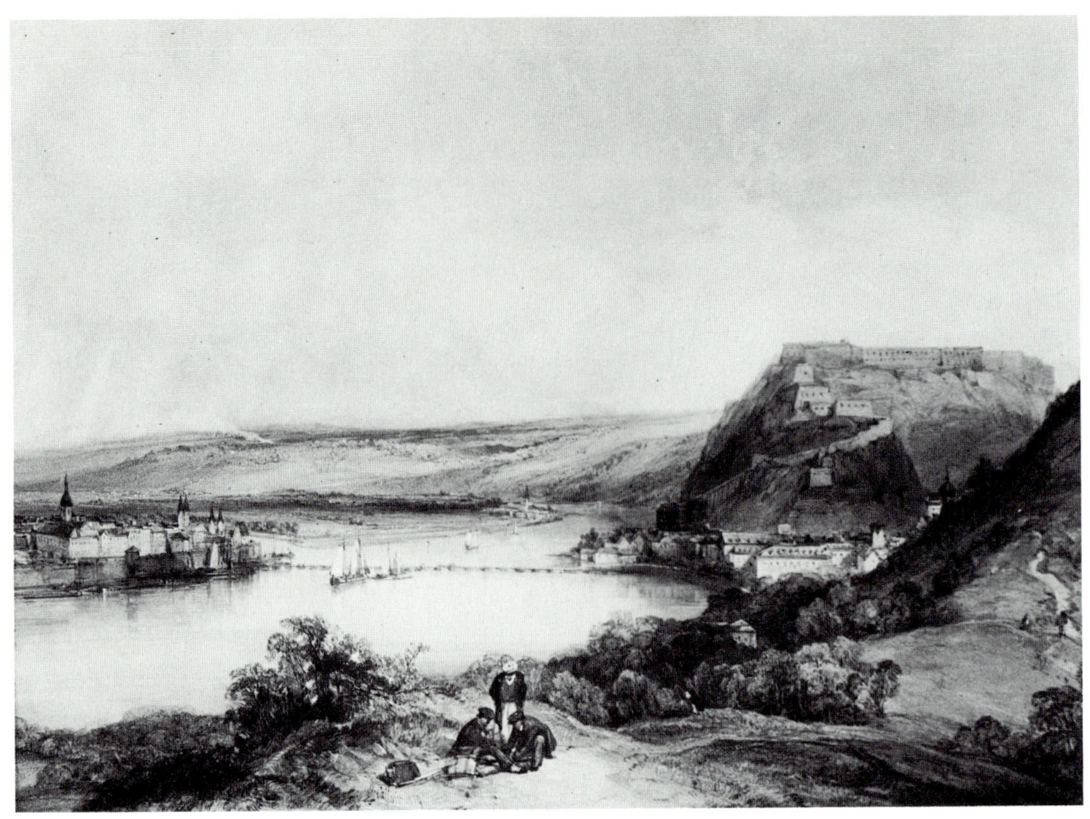

27. 'Ehrenbreitstein and Koblenz from the Heights of Pfaffendorf' Water-colour. ($18\frac{3}{5} \times 25\frac{2}{5}$ in. – 472×644 mm)
Signed and dated 1839.
Exhibited: Society of Painters in Water-colours in 1839
Collection: City Art Gallery and Temple Newsam House, Leeds

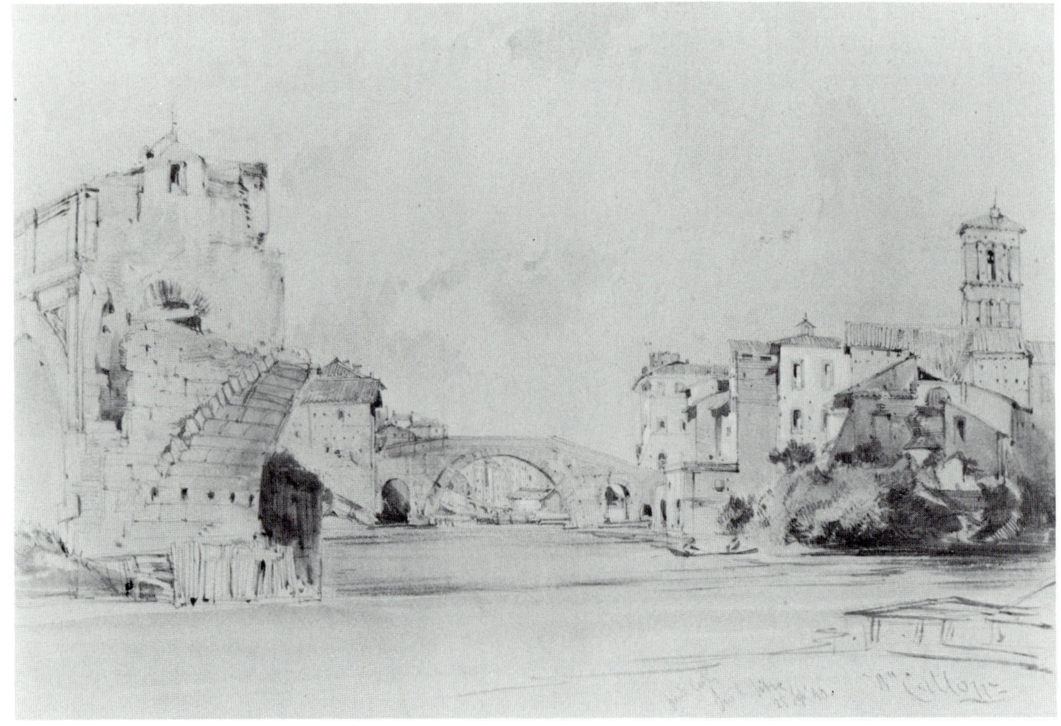

28. 'Ponte Cartro, Rome' Pencil and water-colour ($10\frac{1}{4} \times 14\frac{1}{2}$ in. – 260×368 mm)
Signed: Wm. Callow and inscribed: *Ponte Cartro sur le Tibre 28/Sept. 40* (right)
Collection: Cecil Higgins Art Gallery, Bedford

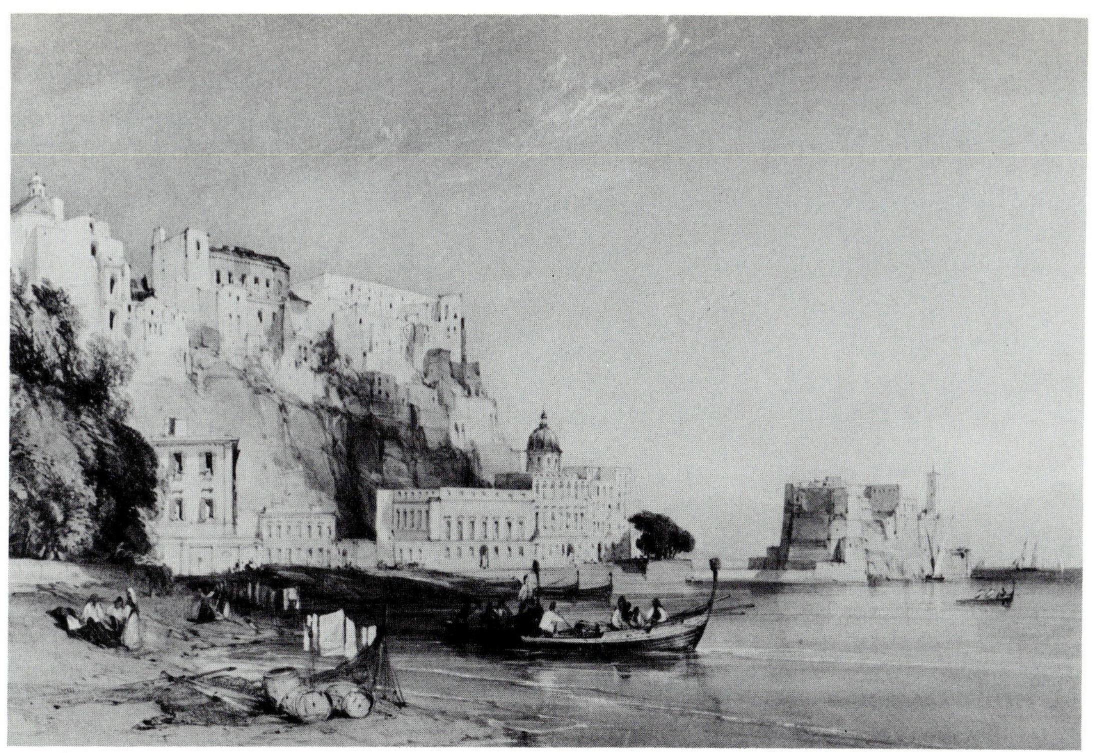

29. 'The Castel dell' Ovo, Naples' Water-colour (13 × 18 in. – 330 × 457 mm)
Signed: W. Callow (on foreground in front of barrels) and dated 1841
Photograph: Christie's

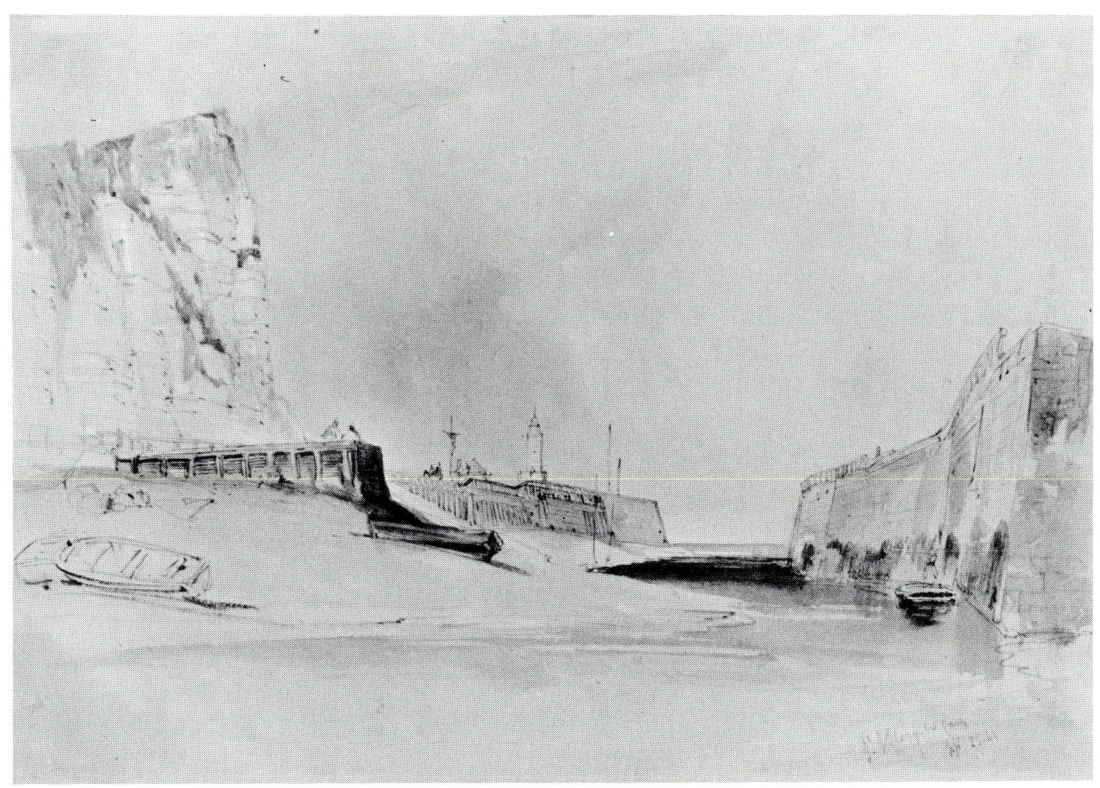

30. 'St Valéry en Caux' Pencil and water-colour and touches of white body-colour on very light grey paper
Inscribed: *St Valéry en Caux/Sept/25.41.* (Similar pencil sketches of St Valéry en Caux are included in the sketchbook, illustration no. 31)
William Spooner Collection: Courtauld Institute of Art

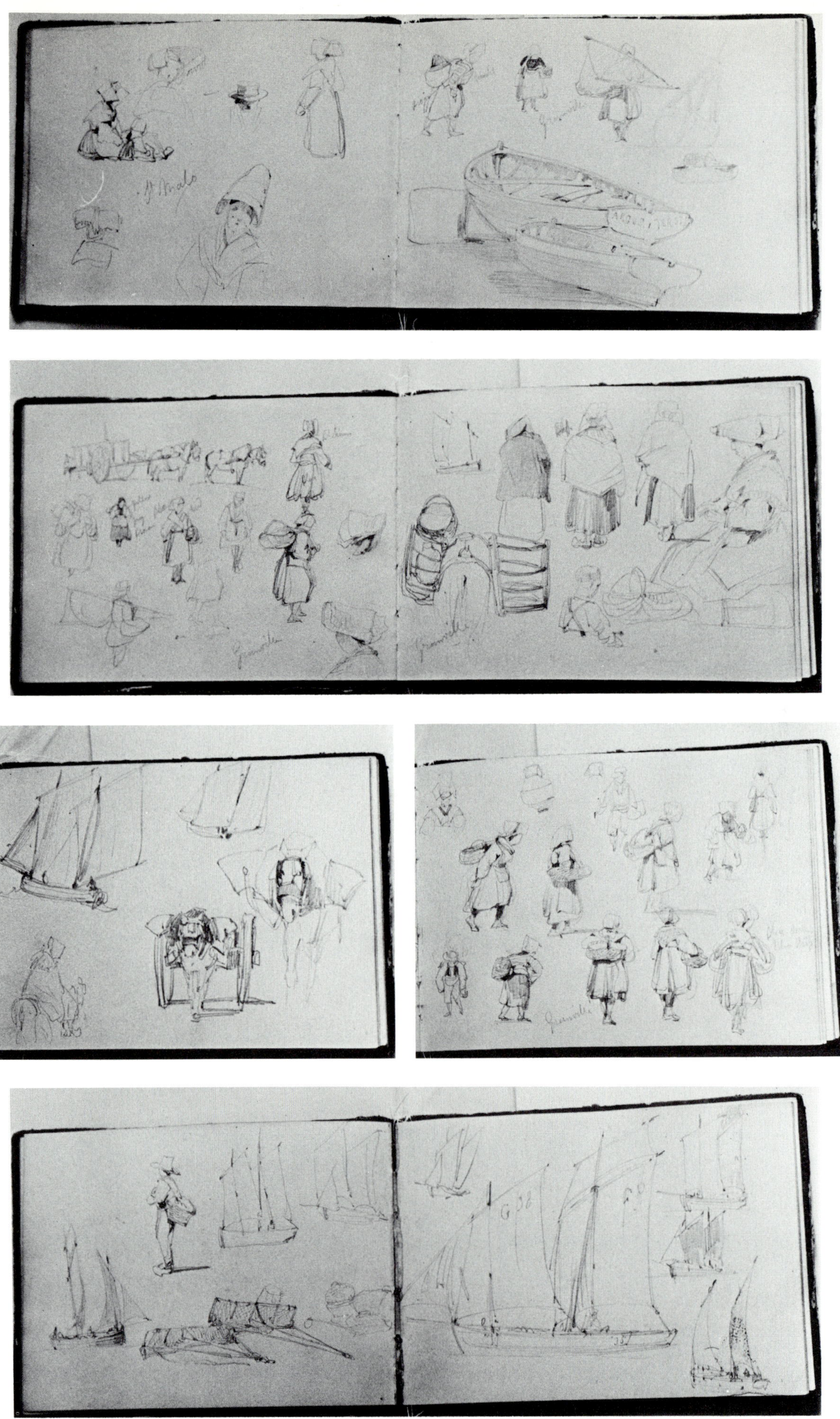

31. Details from pencil sketches executed by Callow, while in Normandy with Charles Bentley in 1841 (each page 5 × 4 in. – 127 × 102 mm)
In possession of the Callow family

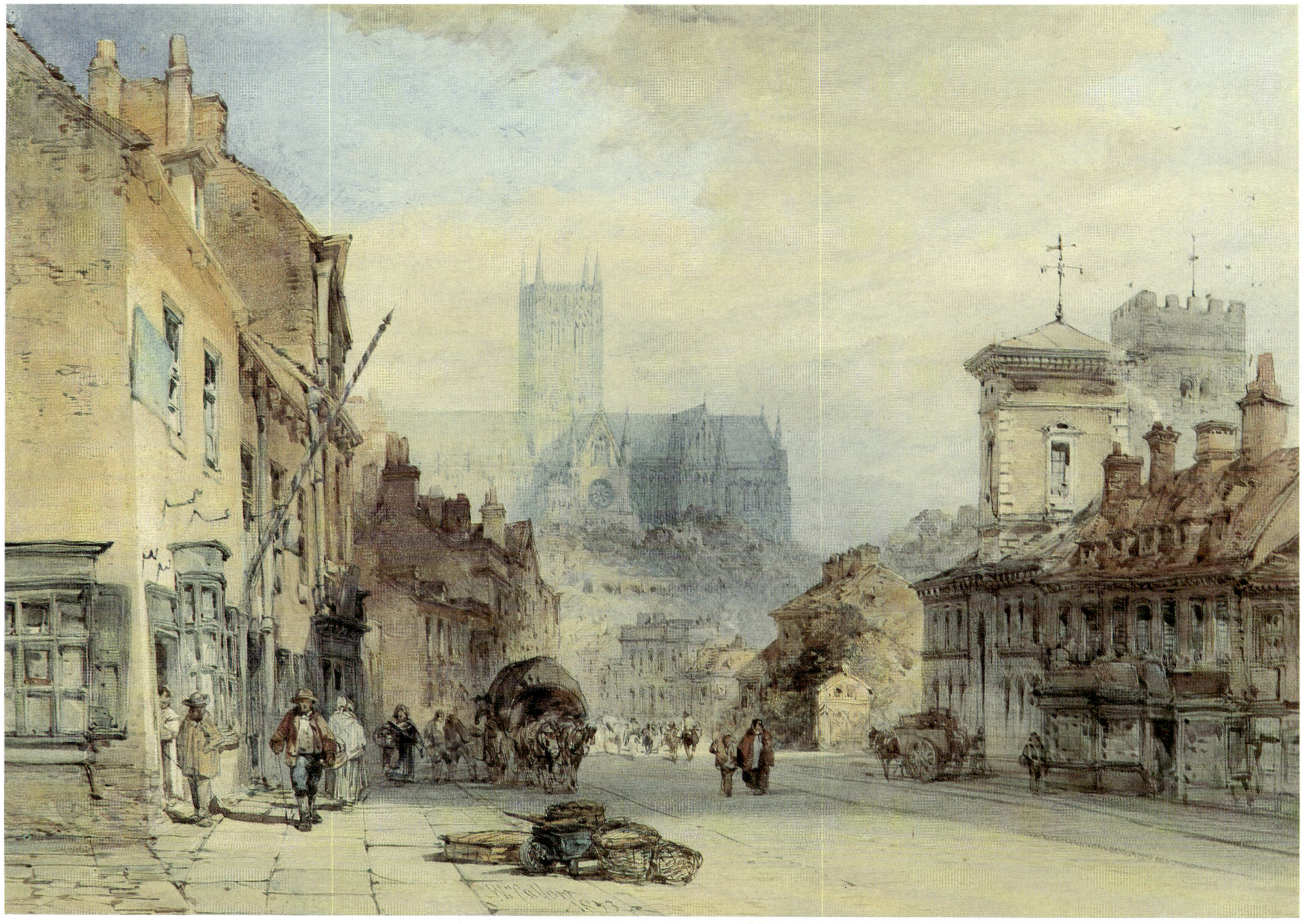

'Lincoln Cathedral from the High Street'
Water-colour ($13\frac{9}{10} \times 20\frac{1}{10}$ in. – 353×510 mm)
Signed: Wm. Callow 1853 (centre foreground)
Collection: Lincolnshire Museums – Usher Gallery, Lincoln

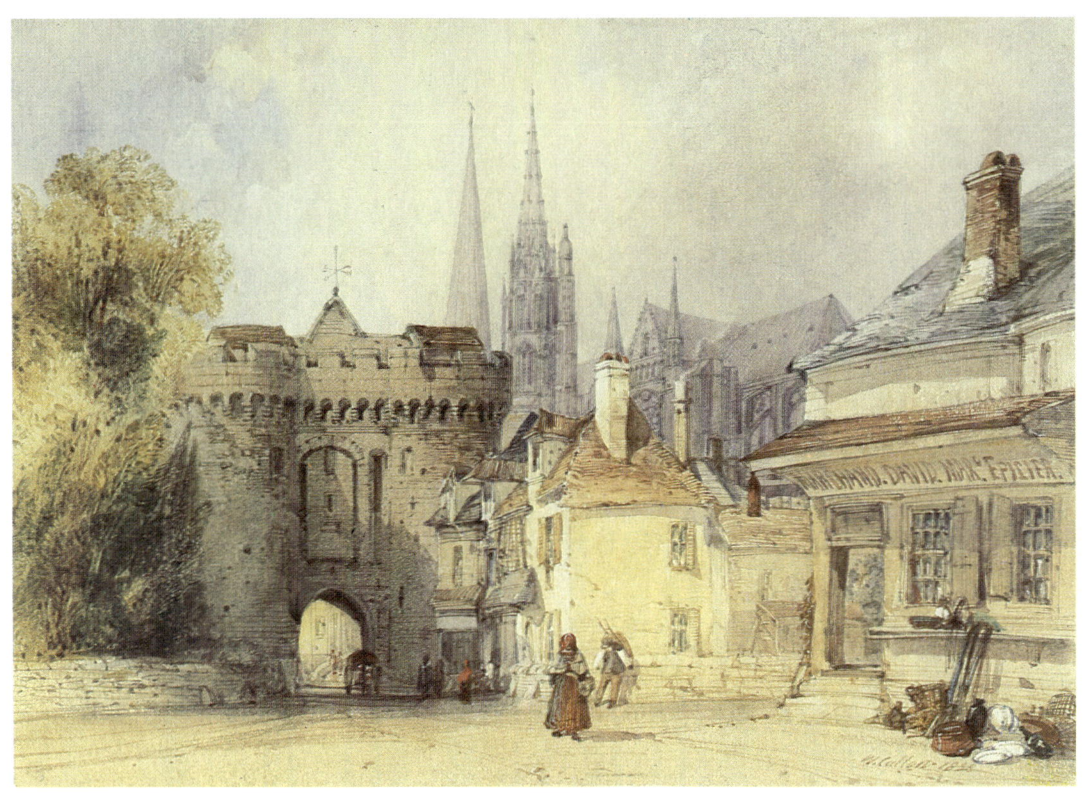

'Chartres, the Guillaume Gate'
Water-colour ($9 \times 12\frac{3}{10}$ in. – 228×311 mm)
Signed: W. Callow 1838 (right)
Collection: University of Liverpool

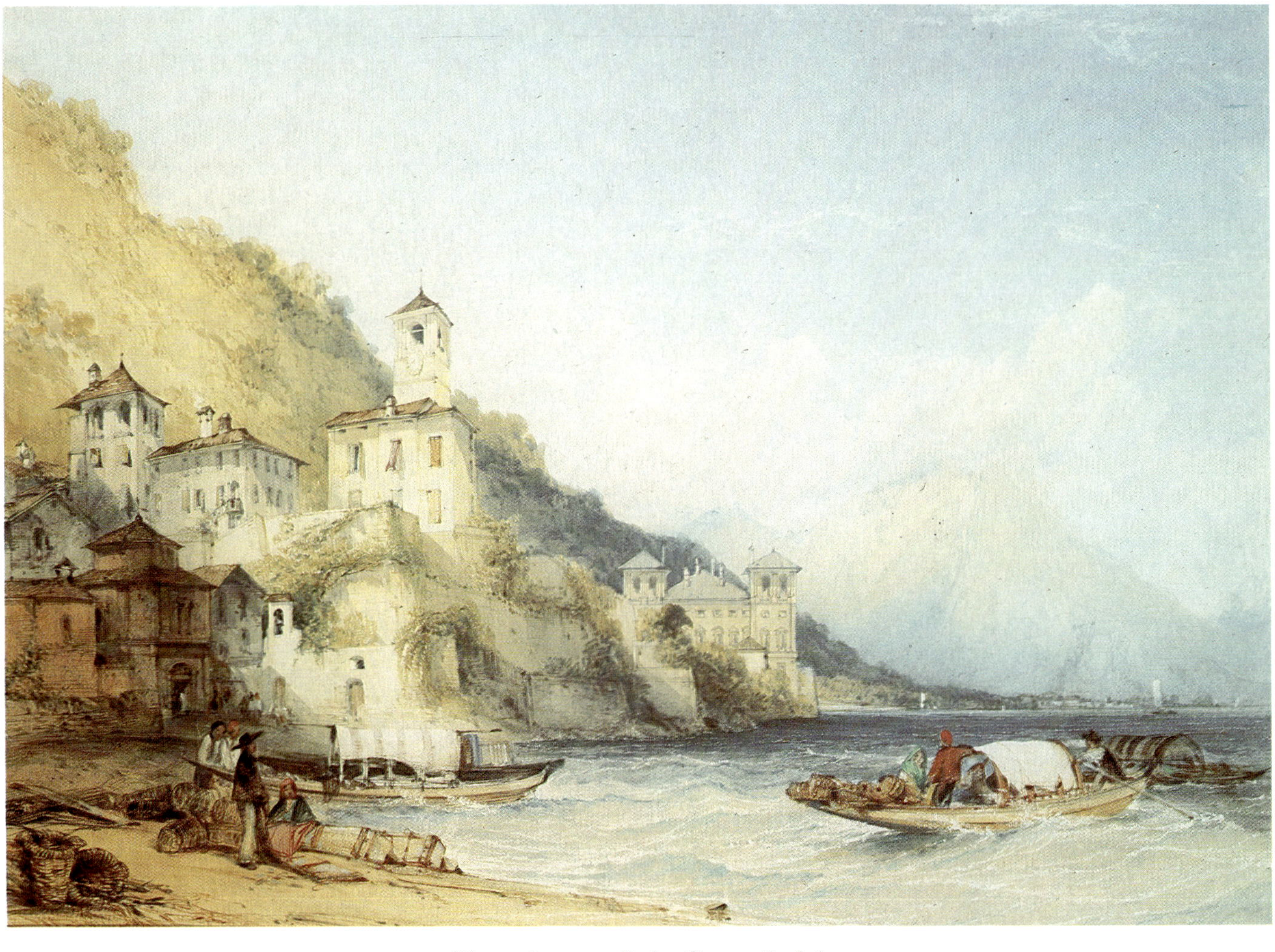

'Gravedona on Lake Como, Italy'
Water-colour (19×25 in. – 483×635 mm)
Signed: W. Callow 1841 (to right of seated woman)
Collection: Mrs M.D. Dubin. Photograph: The Leger Galleries

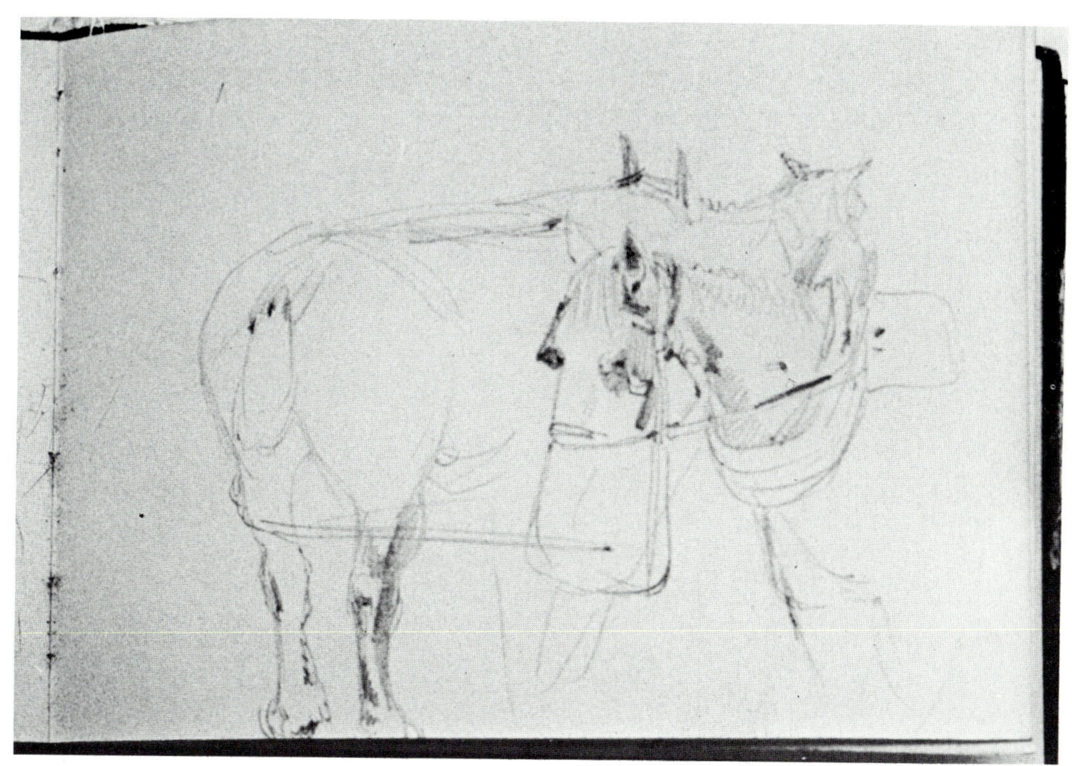

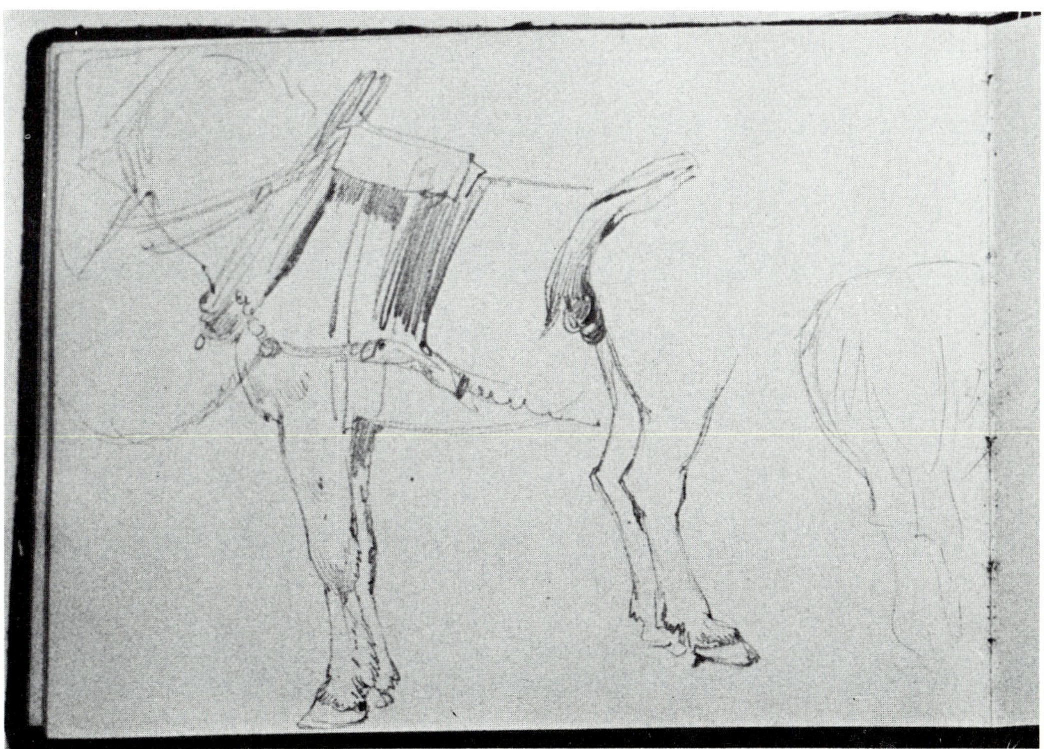

32. Studies of horses. Pencil, also Normandy 1841 (enlarged from 5 × 4 in. – 127 × 102 mm)
In possession of the Callow family

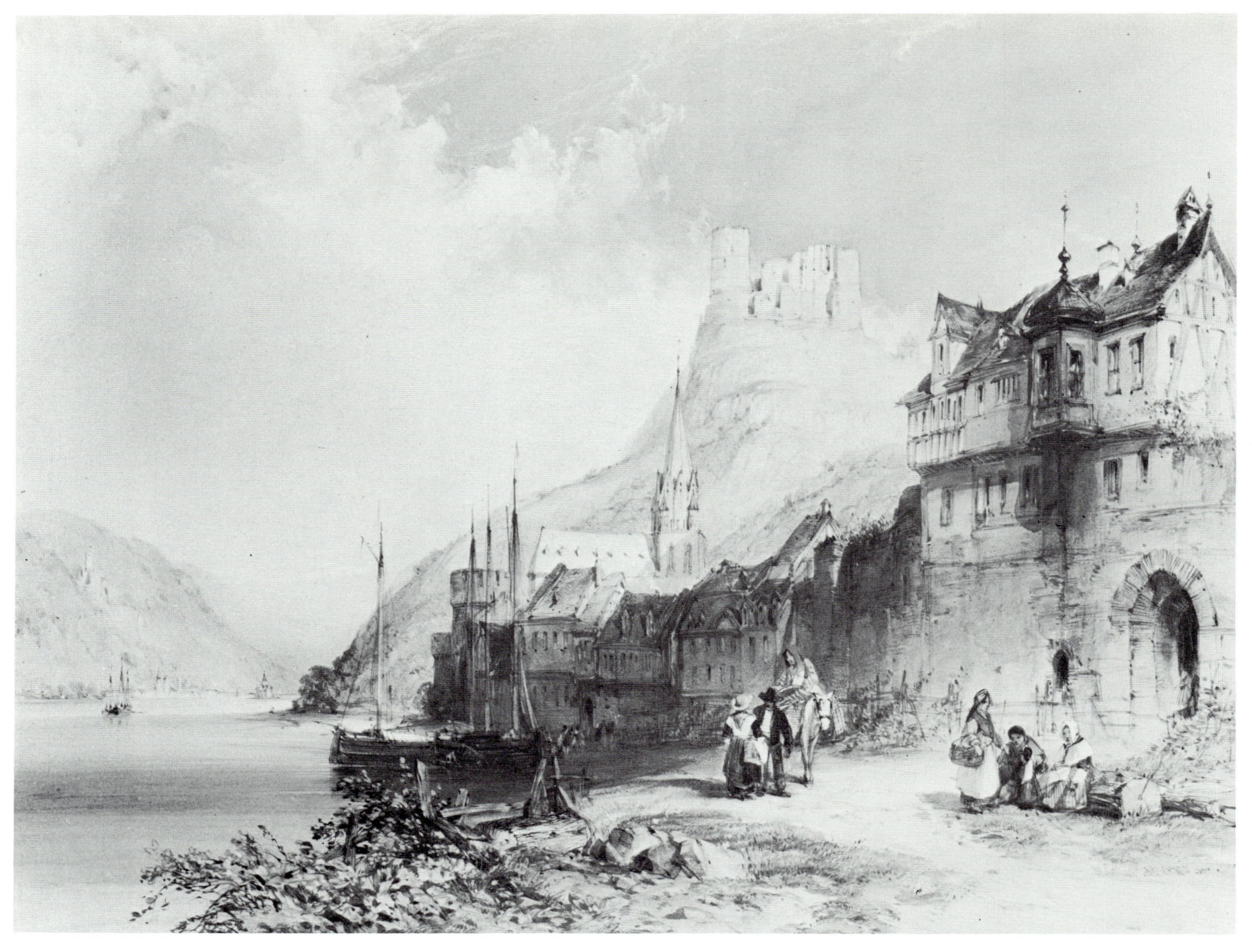

33. 'Oberwesel on the Rhine and the Castle of Schönburg, Germany' Water-colour with touches of body-colour ($19\frac{1}{8} \times 25\frac{3}{8}$ in. – 485×645 mm)
Signed and dated: W. Callow 1841 (right)
Collection: The Whitworth Art Gallery, University of Manchester

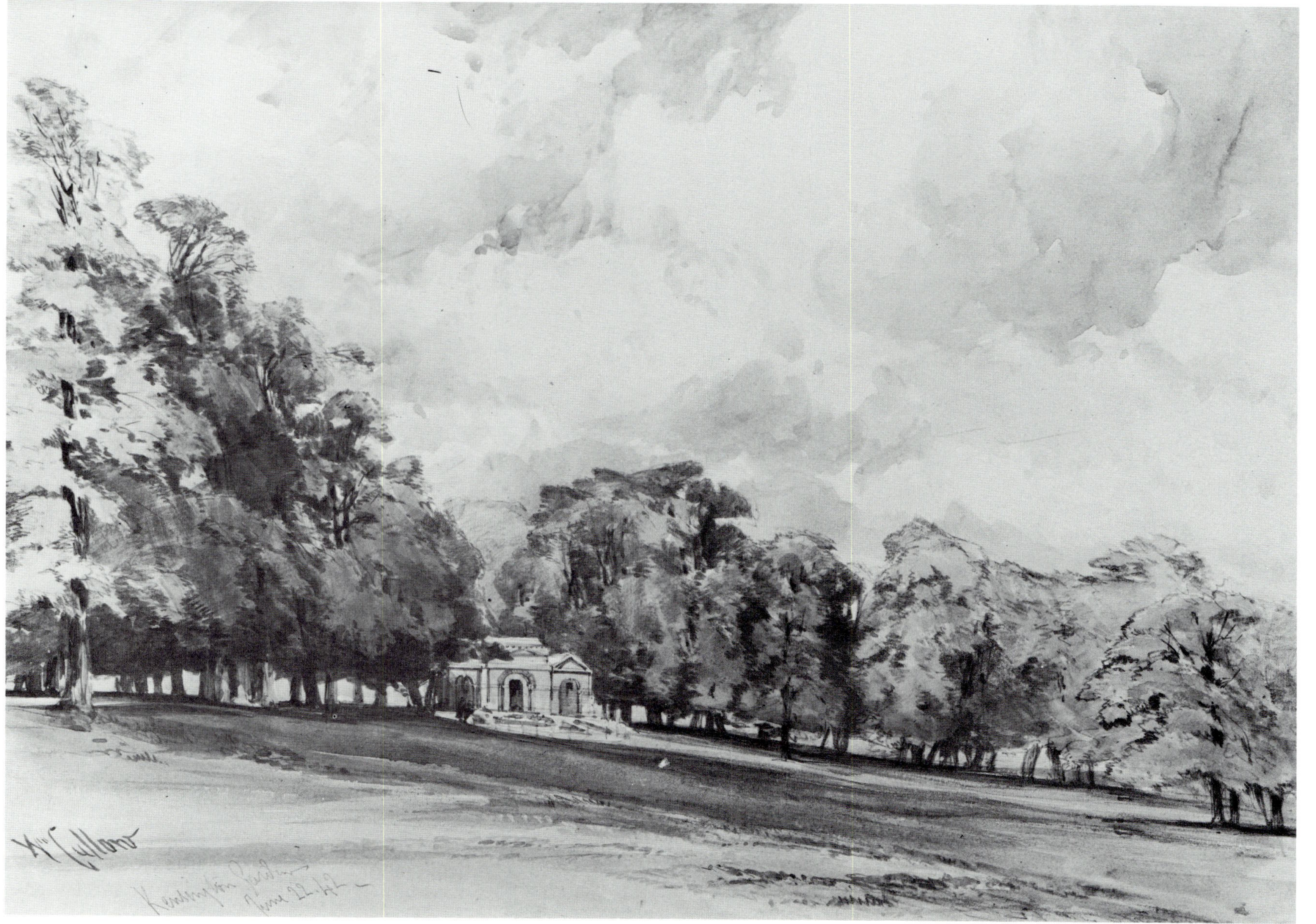

34. 'View in Kensington Gardens showing the "Temple Cottage"' Water-colour ($10\frac{1}{4} \times 14\frac{3}{8}$ in. – 260×365 mm)

Signed: Wm. Callow. Inscribed: *Kensington Gardens June 22 .42*

Collection: Victoria and Albert Museum, Crown Copyright

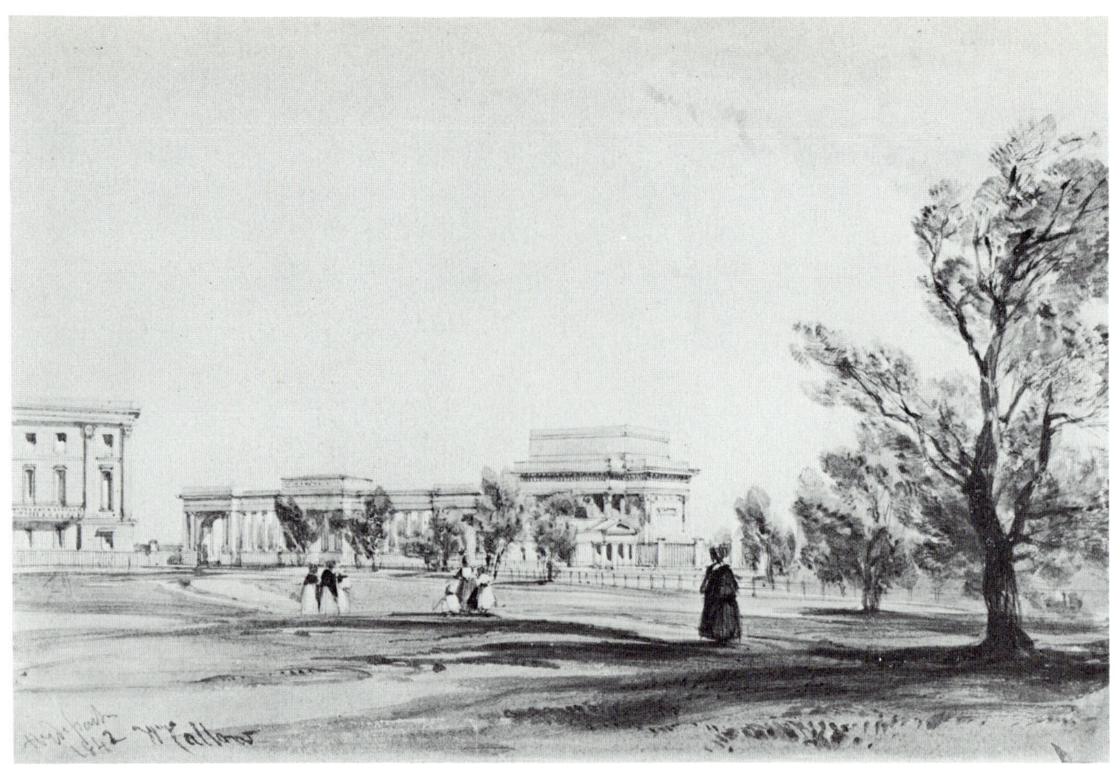

35. 'Entrance to Hyde Park at Hyde Park Corner' Water-colour ($10\frac{1}{4} \times 14\frac{1}{2}$ in. – 260 × 370 mm)
Signed: Wm. Callow. Inscribed: *Hyde Park 1842*
Exhibited: Thomas Shotter Boys Centenary Exhibition, Nottingham University Art Gallery, 1974, which also included 'Rue de Rivoli'
Collection: Victoria and Albert Museum, Crown Copyright

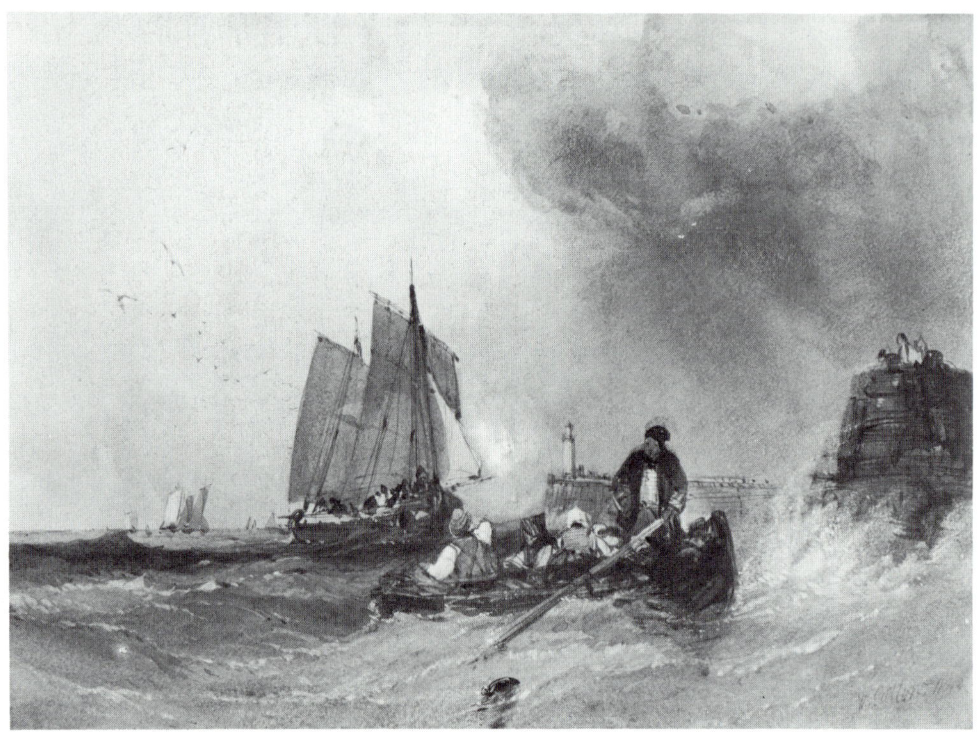

36. 'Entering the Harbour' Water-colour, with touches of body-colour ($9\frac{1}{4} \times 12\frac{1}{2}$ in. – 235 × 317 mm)
Inscribed in lower right corner: *W. Callow 1842*
Reproduced by permission of the Trustees of the Wallace Collection, London

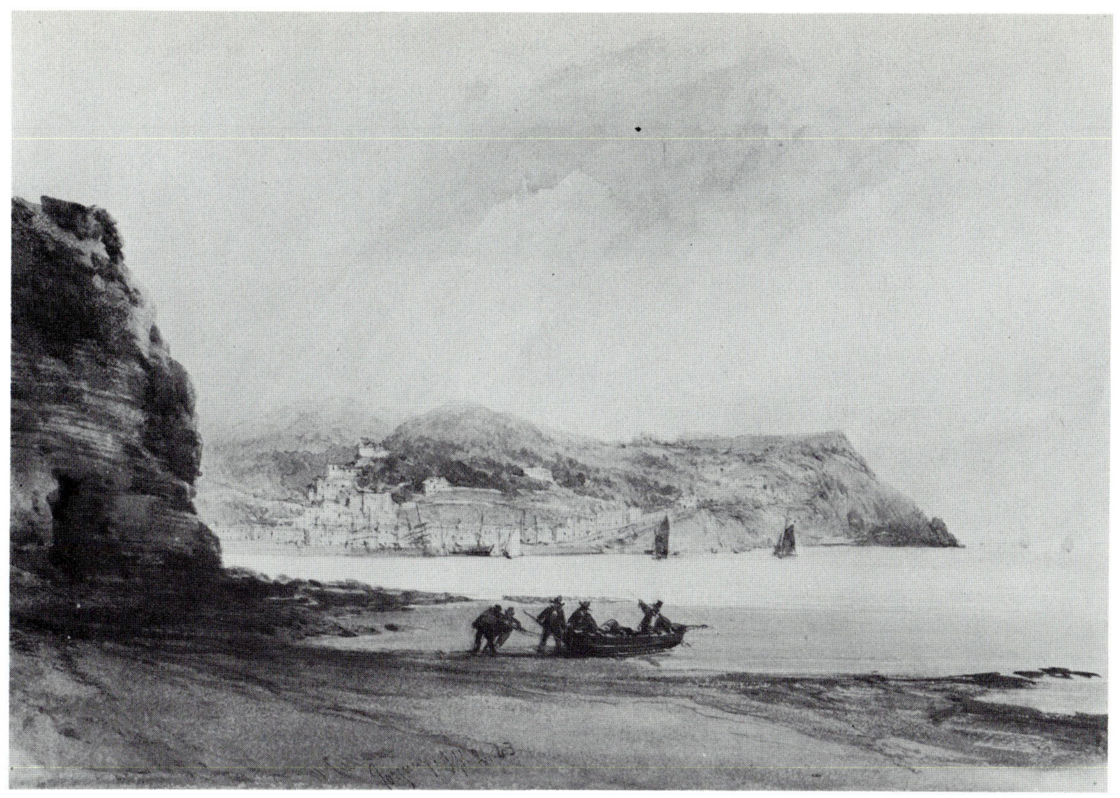

37. 'Torquay' Water-colour ($10\frac{1}{10} \times 14\frac{1}{10}$ in. – 256 × 358 mm)
Signed: W. Callow. Inscribed: *Torquay Sept. 24.43(2?)* (*see* text, page 79)
Collection: The Walker Art Gallery, Liverpool

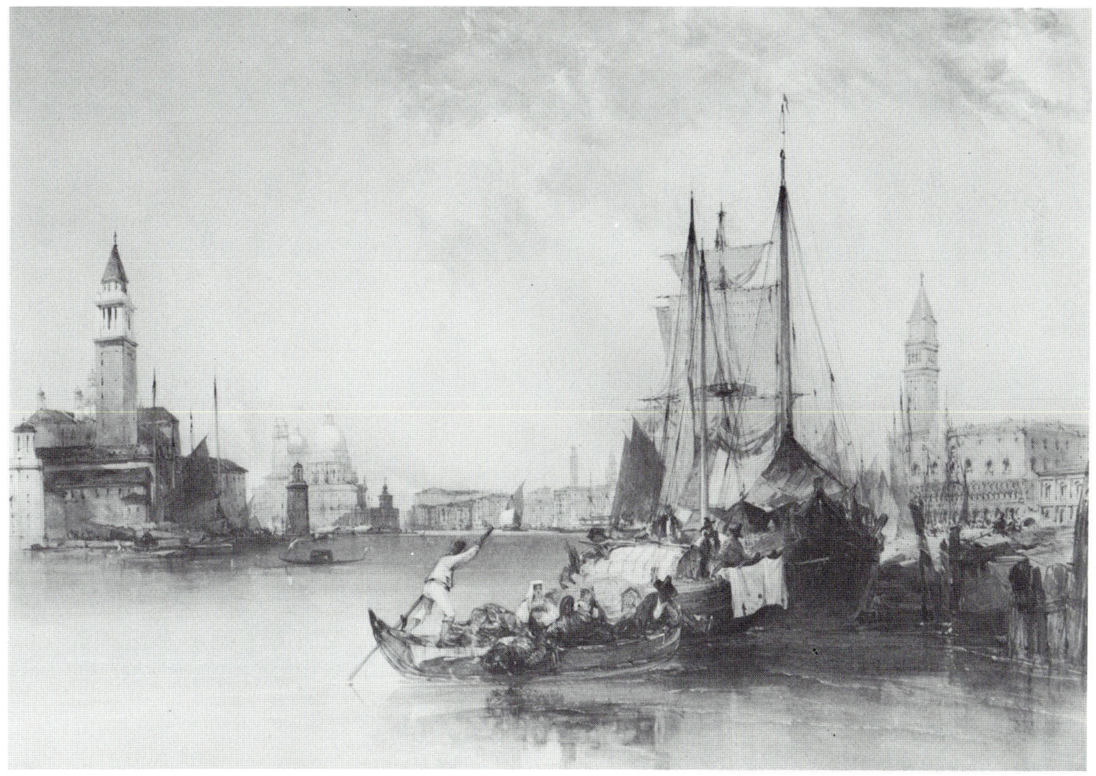

38. 'The Grand Canal, Venice' Water-colour (34 × 22 in. – 864 × 559 mm)
Signed W. Callow
Exhibited: Society of Painters in Water-colours, 1842
Engraved: Plate 7 no. 30 in the London Art Union Prize Annual, 1845
Photograph: The Fine Art Society Ltd

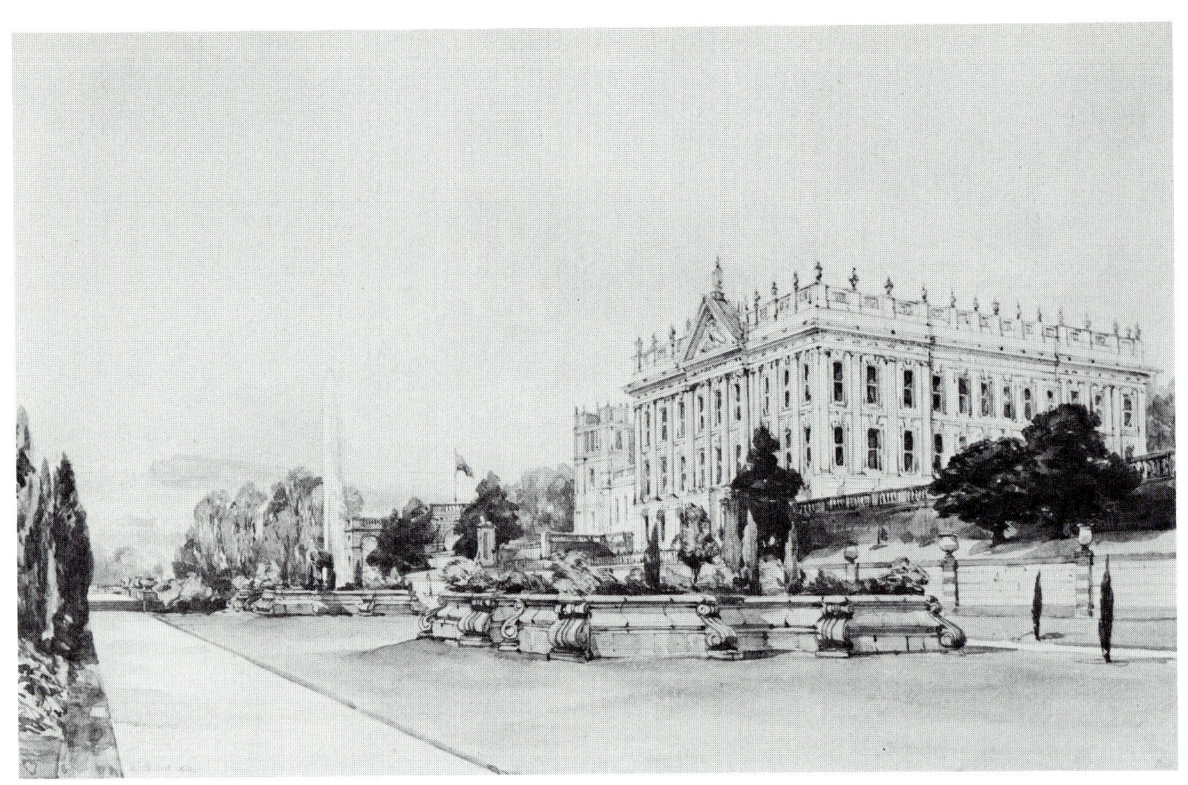

39. 'Chatsworth, the Garden Front' Water-colour (7 × 12½ in. – 178 × 318 mm)
Signed: W. Callow 1843 (left)
Reproduced by gracious permission of Her Majesty the Queen

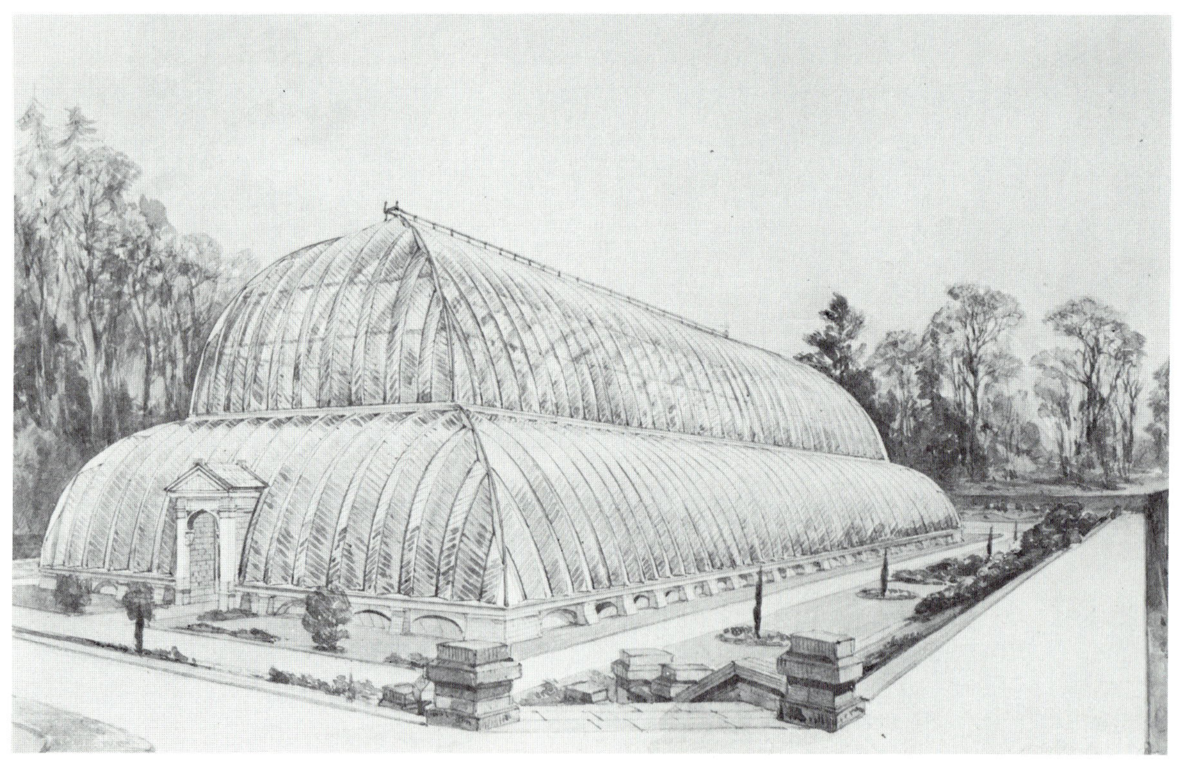

40. 'The Great Conservatory at Chatsworth' Water-colour (7⅞ × 12⅜ in. – 200 × 314 mm)
Reproduced by gracious permission of Her Majesty the Queen

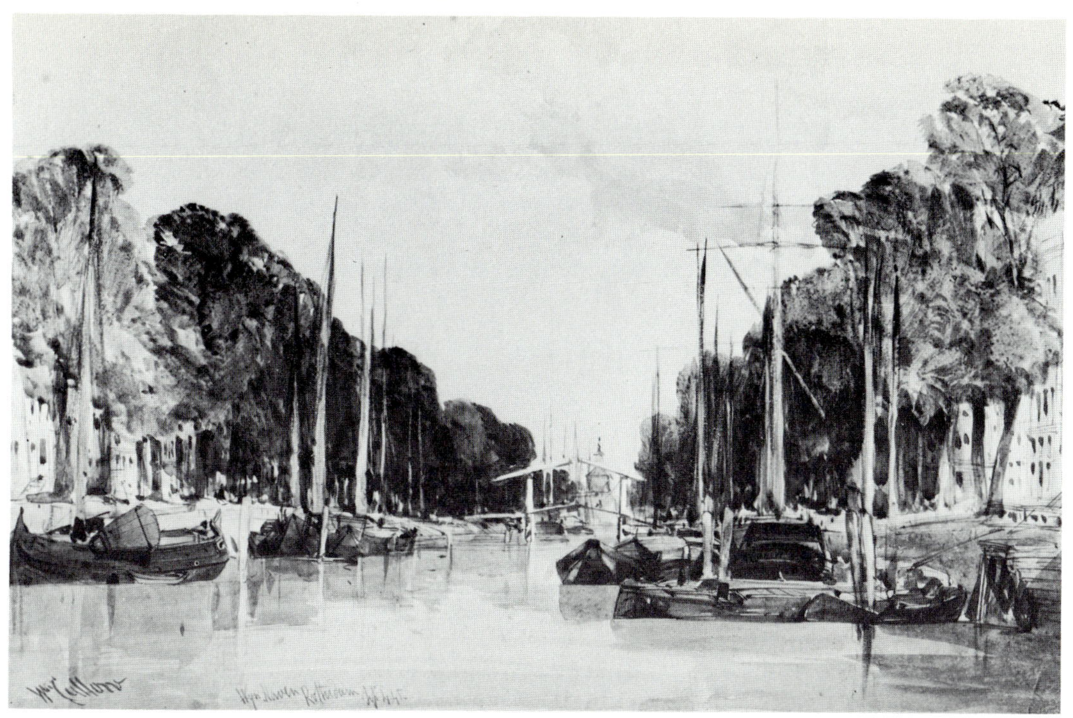

41. 'Wyn Haven, Rotterdam' Water-colour ($10\frac{1}{8} \times 14\frac{1}{8}$ in. – 257×359 mm)
Signed: Wm. Callow. Inscribed and dated: *Sept.4.45*
By courtesy of Birmingham City Museums and Art Gallery
Photo: Courtauld Institute of Art

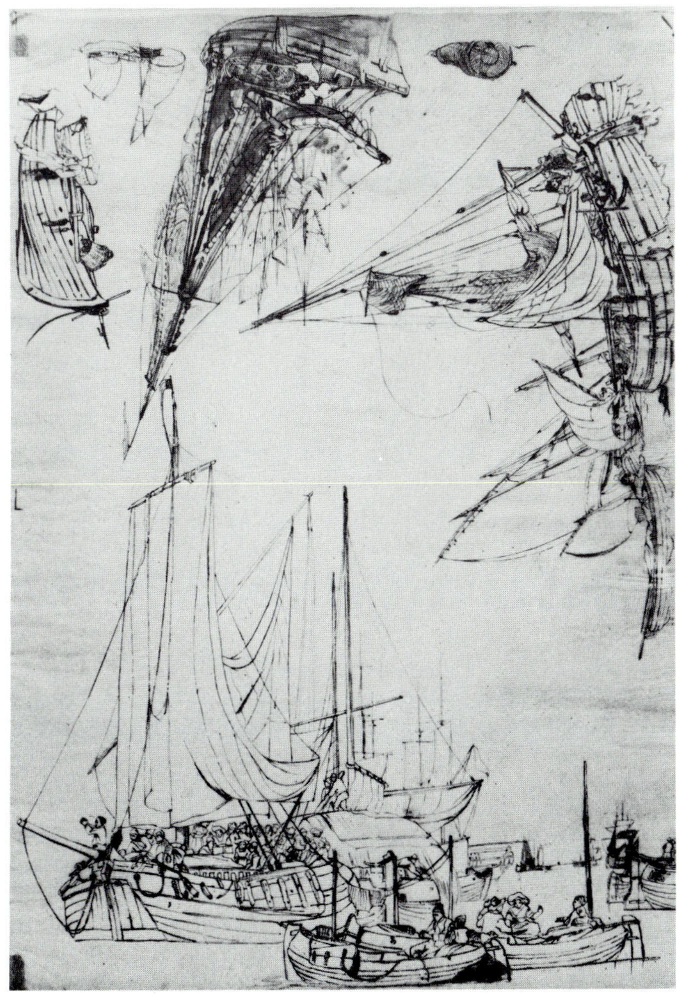

42. 'Dutch Fishing Boats at Scheveningen – 1845'
Sepia ink on tracing paper
(14×9 in. – 356×229 mm)
In possession of the Callow family

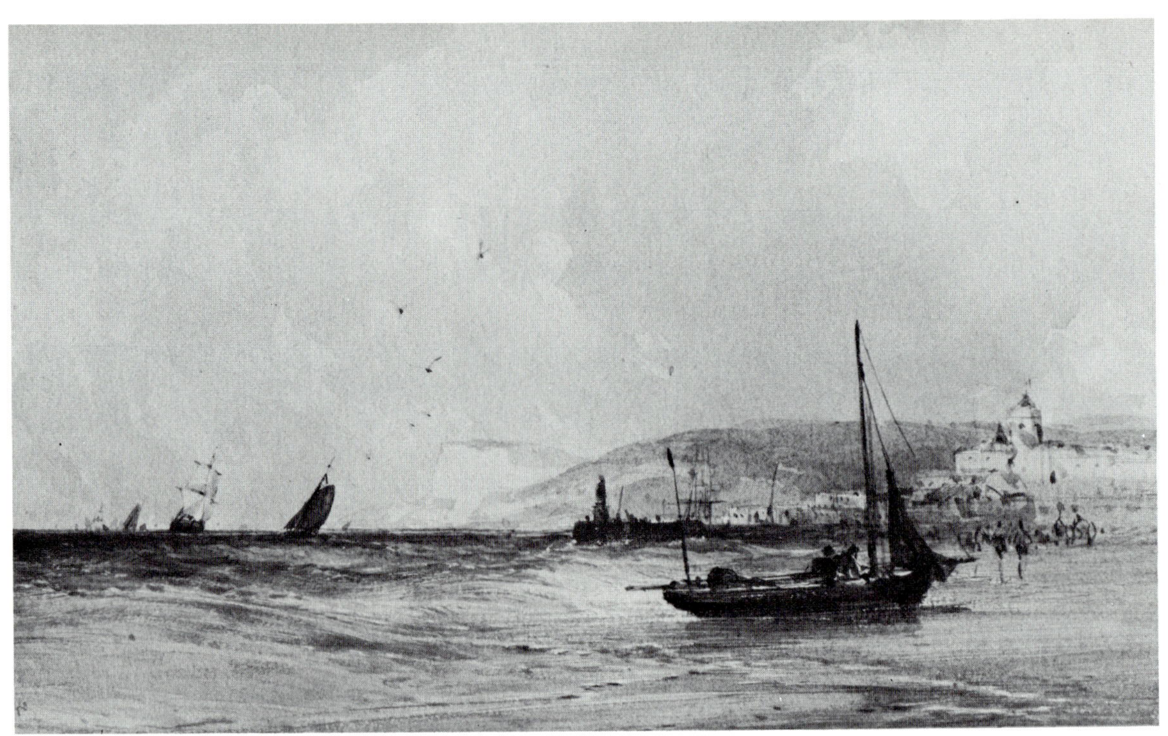

43. 'Fishing Boats at Dover' Water-colour ($7 \times 10\frac{1}{16}$ in. – 178×256 mm)
Collection: The Leicestershire Museum (Leicester County Council), Leicester

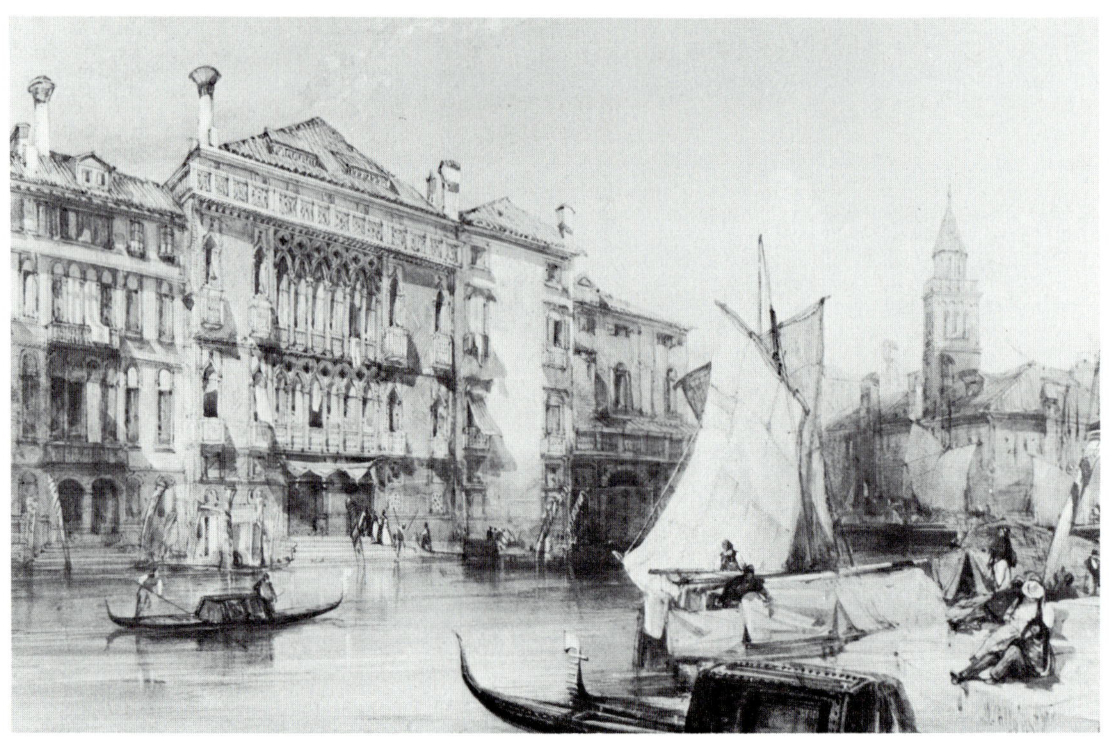

44. 'The Palazzo Pisani-Moretta on the Grand Canal, Venice' Water-colour, heightened with white (12×8 in. – 305×203 mm)
Signed: W. Callow (right)
Photograph: Christie's

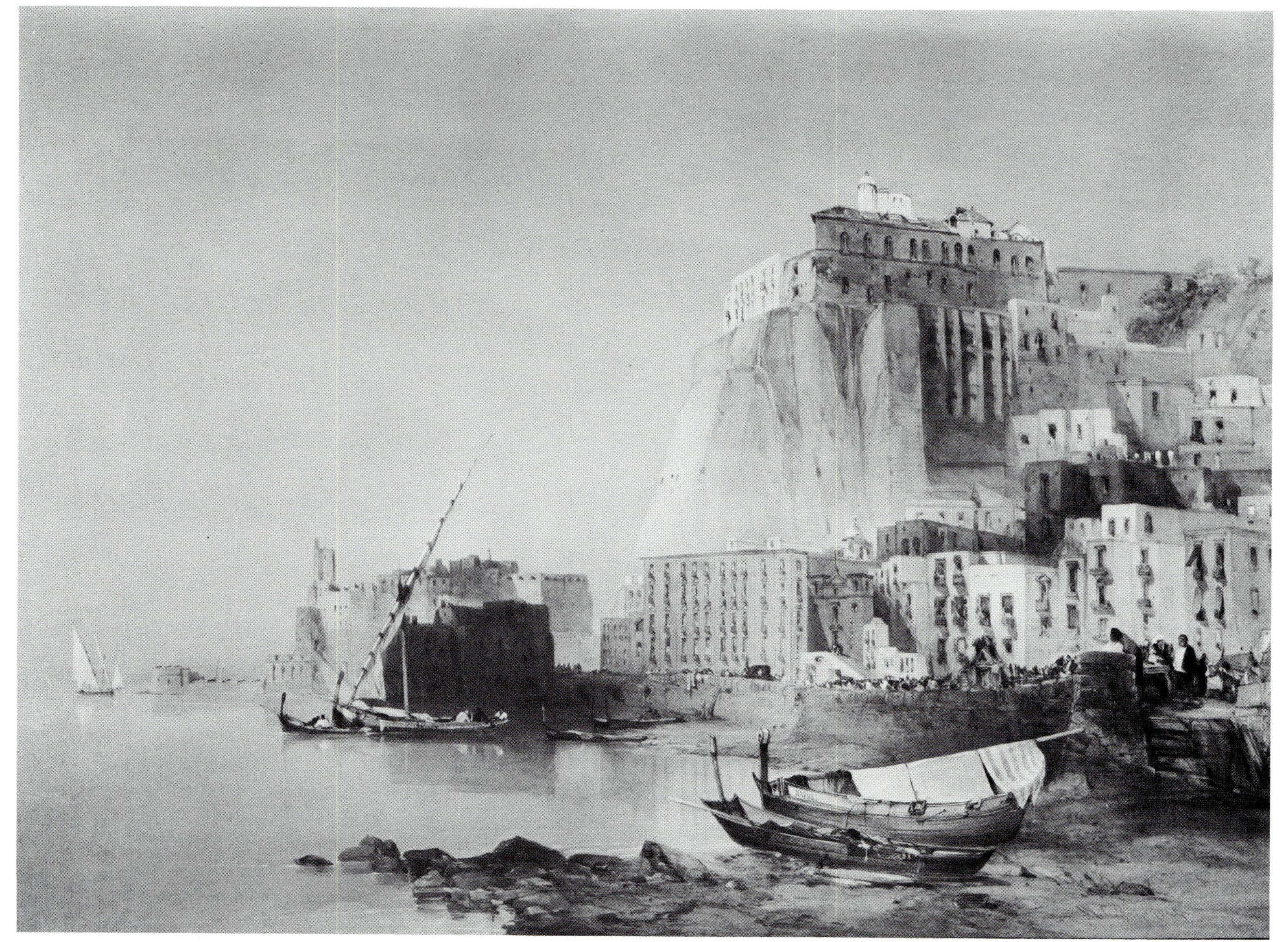

45. 'Piazza Falcone from Quai Santa Lucia, Naples' Water-colour ($21\frac{1}{2} \times 29\frac{1}{2}$ in. – 546 × 749 mm)
Illustrated: *Apollo*, November 1959
With Agnew in 1979

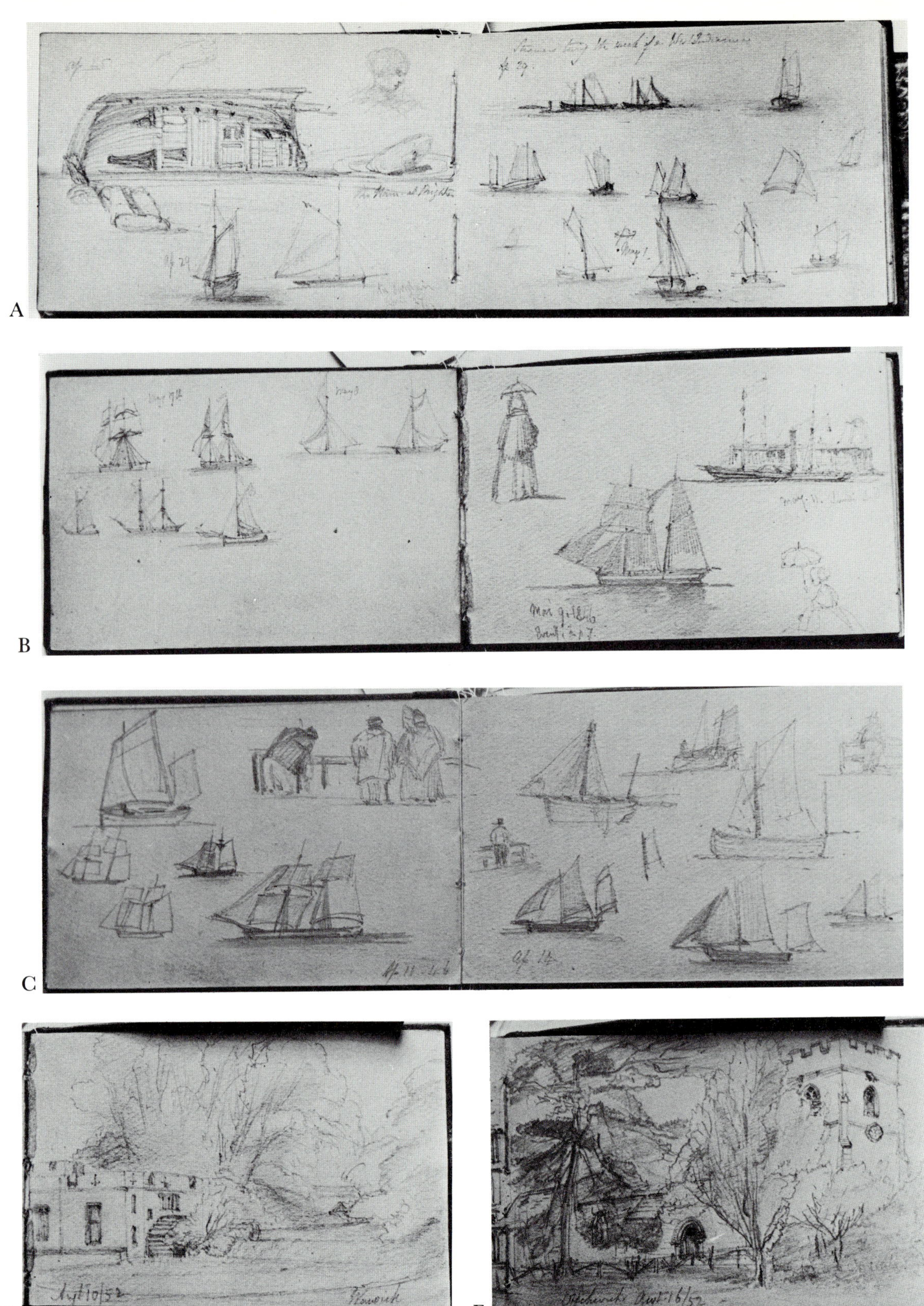

46. Pages from a sketch book belonging to **Harriet Anne Callow** – first wife of William Callow. 'Brighton, 1846' (figures A, B and C), 'Warwick' and 'Offchurch' (Figures D and E)

In possession of the Callow family.

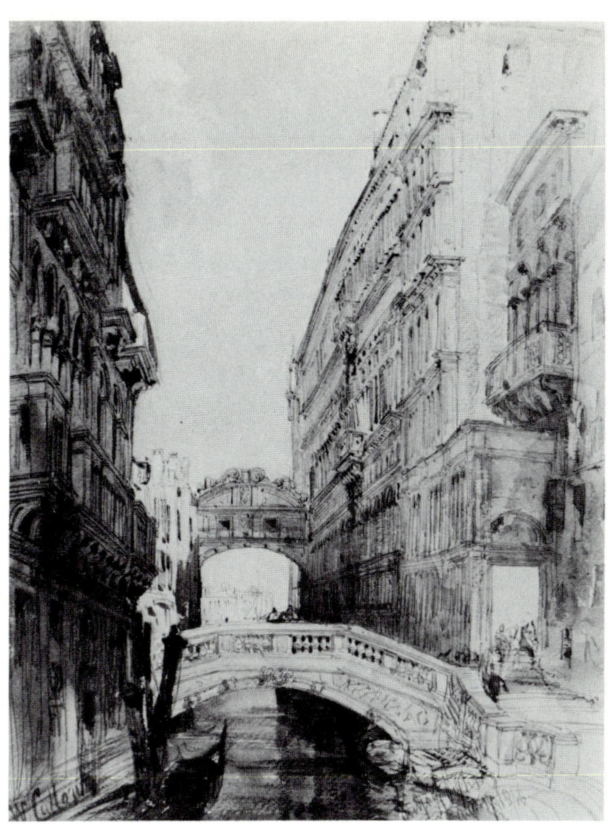

47. 'Bridge of Sighs, Venice' Water-colour and pencil (14¼ × 10¼ in. – 362 × 260 mm)
Signed: W. Callow. Inscribed: *Augt. 17 1846*
In possession of the Callow family

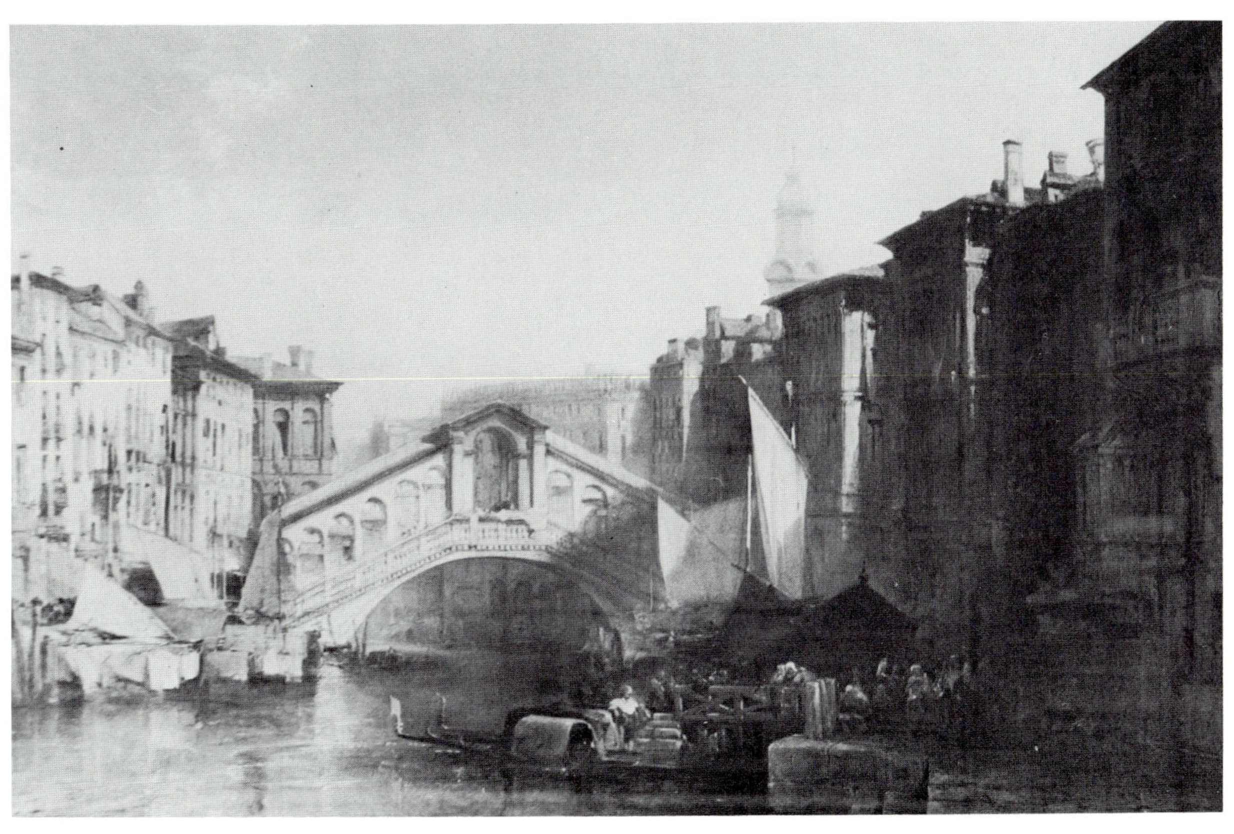

48. 'Rialto, Venice' Oils (29 × 44 in. – 737 × 1118 mm)
Williamson Art Gallery (Metropolitan Borough of Wirral), Birkenhead

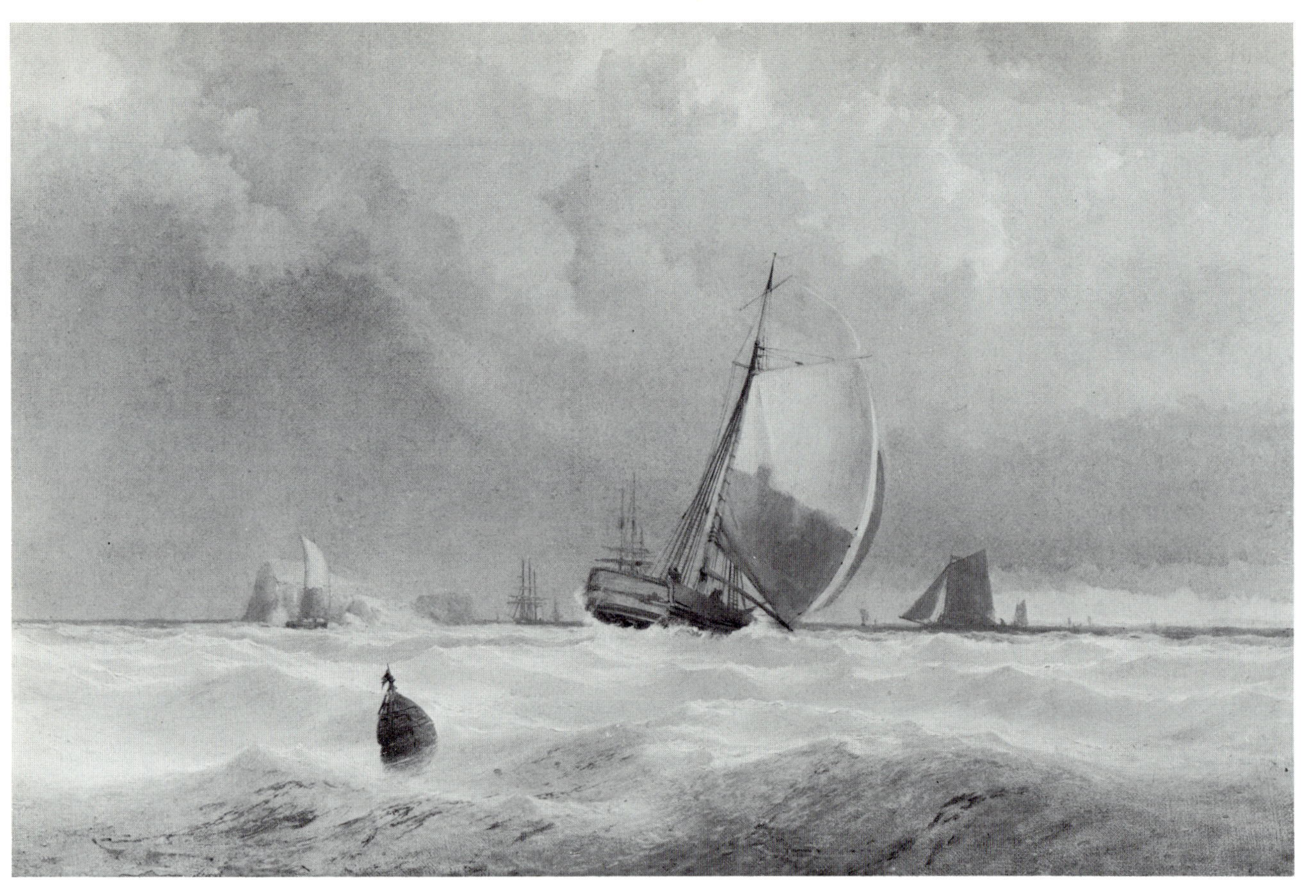

49. 'Shipping off a Coast' Oils
Collection: E. H. H. Archibald

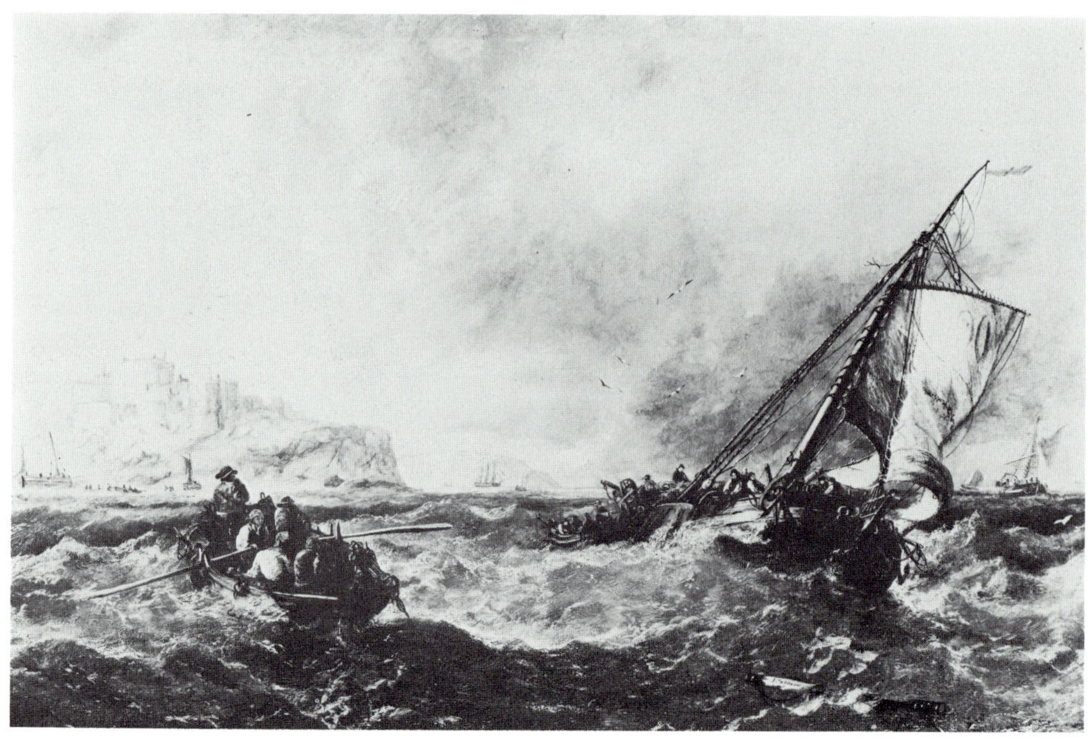

50. 'Seascape, Brittany' Oil painting by **John Callow, A.W.S.** ($33\frac{9}{10} \times 5\frac{3}{10}$ in. – 860×135 mm)
Signed: J. Callow (on piece of flotsam – right foreground)
Collection: Rotherham Art Gallery and Museum

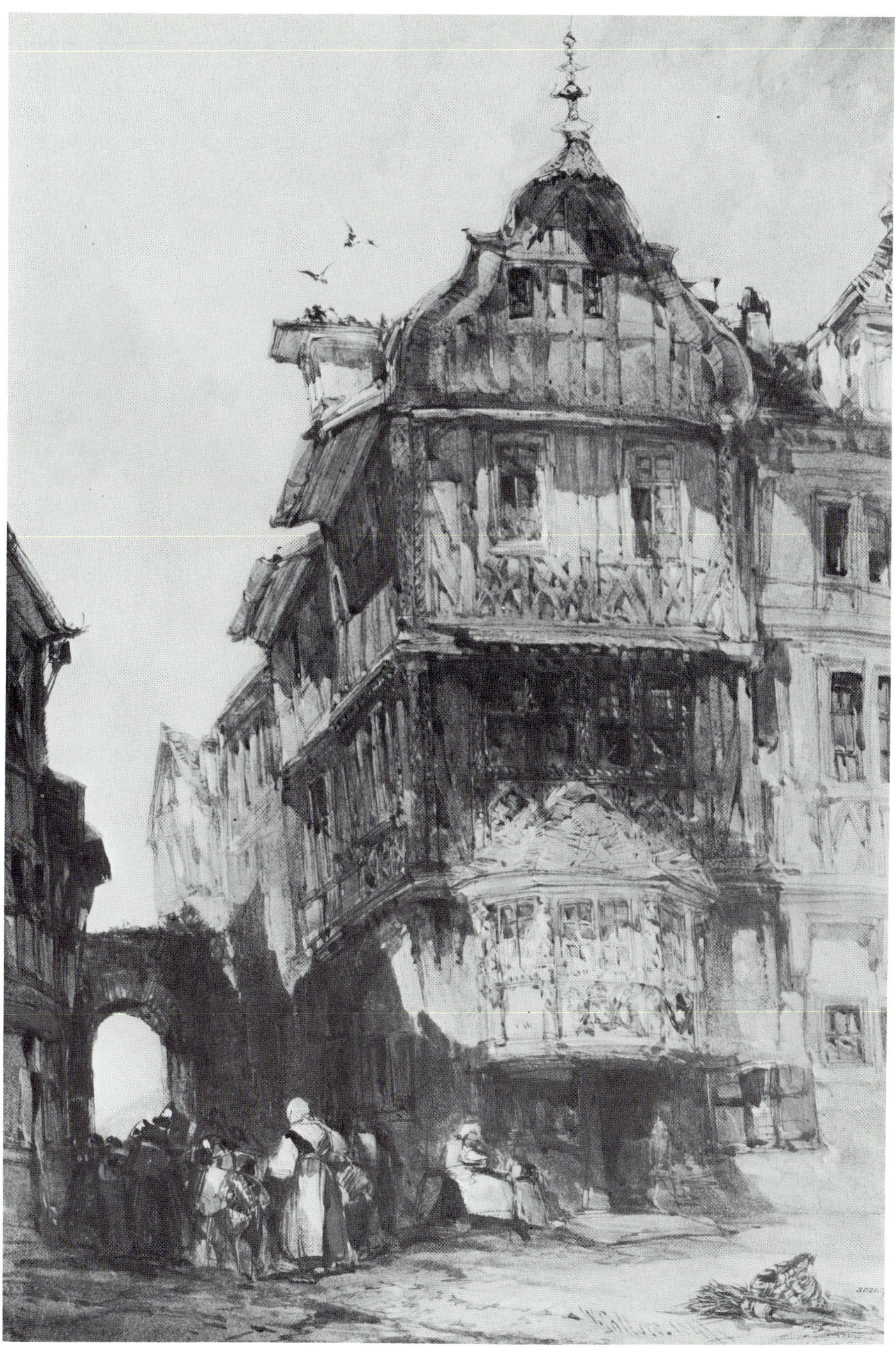

51. 'Old Houses, Berncastel on the Moselle' Water-colour ($19\frac{4}{5} \times 13\frac{3}{10}$ in. – 502 × 336 mm)
Signed and dated: W. Callow 1847 (lower right foreground)
Collection: Victoria and Albert Museum, Crown Copyright

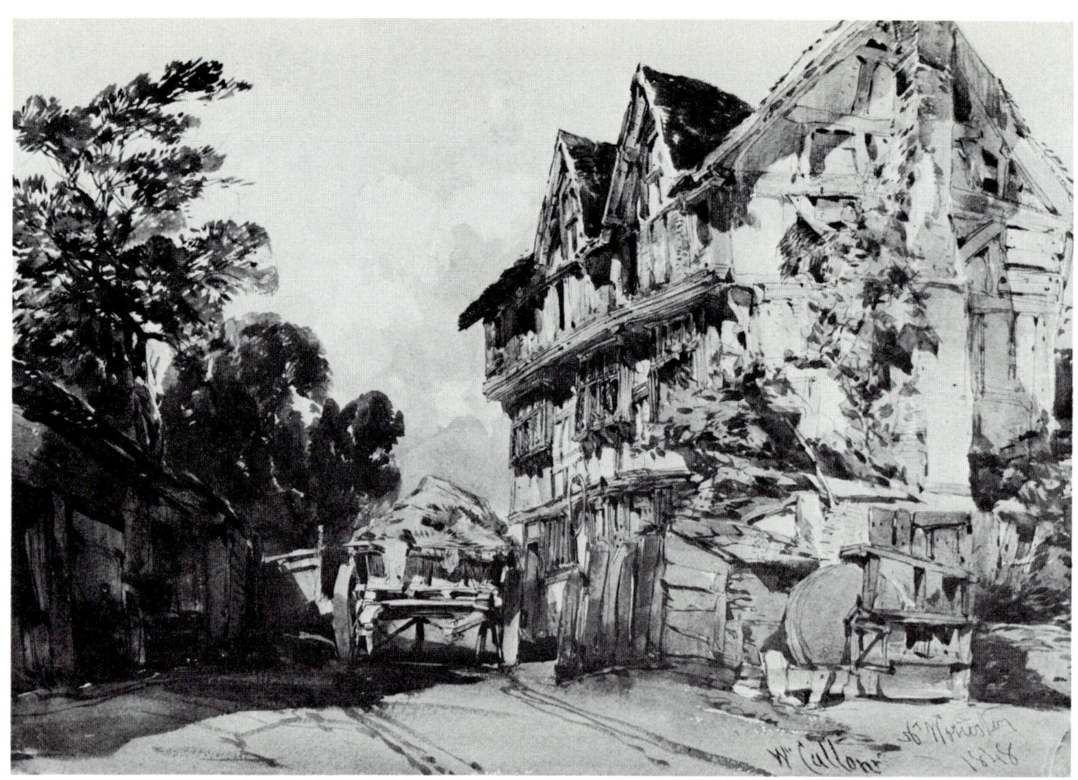

52. 'Old Houses, near Worcester' Water-colour ($9\frac{1}{2} \times 13\frac{1}{2}$ in. – 241 × 342 mm)
Signed: Wm. Callow. Inscribed: *Near Worcester 1848*
Exhibited: Royal Society of Painters in Water-colours, 1907
Collection: Southampton Art Gallery and Museums

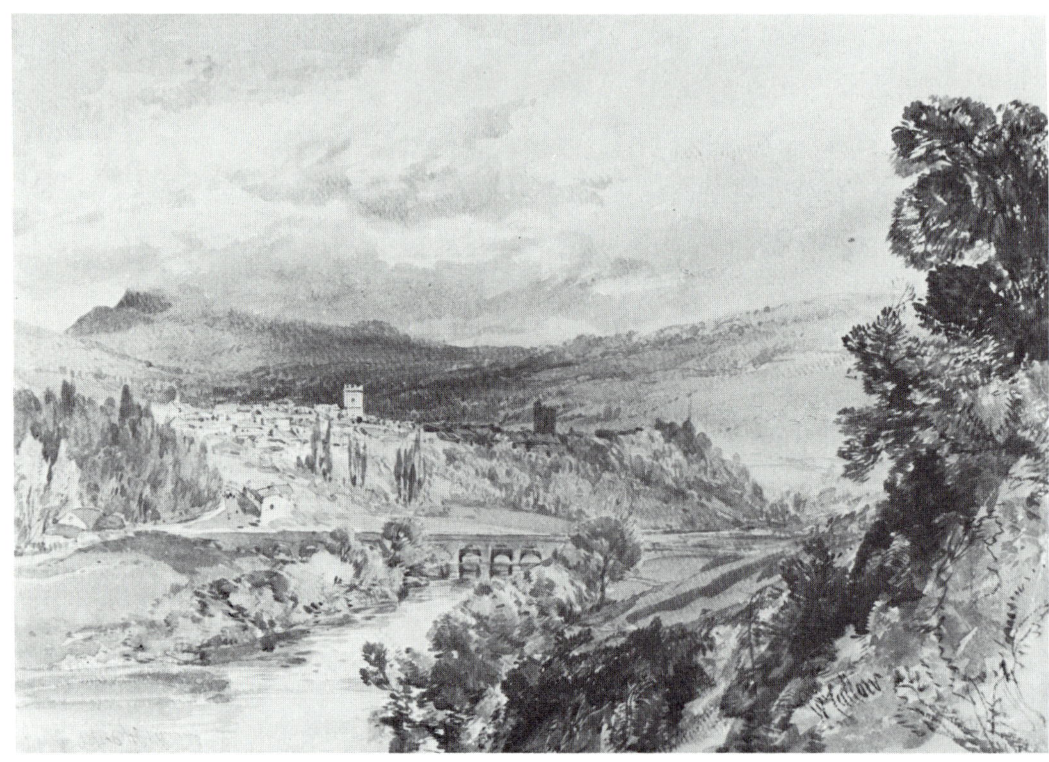

53. 'Abergavenny' Water-colour ($10\frac{1}{2} \times 14\frac{3}{8}$ in. – 267 × 365 mm)
Signed: Wm. Callow. Inscribed: *Oct. 16 1848*
Exhibited: 'Masters of British Water-colour', Royal Academy, 1949
By courtesy of Birmingham Museums and Art Gallery
Photograph: Courtauld Institute of Art

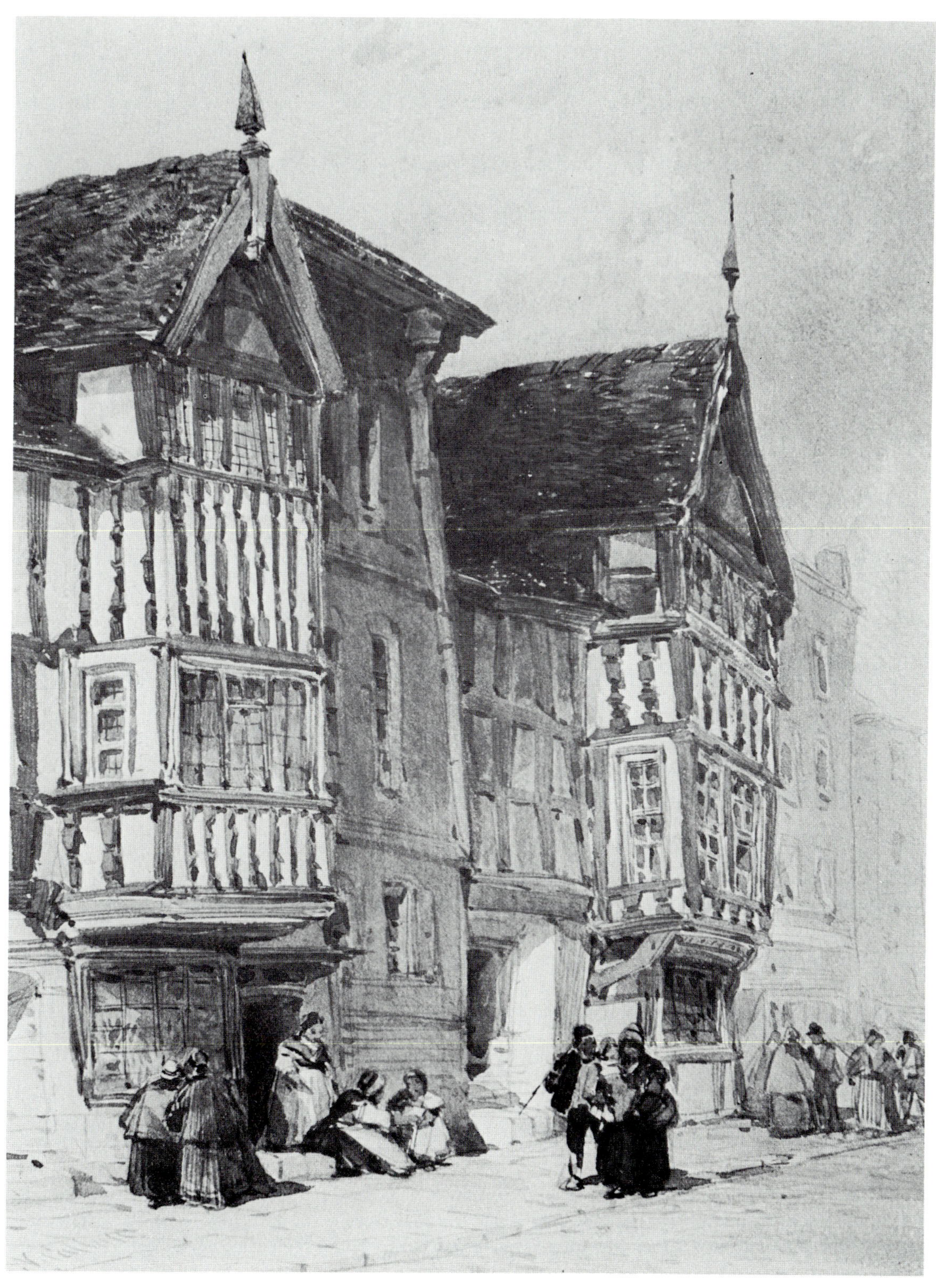

54. 'Old Houses, Pride Hill, Shrewsbury' Water-colour ($10\frac{3}{10} \times 7\frac{3}{5}$ in. – 261 × 194 mm)
Signed: W. Callow and almost certainly dated 1848
Collection: Clive House Museum (Shrewsbury and Atcham Borough Council), Shrewsbury

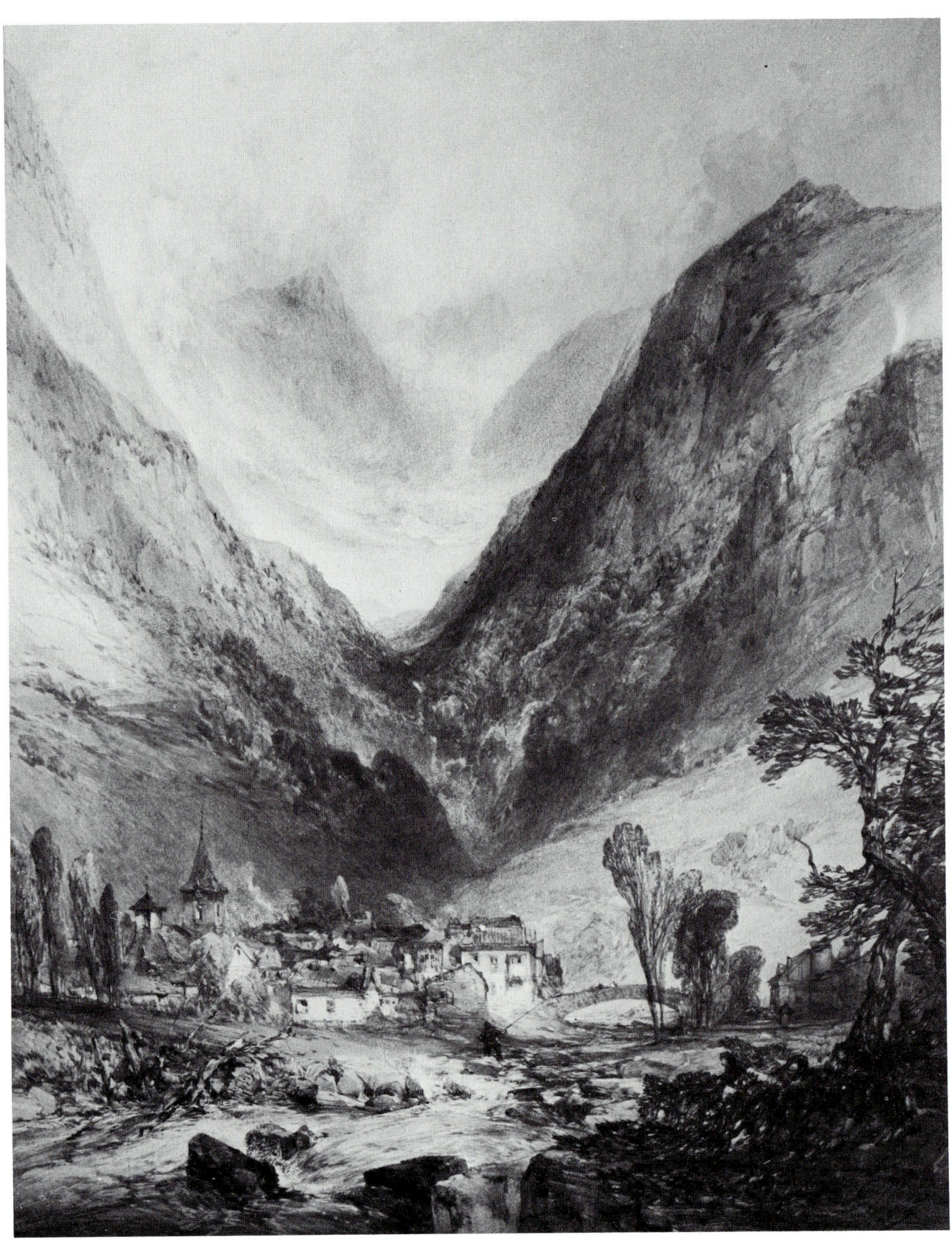

55. 'Glacier du Rhône and the Garlingstock Pass of Furka, Switzerland' Watercolour ($29\frac{1}{4} \times 22\frac{1}{4}$ in. – 743 × 565 mm)
Signed and dated: W. Callow 1849
Collection: City Museum and Art Gallery, Hanley, Stoke-on-Trent

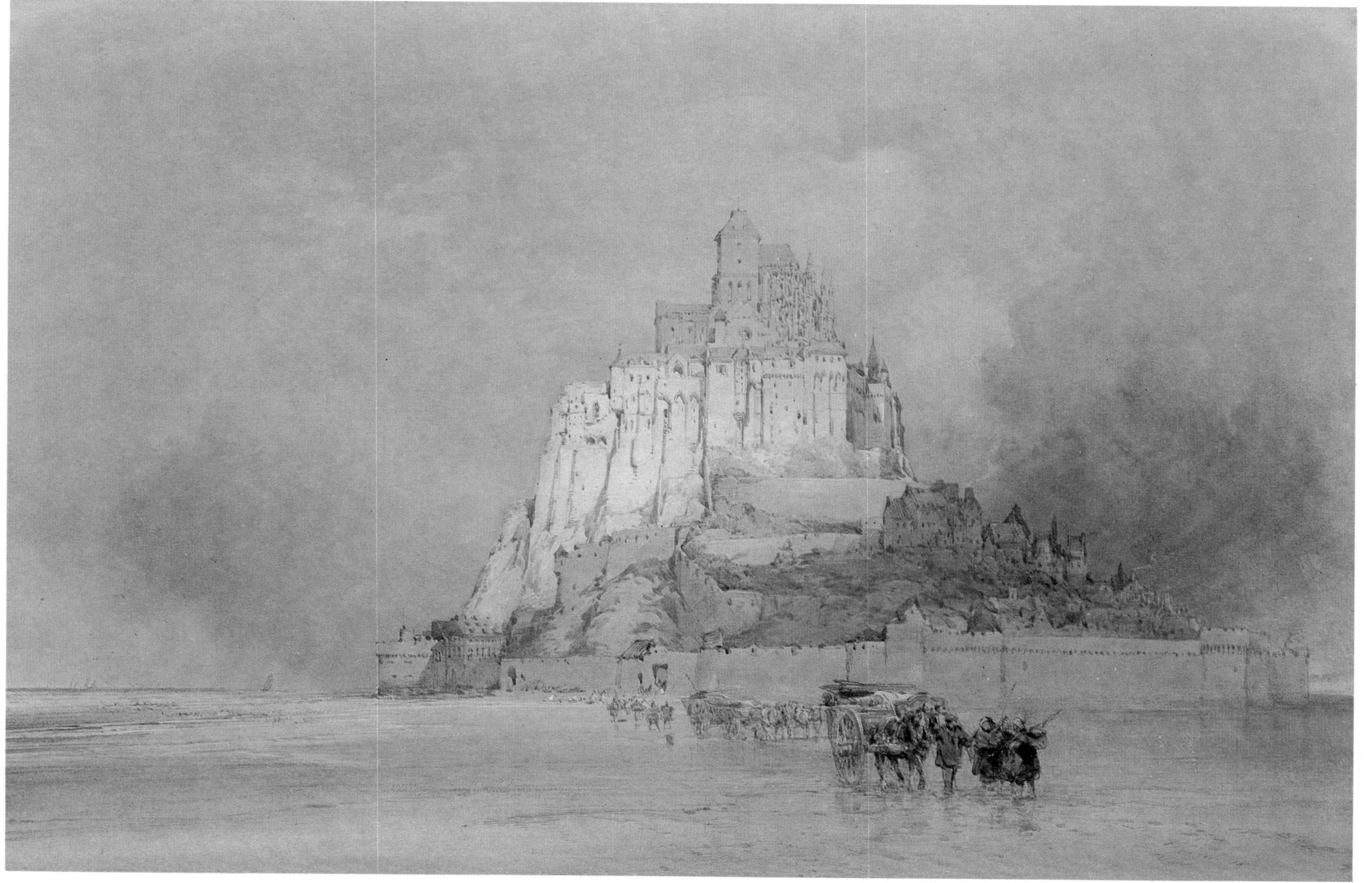

'Mont St. Michel, Normandy, France'
Water-colour ($15\frac{3}{4} \times 24\frac{1}{2}$ in. – 400×622 mm)
Signed and dated: W. Callow 1861
Collection: John Appleby

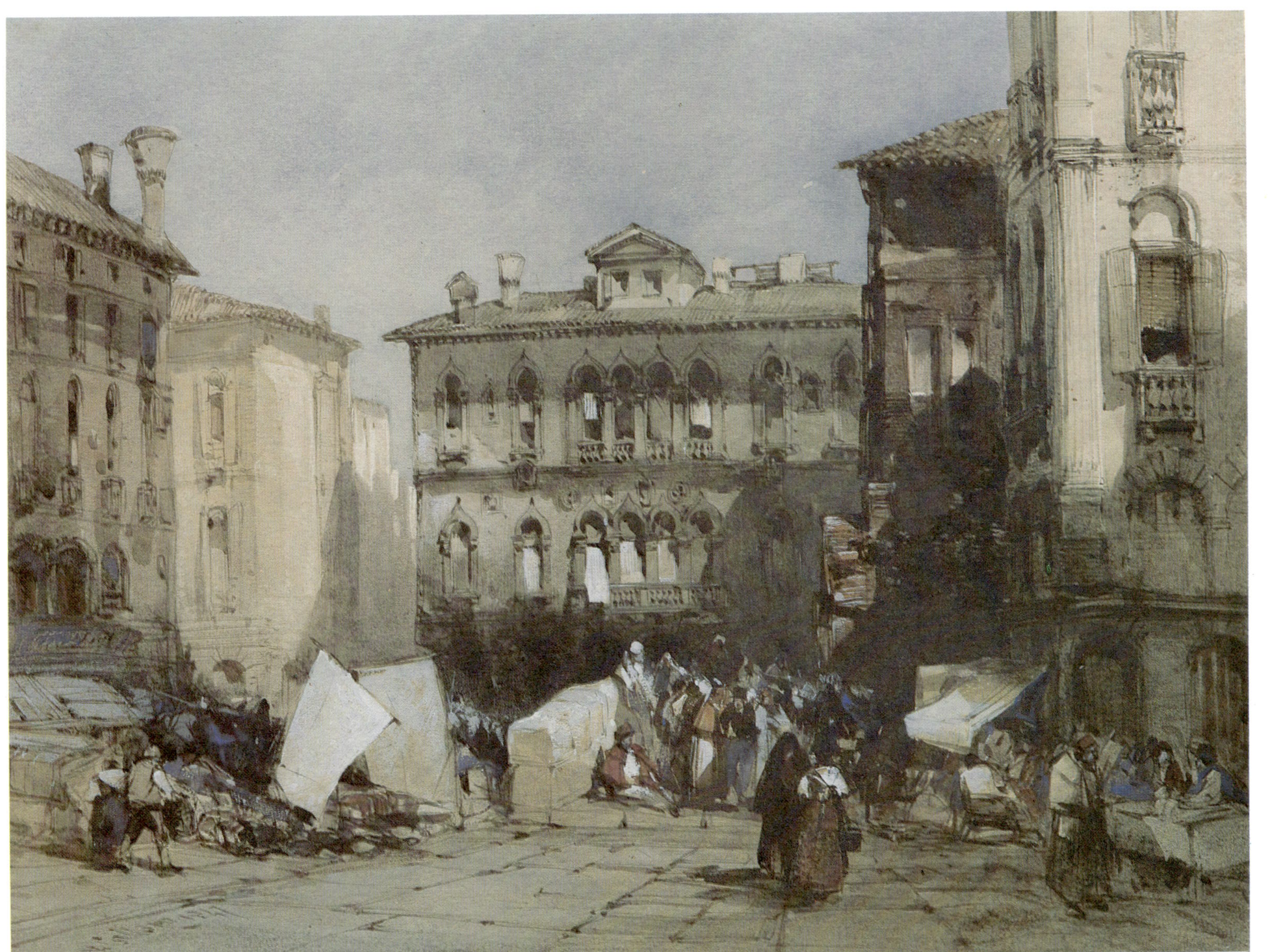

'Palazzo Falier, Venice'
Water-colour ($10\frac{1}{2} \times 14$ in. – 267×356 mm)
Signed: Wm. Callow 1847 (left)
Collection: Laing Art Gallery (Tyne and Wear County Council) Newcastle-upon-Tyne

their passports always with them. Eventually he followed us to the hotel, where we met the maître on the doorstep, who had a lively discussion with the gendarme for about half an hour. Eventually he was sent about his business and we all went to the head office to lodge a complaint. In the evening we had two bottles of wine and invited the maître d'hôtel to join us, as he had so kindly taken our part.

June 15:
Sorry to have to leave at 7 a.m. as we were much pleased with Blois. Passed through Chailles, Monthou, and Sambin, breakfasting at the last-named village, the country now becoming more fertile and rich, and arrived, by a beautiful road, at Montrichard, on the Cher [*illustration no. 23*]. A steep ascent leads up to the village, with houses built on rocks on either side of the road, and the ruins of a fine old castle on the summit. We spent a quiet evening on the banks of the river, a lovely spot.

June 16:
I was up at 5 a.m. and made four sketches before breakfast. Afterwards we walked to Chenonceaux, where, leaving our knapsacks at an auberge, we went to see the château, which still contains the fine old furniture of Francis I and Henry II, who lived here, including the beds of Diane de Poitiers and Catherine de Medicis. We then set off to Amboise, arriving there in time for dinner. In the evening we visited the château, belonging to Louis Philippe; the house being late Gothic is not remarkable for its architecture, but there is a very pretty garden.

June 17:
Arose again at 5 a.m. and made a few sketches, but was very disappointed with Amboise. We set off for Tours [*illustration no. 22*] and ten minutes after we had started it began to rain hard. As it seemed to be set for a wet day, we plodded on through it for four leagues and became soaked to the skin. Fortunately the sun came out and dried us by the time we reached Vouvray, where we stopped to have some refreshments. On reaching Tours we went to the hôtel de France. I was not impressed with the town and the cathedral was nothing very remarkable, excepting some fine stained-glass windows.

June 18:
Did a little sketching, but we could find nothing very interesting. We were detained at Tours for our washing till seven in the evening. Blew up the washerwoman and left for Luynes, where did not arrive until it was quite dark.

June 19:
Up at 5 a.m. and ready to start, but Soherr kept us waiting till eight o'clock whilst he was writing a letter. This was the first little rift in the lute, which ultimately caused our parting company. We eventually set off for Langeais and met a large number of country people going to market at Luynes; the men all wore black hats and many of the girls were very pretty. After passing Langeais on the way to Bourgueil, Soherr said he would take another road because we would not agree to

go with him to Angers; so we went to an auberge to settle the matter over a bottle of wine, and we persuaded him that it was just as near to go to Bourgueil, where we stayed the night.

June 20:
Bid good-bye at 6 a.m. to Soherr, who turned off to go to Candes, whilst Talbot and I kept on the direct road to Saumur,[3] where we arrived very hungry. There is nothing like a five leagues' walk to give one an appetite for breakfast. Went to the castle and had a fine view of the Loire and the country around; later to the Druidical remains; nothing remarkable except for the size of the stones. In the evening Soherr arrived at our hotel.

June 21:
On the previous evening we had half promised the maître d'hôtel to go with him to Candes, and we were called at half-past three in the morning, but made various excuses and let him go alone. After again bidding good-bye to Soherr, who started off to Angers, Talbot and I set off along a pretty road to Candes, meeting our maître on his way back. The church at Candes is very beautiful. We continued on our journey to Fontevrault, where there is a large prison capable of holding fifteen hundred prisoners and an old church of the twelfth century. We obtained permission to see the interior of the latter, in which one of the tombs of Henry II and Richard Cœur-de-Lion of England, with recumbent figures in sandstone. After resting we proceeded to Loudun, a curious old town which had formerly been fortified; a Roman tower, one of seven still exists. The town stands on a height in the centre of a large plain with no village near it. It can be seen for a great distance, and when we were at Fontevrault, five leagues away, the town appeared to be quite close.

June 22:
Left next morning for Mirebeau and on passing through a small village we heard several voices from an auberge calling upon us to stop. We discovered that these were three young conscripts going to join their regiments at Poitiers and that they wished to accompany us on the road; they were surrounded by about twenty of their friends, and there was a good deal of drinking going on. We were obliged to '*trinquer*' some very bad wine with them all, including a dragoon '*en congé*', who said to the conscripts '*souvenez-vous que vous êtes toujours français*'. Eventually, after a great deal of leave-taking, the three conscripts set off with us. We walked two leagues, thinking all the way how we could get rid of our friends when we reached an auberge. Having treated them to some wine, we told them we were going to remain for some time, at which they seemed very sorry and insisted on our having some '*petits verres*' with them; they then left but one, the best of the lot, stayed behind for a few seconds and asked permission to embrace us, '*il était si triste!*' So we could not refuse. Later two carters offered us a lift, which we gladly accepted, though the seats were not

[3] 'Saumur' – pencil sketch ($4\frac{7}{8} \times 9\frac{1}{8}$ in. – 123×231 mm) dated Juin 20.36. (Victoria and Albert Museum, E993 – 1937)

very soft, as the cart was laden with casks. We passed by Mirebeau, not entering into the town, which is surrounded by walls and towers, and went two leagues farther to Etaples, where we put up at an inn. After having some dinner we took a walk in the neighbourhood, and, on returning to the inn, we were greatly surprised to find that our three conscripts had just arrived with numerous others; all very hot and tired out. They suggested that as we were all going in the same direction the next morning, we should start together for Poitiers. When we retired to rest we were greatly annoyed to find a room with five beds, four of which were filled with conscripts, the remaining one being left for us. As there was no help for it, we made ourselves as comfortable as we could.

June 23:
The next morning we were awakened by the conscripts dressing, but we lay quiet until they had all gone downstairs, deciding to remain in bed until they had started, and it was with great pleasure that we heard them tramp off. Later we set out for Poitiers, and while passing through the village of Migné we saw women riding astride on horseback, cleverly tucking in their petticoats. After walking four and a half leagues we reached Poitiers, well known for its battlefield. It is an interesting town, containing many curiosities, including the remains of a Roman amphitheatre. Visited the very fine cathedral of St Pierre and the Church of St Jean. As it was the '*veille*' of the latter saint, bonfires were lit by the priests in the town. Had a beautiful view from the height which is on one side of the town.

June 24:
Made some sketches in the morning, and left Poitiers in the afternoon, and passing through the village of Crontille, with a very pretty country all the way, arrived at Vivonne at nine o'clock.

June 25:
Up at 6 a.m., a splendid morning, so set out from Vivonne at once. The weather became so very hot that we stayed at a village café until late in the afternoon, and then proceeded to Chaunay, where we dined. It was such a lovely night that we decided not to go to bed, but to continue our walk throughout the night. At the village of Ruffec we were asked by a gendarme for our passports. He was a veritable '*grogneur*' [i.e. a grumbler]. Nevertheless we went to his cabin and had some wine with him. After bidding him adieu we continued on our road, getting very sleepy and cold near sunrise; about a hundred conscripts passed us. At last we reached Mansle at five o'clock in the morning; very tired indeed, having walked seven leagues during the day and ten at night. We went to a café to have some hot coffee and milk, and whilst it was being prepared we both fell asleep.

June 26:
Woke up after an hour and had our coffee, then set off for Angoulême, seven leagues further. As we became very footsore, we stopped at a village from 9 a.m. till 3.30 p.m.

Eventually, after mounting a steep hill, we arrived at Angoulême and put up at the Hotel Périgueux. After dinner we turned into bed. What enjoyment! What happiness!

June 27:
Got up for breakfast, but slept nearly the whole of the day. In the evening we went on the ramparts which surround the town; saw a lovely sunset and the full moon rise. In the interesting old town are some towers remaining of an old castle, and the ancient cathedral has some curious sculptures on the exterior. The country around is rich but flat, and the river Charente winds prettily through the plain. Here we first saw oxen used in place of horses for drawing carts.

June 28:
The weather piping hot. A regiment arrived. I never saw soldiers so covered with dust. Made some sketches in the broiling sun. At lunch we met an old military officer who had been through the Russian campaign; he tried to make us believe that he knew everything, and told us that in Holland cows were fastened up with silver chains. There was also a young man who talked very grandly about the number of crimes he would commit for the sake of his country. We had just heard an attempt had been made on the King's life. Took the coach to Barbezieux, passing on the way the ruin of an old abbey at the village of La Couronne and at Roullet an old church of the same period as the cathedral at Angoulême. On arrival at Barbezieux we were followed by a Sous-Préfet, who inquired whether we were Poles, but on learning that we were English he became very polite and apologised for following us. At the inn the host's daughter, who was very beautiful, sang charmingly. We were much taken with her, and made two clerks very jealous because we got into conversation with her.

June 29:
Up at 5.30 a.m. to catch the coach at six, and owing to the stupidity of the maid we had nothing to eat except a piece of bread until the coach stopped at Montlieu for *déjeuner*. There were 10 passengers in the coach, and it being very hot weather, we were nearly stifled. After passing through a beautiful country we reached St André. We walked forward to the banks of the Gironde and saw the ruins of a castle. The river here is very broad, and there being no bridge, we crossed by a ferry, the boat being drawn by a rope attached to a drum, like a mill, turned by horses. We were all packed in the boat, including the coach and horses, and arrived safely on the other side of the river, although there was some alarm amongst the lady passengers owing to the horses getting fidgety. We started on the coach again. Driving through the vine country for two hours, we came to the hills close to Bordeaux on which the best vines are cultivated, then crossed the bridge over the Garonne into Bordeaux [*illustration no. 12*] where Talbot and myself stayed at the Hôtel de Rouen.

June 30:
Spent an intensely hot day seeing the sights of the town, and attended the launch of a vessel at high tide. Could not sleep at night on account of the heat.

July 1:
Got up at 6 a.m. and made some sketches in the early morning; as the weather was extremely hot, could do very little during the day.

July 2:
Walked out to St André and saw the church of St Michael. On our return we met Soherr, who had just arrived, and we talked over our respective adventures.

July 3:
Visited the church of St Severin. I determined to continue my tour in the night on account of the heat. Talbot tried to persuade me to wait another day for him, but as he would only go as far as Agen I adhered to my determination. At 11.30 p.m. Talbot and Soherr accompanied me to the gate of the town, and I started off alone for Langon. Being a lovely night, I rested by the roadside. I never felt so lonely in my life; thought of all those at home. Walked nine leagues and stopped at a village near Castres.

July 4:
Slept nearly all day, and set out for Langon in the evening. Put up at an inn where everyone spoke a patois which I could not understand. Went down to the river and saw steamers arrive from Bordeaux.

July 5:
Up at 4 a.m. and crossed the bridge just as the sun was rising, a charming effect with Langon on one side of the river and a ruin of an old castle on the other; passed several villages in a very pretty country and reached La Réole, where I took the steamer to Marmande.

July 6:
Weather became less oppressive, and I determined to profit by it, making an early start, and at 10 a.m. reached Tonneins, famous for manufacturing tobacco. Was told that on a clear day the Pyrénées could be seen from here. Pressed on, passed the town of Aiguillon, and arrived at Port St Marie, where I stayed the night at an inn overlooking the river which is broad and fine.

July 7:
Started at 4.30 a.m. along a pretty road, with tobacco plantation and a quantity of corn, which was being reaped on either side, the hills were now becoming more lofty. Overtook a regiment on the way to Toulouse, the officers were walking with the men and all were covered in dust. Passed St Hilaire and arrived at Agen at 8 p.m. putting up at the Hôtel de France. Made some sketches, but nearly the whole

of the town is hidden by large trees along a fine promenade beside the river. I had followed the Garonne nearly all the way from Bordeaux.

July 8:
Up late. Visited the very old church of St Caprais and the picturesque Hôtel de Ville which dates from 1665. In the evening took a walk by the river, and saw hundreds of women bathing, quite a usual custom.

July 9:
Took the coach to Auch, and as the road is very hilly and the weather still hot, I am glad of the ride. Had *déjeuner* at Lectoure, a town which has been the birthplace of many generals of the French Army including Montebellow, a maréchal under Napoleon. Auch is prettily situated on a hill, and the cathedral, being built in a prominent position, is seen from a great distance. Went to see the famous stained-glass windows which it contains. As a coach for Tarbes arrived from Toulouse, I decided to continue my journey by it.

July 10:
Arrived at Tarbes at 7 a.m. I had slept on the coach as far as Rabastens. Soon after leaving this place I first saw the Pyrénées, which I had long wished to do; the view made a lasting impression on my mind. A long line of mountains rose from an expansive plain and extended as far as the eye could reach. Above a delicate distant blue, partly hid by mist, could be seen small quantities of snow. The mountains had a grand appearance and I longed to be amongst them. On reaching the Hôtel du Grand Soleil at Tarbes I immediately set off to get a nearer view of the mountains. On my return to the town I once more put my knapsack on my back and left with a light heart for Lourdes. How I enjoyed myself with the beautiful view in front of me! I wished for someone to be with me to partake of my pleasure. I made some sketches, but the scene changed every instant. How happy I felt at seeing mountains for the first time! They were so beautiful. I never felt so happy. I sang for joy. On entering a pass I came to a village which I understood to be Lourdes. Being Sunday all the inhabitants were strolling about the street. I asked for the hotel, but as they spoke only a patois, they did not understand me, but pointed to a place which I discovered to be a low, dirty inn with a lot of men drinking. I was shown by a woman into a room with two beds, and when I expostulated she tried to console me by saying it was only the servant's bed. I ordered some supper, and whilst waiting outside the door of the inn for it to be prepared, all the men who had been drinking jumped out of a window and stood talking and eyeing me in a peculiar manner. Later two drunken men entered; they were going to Lourdes, which I now found out to be a league farther; they were very curious to know all about me and obliged me to drink with them. When they discovered that I was also on the way to Lourdes, they wanted me to accompany them. On my refusing, they whispered to me on the sly that the place was not to be trusted, and told me about a murder and the body being thrown in a pit. I began to be really frightened, and when supper was at last served it was so bad that I could not touch it. Fortunately

a cart was driven up to the door of the inn, and the carter invited me to ride with him to Lourdes, which I instantly decided to do. The woman of the house looked very black when she saw that I was determined to leave, and I put my large knife up my sleeve as a precaution, but the carter soon dissolved my fears. He turned out to be a good fellow, and we had a long talk over his campaign in Spain. We reached Lourdes all safely at ten o'clock at night; the carter directed me to a decent hotel, and after bidding him adieu I entered and ordered a good supper.

July 11:
Up and off by 6 a.m. Am now in the interior of the Pyrénées, surrounded on all sides by beautiful mountains in the greatest variety, with a torrent, the Gave, rushing through the valley of Argèles; in the middle of which are the ruins of several castles. Arrived at Argèles, where I breakfasted, then walked two more leagues to Pierrefitte. After having rested here during the heat of the day, I climbed a very steep road by the side of a mountain, with an impetuous torrent on the other side, leaping from rock to rock and falling in deep cascades; the valley was nearly closed in with mountains, so grand and sublime. It was one of the finest walks I ever had in my life to Cauterets,[4] where I took up my quarters.

July 12:
Started off on a expedition to Lac de Gaube without my knapsack. Met several invalids being carried from the Baths higher up the mountains, and continued to ascend a good road, passing a very pretty cascade, to Pont d'Espagne, which I crossed, and entered into the valley beyond, the wildest I had yet seen; of quite a different character of scenery with huge masses of rocks partly covered with pines. Afterwards I climbed up a path to the lake, beautifully situated, being entirely surrounded by mountains of great height, towering above it. Here I met three Englishmen, with whom I returned to Cauterets. On the way we met some Spanish smugglers – queer-looking fellows.

July 13:
Left Cauterets with great regret at six o'clock in the morning and retraced my steps to Pierrefitte, intending to go to Barèges; but I changed my mind and continued back through Argèles to Lourdes, where I turned off to the right to Bagnères-de-Bigorre. I arrived in the evening, having walked fourteen leagues, but I was not much tired, as so many beautiful views did not give me time to think of fatigue.

July 14:
Remained at Bagnères-de-Bigorre all day, but was disappointed with the place.

July 15:
Up at 5 a.m. and started for St Gaudens along a charming road; passed through Escaliadieu and Lannemezan, having breakfast at the latter village. Arrived at

[4] Water-colour of Cauterets, illustrated in *The Connoisseur*, August 1924 (Callow files, Witt Library, Courtauld Institute of Art).

St Gaudens very tired, having walked all day. Took my departure at ten o'clock the same night on a coach for Toulouse, where I arrived at eight o'clock the next morning, having slept during nearly the whole of the journey.

July 16:
Remained all day at Toulouse and visited the quays and bridges; tried to make some sketches, but a storm forced me to seek shelter.

July 17:
After walking on the promenade of Lafayette, etc. and seeing the churches of St Etienne and St Sernin, I made various sketches. I took the coach to Narbonne in the evening.

July 18:
Travelled all night and the greater part of the next day on the coach. There was little to see on the road excepting the picturesque town of Carcassonne, with its old tower situated on a hill and surrounded by walls. As usual, I was more fatigued by riding than walking, besides being almost stifled by heat and dust. Arrived at Narbonne at last. The town is famous for honey. It is situated on a plain, and has an antiquated appearance. A branch of the Canal du Midi passes through the town, but I was unable to make a sketch of it, as it is so closed in by walls.

July 19:
Up at 5.30 a.m. and set off to Béziers, and soon caught a distant view of the Mediterranean. Stopped at Béziers to lunch and rested during the heat of the day; continued my walk to Pézenas; began to feel very tired, as one of my feet was very painful. Fortunately a man riding a donkey overtook me, and put my knapsack in his basket which was a great relief. We chatted all the way to Pézenas. I went to the Hôtel des Trois Pigeons, and soon to bed as I was never before so tired.

July 20:
Woke at 5 a.m. and started along a pretty road bordered with lime, almond and olive trees; stopped at a spring and rested my foot, which still troubled me, and reached Mèze, in time for breakfast, a pretty place on the Etang du Thau. The boats with lateen sails give it quite an Italian appearance. I decided to rest here for a day.

July 21:
Took the coach to Montpellier, arriving at 2 p.m. Visited the cathedral and the promenade, where there was an exceedingly fine view, the mountains on one side and the sea on another. Met a Monsieur Fils at the hotel and we arranged to go together to Toulon.

July 22:
Up at 5.30 a.m. and made some sketches with Monsieur Fils, who left by coach for Nîmes, where I joined him later.

July 23:
Arrived at Nîmes at 4 a.m. having travelled by coach all night. Visited the Amphitheatre and the Maison Carrée; afterwards we went to the Gardens to see the Temple of Diana and the Bath of Augustus. Took the coach with Monsieur Fils to Beaucaire, with its old castle, prettily situated on the Rhône, with Tarascon on the other side of the river. Had arranged to take the boat in the evening to Arles, but it never arrived, and as the town was so full on account of a fair being held, we were compelled to find some lodgings a little way out of it; even then we could only get a mattress on a floor.

July 24:
We were so disturbed by flies that we were glad to get out of our lodgings at four o'clock in the morning, when we met a man, whose acquaintance we had made on the road to Beaucaire, wandering about in search of his lodgings; on his arrival he had taken some rooms, where he left his luggage and put the key in his pocket, but he forgot to note the name of the street or the number of the house. After helping him for some time without success we left him to his fate. Took the steamer, which arrived in the early morning, to Arles, where we transferred into another steamer for Marseilles. I was delighted with the change from dusty roads. I climbed the foremast and sat on the yard-arm till the steamer reached the mouth of the river. At last I was on the blue Mediterranean. The steamer took a turn out to sea, and in a few hours we arrived at Marseilles, which looks very fine on approaching it from the bay, with the mountains behind it.

July 25:
Strolled about the town and visited the harbour and fortifications. In the evening took the coach to Toulon, along a road which passes through a very mountainous country.

July 26:
Arrived at Toulon at 4 a.m. and put up at the Hôtel de France. Fils having obtained a pass, we visited the Arsenal; the sight of so many criminals was revolting. I never saw such a set of wretches with every crime written on their faces; they were all dressed in red jackets and numbered, and nearly every one had chains on his legs. I was glad to get away.

July 27:
Up early and sketched all day. Saw a man-of-war come into port, and climbed on the heights to obtain a view of the Iles d'Hyères. Returned in a coach to Marseilles. During the night, whilst walking up one of the hills, I saw the full moon through the mountains shining on the Mediterranean – a glorious sight.

July 28:
My twenty-fourth birthday. On arrival at Marseilles went to bed at 8 a.m. Visited the quays and made a number of sketches of merchantmen coming into the harbour.

July 29:
Fils woke me at 2 a.m. to say good-bye; as he was starting for Sisteron. I was to leave by coach at six for Aix, but fell asleep again and did not wake till a few minutes before that hour. Hurried into my clothes, but found the coach had already started, so got a man to carry my knapsack and ran after it, catching it up about a mile out of town as it was ascending a hill; arrived at Aix at 9 a.m. Intended to make some sketches but unable to do so, because of the heat. I had decided to take the coach to Avignon, but it was so full that I went by another one to Orgon.

July 30:
Arrived at Orgon at 3 p.m. Was told the coach for Avignon would pass through at 6 p.m., but they could not ensure my obtaining a seat, so I decided to walk. Had not proceeded far when the coach overtook me, and I was tempted by an offer to take me to Avignon for 30 sous. The picturesque town is entirely surrounded by walls, and has a pretty promenade with lime-trees on the banks of the Rhône, which is very broad here, and over it is a wooden bridge, and there are also remains of one built in the twelfth century. Saw the Palace of the Popes, which has more the appearance of a prison with its severe towers; also visited the cathedral, containing some fine monuments.

July 31:
Tried to sketch, but the wind blew so hard that it was impossible to do anything. Took the coach in the evening to Orange. Having the box seat and no overcoat, I was nearly frozen by the cold wind. Put up at a miserable inn. There was no bolt to my bedroom door, so I placed a chair against it and my money under my pillow. I was just dropping off to sleep when I heard a noise. I jumped out of bed when I saw a man with a lantern. He made an excuse of wanting to fetch something, but I am not sure that he had not some other intention.

August 1:
Roamed about the town and saw a very beautiful Roman triumphal arch. Determined if possible to continue my walk by side of the river – my original intention. I started across the country by a cross-road, but after some time I found myself on the main road only about three miles off Orange. I continued to Mornas, where I made a sketch of the picturesque castle of Montdragon, situated on a perpendicular rock above the village; then proceeded to La Palude, where I stopped the night at the Hôtel des Postes.

August 2:
Had experienced so much heat on the previous day that I got up early and was on the road again by 4 a.m., rested at Donzère. After leaving this village I was overtaken by a '*patache*', the worst description of a coach ever invented, and I was to my sorrow tempted by an offer to take me to Montélimar for ten sous. I was almost

suffocated by heat, and every bone in my body was nearly dislocated by the jolting. Arrived at the Hôtel des Princes at 10 a.m.; took a stroll by the side of the little river which flows into the Rhône, with a charming view of the Dauphiné mountains in the distance.

August 3:
Up again at 4 a.m. and started for Valence, resting at Loriel on the road, which is very beautiful as it approaches the Rhône. My foot began to trouble me again, so I took a seat on a coach, and arrived at Valence in the afternoon.

August 4:
Decided to rest here all day and made some sketches by the river.

August 5:
Started at 4 a.m. for Tain. Just before reaching it the road passes close to the river, and there is a beautiful view with Tain on one side and Tournon, with the ruins of an old castle, on the other. On account of the beauty of the place I had intended to remain at Tain, but I got into such bad quarters that I was quite disgusted. Determined to walk on to St Vallier. The weather now seemed inclined to change, and some heavy black clouds came up and produced some beautiful effects over the hills, but there was no rain. How I longed for a shower! It was now about two months since I had felt a drop of rain, and had hardly seen a cloud; nothing but continuous blue sky and burning heat. Arrived at St Vallier and put up at an hotel which was worse than the one I had left, and as there was no other, I was compelled to stay. Rain came during the night and everybody, including myself, was delighted. Everything was parched up, the grapes were very small and there were neither vegetables nor grain.

August 6:
Took a seat in a small coach to Le Péage, and from there I walked six leagues to Vienne, along a very interesting road close to the river, with a view of the hills opposite and the Dauphiné mountains in the distance. Visited the fine Gothic cathedral. Was much annoyed at being woke up in the middle of the night to admit a traveller to sleep in a spare bed which was in the room.

August 7:
Passed the day making sketches beside the river of the picturesque town.

August 8:
The last day of my tramp. Started at 4 a.m. as usual and walked to Lyons [*illustration no. 15*]. Here I remained for some days waiting for remittances, which arrived on the 13th. I at once booked a seat in the banquette of the diligence for Paris, and started at ten o'clock the same evening. When we had passed Mâcon and Châlons we experienced a tremendous thunderstorm, the lightning being exceptionally

vivid, which frightened the horses so much that the conductor had to get down and lead them.

Callow records that having spent three days and nights on the road, he arrived safely in Paris on 16 August. During the two and a half months that he had been on this walking tour, he covered 681 leagues, or about 1,700 miles (2,735 km) – for a total cost of only twenty pounds.

CHAPTER III

France: the Established Years, 1836–1841

In the Autumn of 1836 my old friend Charles Bentley came over to Paris on a visit. I was delighted to see him as this was the first time Bentley, Edge and myself had met together since we were pupils under Fielding.

THIS IS the last reference by Callow to John Edge. Two pencil sketches of a fishing-boat at Rouen, dated Oct 5.36 (Victoria and Albert Museum, E 986–987 – 1937), relate to a sketching trip which Callow and Bentley made to the area of Rouen and Havre in that year.

Callow had refused interesting appointments because of his teaching commitments and commissions, but in 1837 he was still accepting rather mundane work as an unidentified finisher of wood-blocks and drawings for engravings. He had gained a reputation for skill in this craft and was employed by Giraldon, Bovinet and Co., and several other publishers. T. S. Boys had introduced Bovinet to the Cookes in 1833 and it is also possible that it was his word that brought Callow to this firm. The fact that Callow was known to have been with the Fieldings would commend him to a publisher, in respect of engraving work, although it should be noted that working on wood-blocks was the exact opposite of the intaglio process, which had been his chief experience (in a wood-engraving, of course, the incised lines and areas are those that do *not* print). For an artist to reject a world tour, but to continue touching up drawings and wood-blocks, seems an odd decision, but Callow may have been so determined to succeed that he felt it necessary to accept as much work as he could handle in the studio. In a sense, the correction and improvement of the work of others were an extension of what was required of him when giving lessons – and Callow was a born teacher.

In 1837, Callow is known to have been working on plates for *Reise in das innere Nord-Amerika in den Jahren 1832 bis 1834* which was carried out for Prince Maximilian Alexander Philipp zu Wied. Karl Bodmer was the artist chiefly associated with this extensive project, which included 48 copper-plate engravings, 33 vignettes, many wood-cuts and a map. (Published by Hoelscher, Coblenz, in 1839–41. English edition – *Travels in the Interior of North America*, London, 1843. British Library shelf marks 1785.a.22 and 792.m.17.)

Callow was also re-touching wood-engravings for *Les Galeries Historiques du Palais de Versailles*, published in several volumes between 1839–1848 (Paris, Imprimerie

Royale). This should not be confused with *Les Fastes de Versailles* by H. M. Fortoul, also published in Paris in 1839 (Delloye). Giraldon had introduced Callow to the London publisher, Charles Heath, who commissioned him to make a series of original drawings, 14 of which were engraved for the French edition and nine in the London edition, which appeared as *Picturesque Annual for 1839 – Versailles*. Callow obtained special permission to visit the private gardens and the Trianon while working on this project.

'Versailles' (*illustration no. 17*) is undoubtedly linked with the series commissioned by Charles Heath, although this was not actually used in the *Picturesque Annual*. A number of studies for these drawings are included in the volume of sketches in the Victoria and Albert Museum. 'Vue prise de la Terrasse de Versailles' (*illustration no. 16*) is obviously a preliminary study for the water-colour in the National Gallery of Canada, in which only the grouping of the figures has been enlarged and altered. A study of the two illustrations shows the ability of Callow to utilise his sketches to produce a finished work of beautiful clarity. Every detail has been accurately translated from the sketch and brought into sharp focus by means of the Bonington method of outlining with a fine brush. The figures are still very much a derivation from the style of Boys and Bonington. A smaller Bonington view of Versailles from a slightly different angle (illustration no. 94 in Redgrave's *A Century of British Painters*) shows a dog in the left foreground playing with a child's hoop. We can see that Callow worked the composition of 'Versailles' from his own original observations, apart from the figures and a few very minor introductions. The fact that the left foreground of his finished water-colour also includes a hoop does suggest that Callow had probably received this incidental idea, quite unconsciously, after having actually seen the Bonington work.

'Château de Versailles et l'Orangerie vue de la pièce d'eau des Suisses' (*illustration no. 18*) shows the Bonington style in the foreground washes and a most characteristic group of Boys-inspired trees on the left, but the natural flow of the composition and the minute observations of detail are now essentially Callow. A pencil sketch for this drawing, inscribed 'Mai 28.37', is in the Victoria and Albert Museum, E 957 – 1937.

Other pencil sketches in the *Picturesque Annual* series include:

'The Gardens of Versailles', sketch for plate, engraved by J. Davis, to face p. 110. Inscribed 'Mai 28.37'. (E 955 – 1937.)

'The Gardens of Versailles from the Basin of Latona', sketch for the plate, engraved by S. Bradshaw, to face p. 129. Inscribed 'Juin 4.37'. (E 956 – 1937.)

'The Palace of Versailles from the Paris Avenue', sketch for the plate, engraved S. Fisher, to face p. 80. Inscribed 'Juin 18.37'. (E 961 – 1937.)

'The Lake and Hamlet of Trianon', sketch for plate, engraved by S. Fisher, to face p. 36. Pencil sketch; heightened with white. Inscribed 'Laiterie Suisse. Pt. Trianon. Juin 18.37'. (E 964 – 1937.)

'Bassin de Neptune', sketch for the plate, engraved by W. Watkins, to face p. 160. Inscribed 'Bassin du Dragon. Ver. Juin 18.37'. Pencil, heightened with white. (E 965 – 1937.)

'The Canal of Trianon', sketch for the plate, engraved by E. Radclyffe, to face p. 140. Inscribed 'Vue du Palais de Trianon. Prise du Côte du Canal'. (E 974–1937.)

'The Original Palace of Versailles', sketch for plate entitled 'Louis XIV at the Chace', engraved by E. Radclyffe, to face p. 8. Inscribed 'Arrièr(e) 1st Palais de Versailles. Prise d'une gravure'. (E 975–1937.)

At about this time, the Comte de Noë called on Callow to obtain some drawings for the Société des Amis des Arts, of which he was President. 'The Port of Marseilles', one of two drawings supplied by Callow, was later won by King Louis Philippe in the lottery. On several further occasions Callow sold work to the Comte de Noë as prizes for these lotteries, which were similar to an Art Union. As so often happened from a chance meeting, Callow continued his acquaintance with the Comte, who became a personal friend. Callow was later to meet his son, a caricaturist, who contributed to *Le Charivari*, etc., under the name of 'Cham'.

It is not surprising that, towards the end of 1837, Callow was feeling the strain of such unrelenting application to his work. As a respite, he and his brother went to England, first visiting London, then Great Yarmouth, where Callow sketched boats and shipping scenes. Later, he accompanied Bentley to the Isle of Wight, where they both made studies of marine subjects. At this time, Callow was much occupied with sea-pieces, which were the subjects that sold best to the French dealers.

It has been stated that no painting of shipping by Bonington ever showed the least inaccuracy about the rigging or craft structure. Callow was also exceptionally sound on such details. Some of his earliest memories would be of Greenwich, which he used to re-visit with his father in a Thames wherry and, later, in a steamboat. Although Callow did not have a glimpse of the sea until he was nearly 17, his childhood background must have provided him with many opportunities to absorb a visual knowledge of ships and boats. These are never mere conventions in the work of Callow, but, although handled with an attractive freedom of movement, have a technical accuracy and a keen observation of detail.

In 1838, Princess Clémentine commissioned two water-colour drawings from the sketches that Callow had done in the South of France. Not long afterwards, Alexandre Dumas, the novelist, paid a surprise visit to the atelier in order to ask Callow to accompany him on a long tour of that area. He was aiming to write his *Impressions du Voyage* and wished Callow to undertake the illustrations, but Callow again turned down a commission of scope and interest because of his pupils and the extent of the work in hand.

J. F. Lewis and Charles Bentley continued to urge Callow to submit some drawings to the Society of Painters in Water-colours, which he finally agreed to do. On 15 February 1838, he was told that he had been unanimously elected as an Associate of the Society. George Cattermole (1800–1868) had strongly supported his candidature, but the most important voice was certainly that of Copley Fielding (President of the Society), who had spoken of Callow in terms of high praise. It was a rule of the Society not to elect an artist who was living out of England, but an exception was made in the case of Callow – undoubtedly as a result of the influence of Copley Fielding. '... when the news of my election reached me I could scarcely believe it to be true, not having sufficient confidence in my own powers to think that I should ever succeed.' The following notice appeared in the *Spectator*:

> The Water-colour Society last week filled one of two vacancies by electing a Mr William Callow, a landscape and marine painter, not known in this country, but who has studied in the French School, we have heard, and is of the dashing style of execution. There were several candidates, most of whom possessed as much merit as many of the present members, but the Society has wisely raised the standard of qualification.

The *Athenaeum* concluded a review of the 1838 exhibition with the comment:

> We do not remember to have met Mr Callow before; many of his landscapes are very clever. We must specify one, 'Montpellier from the Aqueduct' (no. 236). But his is the only new name of promise to be found in the catalogue.

'Chartres, the Guillaume Gate' (*colour plate*) dated 1838 (worked from sketches made 7 June 1836) is an excellent example of the work of Callow at this period.

The water-colour technique of the established Callow was essentially based on traditional methods. As with most mid-nineteenth-century water-colourists, he had discarded the practice of laying down a preliminary monochrome wash, but whereas some artists damped their paper with plain water, Callow worked directly onto a dry surface. Transparent colour washes were laid on, allowed to dry, the process being repeated with successive tints, until the necessary graduations of colour and tone were obtained. The placing of water-colour on a dry, non-absorbent support produces 'hard edges', as the high surface tension of the water attracts the pigments to the edge of the wash, forming coloured borders of deeper tone. Callow softened these, between washes, with a brush and plain water.

An influence from Copley Fielding, his original mentor, must have been absorbed into the water-colour style of William Callow, but this is evident only in small tricks of execution, which might equally well have been received from contact with other similar traditionalists. The individual manner of Fielding is not immediately apparent in the work of the established Callow. Copley Fielding had prescriptive methods of dealing with landscape. He would advise the young Callow to suggest perspective by washing near objects with warm colours and distant areas with cool tones (with an individual emphasis on blues). Some of the water-colour drawings of Copley Fielding employ virtually no more than vandyke-brown, indigo and yellows. Callow was to use a more extended palette, but would learn from Fielding the wisdom of obtaining effects from an economy of tints. Callow was never influenced into any constant imitation of the dark and voluminously cloudy skies of Copley Fielding, although he certainly shaded cobalt through rose madder into yellow ochre from lighter sky effects, after the prescribed methods of Fielding. Certain earlier examples show that Callow appears to have crumbled burnt umber onto the surface with a dry brush for foreground and foliage effects – a practice taught by Fielding, although much frowned upon by some purists. Even in later life, if faced with a mountain, Callow often seems to have reverted to the dictum of Copley

Fielding that these should be delineated with a broken scraggy touch, rather than using his own interpretation. This has led to a lack of balance in some compositions, in which the crisply handled foreground and middle distance, full of individual observations, is not fully supported by a distance which is a mere classical convention.

Roger Fry questioned Callow as to his water-colour method for a short piece in the *Burlington Magazine* (1907) which appeared in the form of a rather stilted interview. Callow was then 95 and very deaf, which no doubt accounts for some omissions and for the fact that the article has been widelv misinterpreted, in regard to the use of body-colour by Callow. H. M. Cundall may have used this article as his source when he gave it as his opinion that Callow had experimented with this technique on one occasion only. Roger Fry commented:

> In the face of the body-colour and every device that the ingenuity of modern water-colour artists has discovered to obtain greater power and force, these modest wash drawings have more than held their own, and even the brilliant mastery of men as great as Mr Sargent cannot extinguish their more retiring dignity.

Callow is quoted as saying:

> The modern style of water-colour painting and the change that has taken place in style and method, I attribute to the introduction of opaque or body-colours.

The original rules of the Water-colour Society forbade the use of any body-colour, although this subsequently came to be widely disregarded. It is true that Callow adhered much more closely to this principle than many members of the Society, but he did not paint entirely in pure water-colour. It was a comparison between the work of Callow and such painters as J. F. Lewis (whose technique was essentially based on body-colour) that was intended by the Fry article, but it has erroneously been taken to mean that Callow used no body-colour whatsoever. His method was not that of the complete purist. For instance, such an artist would allow only the use of an area of exposed white paper to define a highlight, but Callow frequently pointed up such details with white paint and also strengthened certain colours areas with the admixture of this body-colour (e.g. touches of an opaque pink on a ship's sail and strokes of solid yellow on the facing of a building). Scratching-out of highlights with a knife and the marking of texture on wet paint with a thumb (e.g. to give surface interest to foliage) are all to be found in the work of Callow, but only as minor practices.

Callow used Harding paper for sketches and preferred a hard, non-absorbent Whatman paper for finished drawings. The degree of absorbency of the support had a marked effect on the appearance of a water-colour. A thick, absorbent paper will give a soft, rich result, but will not produce the fine points of detail that were essential to the style of Callow. Absorbent papers were used for experiments only and tinted papers tend to relate to his earlier period – the 1836 walking tour produced a great many sketches on tinted paper. The water-colourist uses the fact that the white of the underlying paper reflects light through the pigment to increase luminosity. Some of the original sparkle of certain water-colours by Callow has inevitably been lost as a result of soiling and yellowing of the paper. As a counsel of perfection, water-colours should ideally be kept in portfolios. Changes take place when a work is exposed to light and air, leading to fading, 'foxing' (small brown marks) due to damp, also alterations in colour as the atmosphere affects some pigments.

William Callow always used Winsor and Newton materials. His water-colour palette was a fairly limited one and consisted of a basic reliance on tones of blue, red, yellow and brown. The following list of water-colour tints used by Callow has been compiled from an examination of his colour-boxes (in possession of the Callow family). Starred items are colours additionally mentioned by Roger Fry, as named by Callow.

Cobalt Blue   French Ultramarine   Prussian Blue   Indigo*

Crimson Lake   Carmine   Scarlet   Vermilion   Rose Madder   Indian Red

Cadmium Yellow   Chrome Yellow   Chrome Orange   Indian Yellow
Gamboge*

Yellow Ochre*   King's Yellow*

Burnt Sienna   Madder Brown   Vandyke Brown

Sepia   Raw Umber   Burnt Umber and Raw Sienna

Neutral Tint   Chinese White

King's Yellow contained arsenic and was discontinued for reasons of safety. Cadmium Yellow is the nearest substitute. Again we have to take into account the age of Callow when relating the names of his colours to Fry. It is possible that he employed the term King's Yellow for the Cadmium Yellow that he had actually been using. It is also possible that some items are missing from the colour-box. That Callow made very characteristic use of Yellow Ochre is obvious, although Raw Sienna is in this colour group. Callow stated that a colour-box had been named after him by Winsor and Newton for the use of students, although details of such an item do not appear in their present archives.

* * *

In the autumn of 1838, William Callow made his first visit to Switzerland. His own account of this tour provides a useful topographical reference:

In the autumn of 1838 I made my first tour of Switzerland. I took the diligence to Dijon, on which I made the acquaintance of a Mr Forman, and we agreed to travel together. From Dijon we crossed the plains of Burgundy to Besançon and Pontarlier. From the latter place we took the Swiss post over the Jura mountains to Lausanne. Here, shouldering our knapsacks we started off and walked to Vevey, where, after making some sketches, we continued to Villeneuve, on the borders of the Lake of Geneva, and took the steamer to Geneva. We left the next day at 3 a.m. and walked along a beautiful road to Bonneville. Arrived very tired and knocked up by the heat. On the following day, after resting during the heat at

Cluses, we reached St Martin late in the evening. We then proceeded through the valley of Servez and a beautiful gorge to the valley of Chamouni, surrounded by Mont Blanc and other mountains. We made an excursion to the Mer de Glace, taking a mule, which we rode in turns up to Montanvert, then across the ice up to Le Couvercle, and arrived at the Jardin, where we rested and returned to Chamouni. The next day we went with guides up Mont Blanc. We afterwards proceeded to Nantborrant; from there we went down to Les Chapieux, and ascended Col de la Seigne, where I made some sketches of the beautiful view, the Aiguilles and Mont Blanc above us, and Lake Combal and the Allée Blanche below. We then proceeded to Aosta.

Next day we left with a party of eight and two guides for St Rémy, the hospital of St Bernard, where we saw the monks, the famous dogs and the chapel. I thought of Roger's lines 'promising bread to the hungry, and to the weary rest'. From St Rémy we descended to Liddes in a thunderstorm, and reached Martigny the same evening [*illustration no. 20*]. On the following day I and Forman had to part company. I set out to Sion, and then proceeded up to Louèche, where I went with a guide up the rocks. Afterwards I walked to Thon, and took the steamer to Unterseen, beautifully situated on the lake, and proceeded to Interlaken. On the following day I hired a guide, and went through the valley of Lauterbrunnen, visited the Staubbach, where the Jungfrau, covered with snow could be seen, and climbed up the Wengern Alp, arriving at the chalet, where I was the only traveller. The next morning I was called by the innkeeper to see an avalanche. Afterwards I left for the valley of Grindelwald, crossing the Scheidegg at the foot of the Wetterhorn, and stopped at Rosenlaui, a very pretty spot. Saw during the descent the cascade of Reichenbach. Then proceeded to Meiringen, where I hired another guide and started for the Grimsel, turning on one side to see the beautiful waterfall of Handegg, and passing over immense blocks of granite to Grimsel. I next walked alongside the Glacier du Rhône to Andermatt; passed at the foot of St Gotthard and visited the Devil's Bridge. On the following day I started through the valley of the Reuss, passing through Amstag and Altdorf, where William Tell was born, to Flüelen, close to the lake of Quatre Cantons. Visited Tell's Chapel and Brunnen and back to Flüelen, where I took the steamboat to Lucerne, ['Lac de Licerne' – pencil sketch dated 6 September. Victoria and Albert Museum, E 1036 – 1937] and went to see the Lion of Thorwaldsen. The next day by coach to Zurich, where I made some sketches, and afterwards took a steamer to Rapperswil; thence by coach to Wesen and the Lake of Wallenstadt. Proceeded to Ragatz and made an excursion to the Bains de Pfeffers. Next posted to Rorschach on Lake Constance, and down the lake by steamer to Constance.

On the following day posted to Schaffhausen and saw the falls of the Rhine. Then quitted with great regret the mountain scenery of Switzerland and posted to Freiburg, where I took the coach to Strasbourg, reaching there at half-past eleven at night, and being kept for half an hour at the gates of the town by the custom-house officers. Then proceeded by coach to Baden-Baden, Carlsruhe and Heidelberg [*illustration no. 21*]. The last-named town proved so interesting that I remained there for five days making sketches. Proceeded by coach to Frankfort and Mayence. I now commenced walking again with my knapsack on my back, and reached Rüdesheim, where I saw the beauties of the Rhine for the first time, and crossed the river to Bingen. Next proceeded on foot to Bacharach and Pfalz, passing many old castles romantically situated on the tops of hills overlooking the river, and reached Oberwesel with its fine castle of Schönburg [*illustration no. 33* – this was to be a frequent subject]. At the hotel I tried to speak German, and on asking for some wine they brought me cold meat. Continued my walk to St Goar, and crossed the river to see the Castle of Katz. Proceeded along a path beside the river to Boppart and Coblenz, where I crossed the bridge of boats to visit Ehrenbreitstein. Next continued to Andernach and then to Remagen and finished my walking tour at Bonn, where I took the steamer to Cologne and posted on from there to Aix-la-Chapelle and then to Liège, where I took the train – the railway had not long been opened – to Brussels, and thence by diligence via Valenciennes and Noyons to Paris, reaching it after an absence of ten weeks. Travelling in those days was not at all like it is at the present time. English was not understood and having no knowledge of the German language, I was compelled to make signs for nearly everything I required during the three weeks I was in Germany, specially in the Moselle district.

* * *

Callow continued to widen his circle of aristocratic acquaintances to include a Comte Stackelberg, also Baronne Mayendorff and the family of a Polish diplomat named Chernitícheff, all of whom became his pupils. In 1838, Callow records: 'I returned to England to witness the Coronation of Queen Victoria, which I did both at Westminster and in the Park in company with Bentley.' Callow would not realise that the uncle of his future wife was playing the organ for the Coronation ceremony. During this visit, he called on the publisher, Charles Heath, who gave him an introduction to J. M. W. Turner.

> On presenting myself at Queen Anne Street, the door was opened by his old housekeeper, who requested me to wait in the hall whilst she delivered the letter to Mr Turner. To my surprise Turner himself came out to me, and upon my asking permission to see his gallery, he abruptly, though kindly, said 'Go up'. So upstairs I went, delighted not only at getting an opportunity of seeing his wonderful paintings, but at meeting the painter himself. It was a painful surprise, however, to find Turner's gallery in a most delapidated condition. Many of the pictures, some on the ground and others leaning against the wall, were cracked and damaged; the walls were in a deplorable state of damp, with the paper hanging down in strips. I remained a long time admiring his beautiful painting, and on going downstairs no one appeared so I had quietly to let myself out at the front door without having an opportunity of thanking Turner for his kindness. My recollection of Turner is that of a short, dark man, inclined to stoutness, with a merry twinkle in his eye. The next time I met Turner was in Venice at the Hotel Europa, where we sat opposite at meals and entered into conversation.

J. M. W. Turner was in Venice in August 1840 for three weeks.

> One evening whilst I was enjoying a cigar in a gondola, I saw Turner in another one, sketching San Giorgio, brilliantly lit up by the setting sun. I felt quite ashamed of myself, idling away my time whilst he was hard at work so late.

Fraser's Magazine, June 1839, included the following comment by Thackeray, in respect of the Exhibition of the Society of Painters in Water-colours:

> There is no need to mention to you the charming landscapes of Cox, Copley Fielding, De Wint, Gastineau and the rest. A new painter, somewhat in the style of Harding, is Mr Callow, and better I think than his Master or original, whose colours are too gaudy to my taste and effects too glaringly theatrical.

Thackeray would see the work of James Duffield Harding (1797–1863) reflected in the outlines of Callow, strong and clear, with the subject often Continental and showing an influence from Samuel Prout, under whom Harding had studied. Callow was also still using tinted papers, a practice much employed by Harding. The *Athenaeum* commented: 'Mr Callow has some clever drawings of foreign towns' (May 1839, p. 338).

In 1839, the London publishers Moon, Boys and Graves (Thomas Boys of this firm was a cousin of the painter) asked Callow if he would present a copy of *Picturesque Architecture in Paris, Ghent, Antwerp, Rouen, etc.* to Louis Philippe. This lithographic work of exceptional brilliance was one of the most important achievements of Thomas Shotter Boys. Callow duly presented a copy to the French King, via Princess Clémentine. This was accepted and a ring (in the form of a diamond-studded brooch) was sent by Louis Philippe to the publishers.

> My friend, T. S. Boys was terribly disappointed, as he was the person who should have received the present. The mistake occurred through the publishers and not the artist sending the book.

James Roundell concludes that Thomas Boys, the publisher, subsequently forwarded the ring to his cousin. When another lithographic work, *Original Views of London as it is*, was published in 1842, T. S. Boys was careful to make a direct approach to the French King, who sent him a valuable watch and a flattering letter. Editing by H. M. Cundall has to be taken into account when reading the 1908 autobiography, but Callow does present a slight air of aiming to justify his own part in the incident of the ring. By 1839, T. S. Boys could well have reached a point when he had come to resent the constant patronage that Callow was now receiving from the French royal family and other titled connections and may have felt that a former pupil could have done more to effect his introduction into such circles, as an aid to his own career. Boys was known for moods of sudden excitability and, in his understandable disappointment over the ring, some angry words could have caused the rift that seems to have occurred between Callow and Boys. In later years, Callow was to describe Boys as a 'clever, but eccentric artist'. The first adjective is patronising and the second has engendered much speculation among art historians as to the exact meaning. Eccentricity is hard to define, although T. S. Boys certainly appears as something of an original. For instance, the Constable gift probably seemed somewhat odd, not only to the painter, but also to Callow. In his drawings, Boys was given to adding quirky little touches of humour, such as his trick of writing his own name into a shop sign or bill-board, as part of the picture e.g. 'T. S. Boys – *Fripier*', i.e. an old-clothes dealer. The work of this artist frequently included keen observations of everyday life and occasionally went so far as to show a man relieving himself against a wall, albeit as a perfectly valid statement. Callow probably thought the bill-boards were merely quaint, but some of the realism extraneous, even vulgar.

William Callow was a man very conscious of the social niceties. Did he sense that the rotund and somewhat untidy Boys, who was sometimes capable of strong language, might cut a slightly untoward figure if introduced to some of his new associates? It seems feasible that resentment from Boys and mild disapproval of Callow caused him to gradually withdraw from the circle of Boys. The latter did not exhibit with the Society of Painters in Water-colours, but with the 'New' Society (From 1824 to 1873), and this also tended later to exclude him from the immediate circle of Callow. From 1840 there are no further references to Boys in the diaries of E. W. Cooke, which does point to some kind of general disagreement at about this time. Callow, on the other hand, kept up his acquaintance with E. W. Cooke. On 7 March 1849, shortly after the Cookes had moved from Barnes to Kensington, Cooke was to record that Callow was amongst those who called on them in their new home. After Boys returned to London, he fell into real poverty, but he does not seem to have contacted Callow, although he was often forced to appeal to old friends and other painters for assistance. Callow can hardly have been unaware of the sad plight of Boys and it is directly against his character that he should not have been generous to a friend, but their lives were to take very different paths. William Callow always acknowledged that he had been influenced and helped by this painter, but, nevertheless, he possibly never fully realised the extent of his academic debt to Thomas Shotter Boys.

* * *

In the summer of 1840, William Callow made his first visit to Italy; his own account follows:

I was accompanied for some part of the time by Forman, who had been with me two years previously on the tour through Switzerland. We left Paris by diligence for Dijon, and then crossed the Jura mountains to Geneva, where we stopped and sketched. We next passed on the left side of the lake through Lausanne and Vevey to St Maurice, where we changed diligences and arrived at Brieg. The next day we crossed the Simplon Pass and reached Domo d'Ossola at 11 p.m. After sleeping for a few hours on a sofa we took the '*malle post*' in the early morning to Arona on Lago Maggiore [*illustration no. 86*]. Here we stayed and sketched. Afterwards crossed the lake to Angera to see the picturesque castle, and made a trip up the lake by steamer to enjoy the scenery. On the same evening we took a carriage to Bellinzona, and made some sketches in the very picturesque town with its old walls and towers before breakfast the next morning. Later we proceeded to Lugano, passing over Mont Cannero, and witnessing some splendid views on the road. The next day we left by coach for Como, crossed the lake by a boat, and arrived there in the evening. On the following day we took a steamer up the lake, which is smaller but prettier than Maggiore, and went ashore at Bellaggio. Here, although there was no hotel we obtained some very comfortable quarters and stayed the night. We took a delightful sail up the lake, but, owing to a contrary wind, could only reach Gravedona [16 August 1840 – *see* City of Birmingham Collection, also *colour plate* dated 1841], where it was impossible to stay, as every cottage was so dirty; consequently we returned as far as Domasco. Next day, after sailing for seven hours, we managed to reach Cadenabbia, opposite to Bellaggio, then took the steamer back to Como, being very much pleased with the trip. Sketched all next day at Como and left in the evening for Milan in a 'velociferi', a long vehicle holding about twenty people, and after about four hours' jolting arrived at the capital of Lombardy, where we inspected the cathedral, the Scala and other fine buildings. Left Milan at midnight, passing through a splendidly rich country, and, skirting Lake Garda for some distance, arrived at Verona in the evening, after having been almost stifled with heat and dust. We were much interested in this town, with whole streets of fine palaces, intermingled with Roman and other antiquities, the tombs of the Scaligeri, the old bridge and the amphitheatre.

Next we proceeded to Padua [*illustration no. 85*], with its arcaded streets and two remarkable churches, in one of which we saw a beautiful painting by Paul Veronese. Being anxious to arrive at Venice, we took the '*malle post*' to Mestre, where we embarked in a gondola, traversing several miles over the lagoons, and arrived in the evening at the steps of Hotel Europa, delighted with our first view of the Queen of the Adriatic. We stayed for ten days, seeing all the wonderful sights and making many sketches. We left Venice with great regret and returned to Padua whence we posted to Ferrara, and then on to Bologna. Here we saw the castle of the Dukes of Ferrara, a fine fortress, the cathedral, the leaning tower, all of which I sketched [*illustration no. 84*]. The next day we started in a '*vettura*' in company with two others for Florence, having to be drawn by oxen at a snail's pace across the Apennines. We slept in a solitary habitation, Albergo del Nolta, in sight of Monte di Fo, and after two days travelling arrived in Florence. Here we remained for two days, sketching all the wonderful buildings. Forman being obliged to return to Paris, I proceeded by myself in a '*vettura*' to Rome.

The journey took six days. Stopped the first night at Arezzo, the birthplace of Petrarch, then quitted the Tuscan States and entered those of the Pope. From the Custom-House there is a beautiful view over Lake Trasimeno, near to which Hannibal obtained a famous victory over the Romans. Arrived at Perugia on the third day and visited the Cathedral; afterwards took a carriage to Assisi and saw the famous convent of St Francis, remarkable for three churches built one above the other. We then proceeded to Foligno, and then to Spoleto, where I made a sketch of the town and gateway where Hannibal's progress received a check from the inhabitants. Next reached Terni, where I saw the cascade and the villa where Queen Caroline resided. Continued the journey, passing Narni, with the Roman bridge built by Augustus Caesar, and along a splendid road across the mountains and arrived at Nepi. On the last day we crossed the Campagna, beautiful in its barrenness – no trees, no water, no cultivation of any kind, and not even a house, but how many reflections it causes in one's mind – and arrived at last at Rome, entering it by the Porta del Popolo. Here I remained for ten days enjoying all the wonderful sights of that marvellous city.

Afterwards I left for Naples, stopping a night at Terracina by the way, and reached Naples on the following day, visiting Herculaneum and Vesuvius. Next I took the railway to Castellamare and walked to Torre del Greco, where I hired a donkey and went to Castel Lettere and Gragnano; afterwards to Pompeii, in which place I was greatly interested. From there I returned to Torre del Greco and back by rail to Naples. On the next day I took the steamer '*Francisco Primo*' for Marseilles. It came on to blow so hard during the middle of the first night that the steamer was nearly swamped by the heavy seas, which stove in two deck cabins, carried away some of the boats and filled the main cabin half full with water. We stopped at Leghorn and Genoa, and, after a boisterous journey finally reached Marseilles.

* * *

William Callow, like Bonington, was strongly affected by this first visit to Italy. After 1840, his work has an extra colour dimension, and Italian scenes, particularly those in Venice, were to prove some of his most popular subjects.

In 1840, Callow was awarded a second silver medal at the Rouen exhibition. It was also the year of his highest award in France – the gold medal at the Paris Salon. Callow should have been presented with this by King Louis Philippe, but, at the last moment, the ceremony was cancelled, owing to an outbreak of the political rioting that frequently disrupted Paris. The position of the 'Citizen King' was perilously uncertain. Constant attempts were made on his life and the Orléans family were already anticipating that they might have to leave France. In that year, Queen Marie Amélie, the Duc de Nemours and Princess Clémentine commissioned five large water-colour drawings by Callow, from a selection of the Italian sketches, which they had specially requested him to bring to the Tuileries Palace.

William Callow was not only held in private favour, but was also identified with the French royal family in public, receiving tickets for many important events, as the personal gift of Princess Clémentine – the Orléans wished to be surrounded by those whom they knew to be loyal. In 1840, the body of Napoleon was returned to France from St Helena, on board a frigate commanded by Prince de Joinville, and on 14 December, at the invitation of Princess Clémentine, Callow had a privileged view of the magnificent procession that escorted the arrival of the body of Napoleon into Paris.

Callow had never intended to settle in France for the rest of his life and must have realised that his position could become difficult, even dangerous, if Louis Philippe were to abdicate. Consequently, when offers of commissions and enquiries as to his availability began to reach him from England, he decided to return to his own country. Callow now had a considerable sum of money in the bank where he had first deposited 20 francs on the advice of Sigismund Himely seven years before.

William Callow had worked hard for his success and was established, at the age of 28, in a position of recognition that could have taken some artists a lifetime to achieve. He had been happy in Paris and regretted leaving his friends, his pupils and the French royal family, particularly Princess Clémentine, but later events were to prove the wisdom of his decision. He sold his principal furniture, books and prints to Baron Schwiter and other friends, giving the remainder to his brother, John, who remained in Paris until 1844.

> I finally quitted Paris on 28 March 1841 and settled in London, rather nervous as to the result, for having given up my Royal pupil, as well as a good connection as a drawing master among many of the French aristocracy, I had to start afresh, and practically unknown, in London.

CHAPTER IV

London: Life as a Fashionable Artist and Drawing Master, 1841–1855

IN LONDON, William Callow took a lease on 20 Charlotte Street, Portland Place, near Regent's Park (Charlotte Street was to become known as Hallam Street in 1905). Although his drawings were selling well, Callow only obtained one pupil during his first year in Charlotte Street. She was Lady Beaujolois Bury, a daughter of the Earl of Charleville.

In 1841, Callow spent a great deal of time with a very wealthy Russian, named Kalergi, who was also living in Charlotte Street. Their chief mutual interest was music, particularly opera. Callow had heard many famous singers in Paris and had a deep appreciation of all forms of music.

During his first year in England, many old friends from Paris visited his studio, including Comte de Noë and Baron Schwiter. William Callow was a man whose liking for titled company can be misinterpreted as snobbery, but it was the mutual enjoyment of art, music and good conversation in gracious surroundings that attracted Callow only into certain aristocratic circles. As one who was exceptionally sensitive to animal suffering and had a particular dislike of blood sports, it is impossible to see him as a member of a country-house shooting party. In fact it was Charles Bentley, son of a master carpenter, whose friendship meant more to Callow than any other. He is constantly mentioned as having accompanied Callow on visits, excursions, to lectures and on sketching trips, such as the one which they made to Normandy in the autumn of 1841.

William Callow was in the habit of always carrying a small sketch pad. These little books, often with leather spines, pocket-rubbed, are filled with swift impressions and sharp observations of detail. The modelling of the figures in *illustration no. 31* now displays a much more individual character, as distinct from earlier examples, derived from Boys. Sketches made during this Normandy tour were later worked up into finished water-colours, with which Callow was to have particular success in 1842. The final sketches in the illustrated book prove that Callow made another visit to Lowestoft in 1841.

In 1842, he purchased the lease of 20 Charlotte Street and it was arranged that Charles Bentley should share part of the house with him. In this year, Lady Stratford de Redcliffe (the wife of the British Ambassador in Constantinople) visited the Charlotte Street studio with her family, in order to receive drawing lessons.

From then onwards, his connection was to build up rapidly. Some of his success was due to the fact that Callow greatly enjoyed teaching; this brought an extra quality to his instruction, in addition to a very genuine ability to impart skill. Many of his pupils subsequently became close friends. It is also obvious that a tall, handsome man, whose natural charm was now touched with an air of French courtliness, would have an appeal for women. Callow appears to have made a special journey to Madeley Manor in Staffordshire, in order to give drawing lessons to a Miss Crewe, sister of Lord Crewe. 'I unfortunately caught a severe cold on the last day of my visit through sitting on the damp grass, so decided to go to the South Coast to recuperate' – this convalescent trip included a coach journey to Plymouth and a visit to Dartmouth (two sketches, dated 20–22 July, *see* Cartwright Hall, Bradford, page 174), Torquay (*illustration no. 37*), Teignmouth, Lyme Regis and Corfe Castle. 'Torquay' is clearly dated Sept. 24.43. In this year, Callow exhibited a very similar view with the title 'Torquay, looking over Torbay' signed and dated 1843 (Christie's 16 July 1974). The latter showed a more stylised foreground and group of trees to the left with the appearance of having been based on a previous sketch. A pencil drawing in the City of Birmingham Art Gallery proves that Callow was in Durham on 20 September 1843, from where he travelled back to London. It does seem that the illustrated work should be dated 1842 and that the later date was probably added to the inscription, in error, at the time of the execution of the exhibition piece.

By 1841, the style of William Callow had been essentially patterned by the early years in France, where he had encountered not only the topographical style of T. S. Boys and the colourful innovations of the Romantic movement, but also the brilliance of the Continental light. The style of a landscape painter must always be influenced by the climate of his predominant environment. The atmospheric effects in the paintings of Turner and Constable owe a great deal to the prevailing moisture in the climate of England, but, until he was nearly 30, Callow had seen very little of his own country. In consequence, his crisp lines and sometimes exaggerated chiaroscuro reflect the sunshine of France and Italy rather than the more cloudy effects of his native land.

The Art Union of London had been established in 1837. This was a society for the fostering of interest in the Fine Arts and the encouragement of British artists and manufacturers of decorative wares. Members paid an annual subscription of one guinea and for this fee they were entitled to receive a large engraving and to participate in a yearly lottery. Winners in this 'draw' could choose a painting to the value of their prize from one of the current exhibitions.

In 1842, 'On the Grand Canal, Venice' (*illustration no. 38*) and 'Granville, Coast of Normandy' were selected as Art Union prizes (£40 and £25 respectively) from the exhibits of Callow with the Society of Painters in Water-colours. It was only just over a year since he had returned from living in France and his name was comparatively unknown to the English public; the selection of these works as Art Union prizes must have been very much on the merits of the pictures. 'On the Grand Canal, Venice' was a forerunner of many such scenes and displays a fine sense of balance, rhythm and atmospheric colour. 'Granville' was less calm, but again well designed, showing a fishing boat on a choppy sea, handled with an excellent sense of movement, reminiscent of the manner of 'Fishing Boats at Sea' 1833 (*illustration no. 8*). Engravings of 'Grand Canal' and 'Granville' were included as numbers 30 and 74 in the *London Art Union Prize Annual*, published by R. A. Sprigg in 1845. 'The Boulevard du Temple', a further engraving, after the work of Callow (by J. C. Varrall), was to appear in *The Keepsake* for 1849.

1842 marked an advance in the establishment of the individual style of Callow, although it is still possible to detect a very positive influence from T. S. Boys in some work of this date. 'Entrance to Hyde Park at Hyde Park Corner' (*illustration no. 35*) has a marked resemblance to 'Hyde Park, near Grosvenor Gate' by Boys, which appeared as Plate XVI in *London as it is* (Plate 66, p. 152 – *Thomas Shotter Boys* by James Roundell). The fact that Callow made this drawing in the same year of the publication of the Boys lithographs does suggest a direct motivation from this print. 'Entrance to Hyde Park' is noticeably more in the style of Boys than the general presentation of Callow by 1842.

Personal recommendations were now continually increasing his circle of pupils.

> ... amongst them was Lord Dufferin, who, however, was more interested in chemistry than drawing, so much so that his Mother, one of the beautiful Sheridan sisters, told me that she was in constant fear lest he blow up their house. I lost sight of my pupil for many years, but followed his brilliant career with great interest, especially during the time that he was Viceroy of India. Shortly before his death I wrote to condole with him on the loss of his eldest son who was killed in the Boer War. He sent a charming letter to me in reply, saying that he had often noticed my name in the newspapers, and in addition was pleasantly reminded of me by a lovely work of mine hanging on the wall of his drawing room....

In fact, in spite of his absorption with chemistry, Lord Dufferin was later to produce some excellent water-colours.

'Madeley Manor, Staffordshire' reproduced in *Apollo*, November 1962, was executed while Callow was on a second visit to give a further session of drawing instruction to Miss Crewe (during which time he also saw nearby Crewe Hall). He then went by steamer up the Clyde to Glasgow and from there to Edinburgh. After sketching in Edinburgh for a few days, Callow went on to Melrose, Jedburgh, Berwick, Bamborough Castle, Alnwick and Durham; then from Catterick Bridge to Richmond and back to London.

> Travelling by coach in those days was a great pleasure. Stopping at the principal towns, one was welcomed at the inns by the landlords, and was served as travellers never are and never will be again. During this little tour I made many sketches, from which I executed later finished water-colour paintings.

On 1–3 December 1843, Queen Victoria and Prince Albert were visiting Chatsworth House in Derbyshire, seat of the Duke of Devonshire. The Queen particularly admired the Great Conservatory, which had been built to the design of the celebrated Joseph Paxton, who was then head gardener at Chatsworth and afterwards knighted, following the success of a similar design for the Great Exhibition of 1851. Very shortly after the departure of his royal visitors, the Duke of Devonshire commissioned Callow to make two water-colour drawings – one of Chatsworth House (*illustration no. 39*) and one of the Great Conservatory (*illustration no. 40*). As it was bitterly cold December weather, the Duke gave special instructions to Paxton that Callow should be protected. Accordingly, Paxton had a large brazier placed by Callow while he sketched in the grounds, with a manservant in constant attendance.

> When the drawings were finished the Duke came to see them at my studio, and he was so pleased with them that he increased the price originally stipulated.

A search of Chatsworth House records has not revealed what the original fee might have been, but does provide a slight clue as to why Callow was chosen for this particular commission. The Duke of Devonshire had not previously been a collector of his work, but an entry in his diary for 16 November 1843, written while on a visit to Windsor Castle, shows that the Duke was seated next to the Duc de Nemours, while dining with Queen Victoria. It seems likely that he already had it in mind to present the Queen with drawings of Chatsworth for her souvenir albums, which would no doubt be on display for guests at Windsor. It is rather more than coincidental that the Duke of Devonshire should have commissioned Callow, only three weeks after dining in the company of Callow's first royal pupil. A water-colour by Callow of Bolton Abbey, in Wharfedale, Yorkshire, a property owned by the Cavendish family, is now in the Chatsworth Collection.[1]

'Messrs. Bentley and Callow seem to us fast growing duller and more chalky than is desired, although they both have great cleverness of hand'. (*Athenaeum*, 3 May 1844).

All the critics tend to refer constantly to Charles Bentley and William Callow as a pair, which was a charming tribute to their friendship, but not an entirely correct perception of their work. 'Mr C. Bentley and Mr W. Callow, who singularly resemble each other in style, furnish some good sea-pieces, in which the effects of a watery sky are very ably produced' – (*The Times*, 27 April 1846).

Even the foreign press bracketed their work (*Kunstblatt*, 8 October 1846, p. 202). Charles Bentley, R.W.S., showed a total of 209 works with the Society of Painters in Water-colours, in which the most characteristic subjects were coastal scenes with ships. His wind-ruffled seas are full of lively movement, but Bentley also maintains a sense of control within a well-organised composition, using some near foreground object as a pivot for the eye. *Nagler's Künster-Lexicon* (1835) described him as 'a leading London water-colour artist',[2] but, in spite of his acknowledged position as a painter of seascapes, Bentley was never to have the same financial success as Callow, who had a better business head and worked with a greater variety of subject. Sea-pieces had sold particularly well in France, but Callow was now working away from the style of Charles Bentley and into the topographical scenes in foreign towns that were to prove such popular subjects.

> In August 1844, after an exceptionally busy time in London, I was tempted to revisit the Rhine and the Moselle, so I crossed to Calais, and went by diligence to Dunkirk, from there through Bruges and Malines, making a number of

[1] Access to the archives of Chatsworth House by kind permission of His Grace the Duke of Devonshire. The Great Conservatory (*illustration no. 40*) was demolished in 1922, having fallen into a state of disrepair.
[2] 'Charles Bentley' by F. Gordon Roe – *Walker's Quarterly*, April 1921.

sketches at both places, to Cologne, and then up the Rhine by steamer to Coblenz. After staying there for a few days I started in a very small steamer up the Moselle and landed at Carden on a lovely evening. The next morning I proceeded by boat to Cochem, where I remained for several days sketching. The proprietor of the hotel spoke French and very obligingly walked out with me to point out the principal objects of interest, including Schloss Elz. I next went to Trarbach, a secluded spot with no travellers and with few means of communication with other places. I made a number of sketches in this charmingly picturesque old town . . . from Trarbach I visited the pretty village of Alf, where the river runs round a promontory, on top of which is the ruined Castle of Marienburg; then proceeded by Berncastel to Trèves. The three weeks which I spent alone by the banks of the Moselle were most enjoyable, the only drawback being my utter ignorance of the German language. . . .

In 1845, William Callow became engaged to one of his fashionable pupils, Harriet Anne Smart, a niece of the prominent musician Sir George Smart (1776–1867). The son of a music publisher, he was an organist, violinist, conductor, composer and teacher of singing. Smart lived for many years at 91 Portland Place. ('On January 1st, 1811, I received the honour of a knighthood from the Duke of Richmond, in Dublin Castle, the fees for which amounted to £66.13s.' – leaves from the journal of Sir George Smart, 1907.) In 1822, he was appointed one of the organists of the Chapel Royal (where he had been a chorister) and was subsequently organist for the Coronation Ceremony of Queen Victoria (fee £300). Smart was responsible for the introduction to England of many new works by Mendelssohn, Beethoven and Weber. His compositions included anthems, chants and madrigals. One of his glees, 'The Butterfly's Ball', was specially popular with the Victorians. Harriet Anne was a daughter of Henry Smart (1778–1823), the violinist, music publisher and pianoforte maker, who was a brother of Sir George Smart. He had given professional performances on the violin from the age of 14 and was later leader of the orchestra at the Lyceum Theatre, when this was opened as the English Opera House in 1809, and leader of the Drury Lane Orchestra from 1812 to 1821.[3] Harriet Anne Smart was an accomplished pianist, singer and linguist, with a talent for drawing and painting. Callow would appear to have made an excellent choice, leading to a partnership of mutual interest, in view of his own love of music and her enthusiasm for art. The antecedents of William Callow were not humble, but to be the son of someone 'in trade' could be a disadvantage in Victorian society. In fact, his background had been superseded by the man he had become, socially at ease, and highly respected in his profession, through which he had connections equal to those of his prospective bride. However, the Smart family, for undisclosed reasons, requested that the couple should wait a year before marrying, which does suggest a faint air of disapproval. William was then 32 and Harriet was 27.

As suitable preparation for his marriage, Callow busied himself with the supervision of alterations and improvements to his house in Charlotte Street – and finally gave up smoking. He had been an exceptionally heavy smoker, but etiquette had

[3] Information on the Smart family compiled from *Grove's Dictionary of Music and Musicians.*

already made it difficult for him to do so during the day, if there were to be lady pupils in the house. Charles Bentley also made preparations to leave and return to his old quarters at 11 Mornington Road, Hampstead.

During the summer of 1845, Callow made a sketching tour of Holland – *see* 'Wyn Haven, Rotterdam' (*illustration no. 41*), also 'Wharf and Groote Kerk, Rotterdam' included in an album of sketches in the Tate Gallery (listed on page 168).

> From The Hague I visited Scheveningen, where I obtained some good sketches of Dutch fishing-boats [*illustration no. 42*] and then proceeded by diligence to Delft, Leyden and Haarlem. These places were exceedingly dull, there being very few people to be seen in the streets and at the last-named town, I was the only traveller in the hotel, where I dined alone in a room capable of holding 500 persons. I next took up my quarters in Amsterdam which was much more lively, as it was fair time and there were plenty of amusements, besides I had an opportunity of seeing Rembrandt's glorious paintings. I afterwards had a most interesting trip by steamer through the canals to Antwerp and from there I returned to England.

The supplement to *The Times*, Saturday 4 July 1846, included the following announcement: 'On the 2nd inst. at St Margaret's Westminster by the Rev. J. Miller of Park Chapel, Chelsea, Harriet Anne, second daughter of the late Henry Smart to William Callow Esq. of 20 Charlotte Street, Portland Place.' The inside cover of a small pocket sketch book (*see illustration no. 46*) has the pencilled inscription 'Harriet Anne Smart – Brighton 1846' followed by 'Married this year and am now H. A. Callow, 1846'. A slightly less than crisp sketch is inscribed 'leaving Ramsgate, July 3rd, 1846'. The Callows were embarking on a ten-week wedding tour, which was to take them up the Rhine and across Switzerland to Venice. The following extracts from Callow's description of the honeymoon tour, provide background reference to the many finished water-colours which resulted from sketches made in 1846.

> At Cologne we saw the cathedral before its completion.... I was at first disappointed with Nuremberg, but on looking around, I found many capital subjects. The picturesque buildings, were, however, very difficult to sketch. In fact, I experienced the same difficulty with all German towns. At Munich we saw an interesting fair with Tyrolean peasants in their national costumes. I made many sketches of them.... the scenery of the Alps from Innsbruck is charming and we specially enjoyed the view looking down the winding river from the bridge by moonlight. The old city of Trent is also beautifully situated and I found many subjects here for my pencil. We next proceeded to the beautiful city of Verona; to my mind it ranks next to Venice in point of interest. The market place was a great source of interest to us; Italian ladies with black veils wandering about and making purchases at the stalls covered with huge white umbrellas made an animated scene....

From Verona, William and Harriet Callow continued on to Vicenza and from there to Venice.

'Bridge of Sighs', inscribed 'Aug. 17, 1846' (*illustration no. 47*), is one of several fine pencil and water-colour sketches which were executed in Venice over a known period of four days. There is a particularly confident rhythm to the style of Callow in this mood, combining delicately sketched observations and intricate detail with an expressive freedom of movement. 'The Grand Canal, Venice, looking towards the Salute', inscribed 'Aug. 18, 1846' (Christie's, 2 March 1976), and 'Rialto, Venice', also 'Aug 18' (Yale Center), and 'Canal in Venice' inscribed 'Aug 15, 46' (National Gallery of Scotland), have a very similar response. 'Palazzo Falier, Venice' (*colour plate*), based on sketches made during the honeymoon tour, displays a powerful evocation of atmosphere, handled in Callow's most fluent manner. At this period, the strongly contrasting elements of light and shade have not yet become over-exaggerated or details over-emphasised.

The return journey via Flüelen and Lucerne seems to have been made in torrents of continual rain – not sketching weather. The Callows arrived back in England on 12 September 1846 after

> an enjoyable trip, which was, however, to some extent marred by my wife's delicate health, I now settled down to serious work both in teaching and making drawings for the Old Water-colour Society Exhibitions, but owing to my wife's ill-health, our gaieties were few. . . .

Callow was not using a Victorian euphemism for pregnancy, but referring to some kind of chronic condition. This rather plaintive comment is the nearest that he comes to expressing disappointment with his marriage, but, after only ten weeks, a definite pattern had already been established. From then onwards, Harriet Callow appears to have been always vaguely ailing; there is some evidence that she may have been an asthmatic or perhaps suffered from some nervous complaint or phobia. Her ill-health was to cast a shadow over the years ahead, although it was probably in the nature of William that he was able to cope with a rather delicate and dependent wife – even to regard this as being the correct complement. But it has to be noted that, after his marriage, Callow seems to have expanded his enthusiasm for scientific and geographical interests, frequently attending lectures and discussions in spheres that the Victorians considered suitable only to the male intellect; in this way he continued to find good talk and a social life, without seeming to neglect his wife. Amongst the pupils of Callow were the son and daughter of the Bishop of Norwich, who was President of the Linnean Society and a noted ornithologist. Callow frequently attended meetings and soirées at his home in connection with the Society. Ornithology was one of the special interests of Callow, although specific bird studies do not feature in his work.

In spite of poor health, Harriet Callow was to travel extensively with her husband and continued her interest in drawing and painting. Research for this book has revealed that the work of Harriet Callow not only displayed a charming talent, but can have a hitherto unrealised significance in relation to that of William Callow. Collectors should be aware that some unsigned water-colour sketches, attributed to Callow, have undoubtedly been the work of Harriet Callow. As a pupil of her husband, one would expect a similar style, but her fluent manipulation and technical ability were capable of producing work which it has previously been quite sensible to deduce as that of William Callow. However, before any unfounded doubts are engendered as to the authenticity of work attributed to Callow, it is important to understand the area concerned. Harriet Callow was essentially an amateur; confusion with the work of her husband is confined only to certain water-colour sketches, for which there is limited demand on the art market. It is not proposed to discuss any such examples that have already been auctioned or otherwise sold, because this would be invidious and unhelpful, although the writer has knowledge of work which does appear to support a sometimes cautious view.

Examination of known examples of the work of Harriet Callow provides certain guide-lines for the recognition of her style. A woman who could make a tiny pencil drawing, delicately executed with minute hatching lines, of a piece of meat on a plate, inscribed 'The Ham at Brighton', would appear to have an original eye. Note the general manner of these hatching lines, so much finer and more evenly spaced than those of Callow. These crisp little drawings are full of characteristic Harriet introductions, including the figures of parasolled ladies and dumpy gentlemen who appear to have no feet, but it was in the area of the landscape sketch that the work of Harriet more closely approached that of William Callow. 'Cottages in Carter's Field' (*illustration no. 70*) could well have been from the hand of Callow. Space does not permit many illustrations of her work, but collectors should note the tree formations in the pencil sketch of the cottage at Wimbledon (*illustration no. 68*). These outlines are patterned on much that is characteristic of the work of Harriet, often appearing in a similar manner in water-colours. Her brush-work translates into the same rather obvious skeletal trunk and branch structure, with foliage treated in a more understated (even woolly) manner than that of Callow, although the general composition and style retain an atmosphere that inevitably suggests his name. Cottages, castles and buildings nestling amongst trees were favourite subjects of Harriet Callow (*see also figs. D–E – illustration no. 46*). Her palette was clean, cool and restrained.

A complication with regard to the recognition of work by Harriet Callow is that the handwriting of husband and wife is exceptionally similar – and one is also faced with the possibility that Callow could have later inscribed a sketch of Harriet, after her death, as a means of identification. The inscriptions on the illustrated sketch details by Harriet may prove helpful, as a comparison, but it will be noted that both handwritings employ a long 't' crossing and many other marked resemblances of general style. A long ending to the letter 'g' tends to point towards Harriet. It is fortunate that sketches in the Buckinghamshire County Museum (*see* later reference, page 98) were separately identified in the lifetime of Callow.

Other sketches in the illustrated pocket album belonging to Harriet Callow include: 'Back View of Billy, a tom cat', which is not likely to prove a vital term of reference, but is drawn with affectionate observation and gives a glimpse of her love of animals, about which she seems to have felt as strongly as William. As well as other Brighton sketches, this album includes drawings executed during the honeymoon tour, variously inscribed Köln, Coblenz, Drachenfels, Ehrenbreitstein, Frankfort and other place names which are difficult to decipher. The album also shows later sketches of Wimbledon, Arundel, Warwick and Offchurch, with incidental observations of dumpy figures in crinolines and bonnets. The work of Harriet Callow, pupil and wife of William Callow, has an interesting place in the life of this artist, but collectors should not immediately attempt to see her hand in every unsigned example, because it must be emphasised that possible sources of her work are now very limited. However, publication of these new findings will give a rarity value and interest to the authenticated work of Harriet Callow, as a collectors' item in its own right.

In 1847, 'Piazza del Duomo, Trent, in the Tyrol' was particularly well received by the critics. The *Art Union Journal* commented: 'This is a highly picturesque passage of street-scenery and the most important work that we remember to have seen under this name ... rich in those qualities that are most attractive in this *genre* of Art.' The *Athenaeum* was equally enthusiastic:

> It is a capital exemplification of those groups of old buildings which meet the eye on emerging from the mountains southward of the Adige – and of just and fitting employment of the opaque material now so commonly and advantageously dedicated to their representation.

A lively review of the work includes references to frescoed façades, a fountain and a procession of priests, which the critic of the *Athenaeum* describes, with unconscious humour, as being 'ingeniously led out of the picture by the fruit-seller and the melons'. Nineteenth-century reviews could be deliberately humorous at the expense of a painter's work, in a manner that must have been painful for the artist concerned. Callow was generally popular with the critics, but some of his contemporaries did not always receive such bland treatment. The review concludes: 'The drawing is one of great merit and shows Mr Callow's keen appreciation of picturesque combination' – 8 May 1847.

Picturesque is a term which has been frequently used to describe the work of William Callow. The artist himself often used the word colloquially, but in the more academic sense, his drawings were certainly in this idiom. Callow looked for scenes that could be directly interpreted as pictures. Although he usually worked these to a characteristic formula, his general treatment of any subject, marine, landscape, Continental or English, always had about it a genuine sense of enjoyment and communication – but it was a response to form, rather than a subjective or emotional comment. Callow was fascinated by the quaint, jumbled architecture of a foreign market square, decked with awnings and thronged with peasants, but he does not show the same market place on a wet day or comment on the poverty that he must have seen. No one is being cruel to a donkey in a drawing by Callow, in spite of his being always so much distressed by such sights in the streets of Continental cities. In his compositions Callow usually arranged for the sun to shine and the peasants to have an air of jolly bustle.

'Piazza del Duomo, Trent' almost certainly found a buyer from the 1847 exhibition, but Callow was disappointed with his sales, although he could well stand any financial loss as he was now established as one of the most fashionable drawing masters of the day. He admitted that he had more pupils than he could properly superintend, which leads to speculation as to how far his own work was affected by his teaching. A painter can be stimulated in his development, during the course of encouraging talent in others, but Callow had evolved a successful instruction method, which aimed only for a pleasing effect. This was all that was required of him by his pupils, most of whom were essentially amateurs. Copley Fielding had made rapid and showy drawings for the instruction of his many pupils and this practice undoubtedly affected the quality of his own work, giving it an air of having been done by recipe. Callow also taught by means of demonstration pieces (*illustration no. 91*). Like Fielding, much of his everyday concern was with basic technique and small tricks of execution. These repetitions inevitably became patterned into his own style. But it was a manner that the public admired and (even if he had been so inclined) any experimental work, with a risk of failure or ridicule, might have had a very adverse effect on his position as a teacher – and this was a side of his career that meant a great deal to him. However, at about this time there is no doubt that Callow did feel a need for some innovation in his work and made a mild endeavour to break new ground.

The constitution of the Water-colour Society deliberately encouraged members to undertake large works, in a misguided attempt to enhance the importance of their exhibitions. One system had been to provide large frames, complete with glass, in which members might show their work, but this had been given up shortly after Callow became an Associate. A lottery was held for the remaining frames and Callow considered himself fortunate in obtaining one. It was the subsequent practice of the Water-colour Society to offer a premium to three or four members, each season, if they would be prepared to execute a larger than usual drawing. Even the most venerable water-colourists of the day often had a sense of their work being overshadowed by the oil paintings shown at the Royal Academy and with the Society of British Artists and similar exhibitions.

Callow fell into this trap. He began increasingly to use larger sizes of paper, with a resulting loss of some of the earlier delicacy of touch. He appears to have been aiming for display, rather than the more gentle treatment which is so well suited to water-colours. It was certainly with the intention of enhancing the impact of his work that Callow took up oils, probably about 1847. He was to produce some capable work in this medium, but we must regard his general manipulation as that of the water-colourist, more often producing a drawing in oils. The cool greys and greens of his water-colour seas translated well into oils, but his tones when using this medium for Continental street scenes can be somewhat brown and chocolatey. 'The Rialto, Venice' (*illustration no. 48*) has this tendency about the shadowed area to the right, but Callow has picked out the tall sail in effective contrast and employed general tones of ochre and grey, with touches of terracotta, against a pale blue sky, in an attractive composition, very similar to a water-colour version of this scene, dated 1851. Callow exhibited an oil painting with the title 'Rialto, Venice' at the British Institution in 1858. The sea-piece in oils (*illustration no. 48*) has a definite compositional influence from Charles Bentley (note the characteristic foreground buoy on a choppy sea), but it is also a typical Callow treatment of the coastal subject, with finely detailed delineation of the shipping and a clean and unfussy manipulation of the pigment. The picture is not signed, but sketches exist which give an added confirmation of the work as that of Callow. Sales were again poor in 1848, but this was compensated for by the news (brought to him by the faithful Bentley) that he had been elected a full member of the Society of Painters in Water-colours. The great ambition of his life was now achieved. Callow was later to recall:

> How proud was I to think that for the future I was to be included in a body of celebrated men to whom as a boy I had looked up with an admiration approaching awe, and to belong to the Society and the home of water-colour paintings. I wonder how many of the younger generation have appreciated the honour of membership of this famous Society to the same degree as I have done, and still continue to do.

Although he was a man of undoubted presence, Callow obviously retained a charming lack of pretension and an unassuming attitude to his own talent.

At the time of his election the other vacancy for a full member was filled by Francis W. Topham, who had recently resigned from the 'New' Water-colour Society. It has been ascertained that, in addition to Callow and Topham, the 24 full members of the Society must have consisted of the following:

> Copley Fielding (President), Frederick McKenzie (Treasurer), George A. Fripp (Secretary), Charles Bentley, David Cox, Peter de Wint, William Turner (of Oxford), Edmund Dorrell, John Linnell, James Holmes, Samuel Prout, James Duffield Harding, William Evans ('of Eton'), George Cattermole, W. A. Nesfield, William ('Birdsnest') Hunt, John F. Lewis, Joseph Nash, Octavius Oakley, James Stephanoff, Frederick Taylor and Alfred D. Fripp.[4]

In the year that Callow became a full member of the 'Old' Water-colour Society, at the age of 36, some of his fellow exhibitors had been showing their work when he had first visited an exhibition of the Society, as a boy of under 13 years old. In 1848, Callow received good reviews. The *Art Journal* commented: 'No. 52. The New Münster, etc, Würzberg, Bavaria during the fair' – There is much originality about the work of this artist in dealing with his subject matter, which may be said to be always striking ... the drawing is masterly....'

It is interesting to compare this exhibit with a general impression of the pictures that were being shown by some of the other exhibitors. Copley Fielding was taking his annual look at the Sussex Downs and a fine and airy glimpse of the mountains and coast of Scotland, which was also the subject of one of the breezy sea-pieces of Charles Bentley; David Cox, now 65, exhibited a characteristically sombre view of a Welsh valley; Evans ('of Eton') was out with the deerstalkers, while Frederick Taylor (known as the 'Landseer of Water-colours') was inside a Highland larder, weighing a full-grown buck. O. Oakley and F. W. Topham were amongst the Irish peasants and gypsies, while Alfred Fripp chose to depict a somewhat weird story involving an old, blind pilgrim, a young girl and a sacrificial altar. Maria Harrison showed a

[4] Source L Full list of O.W.S. members in 1848, Maurice Callow, catalogue: *Heritage: one hundred years old-English water-colours, William Callow and his contemporaries and some predecessors.* Exhibition: 3 October to 21 November 1976, McClelland Regional Gallery, Langwarrin, Frankston, Victoria, Australia.

basket of roses, and William Hunt more roses and his customary bird's nest. Peter de Wint painted a distant view of Nottingham and George Cattermole exhibited a landscape, with that title only, of an unidentified castle amid a group of trees. Only H. Gastineau and Samuel Prout, with one of his highly detailed pieces, appear to have been showing the more directly topographical style.[5]

It is inevitable that certain aspects of the style of William Callow should recall Samuel Prout (1784–1852), an important force in the English water-colour school. Newton Fielding is thought to have known Prout, but it is clear that Callow first met him in the Rue de Bouloi atelier and that this was only a very incidental occasion. Prout was a most successful exhibitor, lithographer and teacher, a friend of Francia and an admirer of Bonington. It is his towering Gothic façades, his market squares, with groups of peasants (even the same picturesque awnings) that are echoed in the work of Callow, but the latter has a stronger line and a general impression of greater movement. Samuel Prout had some influence on the work of T. S. Boys, which would indirectly be received by Callow, but his individual style was quite formed before he came into any regular contact with Prout as a fellow exhibitor with the 'Old' Water-colour Society.

'Mr Prout returns from cathedral-decked towns with cleanly specimens of architectural drawing. Mr Callow comes from similar localities with his wonted appetite for stronger contrasts of colour' (*The Times*, 6 May 1851). Samuel Prout died in the following year, which left this particular topographical field very much to Callow.

William Callow was officially introduced to his fellow members by Charles Bentley. Callow was always to enjoy meetings and official duties, in connection with the Water-colour Society. For him, it was a congenial social club, where he could discuss art with friends, as well as taking a keenly interested part in the organisation of the Society. At that time members received a fee for attending committee meetings and assisting with the hanging of exhibitions. Callow gives the impression that he would have paid just to be there. His reminiscences provide a fascinating glimpse of some of the well-known names who were his colleagues:

> ... Evans ('of Eton') put forward a motion limiting the number of works to be sent by each member for Exhibition. Copley Fielding who always contributed many drawings felt that the proposal was levelled at him and was much pained by it. He appealed to William Hunt the fruit and flower painter for his opinion. The latter, who was of small stature and slightly deformed and who had a very gentle manner, said he should be sorry not to be able to send any number of drawings he might be able to paint, without limit. Whereupon Evans withdrew his motion and said he had no intention of hurting the feelings of the President or any of the members. I rarely saw David Cox, except on 'touching up' days, as he was then living in Birmingham. He was a very jovial fellow. In the gallery Cox once remarked that he had never received 100 guineas for any one drawing. He was overheard by a stranger, who addressing Cox, said: 'You shall not state that again, for I will give you that amount for the picture hanging on

[5] Information from the *Art Journal*, pp. 181–2, 1848.

> the wall.' [The work was 'Welsh Funeral – Bettws-y-Coed, North Wales', exhibited no. 212 with the Society in 1852.] At one of the exhibitions, a bright drawing of mine, full of Italian sunshine, was placed on the line next to another by Peter de Wint, which although very powerful in colour was dark in tone. He considered that mine placed his at a disadvantage, and suggested to me that I should subdue my drawing by placing a warm tint all over it. Needless to say my brother artists advised me to take no notice of the suggestion, which, if it had been carried out, would have ruined my work.

In the autumn of 1848, the Callows made a tour in the area of Tewkesbury, Worcester (*illustration no. 52*) and Hereford. A small view of Tewkesbury, which Callow subsequently exhibited with the Society in 1849, was purchased by Charles Dickens for eight guineas. Election as a full member of the 'Old' Water-colour Society provided a stimulus to the career of William Callow. In 1849, he had obviously given time and thought to the preparation of exhibits and had judged the market well – all 20 of his contributions found a buyer. Prices did not include the frames, which were an optional purchase. His drawings were now varying in price from the modest eight guineas paid by Dickens up to at least fifty guineas. It was the topographical detail of his work that the *Art Journal* particularly notices: 'No. 109, "An old Street in Frankfurt". The striking feature of this drawing is an ancient and curiously built building ... the whole forming a subject of much picturesque interest.' No. 197, 'Maison des Francs Bateliers at Ghent', was praised because it would be so readily recognised by anyone who had visited the locale. Had Callow taken any licence with the topographical detail this would have been considered a definite fault.

> In 1849, I made a sketching tour in the west of Scotland, arriving at Glasgow whilst the Queen and Prince Albert were there, and afterwards visiting the Kyles of Bute and Inveraray where my wife and I stayed for a month in most primitive but comfortable quarters, being waited on by a maid without shoes or stockings....

> We congratulate Mr William Callow on a decided advance. His style has of late years been gradually refining without losing any of its breadth – and his eye enters more searchingly than it did into the minutiae of his subjects. His tone is still cold, and we have yet to deprecate the prevalance of a leaden colour in his shadows. His hand – always bold – is acquiring grace of execution. His best drawing here is 'Inveraray Castle, the Seat of his Grace the Duke of Argyll' [*illustration no. 56*]. The castle mid-distance, the finely drawn mountains in the background, and the lake on the right are all aided in their air of truthfulness by the look of reality given, as the eye enters the scene, to some trunks of recently felled beeches on which the woodmen are still at work. [*Athenaeum*, 1850.]

Comparison with the other illustrations demonstrates that this water-colour did not represent any significant change in the style of William Callow. It is, in fact a somewhat uncharacteristic work, with a rather interesting suggestion of the style of S. R. Percy in the foreground introductions. The *Athenaeum* added:

> Mr Callow's other drawings have still some of his old faults: – a tendency to strong contrasts – breadth carried into flatness – with a chilly uncongenial tone – perhaps we ought to say a want of it.

But it was just these strong contrasts and clean areas of cool colour that were the mark of Callow – and in this style he successfully continued. The refinements of style detected by the critic of the *Athenaeum* were not improvements, but the precursor of a later tendency to overworking and fuss.

In general, Callow was to continue to receive favourable notices from the nineteenth-century critics for a considerable period, although the somewhat unexpected appearance of 'Trongate, Glasgow' in the 1850 exhibition drew a slightly tetchy comment from the *Art Journal* critic, who felt that it was 'a relief to turn to anything at home, after the everlasting street-scenery of Venice, of the Rhineland and some of the French cities'. The œuvre of Callow was now firmly identified with such subjects. The more frequent introduction of British landscape from about 1848 might have been expected to give an extra facet to his work, but Callow was never influenced into any new development of style by the individual qualities of the English scene, nor was he attracted to any particular county. In fact, it will be noticed that the immediate impression given by 'Trongate, Glasgow' (*illustration no. 87*) is that this is a Continental scene, so much is it patterned to his usual formula, although Callow has been accurate in the presentation of architectural detail and has not taken any liberties with the subject. This work is almost certainly a similar version of the 1850 exhibit.

The 1850 exhibition of the Society of Painters in Water-colours was notable for the sensation caused by exhibit no. 147 from J. F. Lewis, who, in 1834, had first suggested that Callow should submit his work to the Society. Lewis had been living in Cairo and had not contributed any work since 1841, which led to his being asked to resign. In answer to this, J. F. Lewis exhibited 'The Haareem', startingly colourful in both subject and treatment, handled with outstanding technical brilliance, using a minute stippled technique and executed throughout in body-colour. 'This may be pronounced the most extraordinary production that has ever been executed in water-colour ... this work is unique in the history of water-colour art' (*Art Journal*, p. 179, May 1850). This florid piece received extravagant and astonished praise and was inevitably followed by similar works, which were to have a radical effect on the general manner of the 'Old' Water-colour Society exhibitions.

In 1850, the Callows visited Belgium, including the towns of Lille (*illustration no. 61*), Courtrai, Tournai, Bruges, Ghent and Antwerp. 'At all these towns I had little time for seeing the sights, as I found so many architectural subjects admirably suited for my pencil.' Callow executed many sketches in the wood-encased graphite, commonly known as a pencil, but it should be noted that he frequently used the term in the more eighteenth-century idiom, which can mean the painter's brush and general style.

Town and Fortress of Bellinzona in the Ticino' (32), exhibited with the Society of Painters in Water-colours in 1851, drew an interesting comment from the *Athenaeum*, 3 May:

> The subject is rather quaintly described as 'a specimen of the middle-age architecture of those regions.... Mr Callow surrenders himself more freely to the expedients of picture-making; and here as in many other of his able performances, he exhibits the successful use of a style which has tended to render similar subjects in other hands florid and vague. The sketches of Bonington have done much to mislead. The haste with which this justly lamented artist filled his sketch-books has been mistaken for style, – and their imitation has led to vagueness and an irrational dexterity. Mr Callow shows how such practice may be advantageously applied in the drawing already named and some others. Among these, the 'View in the Rue St Honoré, Paris, looking toward the Palais Royal' (147) is a striking expression of his peculiar art: full of character, strong in resemblance and rich in colour.'

The latter was to be named by the artist as one of his favourite exhibits.

William Callow was now 39 and had established an individual style, which had evolved to a point where it was to progress little further. In consequence, some opinion would like to place all the best work of Callow as having been executed during the period up to about 1850. This often repeated assessment needs some qualification, otherwise it can give a very unbalanced view of the work of this artist. It is true that his early style was more exploratory, luminous and fluently handled and that later work tended to repeat popular themes, with a use of heavier washes, and a loss of spontaneity to the demands of finish, but this should not be regarded as an absolute fault. The earlier Bonington-inspired style may now have more esoteric appeal, but subsequent modifications have to be considered as a valid response to the art climate of the mid-nineteenth century. If Callow shaped his manner in order to retain his popularity, in the face of strongly competing trends, surely this should not be regarded as retrogression. Callow was not aiming to make subjective statements, but to sell his work. As will be observed from a study of the illustrations in this book, the collector needs to avoid rigid generalisations and must employ intelligent selection, with regard to the later work of Callow. This will not be the same as that of his youth, yet it is capable of most attractive qualities of craftsmanship and charm. Callow, the picture-maker, cannot be ignored.

Census returns for 20 Charlotte Street in 1851 recorded that John Callow, painter/water-colourist, unmarried, was resident as part of the permanent household of William Callow. John Callow (1822–1878) was born in London on 19 July 1822 and baptised on 27 July 1823 at St Pancras Parish Church. The occupation of Robert Callow was again given as 'carpenter' and the address as Tottenham Place, St Pancras. On joining William in Paris in 1835, John was persuaded to the academic exercise of copying paintings in the Louvre, a practice which Callow himself had also followed (*see* Paul Mellon Collection, page 206). Callow appears to have been a good judge of the potential talents of his brother. After a while John started to have a genuine interest in drawing and painting, and there is no evidence that he ever regretted that he had been diverted from a life at sea, although this attachment was reflected in his liking for seascapes, which were always his most characteristic subjects. John Callow remained in France until 1844. He was elected an Associate of the New Society of Painters in Water-colours in 1845, but resigned in 1848. In the following year, John Callow became an Associate of the 'Old' Water-colour Society, with whom he exhibited 325 works. He exhibited at the Royal Academy (1844–56) and the British Institution (1851–5). His paintings were also shown with the Society of British Artists. In 1855, William Callow was approached to take the vacant post of Professor of Drawing at the Royal Military College at Addiscombe (*see* Theodore Fielding, page 3), but Callow had neither the time nor the inclination for this and advised John to apply for the position, which he held until 1861. From 1865 to 1875 he was joint master of landscape drawing (with Aaron Penley) at the Royal Military Academy at Woolwich. The National Portrait Gallery has a photograph of John Callow and Aaron Penley (neg. no. 20332). From 1875 to 1878, John Callow was Professor of Drawing at Queen's College, London. He also kept up a thriving private practice.

Examples of his water-colours appear as chromolithographs in *Callow's Easy Lessons*, a book of instruction, and also in *Lessons from Callow's Sketch Book*. Sepia and water-colour drawings by John Callow appear in Vere Foster's *Drawing Copy Book* (1871) and in the illustrations for his *Painting for Beginners* (1884). John Callow also collaborated with R. P. Leitch in producing *Easy Studies in Water-colour Painting* (1881).

The style of John Callow was essentially influenced by that of his elder brother, rather in the manner of the earlier sea-pieces of William.

> Mr John Callow has a facile hand for marine subjects. There are fine masses of old hulls in his 'Wrecks Ashore, near Whitby, Yorkshire' (No. 5) and 'Dismantling a Merchantman on the Thames, near Greenwich' (No. 89), both of which are painted with breadth and freedom. The 'Steamer weathering the Caskets in a Storm' (No. 150) is a difficult subject treated in a very masterly manner. In this last picture the stormy sky and heaving sea are forcibly handled; and the position in which the steamer is thrown, on the crest of a huge wave, evinces much boldness and skill. The clearness and crispness of sea water is well shown, too, in the same artist's 'Entrance to Yarmouth Harbour, Norfolk' (No. 92) – where a brig is being towed out during a heavy squall. [*Athenaeum*, p. 493, 1852.]

The above review encapsulates much that is typical of the style and subject matter of John Callow. He produced so many ships on wind-tossed seas that unidentified work of this type is often indiscriminately attributed to his name. 'Seascape, Brittany' (*illustration no. 50*) shows a painting in oils, a medium which John Callow handled very effectively. His general area of subjects includes scenes on the coasts of England, Wales, France and the Channel Islands, as well as some inland views. Only a brief summary of the work of John Callow is intended for the purposes of this book. There is no evidence that the painters George D. Callow and James W. Callow were related to William and John Callow.

The *Ipswich Journal*, 13 September 1851, in a review of the second Annual Exhibition of the Suffolk Fine Art Society, commented: 'We have to notice two productions of W. Callow, in which the aspect of the busy scenes in the cities of Antwerp and Frankfort are well delineated.' In the following year, this publication considered that 'Looking into Henry VII Chapel, Westminster Abbey' was very 'solemn and subdued in tone, ... The drawing bears considerable resemblance in colour and treatment to some of Cattermole's earlier and most effective rendering of a national monument'. The exhibit was undoubtedly too solemn for local Suffolk taste and remained unsold, eventually to appear in Walker's catalogue of drawings (1927). The *Ipswich Journal* much preferred 'Wrecks Ashore, near Whitby, Yorkshire', praising this as by far the better of the two contributions of William Callow, 'in the style that has gained him well-earned fame'. In fact, the exhibit was that of John Callow and would be probably the drawing mentioned in the *Athenaeum* review (see previous paragraph). Painters frequently sent to the provinces unsold works from the London spring exhibitions, in the hopes of attracting a buyer or an Art Union prize winner. Provincial Art Unions were proliferating at this time, although many survived for only a short period, as was the case in Suffolk.

It was now just over ten years since William Callow had returned from France, as an artist little known in his own country. The critic of the *Ipswich Journal* may have confused the work of William with that of his brother, but he was patently aware of their general style, which had become established as familiar to provinces in the span of one decade. The catalogue section gives full details of exhibits by Callow with the Royal Liverpool Academy and the Norfolk and Norwich Association for the Promotion of the Fine Arts, but does not attempt to list work sent by Callow to every provincial exhibition, which included the Society of Birmingham Artists.

On 23 April 1852, Queen Victoria wrote in her diary: '... immediately after luncheon, we went with the two eldest children to the Old, and then the New Water-colour exhibition. The former very good with beautiful landscapes by Callow, Fripp, Copley Fielding etc. .... the New exhibition was less good. ...'[6] The Queen saw the exhibition on the day before the private view and it was on this occasion that Callow was first presented to the royal family, including the young Princess Victoria, who was then aged 12½, and who was later to be associated with one of the most interesting episodes of his career. The Queen and Prince Albert were particularly gracious to Callow. The Queen remarked that she had heard of him from Princess Clémentine and made enquiries as to whether he was now settled in England and, according to the recollections of Callow, asked many knowledgeable questions about his work.

The Prince Consort, with his usual interest in technicalities, had a long discussion with Callow as to the presentation of exhibits, which he considered might have been improved by the use of white mounts. Callow explained that the rules of the Society required that all work be framed up close in order to prove that the medium could stand the gilt as well as oils. In 1841, Prince Albert had purchased Callow's 'Neapolitan Fishing Boat, Sunrise', a version of a water-colour drawing with the title 'Fishing Boat at Naples', which is in the National Maritime Museum. 'Neapolitan Fishing

[6] Entry from the diary of Queen Victoria, 23 April 1852, reproduced by gracious permission of Her Majesty the Queen.

Boat' (also catalogued as 'Neapolitan Fishers') was at Osborne House until early in the present century, after which it was transferred to Buckingham Palace. From the 1852 exhibition, Prince Albert bought no. 113, 'Distant View of Naples – Early Morning' (*illustration no. 59*). Callow stated that Queen Victoria also bought one of his drawings from this exhibition, but, if so, it seems that this must have been purchased as a gift. The Royal Collection does not now appear to contain any other work by Callow from the 1852 exhibition. The *Art Journal* praised 'Bay of Naples' for the usual qualities: '... the drawing is careful in finish and successful for its definition of graduation.' The work of William Callow and John Callow occupied most of an entire column in the *Athenaeum*, p. 493, 1852.

> ... it is within walls of old cities or at the foot of crumbling ruins that Mr W. Callow displays his greatest power. 'Looking into the Grand Place at Lille, from the Place du Théâtre' ... [*illustration no. 62*]. Mr Callow has greatly advanced his reputation not only by this picture, but by 'Grand Entrance to Hurstmonceaux Castle, Sussex', which is remarkable for rigorous drawing and rich colour....

The *Art Journal* also noticed an architectural piece – 'The Stone Bow, Lincoln' (*illustration no. 58*). 'This is the name given to an ancient-looking and certainly not very picturesque façade, but it is by means of chiaroscuro and careful manipulation wrought into a drawing of much substantial beauty.'

The *Art Journal* may not have considered that the Stone Bow was picturesque, but for Callow it would have exactly the right element of quaintness. A study of the preliminary sketch (*illustration no. 57*) with the finished water-colour provides an interesting comparison. It will be noted how accurately Callow has reproduced the topographical detail and how successfully he has translated pencilled information into the solidity of colour wash. The incidental touches are charmingly characteristic and include the trailing window curtain, which is almost like a second Callow signature. 'Lincoln Cathedral from the High Street', 1853 (*colour plate*), is a fine and characteristic work also based on sketches made in 1851.

'Fir Trees at Offchurch', inscribed 'Offchurch Augt 16 1852' (*illustration no. 60*), shows a very similar view of this subject to that of a sketch by Harriet, executed on the same day (*see illustration no. 46*), but the water-colour can be accepted as the work of William owing to the placing of the brush strokes on the trees and the fluid handling of the foreground washes. The signature is a later addition, but absolutely right as that of Callow (*see* further references to signatures in Chapter VI). Callow is thought to have been very reliable in the separation of his work from that of Harriet, when identifications were made in later years. In specific reference to these two views of Offchurch, note that although the handwriting of the inscriptions is so similar, the 'g' has a turn to the left in Harriet's sketch and the figure *5* is much more open in formation. Callow displays a marked tendency to contract the upper part of this figure, as shown in the dating of 'Lincoln Cathedral'. The figure *8* is also subject to distortion and can read as *o*. It is a general characteristic of the painted signatures of Callow that he frequently attempts to show them in perspective, i.e. as if he were laying the letters and figures flat on the ground, as part of the picture. This can have a distorting effect, which must be allowed for, in the reading of dates.

In late August 1852, the Callows toured Germany, starting from Cologne, then on to Düsseldorf, where an exhibition was being held. Callow made sketches in Hanover, followed by visits to Brunswick, Leipzig (*illustration no. 65*) where they were specially interested in the Bach monument, on to Dresden, and home via Cassel and Frankfort.

In 1848, there had been further revolution in France. The mob attacked the Tuileries Palace and the royal family were smuggled out of France (with the direct help of the British Consul) and found refuge at Claremont, Esher. Queen Victoria had offered them this royal residence, where they were to remain for many years.

Princess Clémentine had married Duke Augustus of Saxe-Coburg, brother of Princess Victoire, who was now the Duchess of Nemours. It is of interest to note that the wedding gift from Queen Victoria to Princess Clémentine was a fine water-colour by Thomas Shotter Boys, with the title 'A Terrace of Houses', signed and dated 1833. Early in 1853, while Princess Clémentine was on a long visit from Germany, Callow was summoned to Claremont, in order to give some further lessons to the Princess and to the Prince de Joinville. All the surviving members of the Orléans family were delighted to see William Callow again. Queen Marie Amélie seized both his hands and began to speak in broken English, until reminded by her son that Callow spoke fluent French, when she then exclaimed: '*Il me fait un plaisir de vous voir. Ah! ça me rappelle le bon vieux temps....*' Prince Joinville was now married to Princess Françoise, daughter of King Pedro I of Brazil. He had his children with him, whom he rather charmingly stood on chairs, in order to show them to his old drawing master. He may now have welcomed a few more lessons from Callow, as a diversion, but it must surely have been for the benefit of Princess Clémentine that Callow was asked to go to Claremont. But, in view of the fact that his instruction was of proved merit, but limited range, the Princess must have previously learnt all that Callow could teach her of his water-colour methods. It seems certain that this was a small ploy, by which these two people, so separate in their life styles, could renew their friendship. William Callow and Princess Clémentine undoubtedly had a genuine attachment for each other, but it comes across as a most refreshingly innocent and unaffected relationship. The drawing lessons at Claremont continued for several months until the Princess returned to Germany.

'Mill at Antwerp', an oil painting exhibited No. 231 at the British Institution in 1853, drew the following comment from the *Art Journal*: '... it has much the feeling of the artist's water-colour work.' William Callow continued to be particularly successful in selling his work from the 'Old' Water-colour Society exhibitions and was also in demand for commissions, which were often virtually repetitions of subjects that had attracted popular notice. Callow executed commissions with tradesman-like efficiency. 'Dear Sir, I have completed your drawing and shall be happy to show it you if you will favour me with a call ...' – letter written from Charlotte Street to a client – 16 June 1857. He was enabled to raise his prices and can be considered to have reached his most prosperous level during the next decade.

'Mr. W. Callow is fertile in cleanly representations of continental architecture' wrote *The Times* on 25 April 1853. This comment was repeated almost exactly in the following year, when his work was placed in rather apt juxtaposition with 'the dainty views of land and sea by Mr. Copley Fielding ... the waves of Mr. Bentley ...'. Callow was now recognised as a veteran exhibitor by the critic of *The Times*, who was making the point that it was difficult to tell any difference between the exhibits of such artists from one year to another.

In the early autumn of 1853, Callow visited Yorkshire and made many sketching excursions in that county. He also visited Chester, which he described as 'a delightfully interesting city, with endless new objects for my pencil'. *Illustration no. 64* shows 'Shoemakers' Row, Northgate Street, Chester'. In the following year, he toured Normandy from Dieppe, taking the diligence to Lisieux, Caen, and Le Havre, then by steamer up the Seine to Rouen.

On his return to England, Callow was extremely distressed to learn that his old friend, Charles Bentley, had died from cholera on 4 September. ('It was a great grief to me as he had been a true companion.') The *Athenaeum*, 9 September 1854, commented: 'The Water-colour Society has just lost a valuable member in Mr Charles Bentley and lost him before his time ... in marine landscapes and other subjects of the kind he may be ranked between Messrs Copley Fielding and Callow.'[7]

[7] Extract from letter in possession of J. L. Wybrew.

CHAPTER V

Great Missenden: the Middle and Later Period, 1855–1883

LONDON did not suit the indifferent health of Harriet Callow. Consequently, the Callows had frequently spent quite long periods in apartments in Reigate or country cottages, such as the one in Wimbledon (*illustration no. 68*). Callow travelled up to London from these places, in order to continue his teaching. In 1854, it was decided to purchase a cottage in the country. Callow recollects:

> ... one dark November morning my brother John and I started to look for one of which we had heard, in the Great Missenden parish. We left Euston station at 6 o'clock, travelling third-class in a truck with no seats or covering of any description and, after a tedious journey, the train being shunted into sidings several times to allow fast trains to pass, we reached Berkhamsted.

Just why William and John Callow chose to travel in this inconvenient manner is inexplicable: William could well have afforded first-class fares. They walked the ten miles to Great Missenden and discovered the cottage, about one and a half miles from the village.

> It was a remote spot, away from civilisation and there was a good orchard and three fields, with some beautiful old trees attached to the cottage.

Callow immediately arranged to purchase the property. William and John then walked the ten miles back to Berkhamsted and returned to London. At 44, Callow had obviously retained his remarkable stamina.

The Callows moved into the cottage in the spring of 1855 and both appear to have been delighted with their new surroundings, although the Buckinghamshire landscape was never to inspire any major exhibition work from Callow. It was as if his attachment for this scenery was a rather personal aspect of his life, not to be commercialised. The Buckinghamshire County Museum, Aylesbury, is in possession of an album of sketches, the work of both William and Harriet Callow, depicting the Great Missenden area (1856–78). A water-colour sketch in this volume by William Callow with the title 'Front of Old Cottage – The Firs', dated August 1859 (*illustration no. 69*), shows the first home of the Callows in Great Missenden.

20 Charlotte Street was retained as a town house and studio, where Callow was to give his lessons until 1860, when he moved to 3 Osnaburgh Terrace, also near

Regent's Park. During the London season, he was either driven or rode on horseback to Berkhamsted, from where he took the train to London, returning the same day. This journey was to be part of his regular teaching routine for the next 28 years.

Not long after his arrival in Great Missenden, Callow was saddened by the death of Copley Fielding.

> ... he was a gentle, kind and amiable man, and most courteous in his manner, he was very industrious both in teaching and painting, and was for twenty-five years a most excellent President of the Old Society, at whose exhibitions his drawings were always a great attraction. I remember him saying that he had never received 100 guineas for any drawing which he made, yet in 1872, I saw one of his drawings realise 700 guineas at the famous Gillet sale at Christie's.

In 1854 a water-colour drawing by William Callow had been sold for £126 at the Royal Liverpool Academy.

Life in Great Missenden suited Harriet Callow and her health improved. This was said to be due to the bracing air, but a more likely reason may be found in the fact that she was taking a great interest in the local villagers, which probably gave her a sense of identity and purpose. Most of the local women and children were employed in straw-plaiting, as outworkers for the hat-making industry in Luton and St Albans. There was a dame school, but as this taught only straw-plaiting, the cottagers were almost totally illiterate. Harriet Callow started a small school for the benefit of the women and girls, where she herself taught them to read and write. Callow then bought a cottage, converted it into a school-house and engaged someone to teach. This was one of the many ways in which William was to give financial support to the charitable activities of Harriet.

1855 marked the fifty-first exhibition of the Society of Painters in Water-colours.

> ... perhaps the most brilliant collection that has ever been seen on these walls. The exhibition is rich in figure pictures – works of a very high class. We remember the Society when it was essentially a society of landscape painters – a period when there were no essays in figure-drawing beyond the feeble, mannered and minute impersonations that were employed to give semblance of life to landscape and street scenery. But, now we find not only comparatively large figures, but even life-sized studies executed with marvellous nicety; stippled with a touch fine enough for the most delicate miniature and drawn with the utmost academical accuracy. The stars of the old school of water-colours are setting, one by one, but they leave other lights behind them... [*Art Journal*, p. 185, 1855.]

The first 'stars' of the Water-colour Society had been such men as John Varley, Joshua Cristall, George Barrett and John Glover, all of whose work was very much in the classical eighteenth-century tradition, following fixed principles of style. By 1855 the 12 successive colour washes of John Varley had been succeeded by very different techniques. David Cox and Copley Fielding, pupils of Varley, had followed with their own interpretations of the traditional and these had subsequently been evolved into an essentially nineteenth-century style by William Callow and his generation. For example:

> Mr Callow contributes a rich collection of Continental scenes – 'On the Grand Canal', from Leone Bianco, Venice (6), 'Church of St Pierre, Caen' (36), 'Mayenz on the Rhine' (43), 'Oberwesel' (56), 'San Giorgio, Venice' (157), – all marked by his peculiar clearness and brilliancy of style. [*Athenaeum*, 5 May 1855.]

Callow had now been exhibiting with the 'Old' Water-colour Society for 17 years. He was certainly an established 'light', still very popular with the public, but many new influences were challenging his position. Callow was competing with 'life-sized studies' and the Arabian extravaganzas of J. F. Lewis (recently elected President of the Society). It is not surprising that he made increasing use of even larger paper sizes and began to show a conscious attempt to induce the more meretricious effect.

After half a century of Water-colour Society exhibitions, not only the style of the exhibits had radically changed, but also that of the art patrons. William Callow had commenced with the Fieldings in 1823 – which was two years before the advent of the first railway. There is something of a paradox in the fact that the works of Callow and many similar painters show practically no hint of the rapid industrialisation of the period, although this undoubtedly contributed to their success. The spreading of the railways over the British Isles and abroad made a diversity of landscape much more easily available to the artist; industry had the effect of providing him with a new market. The wealthy manufacturer was replacing the traditional art patron. Callow must have made many sales by reason of the attraction that his pictures had for this new class of collector, with equally new mansions to furnish. The woollen merchant from Bradford and the Sheffield cutler required the latest interior decoration in their houses and this included the pictures on the walls. The crisp lines of Callow would have an attractive air of modernity. One of the higher prices obtained by Callow up to this date had been at the Royal Liverpool Academy in 1856, when he received 150 guineas for one of his typical Venetian pieces.

By the mid-nineteenth century the middle classes were travelling more widely than ever before. A knowledge of foreign countries was considered a mark of education and also of wealth. The subsequent acquisition of paintings of foreign subjects was the Victorian equivalent of the colour photographs of today, reminding the tourist of what he had seen – and his friends of where he had been. A vaguely Italianate view would not do for people who had actually floated along the Grand Canal in a Venetian gondola.

Topography has been called the portraiture of places, as opposed to the imaginative organisation of natural features which is landscape painting. Callow provided the sharp focus on place, for which there was such an obvious market, although this was not entirely a deliberate commercial policy, but a presentation instinctive to the manner of Callow.

> Mr Callow is beyond average in his clever, highly tinted architectural sketches. His 'Venice' (77) with its pink and green shutters and painted stucco, gay boats

and luminous water is true without straining.... [*Athenaeum*, p. 559, 3 May 1856.]

This piece had exactly the qualities that gave the work of Callow such a popular appeal. The Art Union member with a prize to the value of £75 would have almost certainly found a red tab on this work, but chose instead 'Hôtel de Ville, Brussels' from the 1856 exhibition (*illustration no. 66*). This essentially topographical work was included in his own choice of favourite exhibits when Callow was asked to name some of these in 1904. The full list was as follows:

'Naples from the Sea'; 'On the Riva dei Schiavone, Venice' (1841); 'Rue St Honoré', 1851; 'Grand Place, Lille', 1852 [*illustration no. 62*]; 'Hôtel de Ville, Brussels', 1856 [*illustration no. 66*]; 'Santa Salute, Venice, 1869; 'Mont Richard', 1871; 'Weighing House, Amsterdam', 1882; 'Port of Marseilles', 1884 [*illustration no. 96*]; 'Palaces on the Grand Canal, near the Rialto, Venice', 1886; 'Entrance to the Grand Canal, Venice', 1897; 'View of the Town and Lake of Lugano', 1899; 'Dutch Boats running into Ostend – Stormy Weather', 1900 [*British Water-colour Art*, Marcus B. Huish, 1904.]

The work of William Callow was represented by two water-colours of marine subjects at the 33rd Annual Exhibition of the Pennsylvania Academy of the Fine Arts in 1856. In that year, the Callows visited Tours, Nantes (*illustration* no. *67*) and places beside the river Loire, as far as Blois. In 1857, they were in Edinburgh, Stirling and Aberdeen.

On 2 May 1857, the *Athenaeum* remarked that 'Messrs. Gastineau, Richardson, D. Cox jun., Naftel, Callow and Collingwood fill their usual places – hardly however, with their usual success', but *The Times* (26 April 1858) commented: 'H. Gastineau, the Callows and W. Turner send subjects of the classes with which we are so familiar from their hands and which hold their own well with younger competitors. ...' The reference to William and John as the Callows marks a new tendency to treat the brothers as of equal status. John Callow had begun to approach his brother, but only because William had remained for so long in the same position.

Mr Callow gets more solid and rich in colour, but still quite cold. 'The Keep, Castle Rising' (217) has quite a grand Macbeth thunder-cloud darkening its walls with a sense of doom. Verona (198) is strongly painted, but has an English atmosphere about it. The shadows are too black. [*Athenaeum*, 1 May 1858.]

In the summer of that year, the brother of Harriet Callow, Henry Thomas Smart (1813–1879), the organist and composer, gave the inaugural performance on a magnificent organ which he had designed for Leeds Town Hall. The Callows were present and afterwards visited Lincolnshire and Yorkshire. During this time Callow was invited to Aske Hall, where Lady Zetland gave him several commissions for water-colour drawings.

It was also in 1858 that Callow underwent an operation for the removal of a small cyst on his cheek. This was performed by Caesar Hawkins, one of the most celebrated surgeons of the day, but the incision was slow to heal and Callow was ordered that classic Victorian prescription, a change of air. While he was still recuperating at Folkestone, he received a letter from Lady Anthony de Rothschild, requesting that he would give her some drawing lessons at her home in Aston Clinton (*landscape illustration no. 72*). William Callow was always enthusiastic at the prospect of a new pupil and hastened home, although he still had a bandaged face, which caused Lady Rothschild to remark that he could be taken for a Crimean hero. The Callow charm had obviously turned a potential disadvantage into a positive asset. Shortly after this, he was asked to give some lessons to the Baroness Meyer de Rothschild at Mentmore Towers, which he did for some time. Again, William Callow was accepted on a level that was very much more than that of an ordinary drawing master. Callow recalled:

> In the spring of the next year, my wife and I accompanied by two nieces, daughters of Henry Smart, went to a ball at Mentmore, where I met my old pupil, the Princess Clémentine. It was a most gorgeous affair, everything being carried out in royal style, and our party did not get home until 4.30 a.m. to the accompaniment of the singing of the birds.

William Callow always delighted in the elegant social occasion. It was said that no hostess in Great Missenden settled the date of a dinner party, until she had made sure that Callow was able to be present, such was his reputation as a raconteur and wit. This must have tended towards somewhat repetitive dinner parties, but one does detect a genuine humour in Callow, which adds just that touch of salt to his character, without which he could seem a little too bland. For instance, while describing the paucity of musical accompaniment for the services at the church of St Peter and St Paul, Great Missenden (a violin and a clarionet, with no choir), Callow related: '... the tuning of the latter was a wonderful performance. One hymn was a particular favourite – "Travelling through the wilderness". This was repeated so frequently that we often wondered if the wilderness would ever be got through....' Callow was a regular churchman at a time when many artists were assuming the pose of Free-Thinkers. Great Missenden Church had become very dilapidated and had no vestry. It was an obvious charitable focus for Harriet, who launched the inevitable appeal to the accompaniment of bazaars. On the instigation of Callow, plans for an extension were drawn up by Augustus Frere (an architect well known in Buckinghamshire), but these met with strong initial disapproval from the Bishop of Oxford. However, William Callow, son of the building trade, knew what he was about and remained obdurate. The fact that the plans were eventually passed without alteration does suggest that the Callows were probably making a substantial financial donation towards the project. William and Harriet also attended Lee Old Church (*illustration no. 73*) near Missenden. Other drawings in the Aylesbury album show an interior, inscribed 'Our Seat, Lee Old Church', July 28/1864. These drawings also include sketches of a horse called 'Old Grey' and a dog called 'Quixote', obviously family pets.

After the Callows had been in Great Missenden for about five years, it was decided to demolish their cottage and erect a new house on the site. Water-colour sketches in the Buckinghamshire County Museum suggest that the county lost a very charming period building, which could have been saved by the necessary repairs and renovations. In the meantime, they rented another cottage with stables and an orchard for £16 a year. Drawings there by Harriet Callow are also contained in the album in Aylesbury, including 'Missenden Mill, from Douglas's Cottage' – August 7.60, 'Missenden, Abbey Park from Douglas's Cottage' – Oct. 25.60.

The new house, designed by Augustus Frere, was completed in 1861. This was named 'The Firs' owing to the large number of such trees which surrounded it (*illustration no. 106*). William Callow and his wife were now established as local benefactors and 'The Firs' assumed a central position in the life of Great Missenden. Callow subsequently purchased several cottages in the vicinity of the house.

> These I had enlarged and improved in many ways, in order to encourage morality and cleanliness amongst the labourers and to brighten up their homes. We also commenced holding small flower and vegetable shows in our grounds to induce the cottagers to take an interest in their gardens. These shows increased in size and importance every year, until the occasion became quite a gala day. All our neighbours attended and a distribution of prizes terminated the proceedings.

On 27 April 1860, Queen Victoria wrote in her journal: 'After breakfast we went to the Old Water Colour Exhibition with the four eldest children, etc. Some fine landscapes by Brandwith, Newton, Fripp, B. Foster and Callow, four very fine ones by Carl Haag.'[1] The memoirs of Callow mention that he was specially sought out for notice during this royal visit. In that year, Callow was also well noticed by the critic of *The Times*: 'It is a long time since we have seen any work by William Callow so finely conceived as his "Castle of Wartburg" (No. 159), as picturesque as his "Old Houses at Brunswick" (No. 72) or as placid and serene as his "Evening on the Avon at Evesham" (No. 257).' However, it was 'Venice from the Rialto – Morning' (No. 91) that was chosen by an Art Union member with a prize to the value of £60. A study of some of the other selections places the work of Callow in the context of what was currently popular with Art Union members. The two most favoured exhibitions from which to make a choice were the Royal Academy and the Society of British Artists. 'An English Pastoral' (£200) by H. B. Willis, 'Morning on the River Dee' (£100) by H. J. Boddington (member of the highly successful Williams family of painters) and 'The First Step in Life' (£75) by Mrs E. M. Ward were amongst those chosen from the Royal Academy, as were three of the £60 prizes. In the five selections from this category, only Callow's 'Venice from the Rialto' was not in oils. The *Athenaeum* was of the opinion that the work was 'much too hot in colour: the shadows are quite lurid', but there can be little doubt that an Art Union member who obtained one of the higher prizes was inclined to choose a picture of large size and strong manner, equating this with value for the sum allowed.

In general, water-colour was the least-favoured medium for these prizes, but the style of William Callow had an air of authority, which not only held its own with

[1] Extract from the diary of Queen Victoria, 27 April 1860, published by gracious permission of Her Majesty the Queen. This entry could also have made further mention of Callow, but, after the death of Queen Victoria, her youngest daughter copied out these journals, deleting some material and destroying the originals.

oils, but was also able to compete, for at least the next decade, with an increasing diversity of innovation within his own water-colour field.

Since the exhibition of 'Haareem' the trend had been very much towards the opaque; some artists were even using body-colour over pure water-colour and water-colour over body-colour, with decidedly mildewed effects. Popular taste was now also very much in favour of works of 'genre' (narrative pieces, scenes of domestic incident). This is not a category in which one places the work of William Callow. Myles Birket Foster (1825–1899), whom the Queen mentions in her journal entry, was elected a full member of the Society in 1862. His finely detailed compositions, lively with pinafored children in a flowery countryside, were to achieve immense popularity. By 1864, the strikingly individual paintings of Edward Burne-Jones (1833–1898) were appearing on the walls of the 'Old' Water-colour Society. Some critics derided these romantic expositions of literary medievalism, with their flat technique, so closely resembling oils, and their 'greenery-yallery' colouring, but the general public was soon to recognise the knights in armour and ripple-haired maidens of Burne-Jones in designs for tapestry wall hangings, painted furniture and stained glass. Many of these were produced for the firm of William Morris (founded in 1861) which was to herald an entirely new era in Western art and domestic taste. The Victorian water-colourist was inevitably affected by the repercussions of such changes.

In April 1860, Holman Hunt's 'The Finding of the Saviour in the Temple' created a sensation when exhibited at the German Gallery in Bond Street: 800 to 1,000 people each day paid 1/– admission to see the picture. An unusual sidelight on this work by the most famous of the Pre-Raphaelites is provided by Callow, who recalled that the model for the figure of the young Christ had been Cyril Flower, who later married a daughter of Lady Anthony de Rothschild, who had been one of Callow's pupils.

In the autumn of 1860, William and Harriet made a journey from Coblenz up the Moselle, as William had done alone in 1844. Callow was horrified to find that Trarbach was an entirely new place, with bright green doors and brass knockers, to which he seemed to take a particular exception. Old Trarbach had disappeared, having been destroyed by fire. In consequence, Callow regarded his 1844 sketches as specially valuable to him.

In 1861, 'Martigny' was taken as one of the smaller Art Union prizes (£20) and in 1863 'At Antwerp' (£15) was selected. Callow was maintaining a successful level of sales, but there was a general decline in the amount of notice that he received from the critics. 'Mr William Callow in "The Ruins of the Palace of the Dukes of Burgundy, Malines" (167) paints a picturesque building, with the telling contrast of colouring to which he is addicted' (*Art Journal*, p. 118, 1863).

Blackwood's Magazine, Vol. 92, July 1862 (p. 70), quoted *Le Moniteur* of 1855, which had commented on the unrivalled position of the English water-colourist in this branch of art:

> They have indeed, in this style, attained a vigour, a brilliancy and an effect quite incredible . . . they possess indeed colours of a manufacture irreproachable,

> forming a gamut the most extended: papers also they have smooth as ice, and granulated as a wall, according to the effect desired; papers which permit an execution the most varied, from the thinness of a transparent wash to the thick embroidery of pack thread!

William Callow was almost totally unaffected by such technical advances, but did consider that colours had been more pure in the early days of his career, when the painter had to 'rub' them before use, i.e. cakes of hard paint were crumbled against an abrasive surface, such as a ceramic tile, into a small quantity of water. This method became obsolete after the introduction of 'moist' (added glycerine) colours in pans. Callow also felt that Whatman paper underwent some slight alteration of texture, which was not an improvement. The innovations of artists' colourmen could be a disadvantage.

In 1864, George Rowney and Co. published a catalogue of *Chromo-lithographs or fac-similie water-colour drawings*, from which this quotation comes:

> Chromolithography has recently become one of the most popular arts in this country, from its having been adopted as a means of multiplying copies of Oil Paintings and Water-Colour Drawings: and so admirably is it adapted for this purpose, that not only is each colour and graduation of light and shade rendered with remarkable accuracy, but even the very texture of the paint and the rough surface of the paper is copied with strict fidelity.

Messrs Rowney were not exaggerating the excellence of their wares. Many artists of a less strong manner than Callow were now adversely affected by the quality and availability of such reproductions. This particular catalogue advertised 'fac-similie water-colour drawings' from the work of most of the leading water-colour artists of the day, including William Callow, who was represented by 'Venice' (19¾ × 14 in. – 501 × 355 mm), priced one guinea; 'Como' and 'Jüdenstrasse, Frankfort' (8 × 14 in. – 203 × 279 mm), both priced seven shillings and sixpence. Copley Fielding, Charles Bentley and J. D. Harding were also included in this last series, which was not the lowest price range. Chromolithographs were also advertised at 5/–, 2/6 and 1/–.

Callow met the challenge of these 'fac-similie water-colour drawings' with an increasingly deliberate finish and strength of colour, which renders some later examples almost indistinguishable from chromolithographs. The writer has known such a reproduction (framed) to be bought in the genuine belief that it was an original water-colour drawing.

William Callow had a very sound commercial sense, with regard to royal patronage. After the death of the Prince Consort, he wrote to Princess Clémentine, in her position as Duchess Augustus of Saxe-Coburg, asking if she could obtain permission for him to make some drawings of Coburg and various other palaces which had formed part of the family background of Prince Albert. While Callow was working on this project, Princess Clémentine took some of his sketches to show to Queen Victoria who was staying at Rosenau, near Coburg (*illustration no. 79*). Prince Albert had been born at Rosenau, a summer residence of his father, Ernest, Duke of Saxe-Coburg-Gotha. This drawing was included in a portfolio, marked with Callow's name in gilt letters and inscribed on an inside cover: '20 sketches of Coburg, Rosenau, Reinhardsbrunn, Callenberg, Gotha, etc. Wm Callow.' (Christie's, 12 October 1976.)

On 24 August 1863, Queen Victoria wrote in her journal: '. . . a fine warm morning, walked a little with Augusta B[ruce] and then sat writing and looked at some lovely sketches of the neighbourhood by Mr Callow who had brought them himself.' She had specially asked to see Callow and received him in the garden, seated under an open tent. As he was being presented, the Queen remarked with a gracious twinkle, 'But I remember Mr Callow perfectly.'[1a] It was obviously a very successful interview. Queen Victoria not only admired the sketches, but also suggested some other locations that he should visit, writing the unfamiliar German place names down for him on pieces of black-edged writing paper, which Callow was to treasure for the rest of his life.

The eldest daughter of Queen Victoria, Princess Victoria, was now the Crown Princess of Prussia. Shortly after the audience at Rosenau, Callow was requested to take a portfolio of sketches to the Coburg Palace, where the Crown Prince and Princess were staying. Callow seems to have received a particularly friendly reception, in which we can see an influence from Princess Clémentine, who would certainly have given the Crown Princess a very favourable report of her former drawing master. She now asked if he would give her some lessons in water-colour painting at the Neue Palais, Potsdam, an idea that was warmly supported by the Crown Prince, who is said to have remarked: 'Do come, Mr Callow, and the Princess will show you all that there is to be seen.' Princess Victoria, a very intelligent and cultured woman, is known to have been often homesick and irritated by the aimless pursuits of the German court. No doubt the Crown Prince felt that the presence of this charming English artist would please his wife, who had a real talent for drawing and painting.

After leaving Coburg, Callow visited Reinhardsbrunn (*illustration no. 80*) and Gotha, making numerous sketches at both places. He must have reached Potsdam on 2 September 1863 and was asked to be at the Neue Palais (a summer residence of the Crown Princess and Prince) at 8 a.m. the following morning.

> This necessitated an early rising, as the Palace was half an hour's drive from the hotel. On my reaching the Palace I was told by a footman that I was one minute late and on being conducted into the presence of the Princess, I found her waiting for me and I apologised for the delay. We then proceeded to look for a subject to sketch and found a suitable one just outside the grounds.

'Neue Palais' (*illustration no. 81*) would be executed at some time during that day.

> We had not been working long before a lady-in-waiting came and informed the Princess that breakfast was ready. They left me busy sketching and returned to the palace. Presently a manservant brought my breakfast, consisting of cutlets, claret, coffee, etc. on a tray.'

The servant told Callow that the Princess wished him to dine with her at 3 o'clock

[1a] Extract from the diary of Queen Victoria published by gracious permission of Her Majesty the Queen.

and added, rather pointedly, that he would be required to wear evening dress. Callow explained that there would be no time to fetch such items from his hotel; one receives a definite impression that this servant was being as rude as the footman. After Breakfast, Callow set off with the Princess and two of her ladies-in-waiting to visit Sans Souci (*see illustration no. 89* with reference to a later visit). The party sketched and climbed to the top of the Belvedere to view the surrounding countryside (*see* reference to sketch in the Henry E. Huntington Collection, page 200). 'On arriving back at the Palace I was shown to a room upstairs and told that I had three minutes to get ready for dinner.' The Palace servants were obviously being insolent, but Callow never states that he was aware of it. After dinner, they drove to the Ile des Faisans, which had to be reached by punt across a narrow river.

> After the ladies had got into the punt, I followed, laden with sketch books etc, and one of the ladies punted to the island. On reaching it, they landed and the last one hastily pushed the punt back into the river and they all walked away, laughing merrily, leaving me standing up in the punt, arms full of impedimenta. There was nothing for it, but to put down my burden and punt to the bank. Eventually I landed and caught up with the Princess and her ladies.

This must surely be one of the most delightful of all Callow anecdotes, although only a genuinely unpretentious man would have included it in his memoirs. Callow was driven back to his hotel, accompanied by one of these prankish ladies-in-waiting, who presented Harriet with some flowers from the Princess and an invitation to go to the Palace on the next day. This invitation seems to have marked a subtle change in the manner of the Princess to Callow. This had always been pleasant, but she now seems to have begun to treat him as a friend. Next morning she was waiting for them in the Marble Hall and had arranged for her three children to be brought down, in charge of their English nurse, for them to see. Prince William (the future Kaiser) was then four years old. As it was a wet morning, the Princess suggested that they should work inside the Palace. Callow made a small interior sketch of a view looking through a suite of rooms and the Princess completed this by adding a figure (posed by a lady-in-waiting). One would have expected the Princess to have kept this drawing, but, in fact, it was retained by Callow (*see* Leicester Galleries – 1907, page 240) and is still in possession of the Callow family.

> During these visits the Crown Prince was most genial and friendly. He showed me his private rooms, which were furnished with the greatest simplicity. Beside the writing table in his study was a seat in the form of a saddle, so that he sat to write as if he were on horseback. There were a large number of photographs of the Princess in his rooms and the Prince pointed out the one that he considered most pleasing.

The Callows left Potsdam on the day after their last visit to the Palace. On her return to Berlin, the Princess asked Callow to visit her at the Kronprinzenpalais, where she presented him with a breakfast service of Royal Berlin procelain, in blue and gold, decorated with views of the various royal palaces. Callow was also commanded to the Royal Palace in Berlin, where he was received in audience by the Emperor, who treated him very kindly, speaking in French. Callow received a commission to paint two large water-colour drawings from his sketches of the Babelsberg and Potsdam Palaces.

Before returning to England, the Callows spent a few days on the Baltic coast, at Stettin, where an old friend was British Consul.

> On our way home we stopped again for a short time in Berlin, where after a great deal of trouble, we succeded in finding Mendelssohn's grave in the Dreifaltigen Kirchhof. We placed a wreath on it and brought away a sprig from the ivy that was growing there. This sprig we brought home with us and planted in front of the house, where it grew rapidly. Hundreds of slips have at times been given to friends and admirers of the great musician, including Mendelssohn's own daughter.

Callow does not actually say that she visited them at The Firs, but this seems highly likely in view of the fact that Harriet's uncle, Sir George Smart, had been a friend of Mendelssohn and was responsible for the introduction of several of the composer's most important works to England, e.g. the Oratorio 'St Paul' at the Liverpool Music Festival in 1836.

Shortly after his return to England, Callow sent a drawing of Lancaster (from a sketch that she had admired in Germany) to the Crown Princess, who had arrived on a visit to Sandringham. Towards the end of 1863, he was summoned to Windsor Castle, where the Queen studied a full portfolio of the German sketches. It is not certain whether Callow actually had an audience with the Queen, but she is recorded as being very interested in the sketches, from which she commissioned several water-colour drawings, including one of Rosenau, a side view, in which the castellated tower is the main feature. A larger version of that view of Rosenau was contained in the portfolio of drawings, auctioned in 1976. A smaller version of the illustrated Rosenau is included in the collection of the Victoria and Albert museum. The composition lacks the sapling in the foreground on the lawn. The five water-colours in the Victoria and Albert Museum (661 a–e) were probably those exhibited by Callow with the Society of Painters in Water-colours in 1864 as 'Souvenirs of Rosenau'.

'Leaning Tower, Bologna' signed and dated 1864 (*illustration no. 84*) shows a remarkable similarity to a version of this subject by Bonington (Wallace Collection – fig. XVI, p. 40, *Thomas Shotter Boys* by James Roundell). Callow had adopted a view slightly more to the right, showing the smaller tower at less of an angle, but otherwise the composition and general treatment have a marked influence from the Bonington work. It is not known whether Callow had seen this, but it would appear extremely likely that he was familiar with the etching on this subject by Bonington, who left the plate unfinished. This was completed by T. S. Boys for publication by Colnaghi and Co., in October 1828. A proof (now in the British Museum) from this plate was originally in the private collection of Baron de Triqueti, who had acquired it from Boys.

In spite of the similarities of these two water-colour compositions, Bonington is more concerned with expressing the romantic atmosphere of the scene, rather than providing an exact description. Comparison with a photograph of the subject shows that the Garisenda Tower (left) in the Bonington not only leans, but is out of true to a point beyond which the laws of gravity would have caused it to fall down. Callow gives the more accurate study. The sharper lines of Callow, always the more elaborate artist, express the minutiae of the scene – roof tiles, gutters and the exact spaces between windows, with a more deliberately balanced arrangement of the foreground figures than in the Bonington.

In 1865, George Fripp resigned the position of Secretary of the Society of Painters in Water-colours and William Callow was unanimously elected in his place. Reviewing the Annual Exhibition of the Society, the *Art Journal* remained kind, but slightly weary: 'The production of the brothers W. Callow and J. Callow, the one among the quaint old towns, the other on the waters of our sea-girt coast, are in the manner usual to these artists.' Again, note the equal status accorded to John, whose name actually appears first in 1866: 'John and William Callow are in their several departments of sea and land a little inky in the shadows, yet the brother, Mr. William, in a fortunate moment at 'Bellaggio' attains an unwonted brilliancy which recalls the romantic glow of Richardson.' Mr William was probably none too pleased at having attracted a second glance, only in respect of a work that suggested the style of another artist.

In the autumn of 1865, the Callows were again in Venice, but this time accompanied by their friend and neighbour Sidney Richard Percy (1821–1886), the landscape painter, who lived at Hill House, Great Missenden, from 1863 to 1872. He was the fifth son of Edward Williams ('The Moonlight Painter' 1782–1855), whose six sons had all become successful landscape painters, three of them changing their name to avoid confusion, including Henry John Boddington, Arthur Gilbert and S. R. Percy. The latter was a man of gentle disposition and quiet humour, whose personality obviously appealed to William Callow. His wife, Emily, had been the daughter of a Barnes jeweller, to whom she had stipulated that she would not consider any suitor with less than £2,000 per annum – Percy was easily able to exceed this qualification. Hill House was a rather grander establishment than The Firs, in keeping with the extravagant tastes of Emily Percy. However, she did take some interest in sketching and painting, and must have been congenial to Harriet, because the friendship between the Callows and the Percys was a lasting one. It is certain that Callow must have met some of the other Williams brothers. Arthur Gilbert and Alfred Walter Williams were frequent visitors to Hill House.[2]

At the time of the 1865 trip to Venice, S. R. Percy was 44 years old and one of the most popular landscape painters of his day, but, rather surprisingly, this was his first journey abroad. William Callow was 53, with a less advantaged start to his life and career, but he was now a much travelled man, whose experience of landscape was much more diverse than that of S. R. Percy, whose work was never that of the topographer. However, the two men, as well as a mutual liking, also had something in common as artists. The style of S. R. Percy displayed an excellent sense of balance, a deft and fluent manipulation of line and a tendency to strong colouring.

[2] *The Williams Family of Painters*, Jan Reynolds (1975).

His powerful oil paintings of Wales and Scotland have a counterpart in, for instance, the large Venetian water-colours of Callow – and both attracted attention on the same level of popular taste.

In 1865, there was an exceptionally severe outbreak of cholera in Italy and the Callow party had to undergo no less than four 'fumigations' before reaching Venice. There Callow found his old gondolier, Jacomo, still alive and delighted to see him. He had employed the same man, on each occasion, since his first visit to Venice in 1840. The return journey was made through Switzerland and also included a few days in Paris, where Callow was able to show Sidney Richard Percy his old haunts. The latter exhibited 'Angera, Lago Maggiore' (British Institution) and various other foreign subjects in 1866, which all relate to the journey with William Callow, but his paintings were soon to revert to the more characteristic scenery of the British Isles. No further travel abroad was to be possible for some years, owing to the outbreak of the Franco/Prussian War in 1866. Consequently, there was an intensive exploration of Scotland and Wales by many landscape painters. Callow also found new subjects at home, but was even more inclined to draw on the wealth of foreign sketches accumulated from previous years. It will be noticed that the illustrations in this book are arranged in chronological date order, but often show a sequence of totally diverse and unrelated subjects, unlike the œuvre of some artists, who might be expected to demonstrate a 'Venetian period' or a preoccupation with their recent experiences. To have placed the work of Callow in sections by subject (e.g. France, etc.) would have been to negate his method of working. Callow would browse through literally hundreds of sketches, often for a considerable time, as if waiting for inspiration, before making the final selection of a subject which he felt ready to work up into finished water-colour. It was of no matter to him how long ago the sketch had been executed or how many years it was since he had orginally studied a scene. Although he annotated some sketches, his memory for colour was exceptional and mere pencilled information was sufficient to recall this accurately to mind. Once the subject was decided, Callow was anything but a browser, but knew exactly how he proposed to handle the work – there was no fumbling for the right effect in his technique. He invariably completed one water-colour at a time (i.e. not working on different subjects, between the drying of washes). This method must have aided his clean and concentrated results. As the *Athenaeum* remarked: ' "Lyme Regis" (No. 4) is a capital specimen of Mr W. Callow's sparkling manner. "Venice looking up the Grand Canal" (41) is delightful: see the tender rosy light on the Palace of the Doge, the harmonious tints throughout. Other Venetian drawings by this painter justify his reputation' (19 May 1866). This reputation made Callow sufficiently well known for a complete stranger to call at The Firs, express great admiration of his work and ask to see some drawings, from which he selected one for £60, paid for it on the spot and departed with it under his arm.

In 1869, the election of William Holman Hunt (1827–1910) as a member of the 'Old' Water-colour Society was nodded through, without the usual voting formalities. The Pre-Raphaelites had established a strong following within the Society, although this was to receive something of a blow from the traditionalists in 1870. In that year a water-colour by Edward Burne-Jones, entitled 'Phyllis and Demophoön' was withdrawn from the walls of the Society, after having been on display for two weeks. This picture had caused a great furore, chiefly owing to the nudity of Demophoön, which scandalised certain visitors to the exhibition, who were rumoured to include a lady of very high position. One can well imagine the reaction of William Callow. What if the Queen were to honour the Society with a royal visit? It would never do. Influential members, with Callow obviously well to the fore, were determined to have the offending piece removed, although there would be a strongly opposing faction which had supported the original selection of the work. Callow must have derived a particular satisfaction from seeing Phyllis and the flagrant Demophoön replaced by one of his cosy Continental pieces, tradition encapsulated, guaranteed not to offend, a view of Frankfurt from Mr Callow, always such a favourite with the dear Queen. Burne-Jones resigned from the Society of Painters in Water-colours in July 1870, after this spat with the traditionalists, but, later in that year, William Callow also resigned as Secretary, on the same evening that Frederick Taylor resigned as President. Internal strife there undoubtedly was and Callow appears to have been making a point of principle.

From about 1870, the Callows again made frequent tours broad. In 1871, they were in Germany, visiting Bonn, in order to attend the Beethoven Festival, afterwards staying in Ems. From there, Callow made numerous sketching expeditions to Limburg, Runkel, Weilburg, Giessen, Marburg and other towns in the valley of the Lahn. Three years later, the Callows were on an extended tour of Germany, starting from Cologne. At Heidelberg, Callow made a sketch of a particularly vivid sunset from the castle terrace. From there, they visited Würzburg, Ratisbon and Passau. The latter town was decorated with flags in commemoration of the victory of Sedan. A steamer took them down the Danube to Linz, after which they visited Salzburg, arriving on a 'Mariafest' day, when the town was full of people in national costume. On arriving at Berlin (via Prague and Dresden), Callow received a telegram from the Crown Princess of Prussia, requesting him to call at the Neue Palais, Potsdam, on the following afternoon.

On 25 September 1874, the Crown Princess wrote to her sister, Princess Louise, Marchioness of Lorne: 'The artist, Mr. W. Callow has been here for a few days and I went out sketching with him.'[3] 'Sans Souci' (*illustration no. 89*), inscribed 'sketched with the Princess of Prussia, Sept 23 1874', was one of the German royal residences outside Potsdam.

The Crown Prince and Count Seckendorf had also been on this expedition, after which Callow dined at the Neue Palais. The Crown Princess showed him some of her paintings and sketches in oils, which Callow genuinely considered were excellent. In the following year, Christmas 1875, the Crown Princess of Prussia sent Callow the first part of a series of chromolithographs of Potsdam with views of Sans Souci and the Neue Palais (*Architektonisch-Landschaftliche Darstellungen von Sans Souci und Umgebung* – an 8-part series, after the water-colours of Carl Graeb). Callow was charmed with the gift, although he thought the colours rather too strong. The Princess later sent him the second volume of this work.

[3] Extract from a letter written by the Crown Princess of Prussia, 25 September 1874, published by gracious permission of Her Majesty the Queen.

'The Grand Canal, Venice, looking towards Santa Salute' and 'Menaggio on the Lake of Como' were exhibited between 10 May and 10 November in the British Section of the Philadelphia International Exhibition in 1876. Callow was awarded a citation and a bronze medal for each work.

Also in 1876, William Callow and his wife were again in Italy, travelling to Rome, by way of Turin, Genoa and Pisa. In Rome he met Penry Williams and Arthur Glennie, expatriate English painters who had been resident in that city for many years. Penry Williams (1798–1885) was living at 64 Newman Street during the years that Callow was with the Fieldings. This tour included visits to Naples and Pompeii.

> Our tour in the following year, 1877, was once more to lovely Venice, where I never grew tired of sketching its glorious buildings and where we were welcomed by our old gondolier, Jacomo. He did not recognise us at first, but suddenly exclaimed to my wife: 'Ah! you are the lady who gave me this, pointing at the same time to the bright scarf that he was wearing. It had been a parting gift to him on our last visit in 1865. He was a most devoted servant and used to attend to my wife with the greatest care during my absence while sketching. At Jacomo's earnest request we paid a visit to his cottage, where we found his handsome wife and her sister engaged in bead work.

'Bathing Machines, Swanage', inscribed 'Nov 5th 1875 (*illustration no. 92*), demonstrates a quality of personal statement, an almost amused observation of the details of these quaint contraptions, a subject which gives such an authentic glimpse of the period. Drawings such as these, lightly washed with colour, came from Callow until almost the end of his life. Their spontaneity and lack of pretension, allied to an underlying masterly technique, have produced works of real interest and value to the collector.

In the autumn of 1877, William and Harriet were in Devon, visiting Dartmouth, Salcombe (*illustration no. 93*) and Kingsbridge, with Callow still sketching indefatigably at each place. The illustrated water-colour sketch is a beautiful example of the naturally fluent manner of William Callow, at the age of 65, when working for his own pleasure. These same qualities are also evident in the sure and peaceful lines of a cornfield, near Missenden (*illustration no. 94*), which Callow had sketched only a few weeks previously. There is a subjective quality about these water-colour drawings, so often absent from the more finished exhibition pieces. 'Hampden', inscribed on the cornfield sketch, is linked with Hampden House, seat of the Duke of Buckinghamshire, near Great Missenden. In August 1875, the Callows had been invited to stay there by some friends, who had rented the property. They occupied the inevitable Queen Elizabeth's Bedroom, which had a view looking towards Missenden. The house party included Count Seckendorf, whom Callow had met at Potsdam in 1874. The Aylesbury album includes sketches executed by both William and Harriet during the Hampden House visit.

The ill-health of Harriet Callow was a constant consideration in their marriage and yet she appears to have shown a remarkable stamina for travel. In 1879, the Callows were in Italy, visiting the Rome area. A small sketch of Narni, dated April

23/79 and rather charmingly inscribed 'nightingales' (Callow collection), shows this to have been a spring visit. It will have been noted that it was much more usual for Callow to go abroad in the autumn, a factor which may have induced a colour imprint on the mind of Callow for the strong, yet mellow tones that he so constantly employed for Continental scenes. In the following year, William and Harriet were in Venice, where the old gondolier was still there to greet them. It was in 1880 that Callow first saw steamboats on the Grand Canal to the equal disgust of artist and gondoliers. It was also in this year that he was selected a Fellow of the Royal Geographical Society, a recognition which always gave him much pleasure. A water-colour by Callow, with the title 'A Distant View of Nice, from Antibes', was sold by the Royal Geographical Society at Christie's, 8 June 1976.

In 1882, William Callow reluctantly gave up teaching, at the age of 70, after over half a century of instructing in drawing and water-colour painting. An occupation that would have been a tiresome financial necessity for many artists was always a source of pleasure to Callow – but the days of the traditional private drawing master were now over. Callow had started his class in the Rue de Bouloi atelier in 1834, which was half a decade before Louis Daguerre demonstrated the first successful photographic process to the French Academy. The years that followed had been ones of unprecedented social change, including the discovery of antiseptics and chloroform, the development of a vast railway system and the foundation of the firm of William Morris (born in 1834). In the year of Callow's retirement from teaching, Morris published *Hopes and Fears for Art*, a plea for simplicity in art and life, a direct challenge to the patrons of the artificially picturesque. Photography flourished. Even modest households now had a family album and the superb work of the Victorian landscape photographer had permeated into the realms of art and publishing. Also in 1882, the French Impressionists held their penultimate exhibition, having exerted a far-reaching influence on style during the preceding decade. The passive woman, hampered in crinoline and layers of petticoats, hardly capable of any more strenuous leisure occupation than embroidery, croquet or a gentle dabble in water-colours, was now being replaced by spirited females, soon to be bicycling in bloomers, playing tennis and taking up energetic socialist causes, often as a result of the ideals propagated by William Morris and his followers. In such a changing world, the works of William Callow were gradually to decline in popular appeal and became associated with a past era, old-fashioned as button-back chairs and Berlin woolwork embroidery.

However, in spite of this trend, one important factor operated as a counterbalance. The nineteenth-century water-colour never underwent the almost total oblivion (or downright ridicule) that was to be suffered by the majority of oil paintings of the period. For instance, from about 1910, S. R. Percy's massively gilt-framed Highland Landscapes with Cattle were being consigned to the attic, having become too overpowering and ornate for a style of interior decoration in which the vogue was for all things new. The very title of such works was to become synonymous with a school of painting which most people erroneously considered would never again revive in popularity. During the first 30 years of this century oil paintings often mouldered in junk shops or even disappeared for ever in the flames of a bonfire.

There was not the same overt dislike or neglect of the Victorian water-colour, a much less dominant, less challenging form of art, more able to co-exist with other styles – easy to store in portfolios. Artists, such as William Callow, who had never been seduced into a modish and immoderate use of body-colour were always to retain a quiet following, with those who admired a pure technique and the traditional style. There has never been any period when the work of William Callow was not to some degree saleable.

Recent trends on the fine art market have shown that the Victorian water-colour is likely to be one of the most rapidly increasing values in the current revival of interest in the period. Water-colours by William Callow have tended to anticipate this movement, ahead of the work of many of his contemporaries. It is not proposed to discuss in this book any more than a few representative auction prices, because such details soon become out-of-date and cannot adequately demonstrate the many factors that contribute to the making of a price. The figures quoted are intended to provide only a very general guide line.

A study of recent auction prices proves that works from the entire span of the career of William Callow are capable of holding up well on the art market. 'A Squall over Croydon' ($4\frac{1}{4} \times 6\frac{1}{4}$ in. – 107 × 158 mm), dated 1829, obtained £500 at Christie's on 20 June 1978. The work must have been executed during his visit to Theodore Fielding, just before Callow first went to France, when not quite 17 years old. This small water-colour showed an open landscape, with emphasis on a rather dramatic and stormy sky, an obvious influence from Copley Fielding. In the same auction, 'The Shakespeare Cliff from Dover Beach' (6 × 10 in. – 152 × 254 mm), water-colour on Whatman paper, an example from the middle period, fetched £550, while a much later work, executed when Callow was 65, during the 1877 visit to Salcombe, was sold for £950. This was 'A View of Salcombe Castle, from near East Portlemouth looking South towards Bolt Head', pencil and water-colour, inscribed and dated 'October 16/1877'.

On 5 June 1973, a fine topographical view of 'Rouen' (8 × 12 in. – 203 × 304 mm) fetched £2,100 at Christie's, where 'The Mouth of the Dart' (12 × 19 in. – 304 × 482 mm) was sold for £1,050, also at the same sale. 1973 had marked a sharp increase in auction prices for Callow, as compared with the previous year, varying from about £150 up to the quoted levels.

As in the lifetime of Callow, his Italian scenes are likely to fetch some of the highest prices. One of these was £2,500 for 'Castel dell'Ovo, Naples' (*illustration no. 29*) signed and dated 1841 (Christie's, 9 November 1976). Good examples from about this period are usually considered to be the most gilt-edged in market value for Callow. 'The Grand Canal, Venice' (10 × 14 in. – 254 × 355 mm) signed, inscribed and dated 'Aug 18/46', had made £2,200 at Christie's in the spring of 1976. 'The Palazzo Pisani-Moretta on the Grand Canal, Venice' (*illustration no. 44*) reached £1,800 at Christies in March 1977 – an excellent example, which would probably have made more had it been dated.

'Rosenau' (*illustration no. 79*) made £450 in 1976 (Christie's sale, as mentioned) with prices for other examples in the portfolio varying between £160 and £280. Most of the initialled signatures, although perfectly authentic, were badly rubbed, a factor which may have slightly affected prices. There are many such considerations, which cannot adequately be demonstrated from a mere list of prices. For instance, an unidentified Italianate view, signed, but not inscribed or dated, will not be expected to do as well as a work with exactly the same execution, but a better provenance. Water-colours having a known link with events in the life of Callow always have added value. Detriments to price may be 'foxing', fading or very soiled condition. Prices in galleries can be expected to be higher than those at auction (up to at least £5,000), but it must be realised that a dealer may have been at considerable trouble and expense to obtain a work and have subsequently further researched the provenance in order to provide a guarantee, and this can have many advantages.

Interest in the work of William Callow has recently induced many later works onto the market. 'Street in Verona, near the Piazza delle Erbe', a subject frequently repeated by Callow, dated 1886 ($15\frac{3}{4} \times 12\frac{1}{2}$ in. – 400×316 mm), was sold at Christie's on 16 March 1978 for £900. Decorative street scenes with a crowd of figures usually find a ready market, whatever the date. During 1978, 'The Belfry at Bruges', dated 1882, another popular theme, provided an interesting example of a late work, with a very sound market potential. This was one of Callow's large pieces ($25\frac{1}{2} \times 18\frac{1}{2}$ in. – 647×469 mm) which had been illustrated in the 1908 autobiography. The belfry stands in the middle distance, with a characteristic, oblique presentation of towering façades on either side of the composition, a bustle of peasantry and the inevitable white awning. This water-colour obtained £1,400 at Christie's on 11 November 1978. An even later example, 'Ehrenbreitstein', 1894, fetched £780 at Bonham's on 1 March 1978, followed by 'Leipzig', signed and dated 1902, which was sold for £820 on 5 July 1978, also at Bonham's.

The fact that Callow was such a prolific artist must reduce rarity value, but the wide scope of his subjects, the charm of many of the slighter pieces, allied to a consistent technique, afford the collector with an opportunity to make a discriminating and worthwhile choice, within a very varied price level. Some painters can have a sudden revival in fashion, but then fade. The work of William Callow has such a sound history of steady market value that his pictures must provide one of the most firmly guaranteed investments in Victorian water-colours.

CHAPTER VI

Great Missenden: the Final 25 Years, 1883–1908

IN May 1883, Harriet Callow became acutely ill while staying at 25 Cambridge Terrace, their London apartment in Kensington. She was attended by the Queen's Physician, Sir William Jenner, as well as Dr Churchill of Great Missenden, but in spite of these ministrations, Harriet Anne Callow died on 30 June 1883. The somewhat vague details on the death certificate are those of a symptom rather than a disease, but do tend to confirm the possibility of some kind of allergic condition. There was a short announcement in *The Times* on 4 July 1883 and in the *Bucks Herald*, 7 July, but no detailed local obituary has been traced.

Under the terms of her will (made in 1862) Harriet Callow left £2,104, fifteen shillings and tenpence. Apart from an undisclosed sum, related to her original marriage settlement, which went to Callow, the bulk of her property was in jewellery, Genoese silver ornaments, etc., all of which were bequeathed to various connections of the Smart family, with the exception of an 'antique' ring and an emerald ring, which she left to her husband, and her diamond ring, which went to her brother-in-law, John Callow.

Just over six months after the death of his first wife, William Callow married Mary Louisa Jefferay, on 8 January 1884, at St Nicholas Church, Plumstead, a district of Woolwich, near Greenwich. William Callow was then 71 years old, his bride only 27. At the time of the marriage she was recorded as being resident in Plumstead, although her father was a saddler and harness-maker in business in High Street, Wendover, about four and a half miles from Great Missenden. Jefferay was first entered in *Kelly's Directory* in 1864 (last entry 1899). The 1851 census shows that Mary Louisa's parents and grandparents were all born and bred in Wendover. The The Greenwich poll books record a William Callow (probably the uncle of Callow) as being a householder in Plumstead in 1837. William Callow would hardly have chosen to be married in Plumstead in 1884, unless he still had connections in the area. No doubt Mary Louisa established residential qualifications by staying with some Callow relations. George Jefferay was a witness at the marriage of his daughter, so would appear to have given his approval, but one has to draw a definite inference from the fact that the event took place away from Great Missenden. It seems possible that Mary Louisa had been in domestic service at The Firs, maybe as a cook or housekeeper. Details from the 1881 census returns will not be available until 1981, but could well confirm this. There can be little doubt that his second marriage must have been the subject of some comment and gossip, in view of the disparity

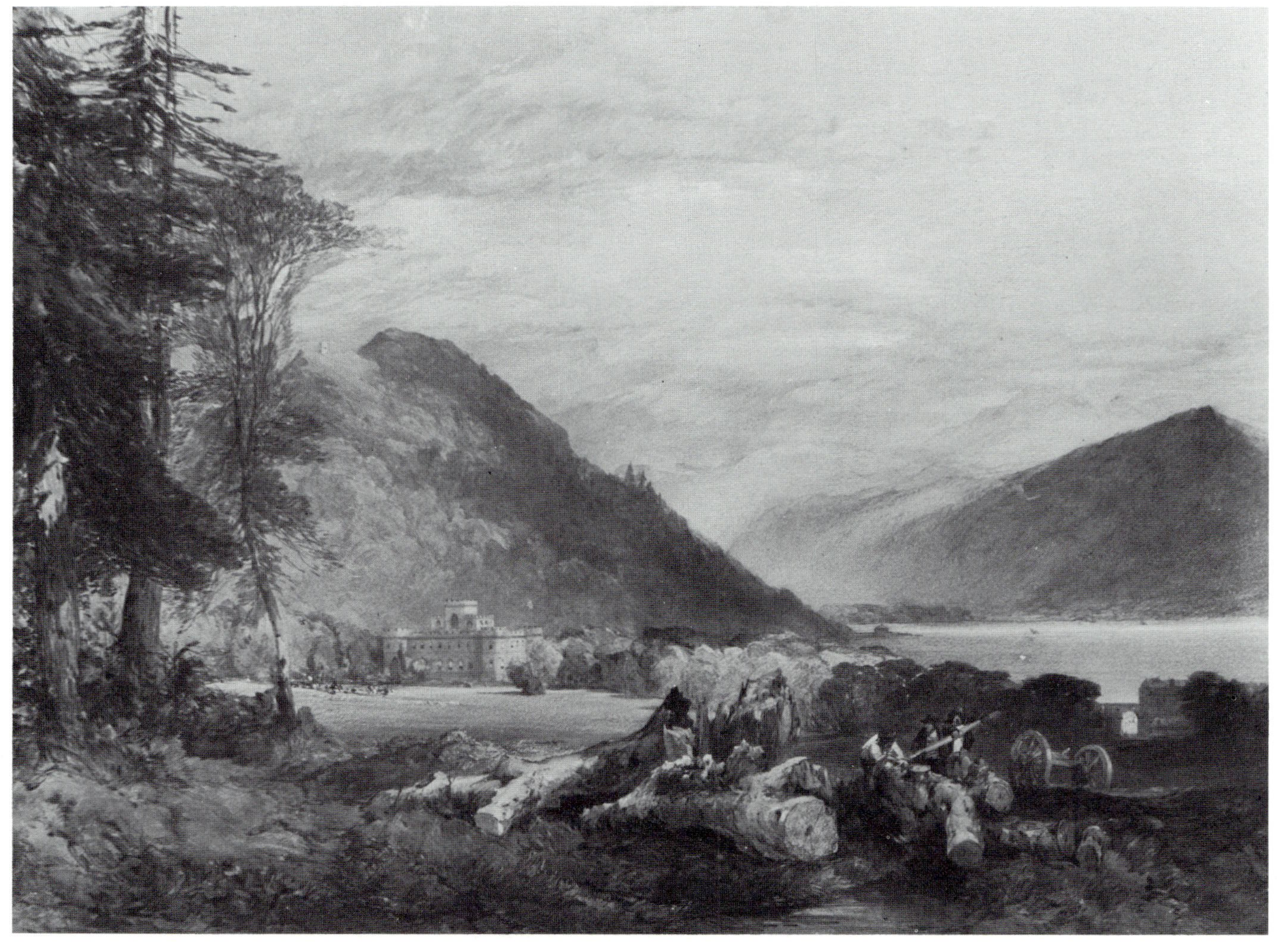

56. 'Inveraray Castle' Water-colour ($21\frac{1}{4} \times 29\frac{1}{4}$ in. – 540×743 mm)
Signed: William Callow (left)
Exhibited: No. 4 Society of Painters in Water-colours, 1850
Collection: St Helens Museum and Art Gallery (Guy and Margery Pilkington Bequest)

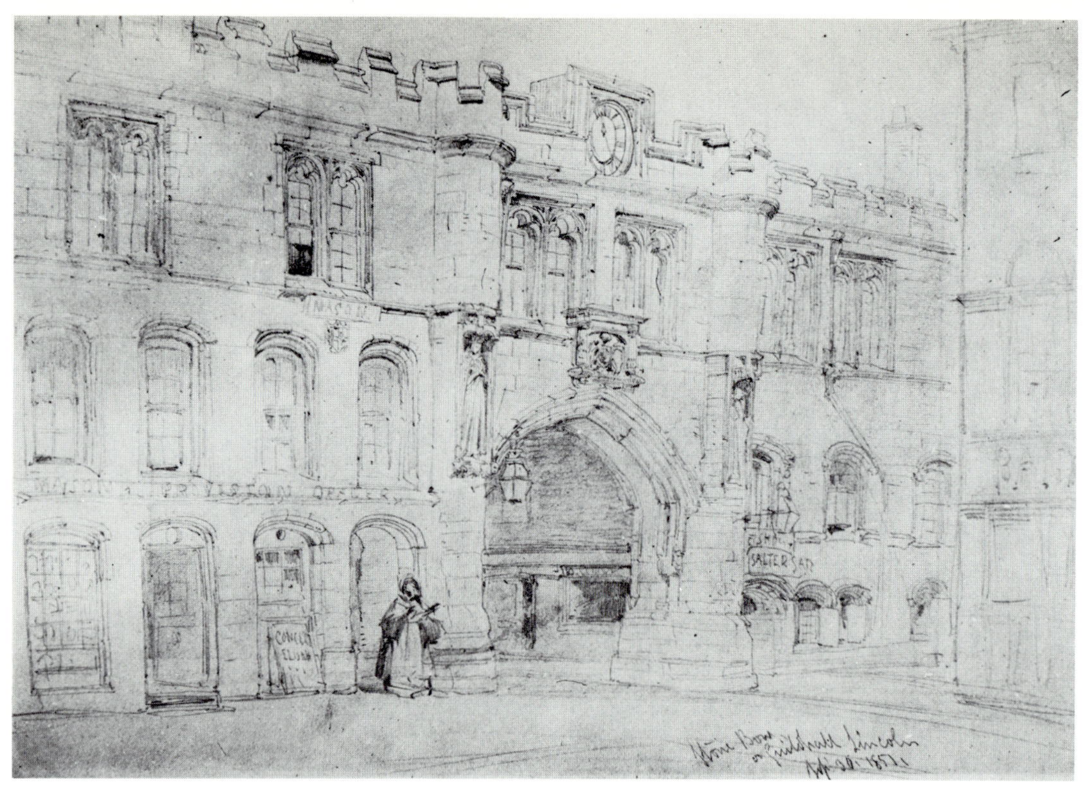

57. 'Stone Bow, Lincoln' Pencil drawing ($10 \times 14\frac{3}{8}$ in. – 255×365 mm)
Inscribed and dated: *Sept 30th 1851.* Original sketch for illustration no. 58
Collection: Usher Gallery, Lincoln

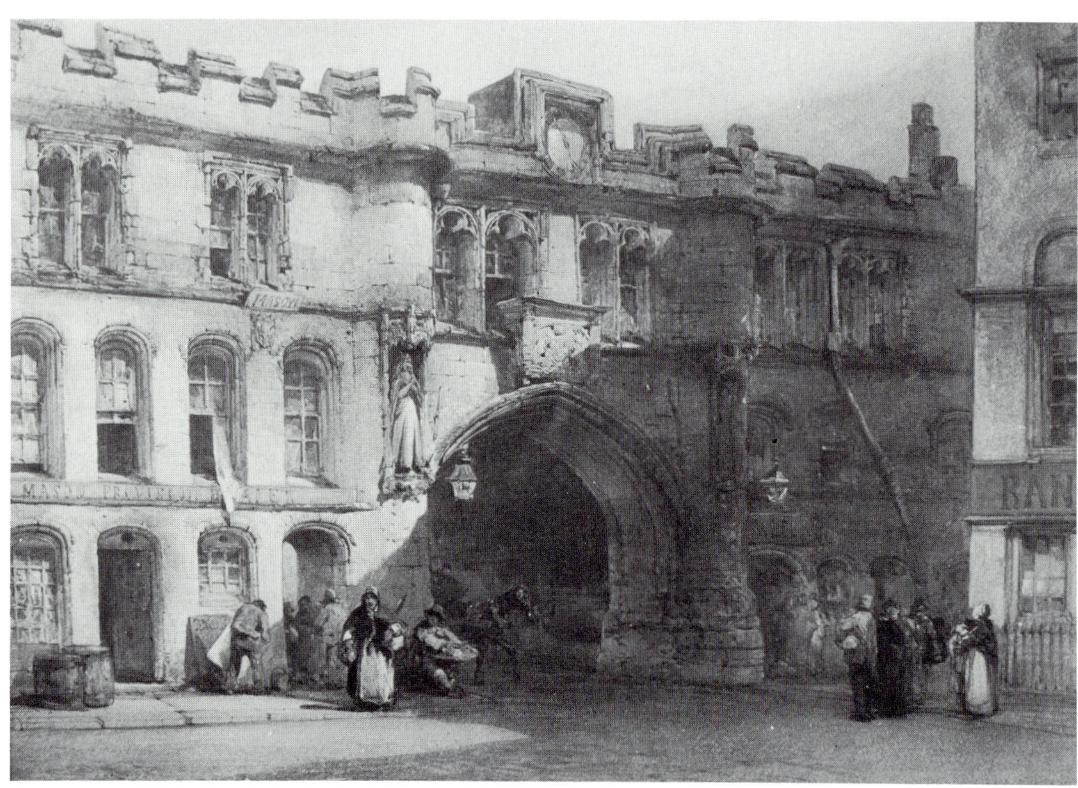

58. 'The Stone Bow on the Guildhall, Lincoln' Water-colour
Signed: W. Callow and dated 1852
Art Journal, p. 178, 1852 – exhibited No. 162, Society of Painters in Water-colours, 1852
Collection: In the Mayor's Parlour, Lincoln. Reproduced by courtesy of the Lincoln City Council

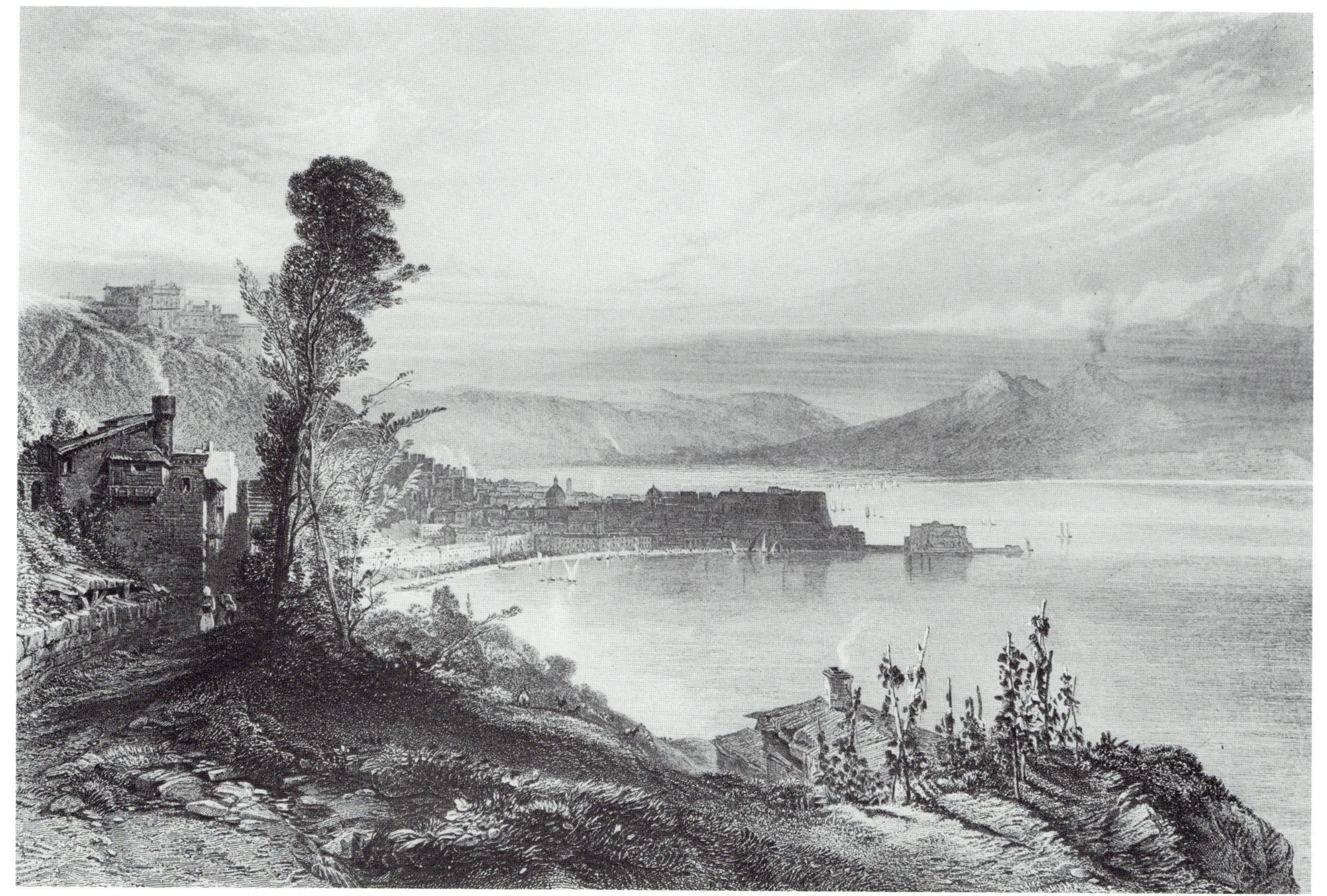

59. 'The Bay of Naples: Early Morning' Engraving by R. Wallis, published in the *Art Journal*, January 1856, p. 16. Series – The Royal Pictures. From the water-colour ($27\frac{3}{4} \times 20$ in. – 705×508 mm) exhibited No. 113 with the Society of Painters in Water-colours in 1852 – purchased by Prince Albert in August 1852
Photograph: by permission of the Sheffield City Libraries

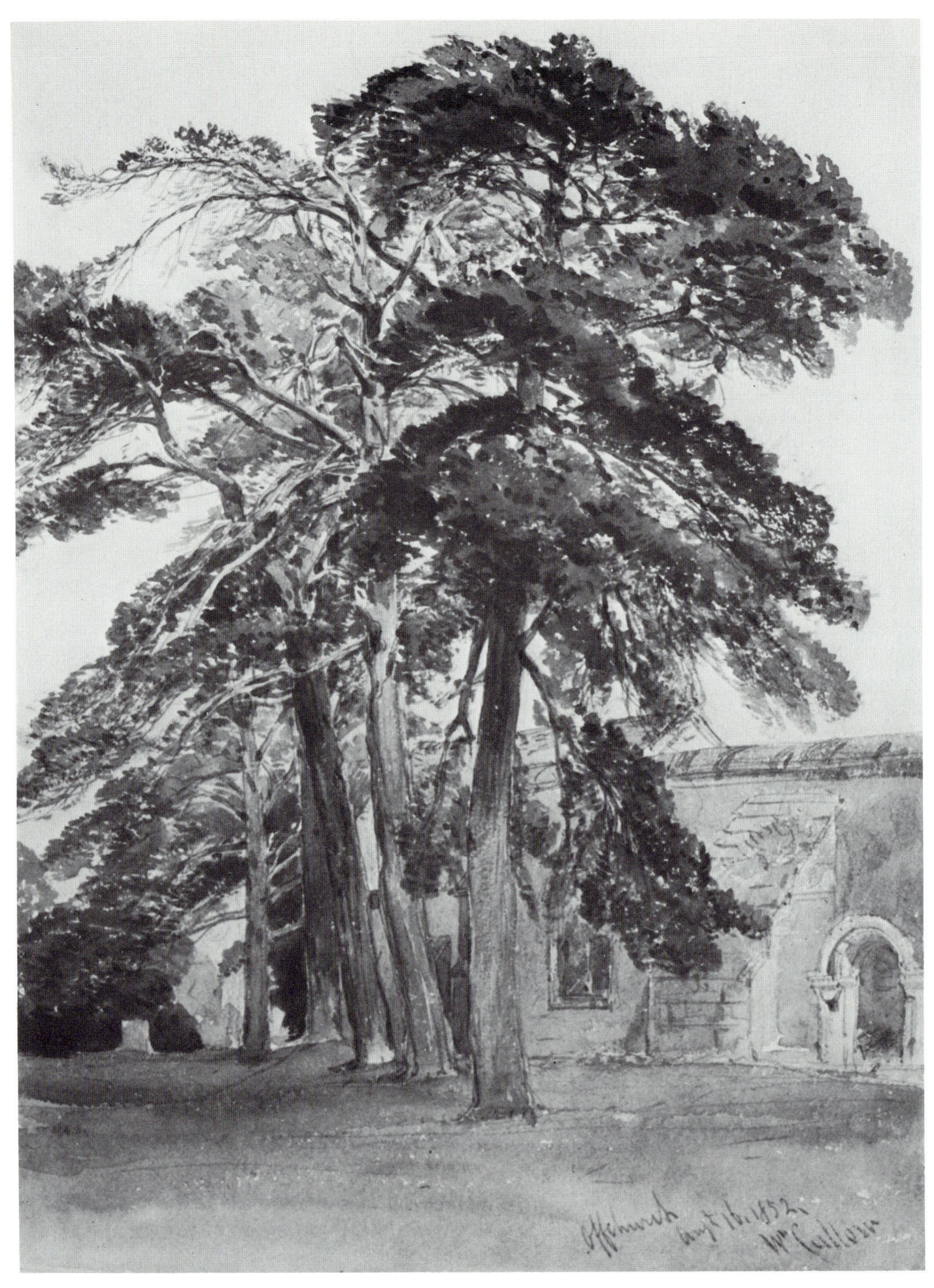

60. 'Fir Trees at Offchurch' Water-colour ($12\frac{4}{5} \times 9\frac{3}{10}$ in. – 325×235 mm)
Signed: Wm Callow. Inscribed: *Offchurch Augt. 16 1852* (*see* text, page 95)
Collection: Herbert Art Gallery and Museum (City of Coventry), Coventry

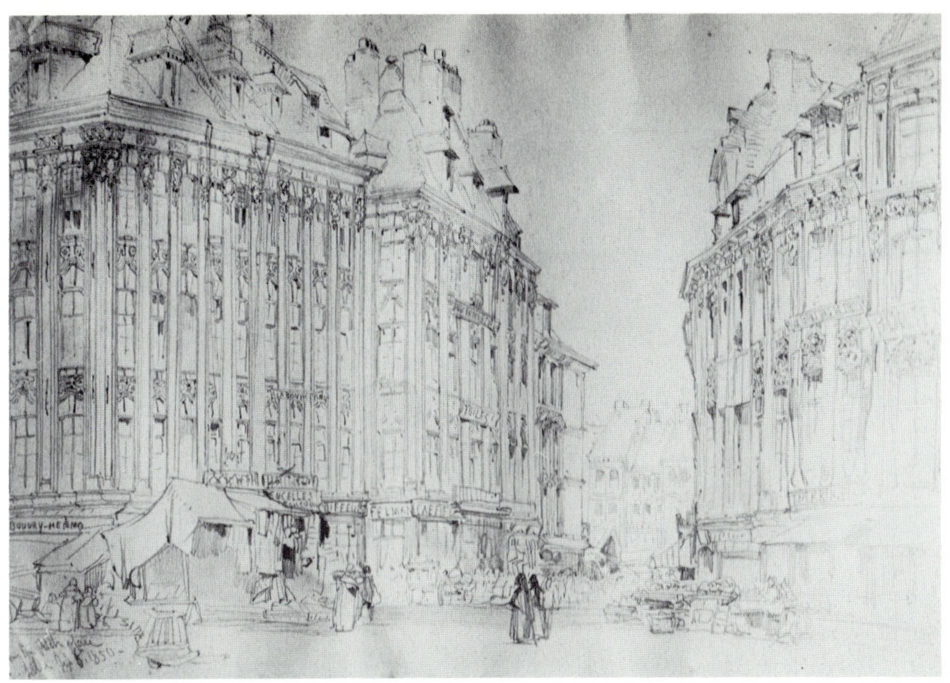

61. 'Lille' Pencil drawing (10 × 14 in. – 254 × 356 mm)
Inscribed: *Sept.8.1850*
Collection: City Museum and Art Gallery, Hanley, Stoke-on-Trent

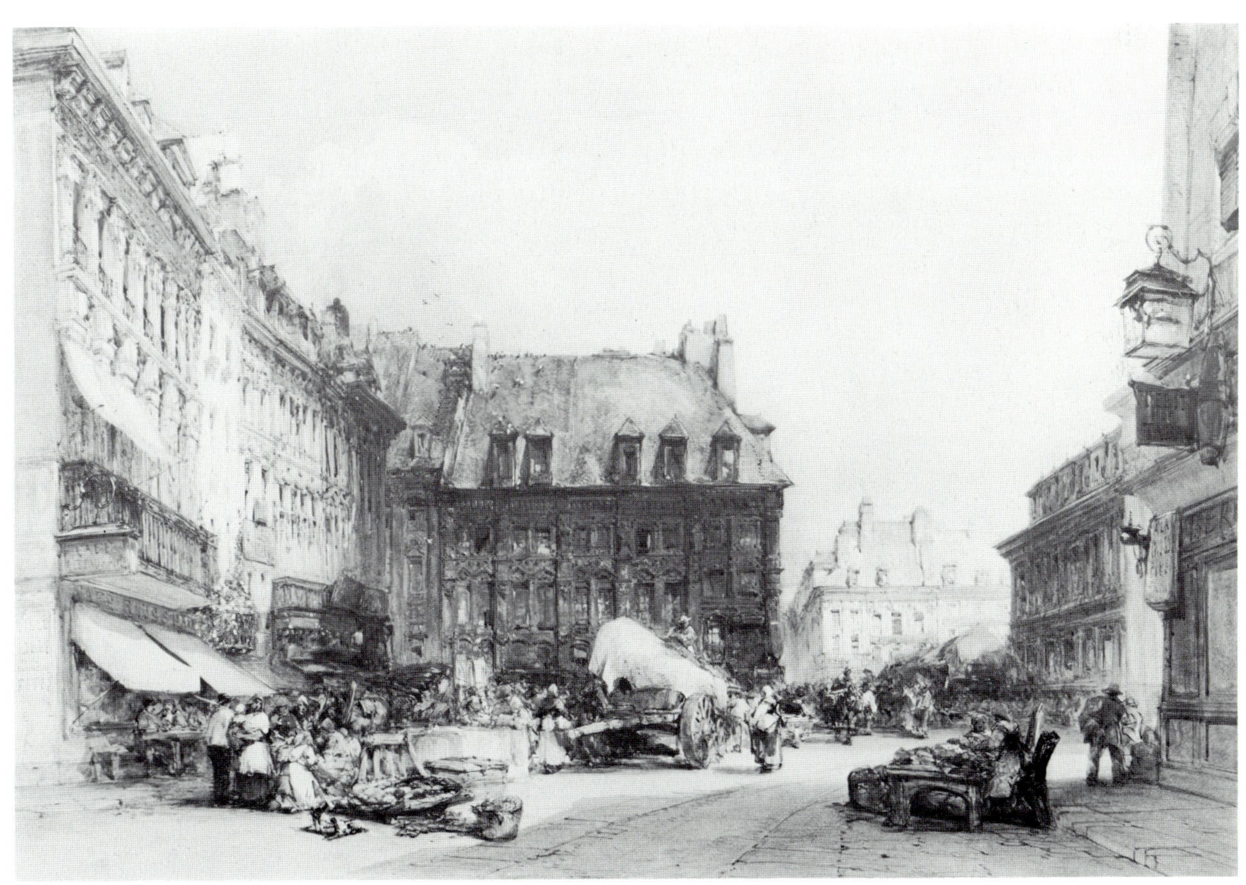

62. 'Looking into the Grande Place, Lille from the Place du Théâtre' Watercolour (25 × 35⅜ in. – 635 × 900 mm)
Signed and dated: W. Callow 1852 (left)
Exhibited: No. 22, Society of Painters in Water-colours in 1852
Collection: Astley Cheetham Art Gallery (Tameside Metropolitan Borough), Stalybridge

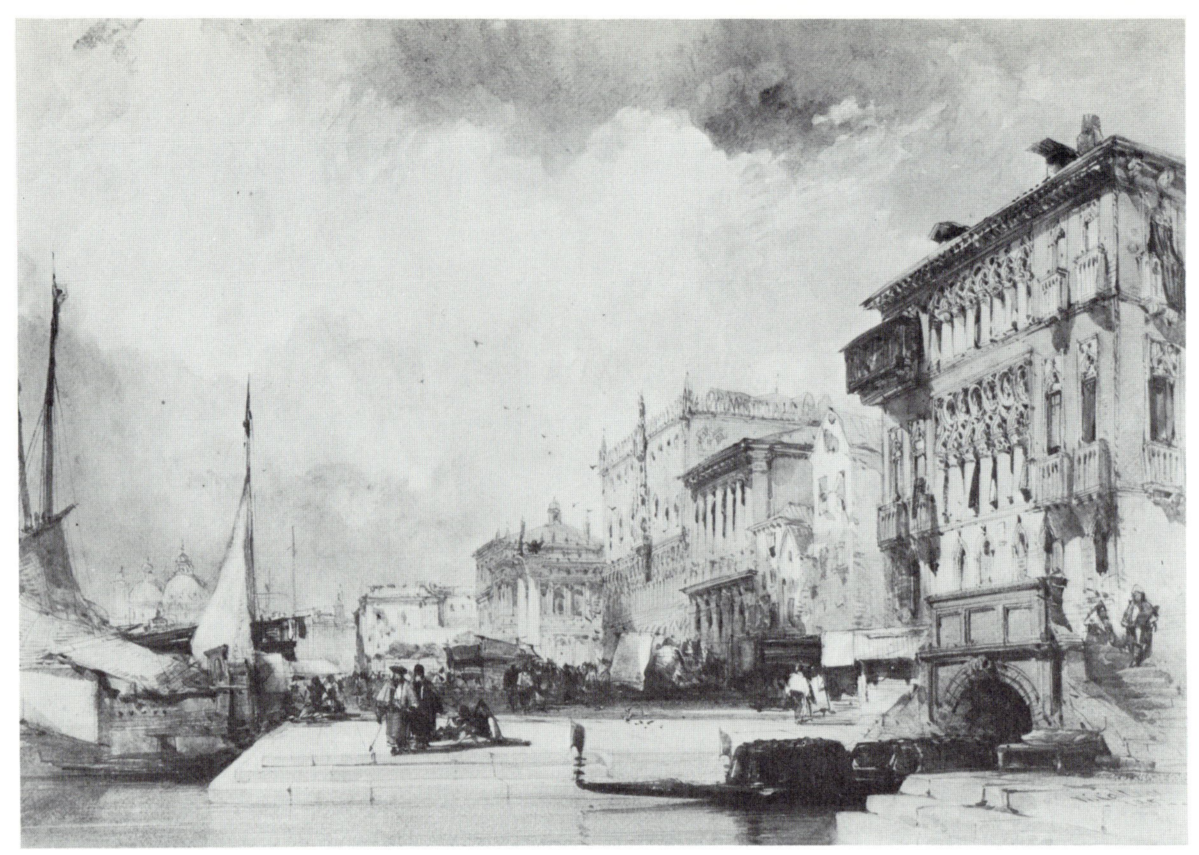

63. 'View along the Molo to the Ducal Palace, Venice' Water-colour
Signed: W. Callow 1852 (right)
Photograph: Sotheby Parke Bernet and Company

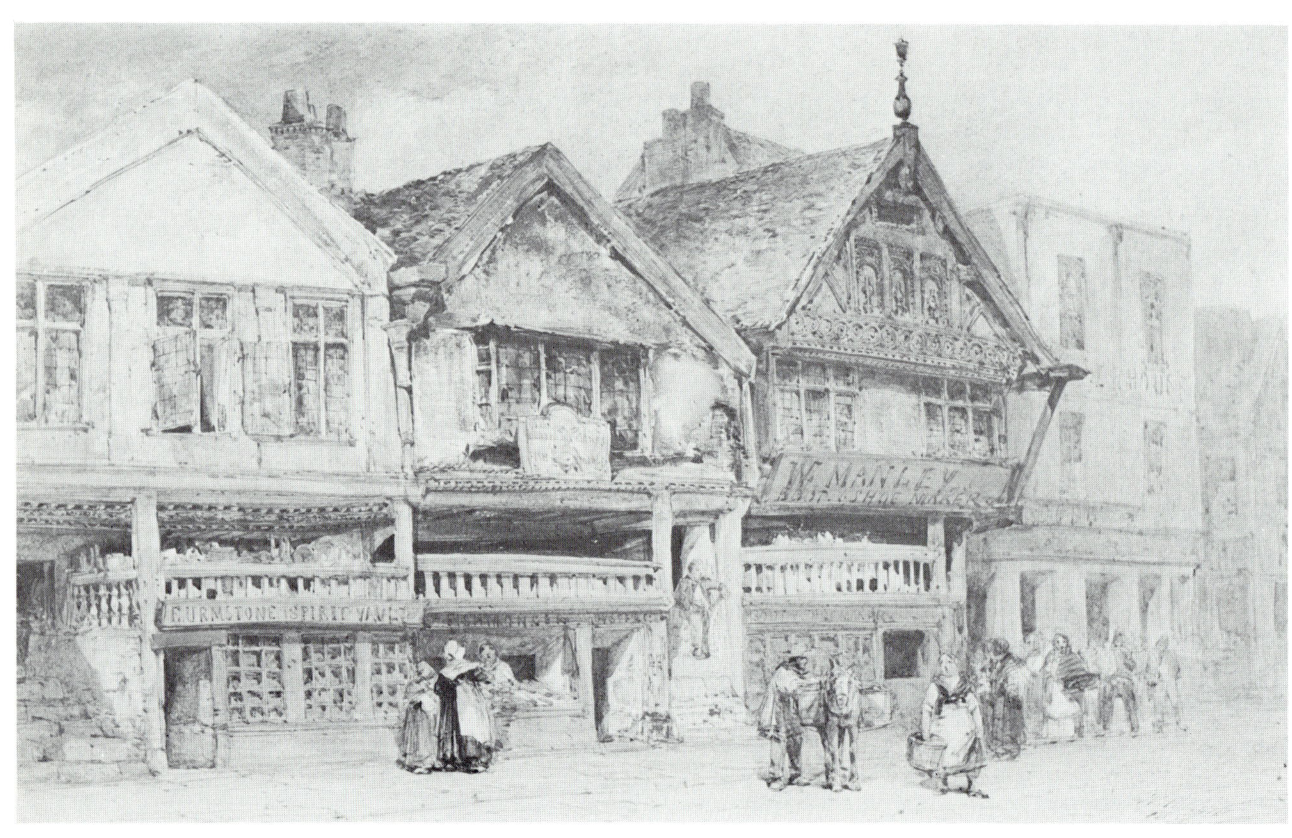

64. 'Shoemakers' Row, Northgate, Chester' Water-colour ($15\frac{2}{10} \times 24$ in. – 385×610 mm)
Signed: W. Callow 1854
Collection: Grosvenor Museum, Chester

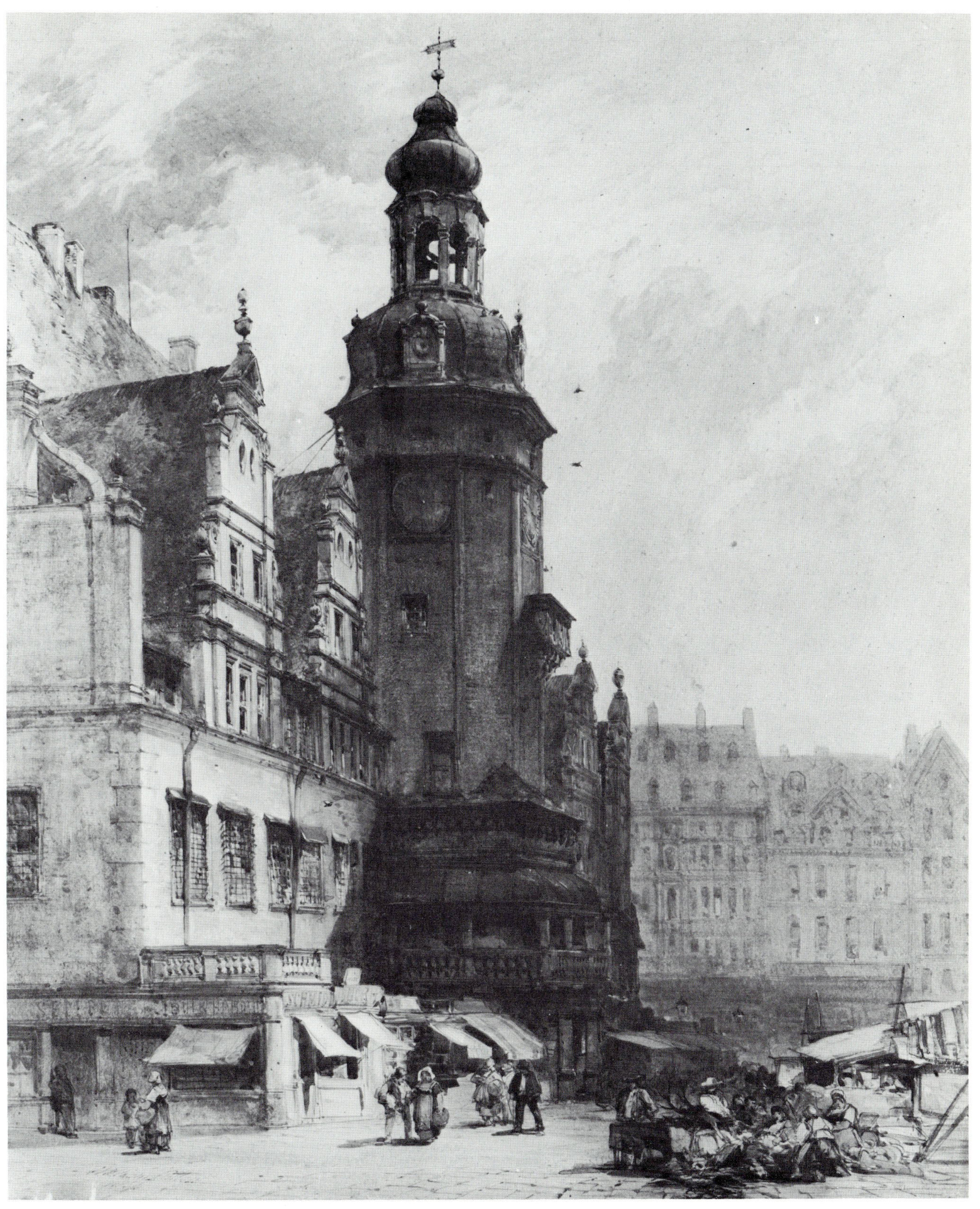

65. 'L'Hôtel de Ville de Leipzig' Water-colour ($28\frac{9}{10} \times 22\frac{4}{5}$ in. – 735 × 579 mm)
Signed and dated: William Callow/1854
Collection: Fondation Custodia l'Institut Néerlandais, Paris

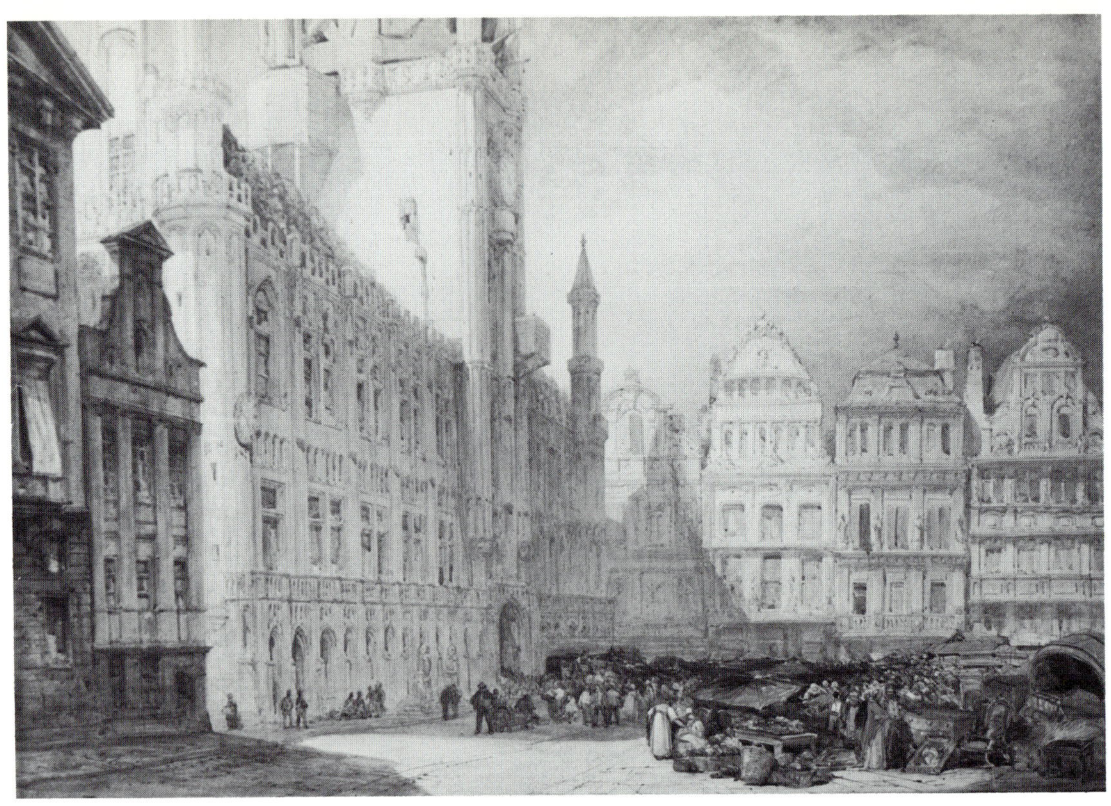

66. 'L'Hôtel de Ville, Brussels' Water-colour ($25\frac{1}{5} \times 35\frac{2}{5}$ in. – 640×900 mm)
Art Journal, p. 175, 1856; Art Union Prize, 1856
Exhibited: Walker's Galleries, 'Early English Water-colours', 1934, and 'The Nineteenth Century Scene' – M. Newman, 1972
Photograph: M. Newman

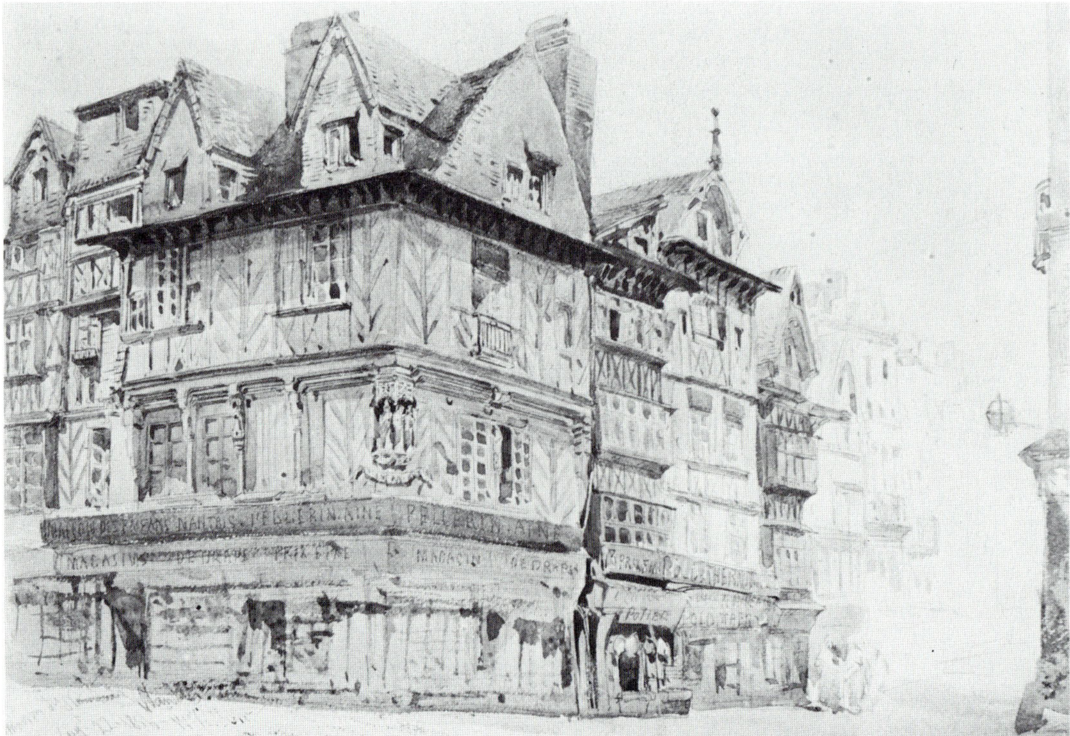

67. 'Old Houses, Nantes' Water-colour (unfinished) (10×14 in. – 254×356 mm)
Signed: Wm. Callow. Inscribed: *Augt. 22nd 1856 – Maison du Nantes*
Collection: Cartwright Hall (Bradford Metropolitan District) Bradford

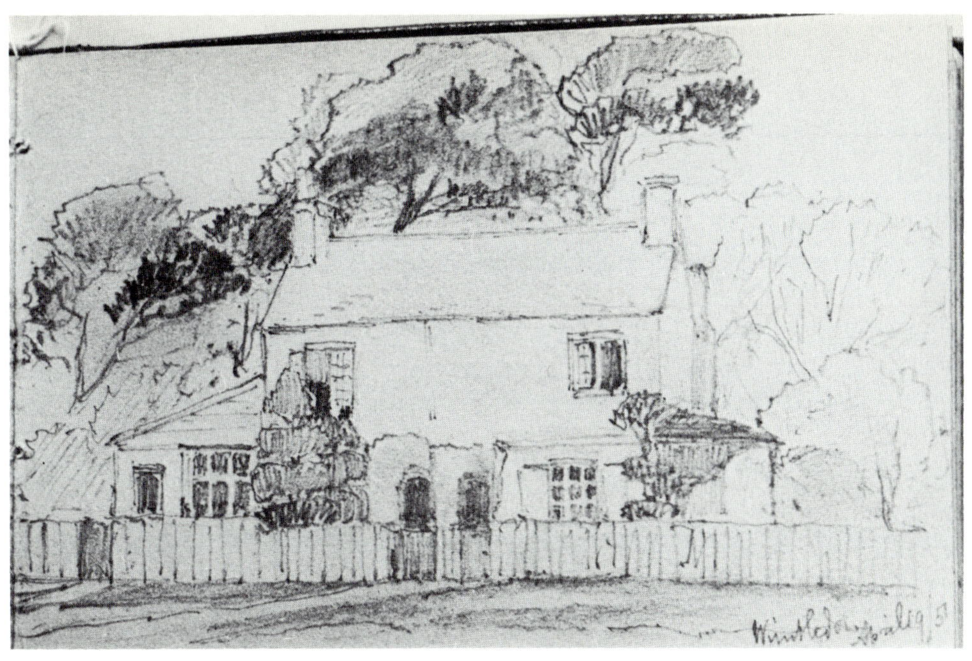

68. Pencil drawing by **Harriet Anne Callow**, first wife of William Callow
Inscribed: *Wimbledon April 19/51*
In possession of the Callow family

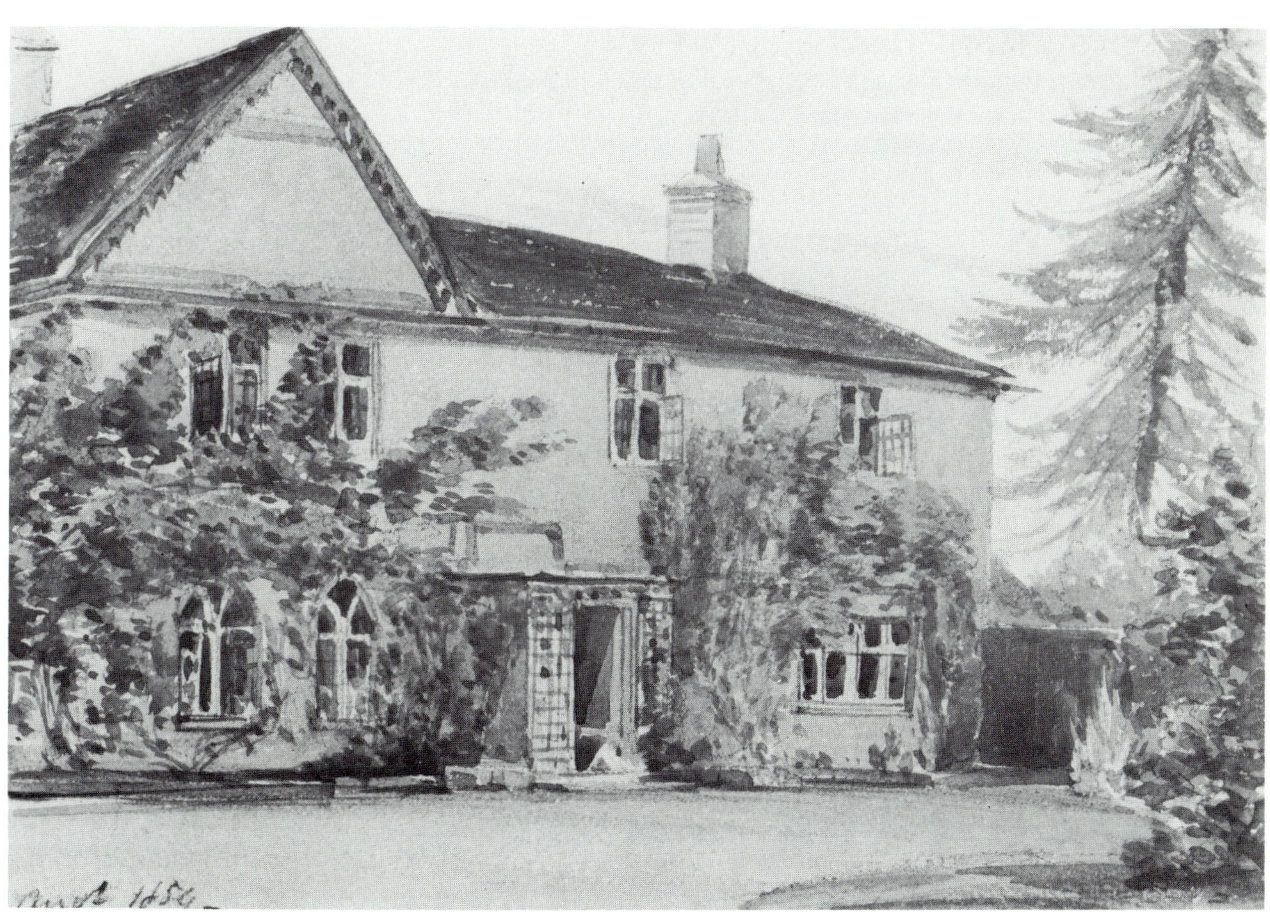

69. The Buckinghamshire home of William and Harriet Callow from 1855 to 1860, on the site of The Firs, Great Missenden. Pencil and water-colour sketch by William Callow, inscribed: *Augt. 1859*
Collection: Buckinghamshire County Museum, Aylesbury

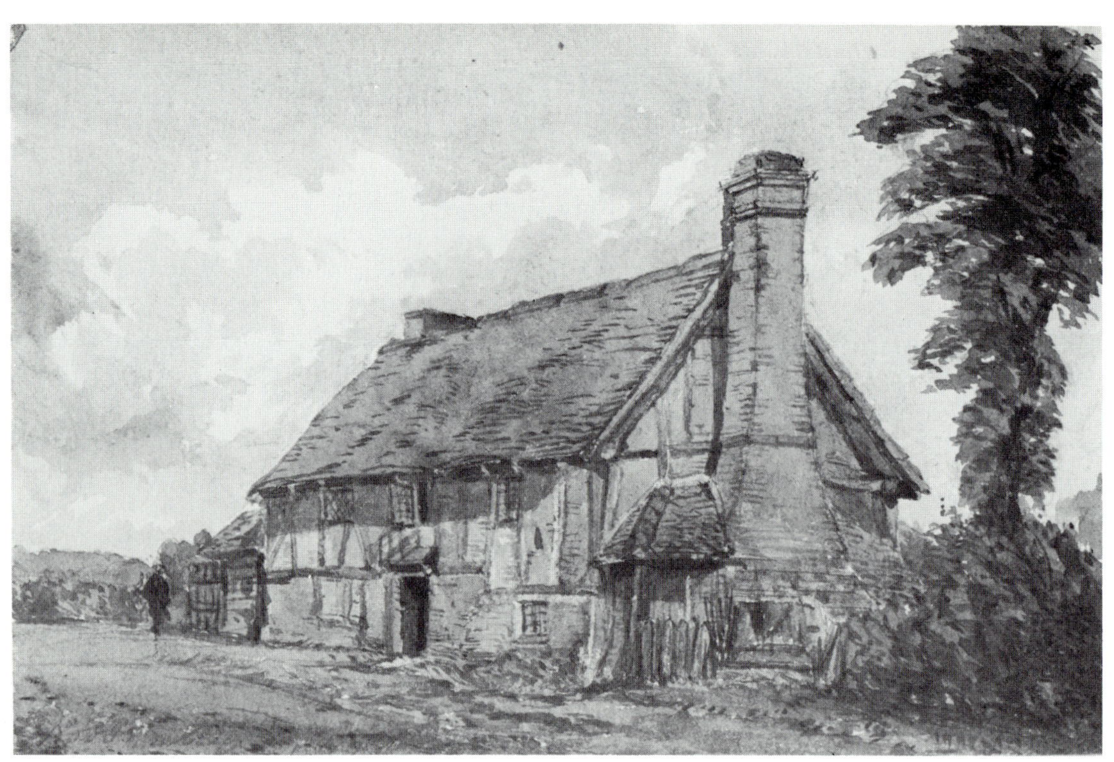

70. 'Cottages in Carter's Field, giving access to Bellinger' Pencil and water-colour sketch by **Harriet Anne Callow**
Collection: Buckinghamshire County Museum, Aylesbury

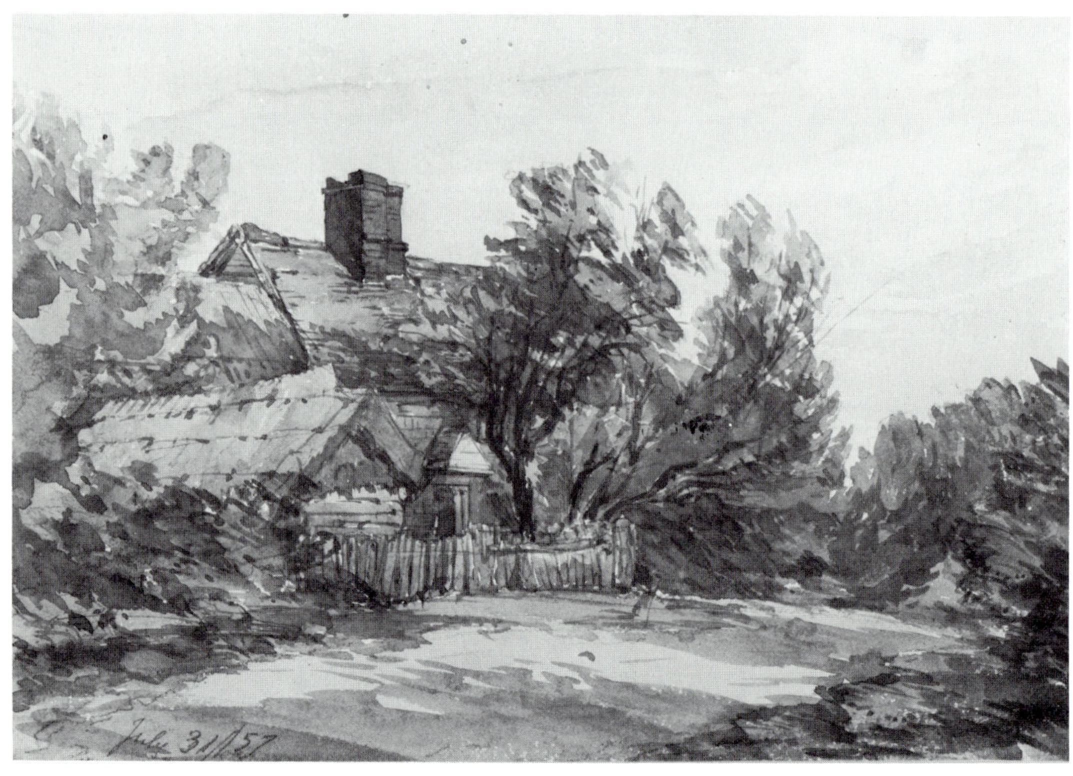

71. 'Wright's Cottage, Barley Mow Lane, Great Missenden' Pencil and water-colour sketch by **Harriet Anne Callow**
Inscribed: *July 31/57*
Collection: Buckinghamshire County Museum

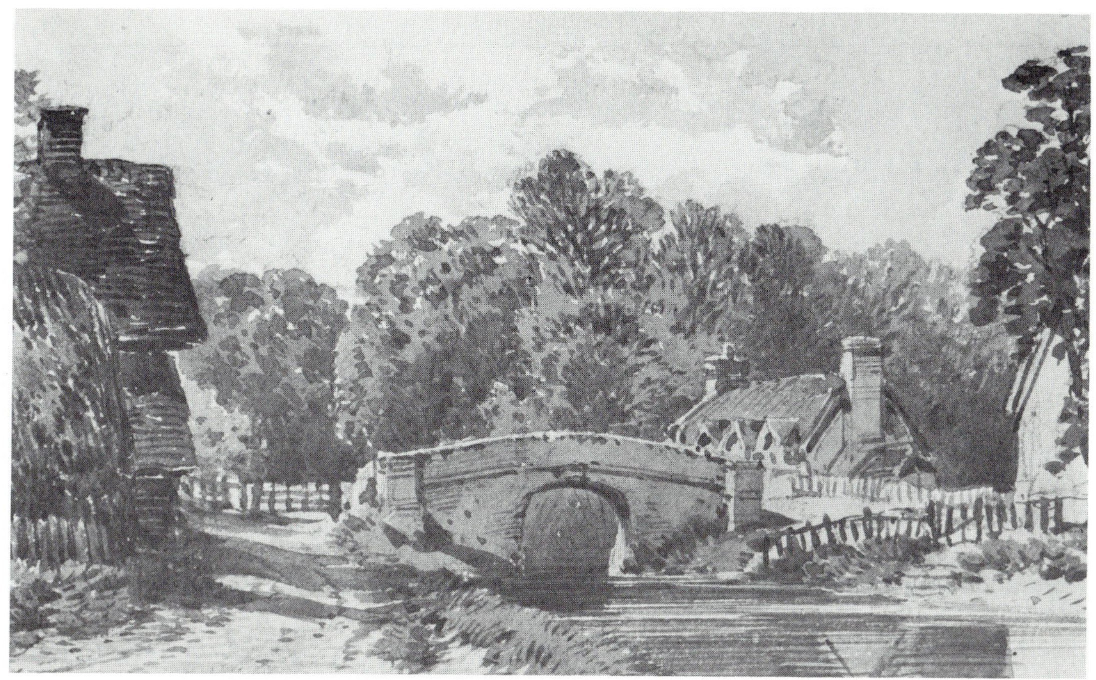

72. 'Canal, Aston Clinton' Pencil and water-colour sketch by William Callow
Collection: Buckinghamshire County Museum

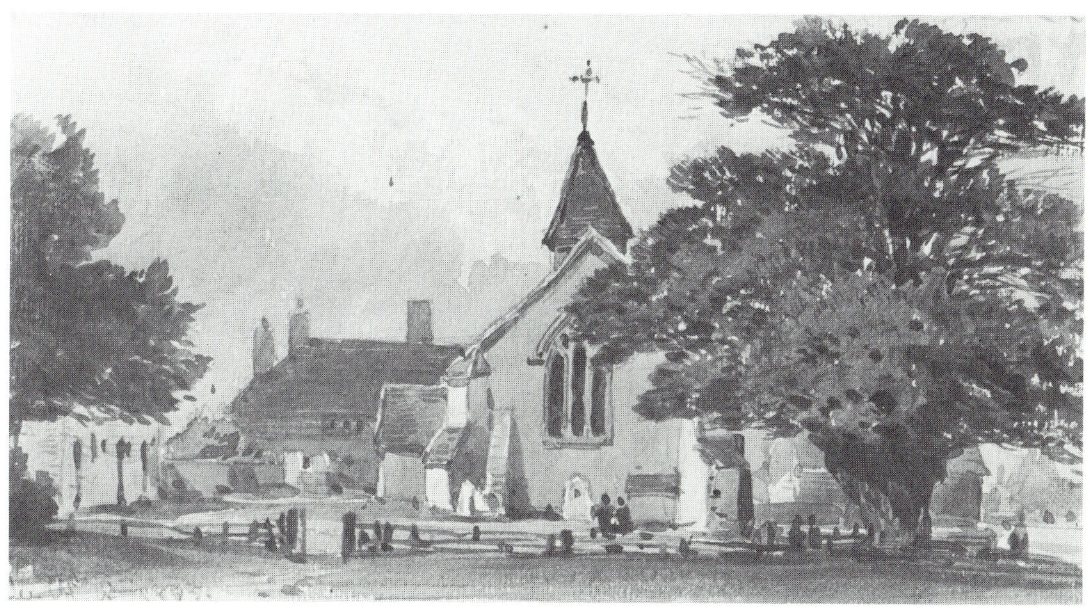

73. 'Lee Old Church and Farm' Pencil and water-colour sketch by William Callow
Collection: Buckinghamshire County Museum

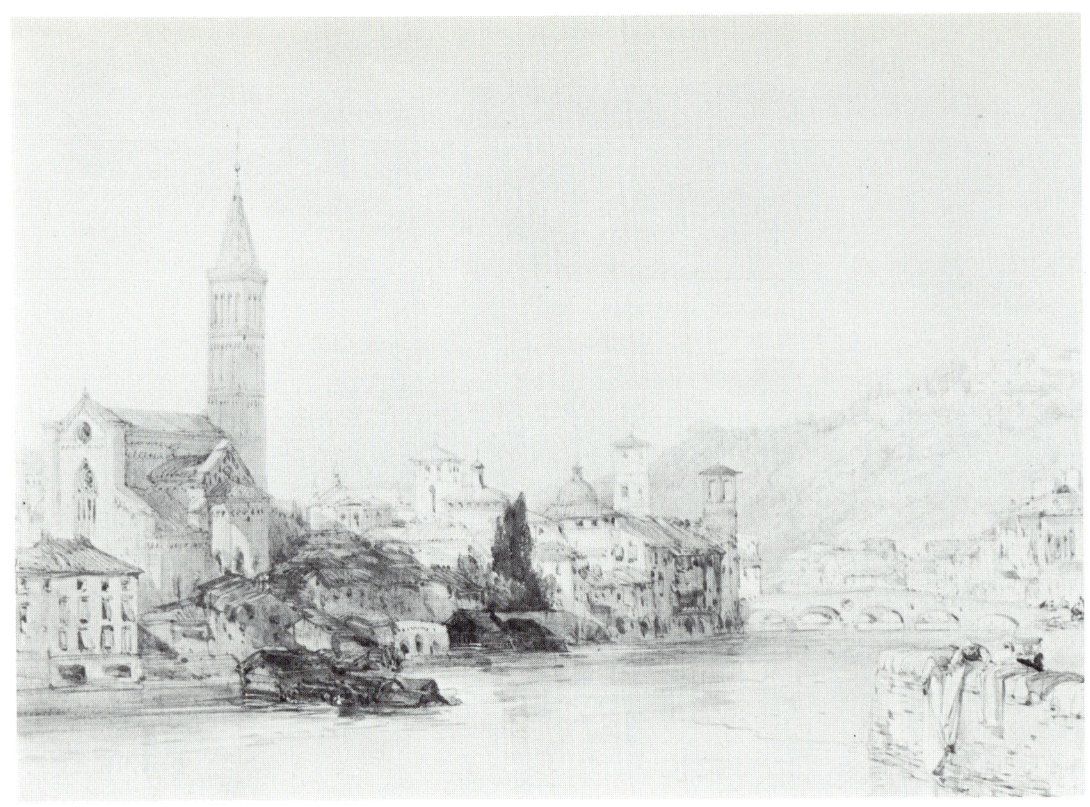

74. 'Verona' Water-colour
Signed and dated: Wm. Callow 1858
Collection: Astley Cheetham Art Gallery (Tameside Metropolitan Borough), Stalybridge

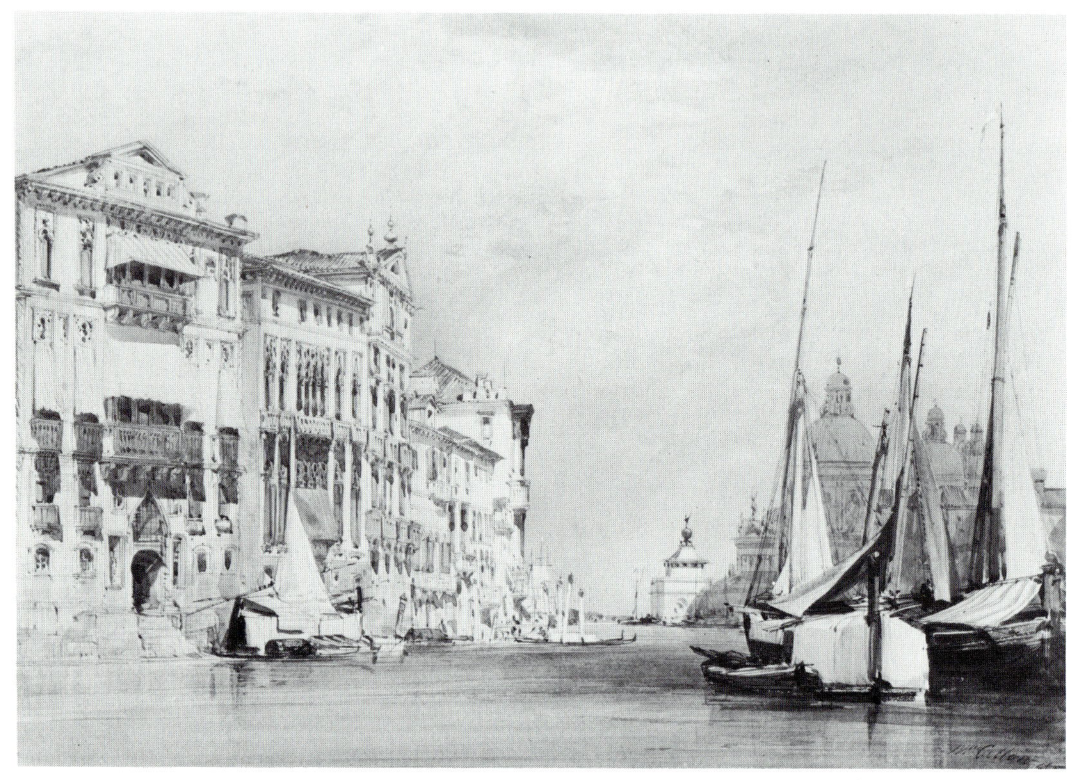

75. 'On the Grand Canal, near the Salute, Venice' Water-colour ($10\frac{3}{4} \times 14\frac{3}{4}$ in. – 273×375 mm)
Signed and dated: Wm. Callow 1859 (right)
Photograph: The Leger Galleries

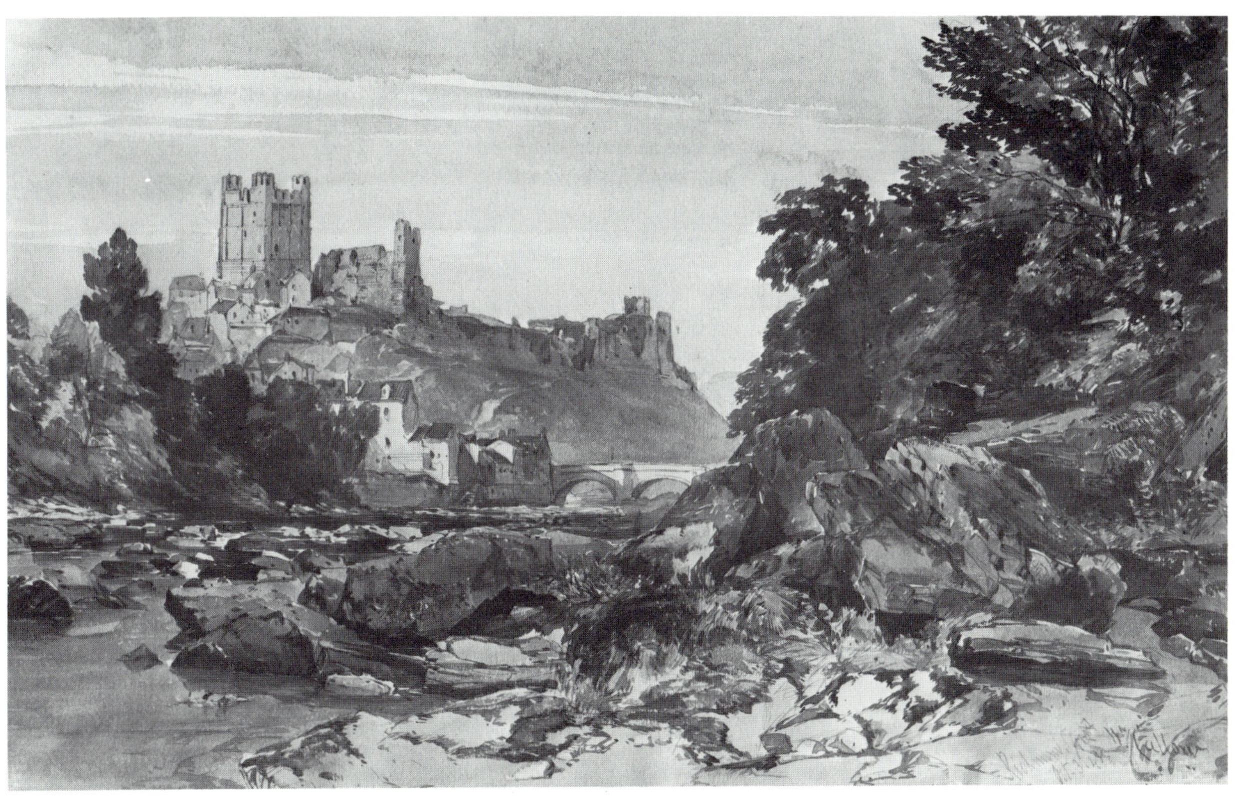

76. 'Richmond Castle, Yorkshire' Water-colour
Signed: Wm. Callow. Inscribed: *Oct 3 1853* – appears to read *48*
Collection: The Tate Gallery, London

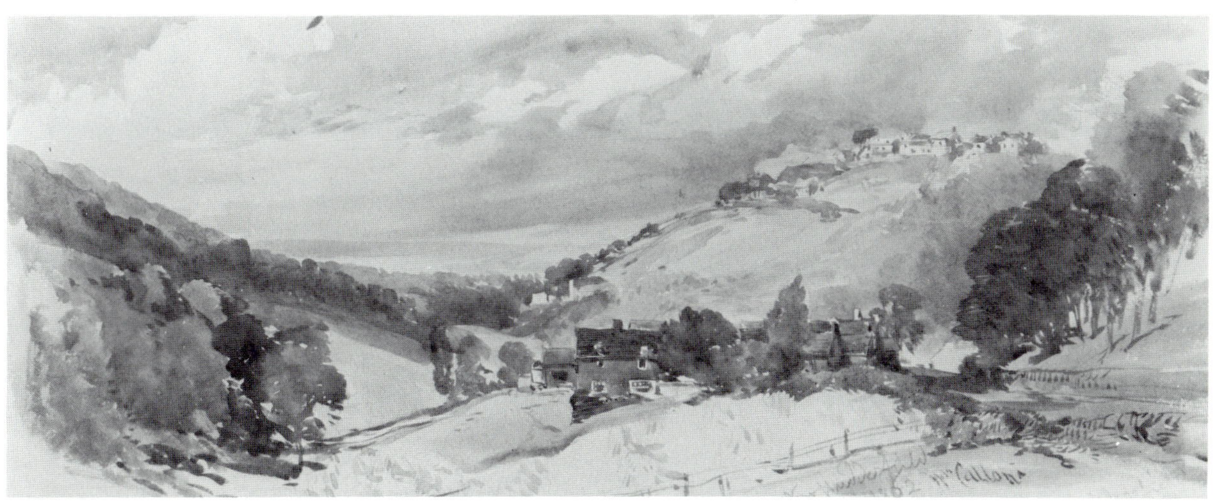

77. 'Near Huddersfield' Water-colour (8 × 19¾ in. – 203 × 502 mm)
Signed: Wm. Callow (right). Inscribed: *Near Huddersfield 1862*
Exhibited: Royal Society of Painters in Water-colours in 1908
Collection: Cecil Higgins Art Gallery, Bedford

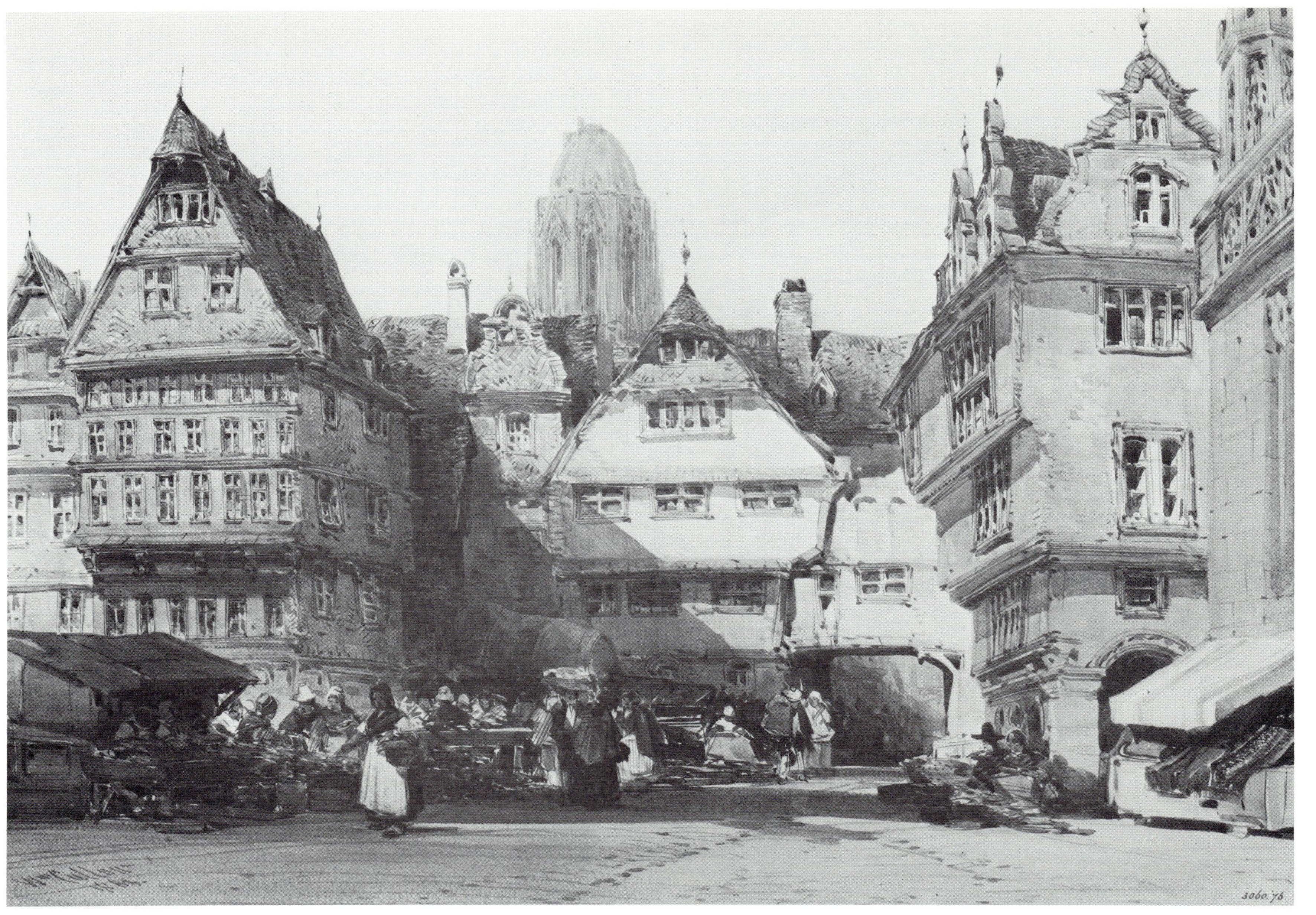

78. 'Market Place, Frankfort' Water-colour ($13\frac{1}{10} \times 19$ in. – 333×483 mm)
Signed: Wm. Callow 1863 (left)
Collection: Victoria and Albert Museum, Crown Copyright

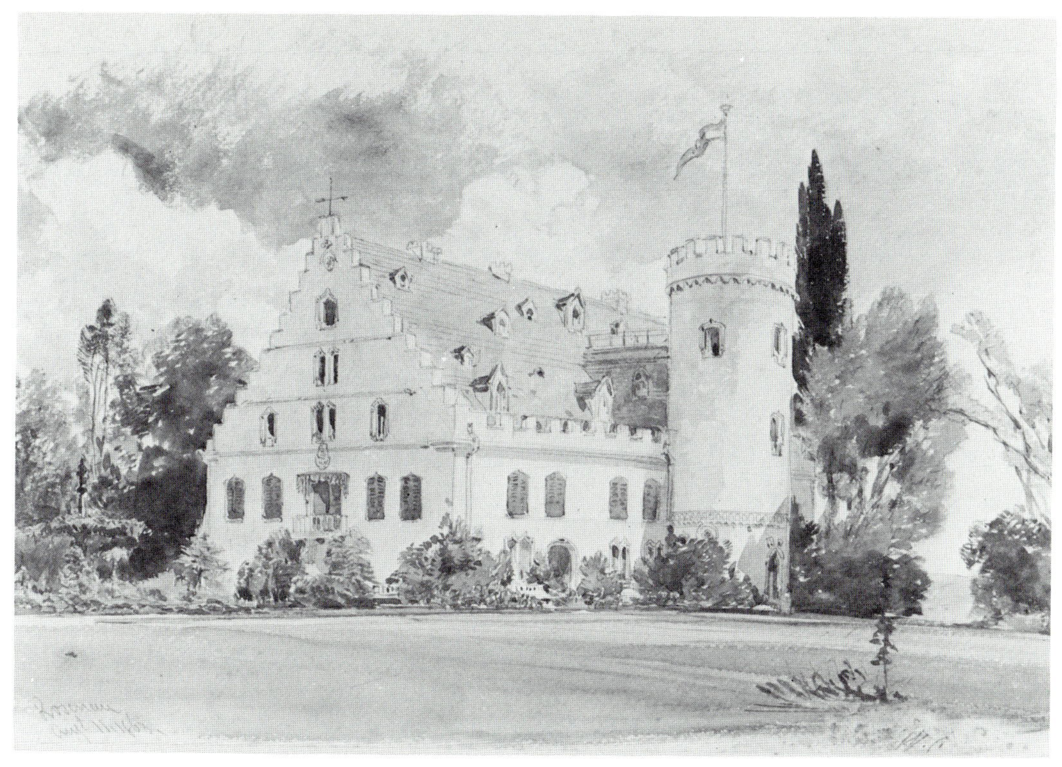

79. 'Rosenau' Water-colour ($14\frac{1}{8} \times 10$ in. – 359×254 mm)
Signed with initials and inscribed: *Rosenau August 11 1863*
Photograph: Christie's

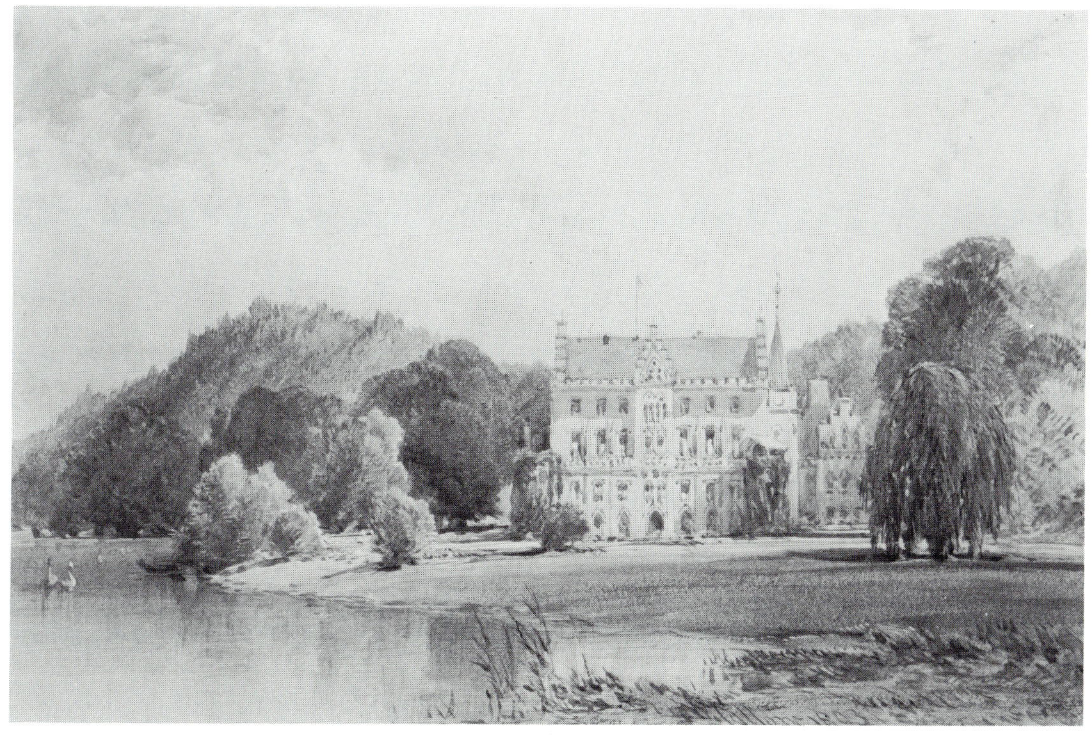

80. 'View of the Palace and Grounds of the Schloss Reinhardsbrunn' Water-colour ($8\frac{5}{8} \times 12\frac{3}{4}$ in. – 219×324 mm)
Signed: W. Callow 1863
Reproduced by gracious permission of Her Majesty the Queen

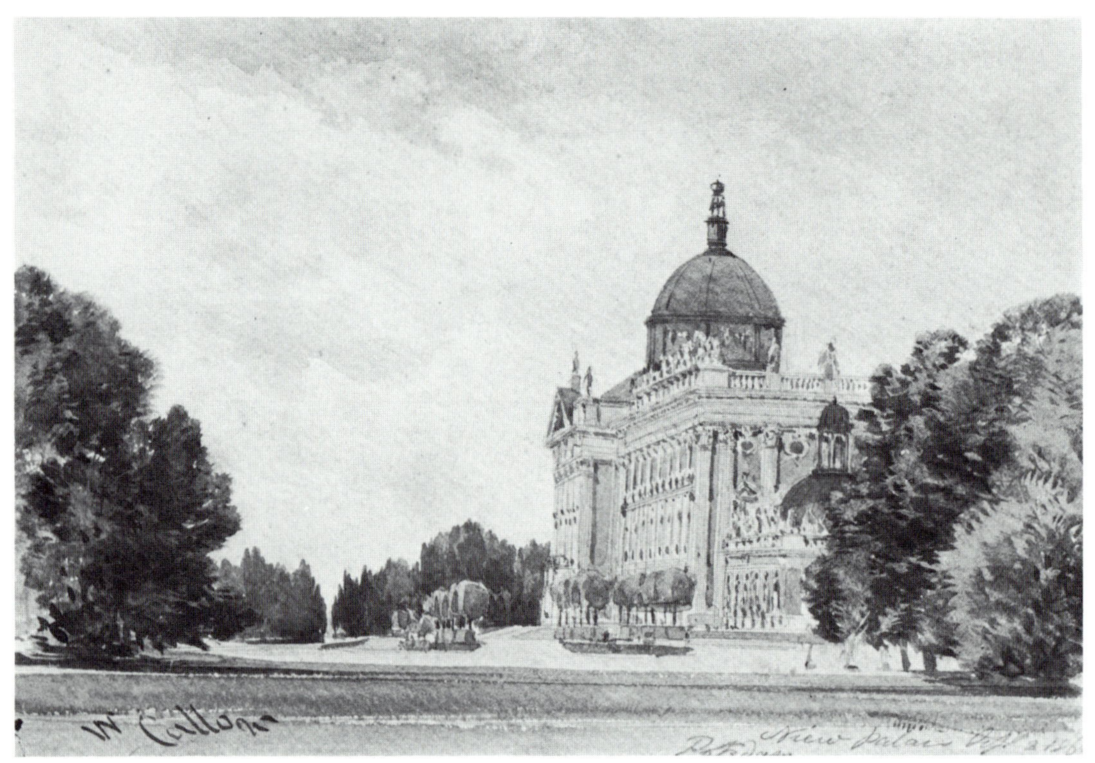

81. 'Neue Palais, Potsdam' Water-colour (10×7 in. – 254×178 mm)
Signed: W. Callow. Inscribed: *Niew [sic] Palais, Potsdam Sept 3 1863*
Collection: Wilhelm H. Köhler
Photograph: Agnew

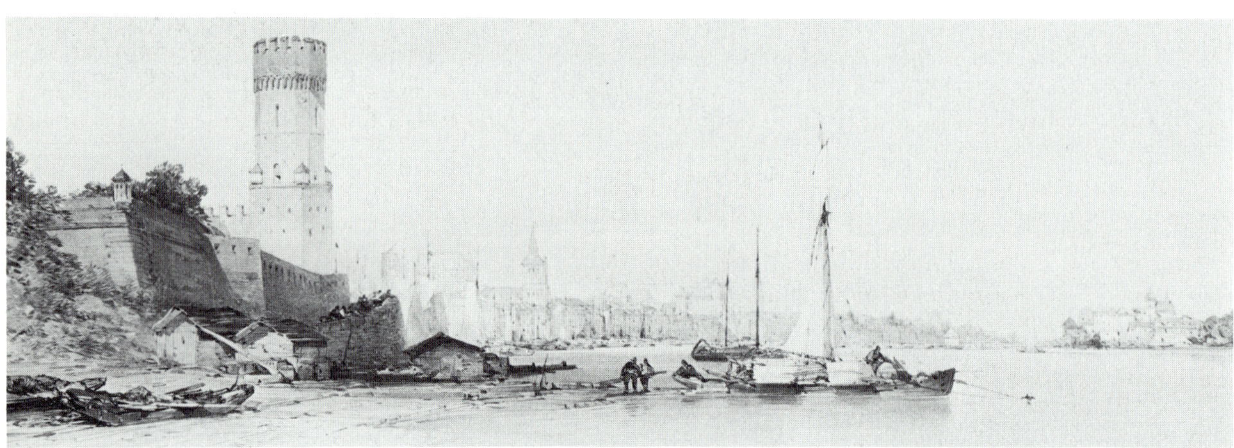

82. 'Beilstein on the Moselle' Water-colour ($9\frac{1}{10} \times 30\frac{1}{10}$ in. – 230×764 mm)
Signed: William Callow 1864 (left)
Exhibited: Victoria Art Gallery, Bath – 'Marine Painting', 1970
Collection: Royal Albert Memorial Museum, Exeter

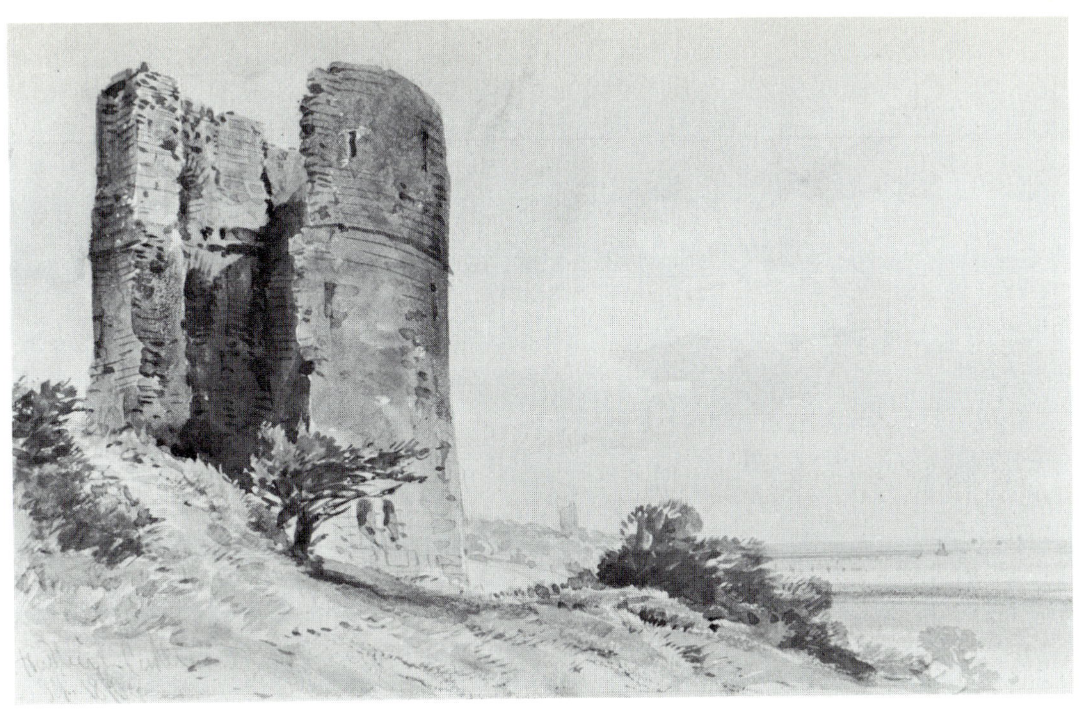

83. 'Hadleigh Castle, Essex' Pencil and water-colour ($6\frac{7}{8} \times 10\frac{1}{2}$ in. – 175 × 254 mm)
Inscribed and dated: *Hadleigh Castle/Sept 18/64*
By courtesy of Norfolk Museums Service (Norwich Castle Museum)

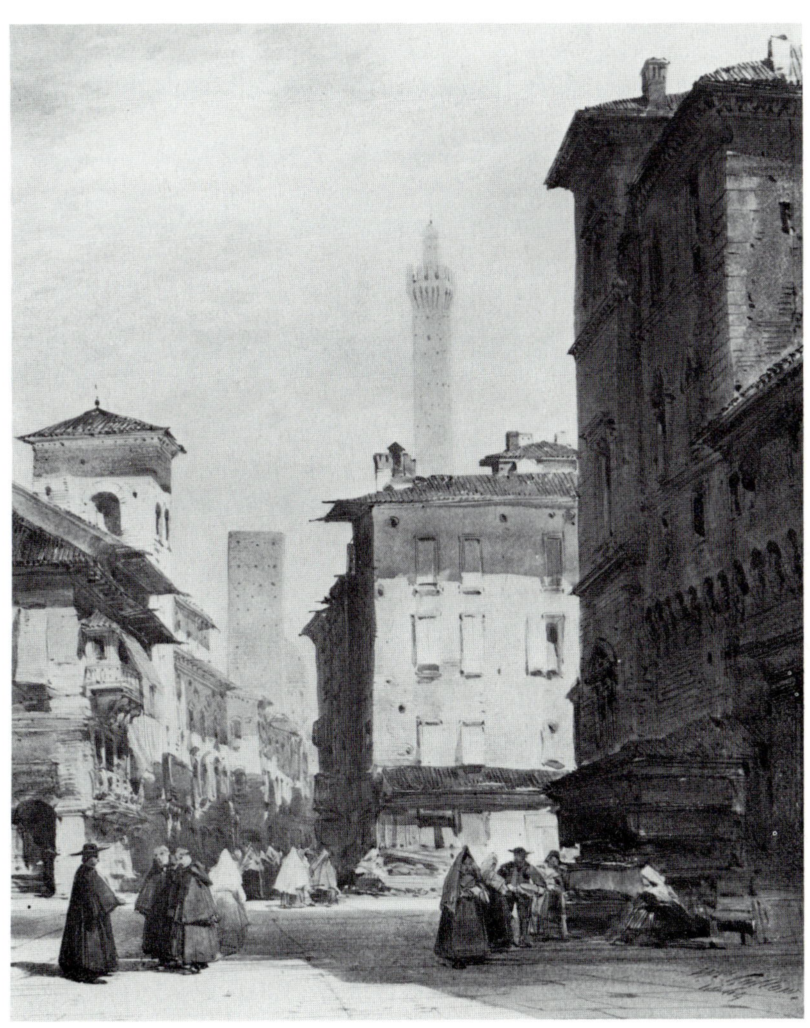

84. 'Leaning Towers, Bologna' Water-colour ($16 \times 12\frac{5}{8}$ in. – 406 × 321 mm)
Exhibited: Society of Painters in Water-colours, 1864
Collection: Victoria and Albert Museum, Crown Copyright

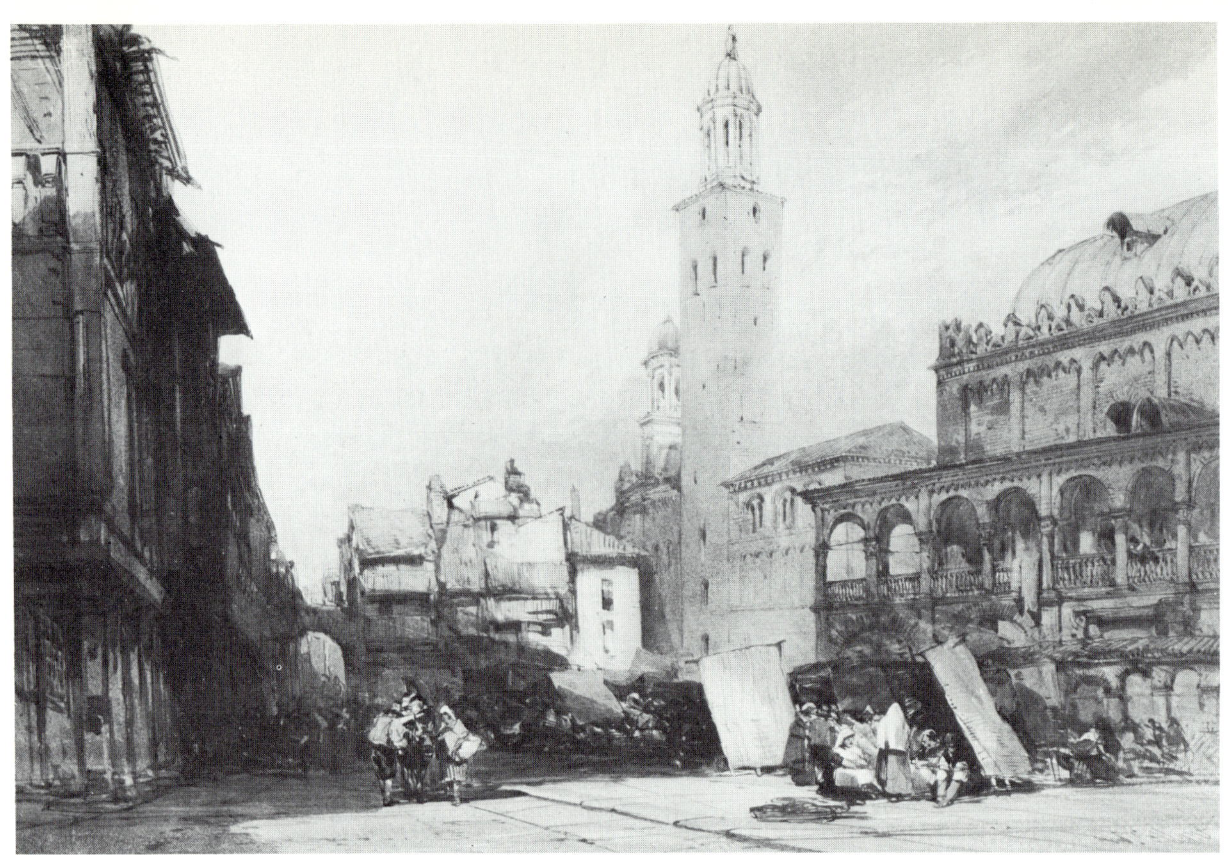

85. 'Market Place and Palazzo Ragione, Padua' Water-colour ($12\frac{3}{4} \times 18\frac{7}{8}$ in. – 324×479 mm)
Reproduced by permission of the Provost and Fellows of Eton College

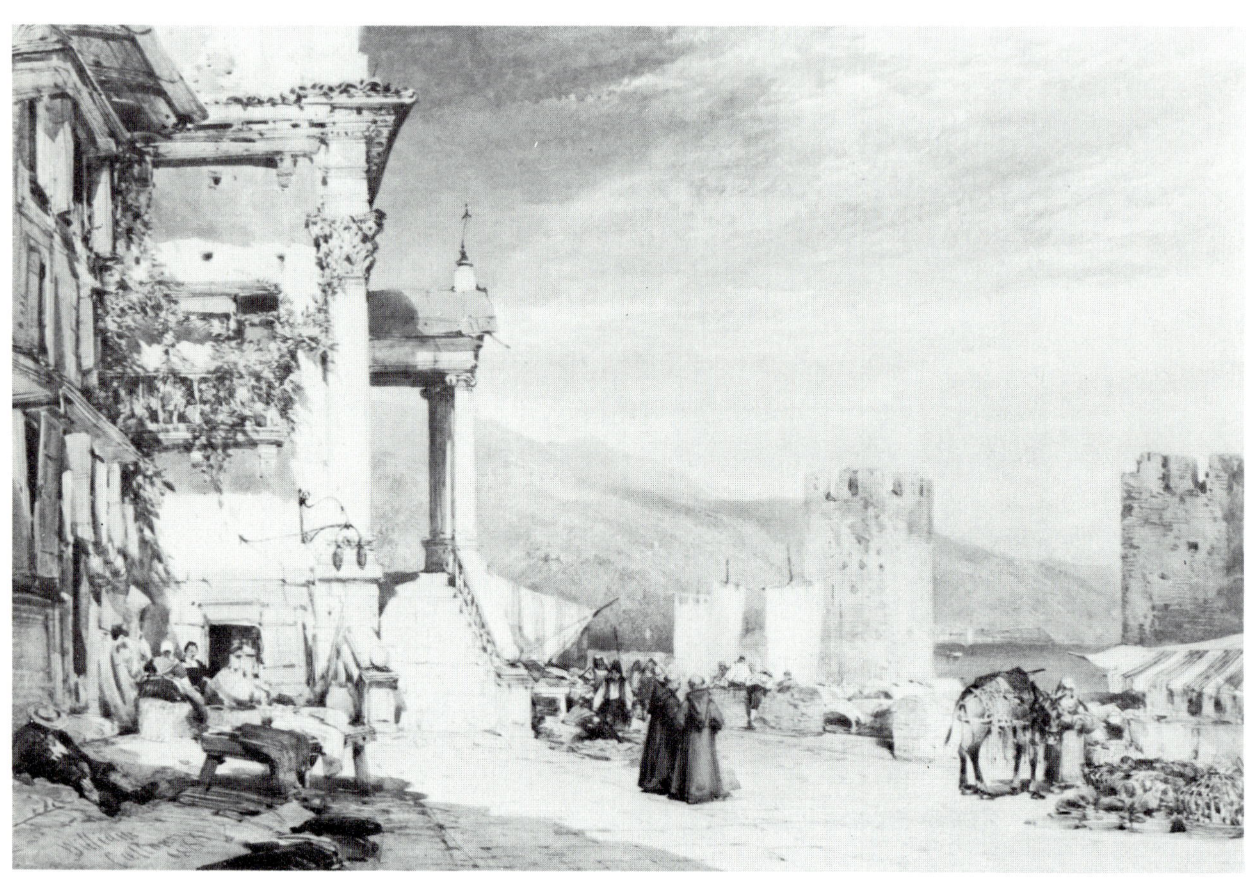

86. 'Arona on the Lago Maggiore' Water-colour ($13\frac{1}{2} \times 19\frac{3}{4}$ in. – 343×502 mm)
Signed: William Callow 1866 (left)
Photograph: Sotheby Parke Bernet and Company

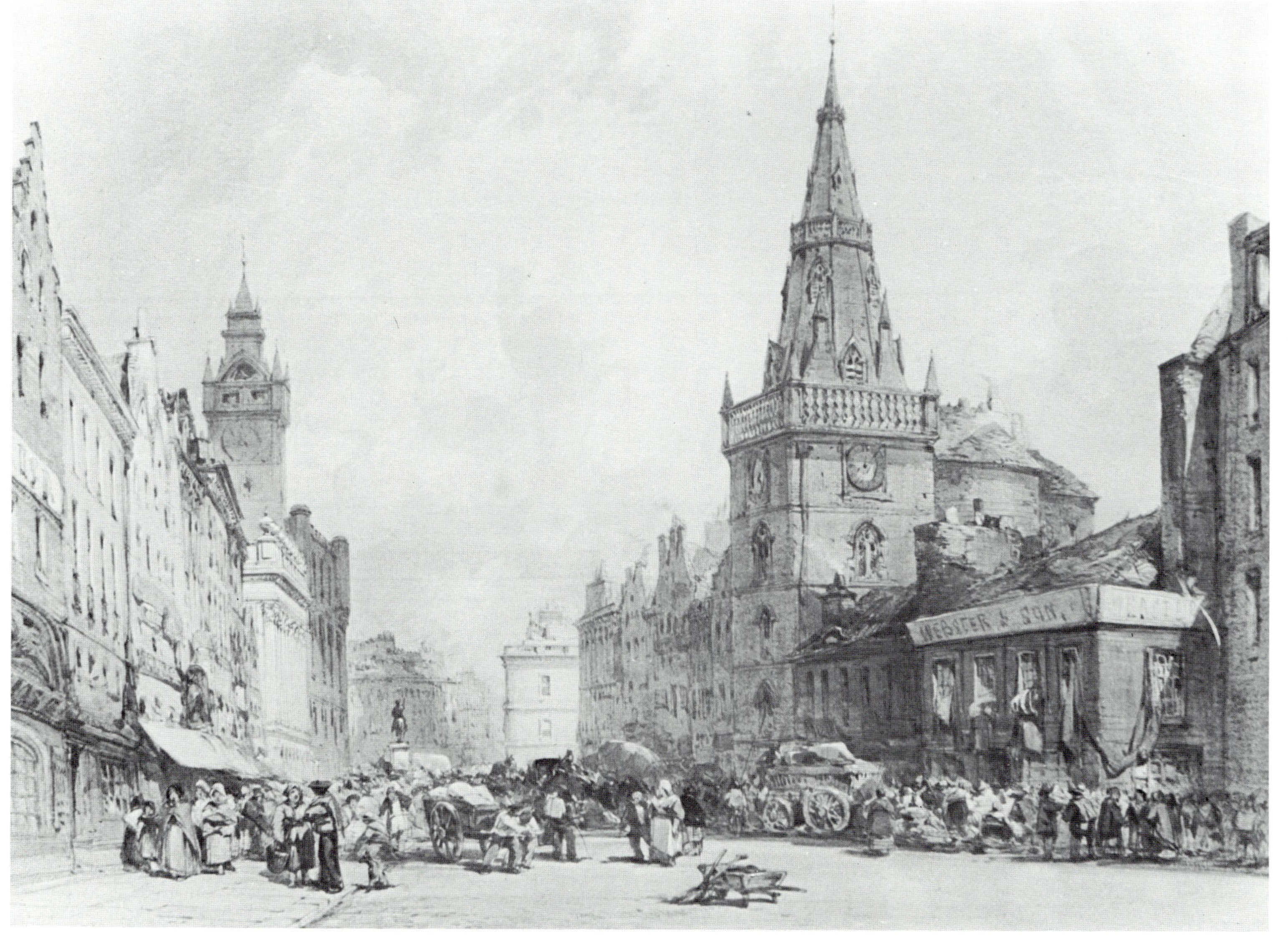

87. 'Trongate, Glasgow' Water-colour ($18\frac{9}{10} \times 25\frac{3}{5}$ in. – 480 × 650 mm)
Signed: W. Callow 1870 (centre foreground, under barrow)
Collection: Royal Museum and Art Gallery, Canterbury

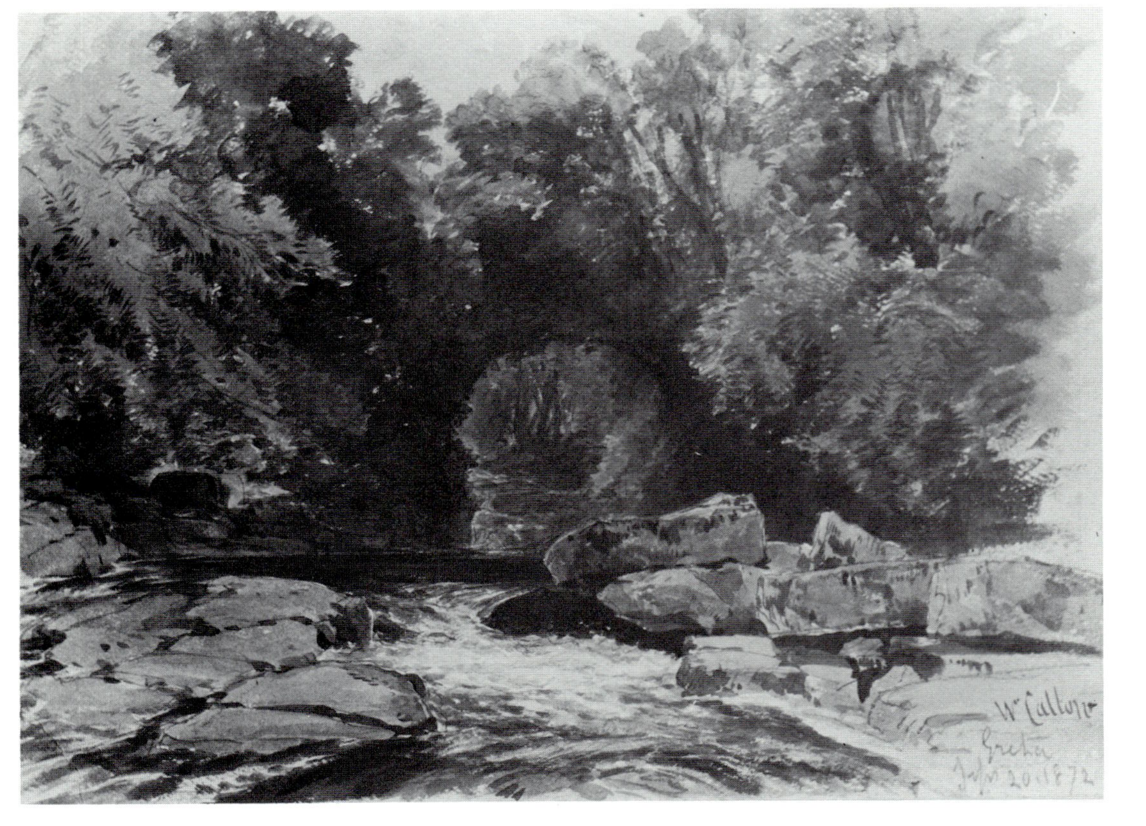

88. 'The Meeting of the Waters' (confluence of the Rivers Tees and Greta) Water-colour ($9 \times 13\frac{1}{4}$ in. – 229×337 mm)
Signed: Wm. Callow. Inscribed: *Sept. 20 1872*
Collection: The Bowes Museum, Barnard Castle, County Durham

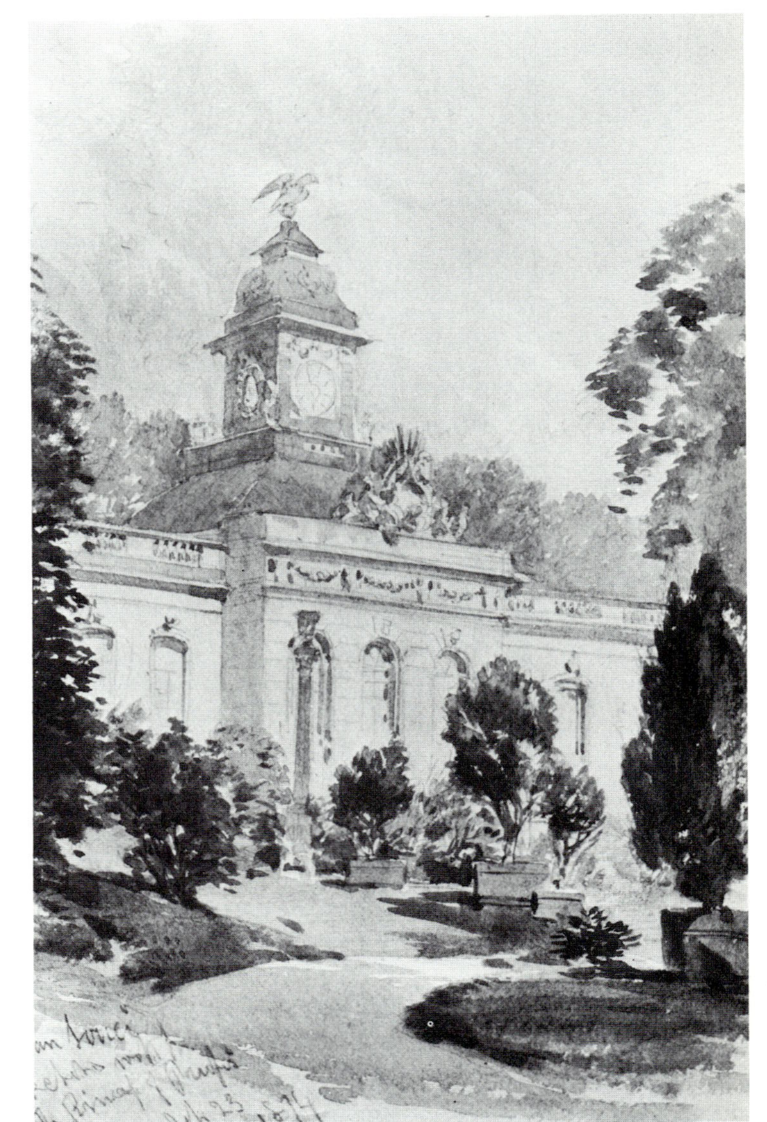

89. 'Sans Souci' Water-colour ($9\frac{3}{4} \times 6\frac{1}{2}$ in. – 248×165 mm)
Inscribed: *Sketched with the Princess of Prussia Sept. 23 1874*
With Agnew, 1977

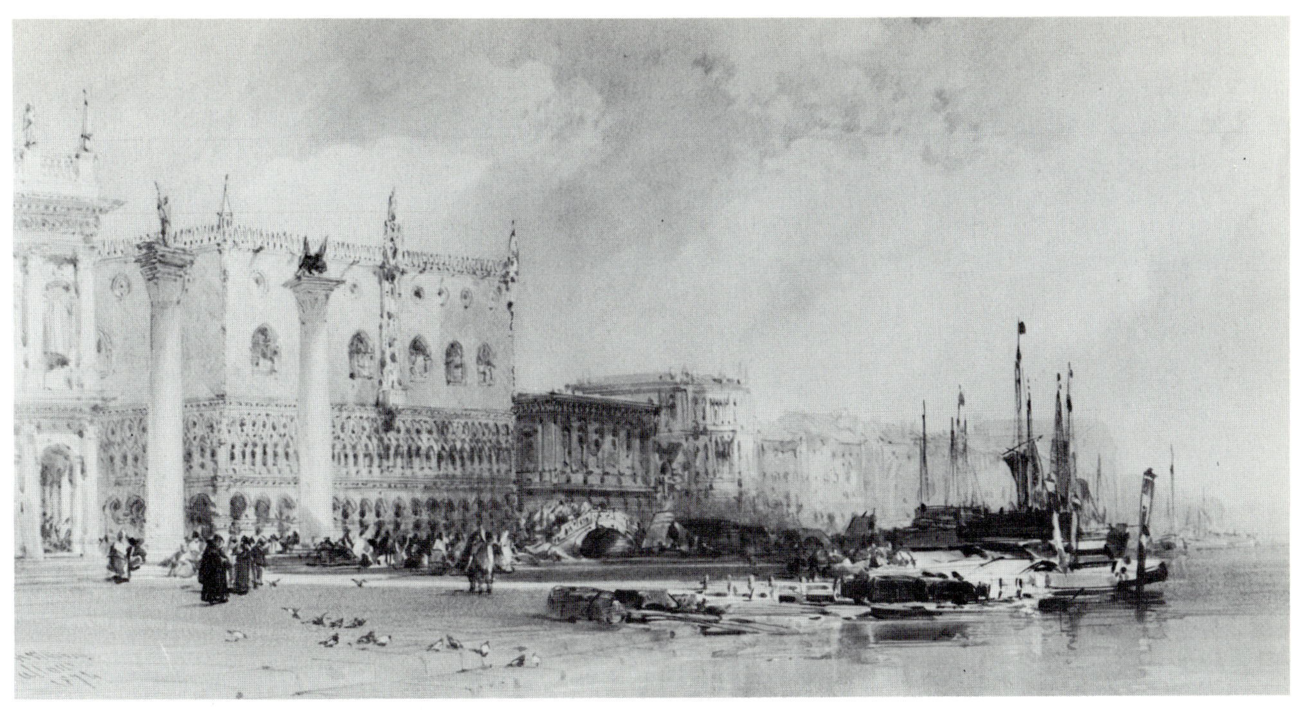

90. 'The Doge's Palace, Venice' Water-colour ($11\frac{3}{10} \times 19\frac{9}{10}$ in. – 286 × 506 mm)
Signed: William Callow 1874
Donated by the artist in 1879
Collection: National Gallery of Ireland, Dublin

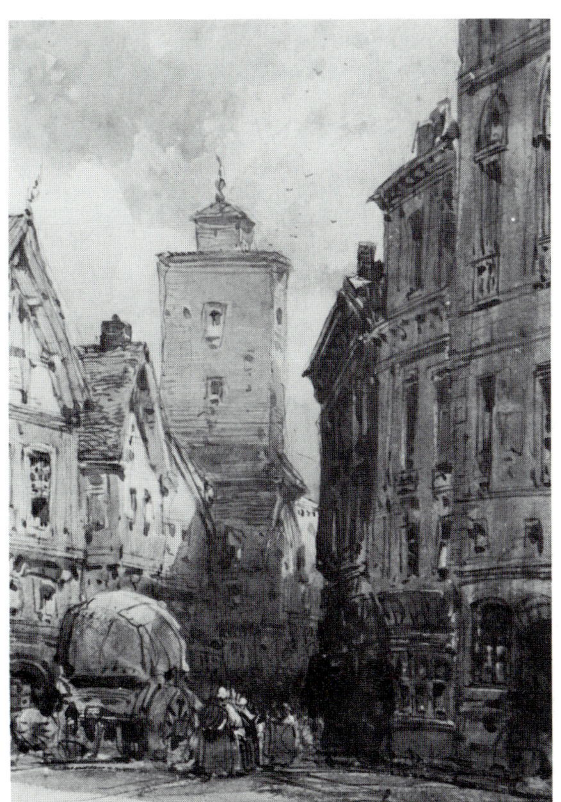

91. Demonstration sketch for a pupil, inscribed: *Done by Wm. Callow in a lesson to me I.G. when Conny Bayley 1870/75 or 6* Water-colour ($6\frac{1}{2} \times 9\frac{3}{4}$ in. – 165 × 248 mm)
Collection: Haswell Lamdin

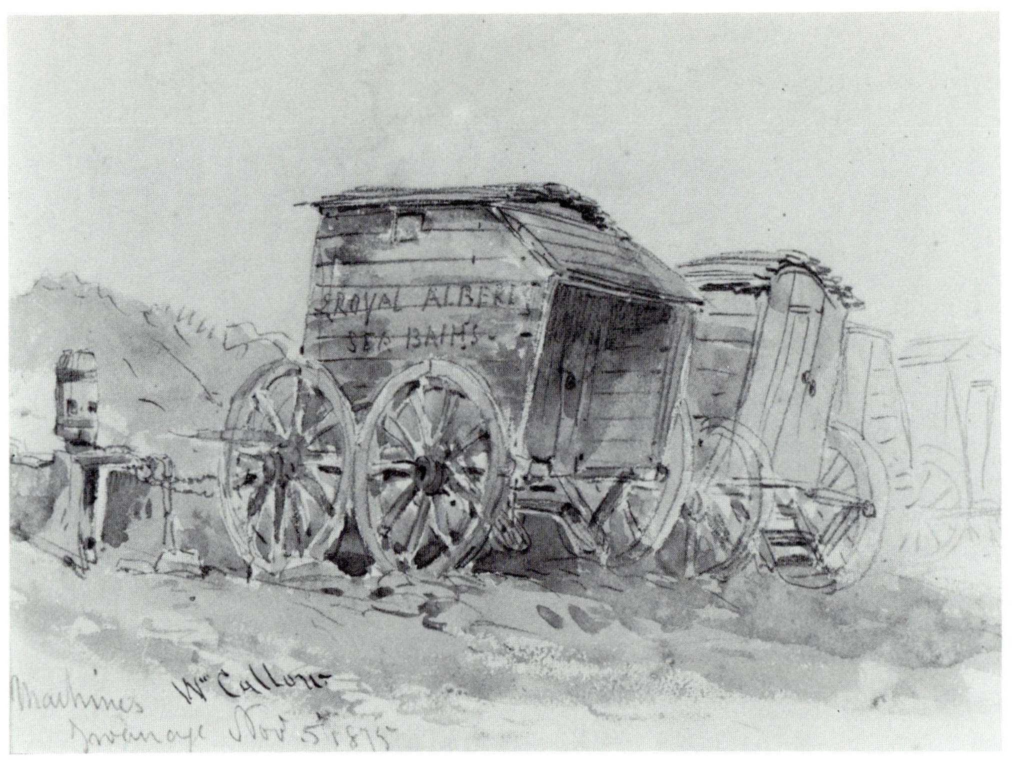

92. 'Bathing Machines, Swanage' Pencil and water-colour ($9\frac{1}{2} \times 7$ in. – 241×178 mm)
Signed: Wm. Callow. Inscribed and dated: *5 November 1875*
In possession of the Callow family

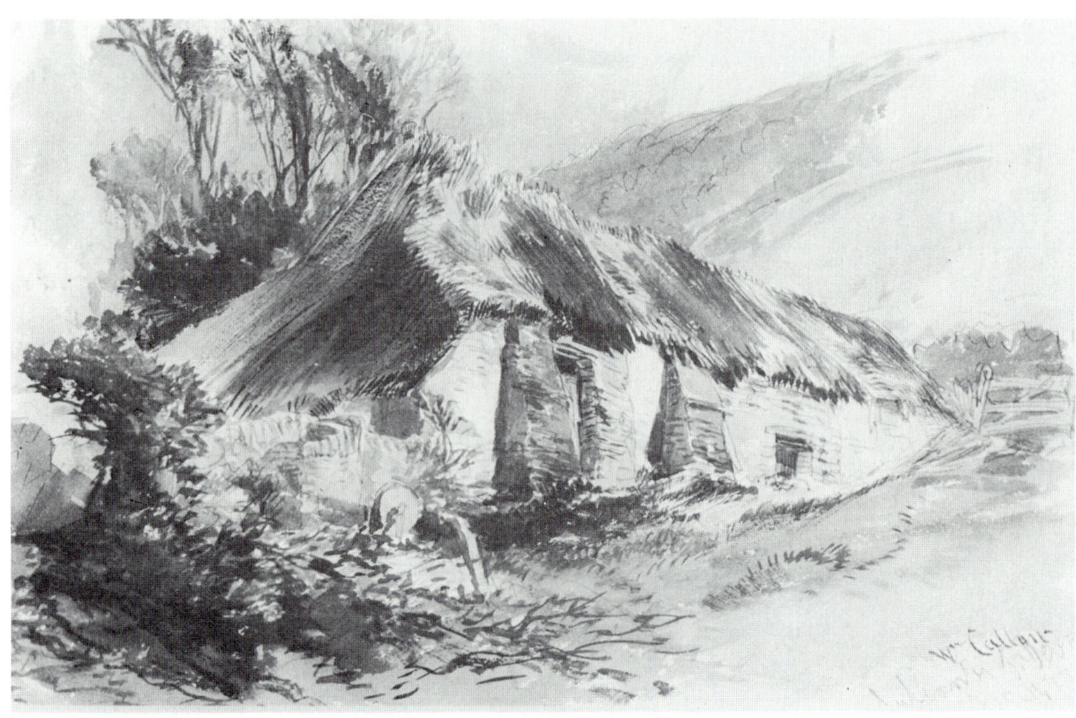

93. 'Cottage at Salcombe, South Devon' Water-colour ($9 \times 13\frac{3}{4}$ in. – 229×349 mm)
Signed: Wm. Callow. Inscribed and dated: *Oct. 15/1877*
Private collection
Photograph: Courtauld Institute of Art

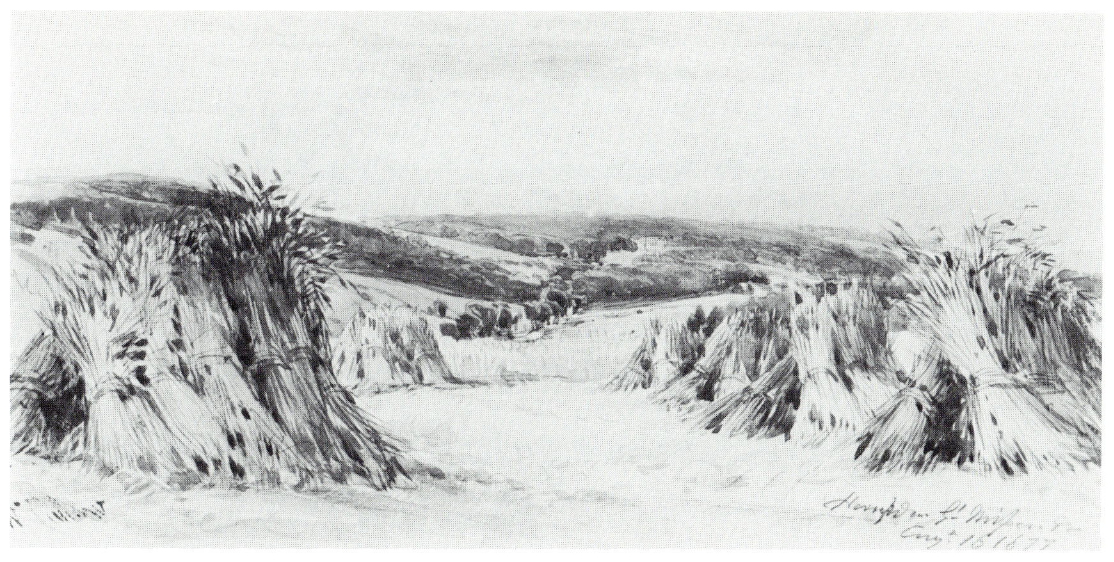

94. 'Hampden, near Great Missenden' Water-colour ($6\frac{1}{2} \times 13\frac{3}{4}$ in. – 165×349 mm)
Signed: Wm. Callow (left). Inscribed: *Hampden, Gt. Missenden August 16 1877*
By permission of the Trustees of the Estate of Miss Helen Barlow
Photograph: Courtauld Institute of Art

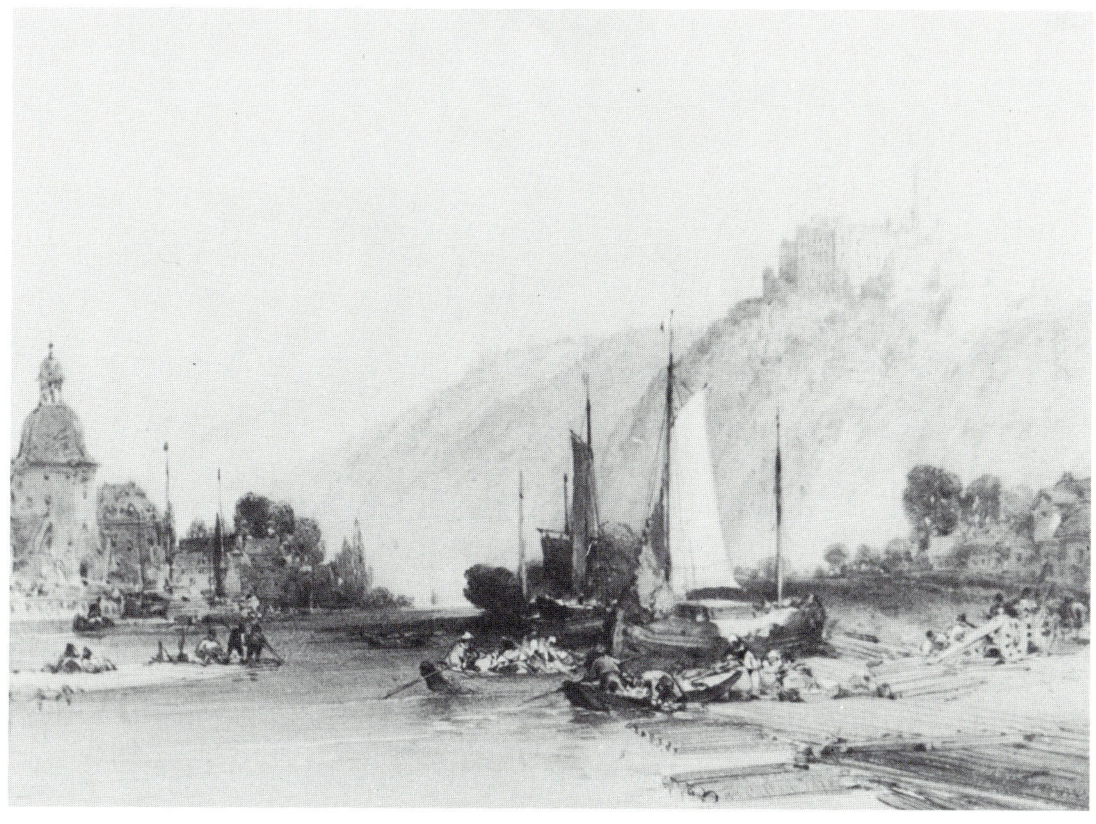

95. 'On the Rhine' Water-colour ($12\frac{4}{5} \times 18\frac{1}{2}$ in. – 325×470 mm)
Signed: Wm. Callow 1878 (on logs on river – right)
Exhibited: Society of Painters in Water-colours, 1879
Collection: Atkinson Art Gallery (Metropolitan Borough of Sefton), Southport

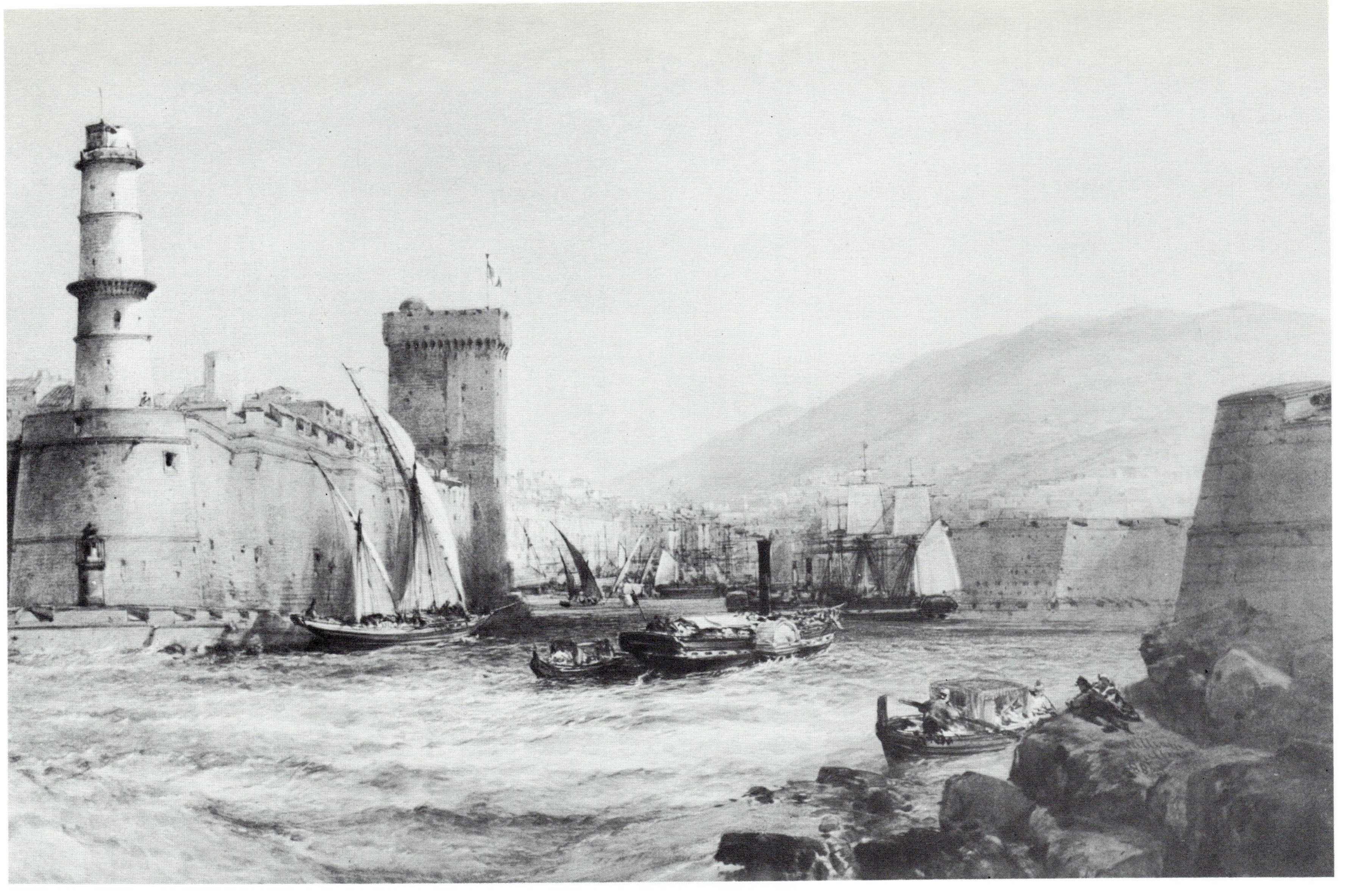

96. 'Entrance to the Port of Marseilles' Water-colour ($21\frac{1}{2} \times 32\frac{1}{2}$ in.) – 546 × 813 mm)
Signed: William Callow 1884
Exhibited: Royal Society of Painters in Water-colours in 1884; Whitworth Institute, Manchester, 1912, No. 218
Collection: Towneley Hall Art Gallery and Museums (Burnley Borough Council), Burnley

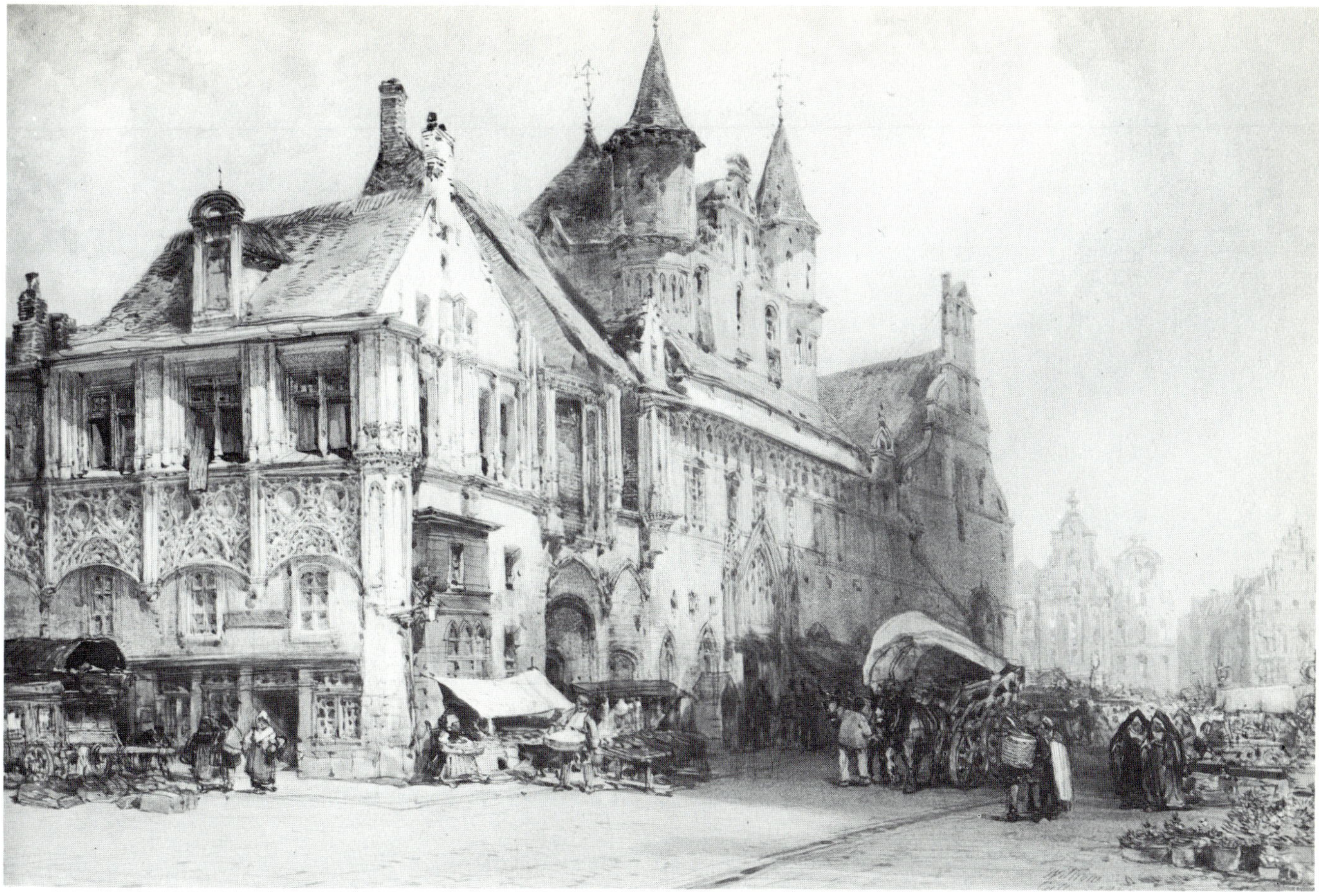

97. 'Market Place, Malines' Water-colour (30 × 20½ in. – 762 × 521 mm)
Signed: William Callow 1884
Illustrated in colour, facing p. 70, *William Callow*, edited by H. M. Cundall, 1908
Collection: The Lady Lever Art Gallery, Port Sunlight

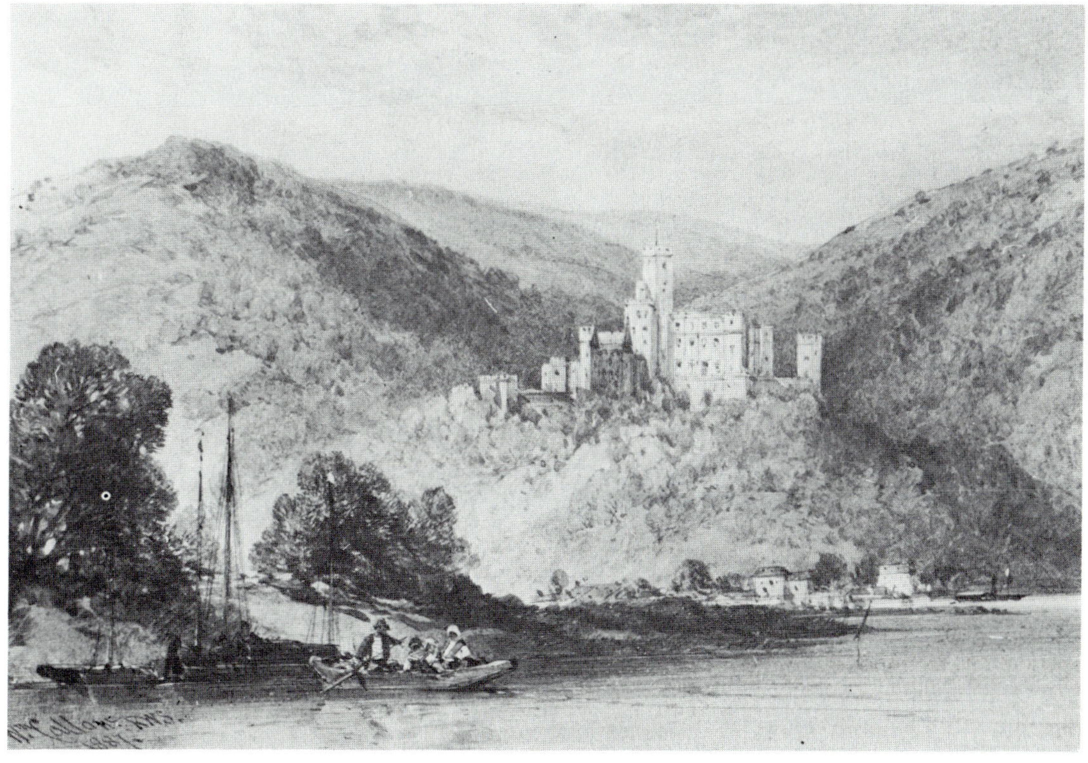

98. 'Stolzenfels on the Lahn' Water-colour (7⅜ × 10¾ in. – 187 × 273 mm)
Signed: W. Callow, R.W.S.. 1887
Included in an album of water-colour drawings presented to Queen Victoria by the R. W. S. to mark the 1887 Jubilee
Reproduced by gracious permission of Her Majesty the Queen

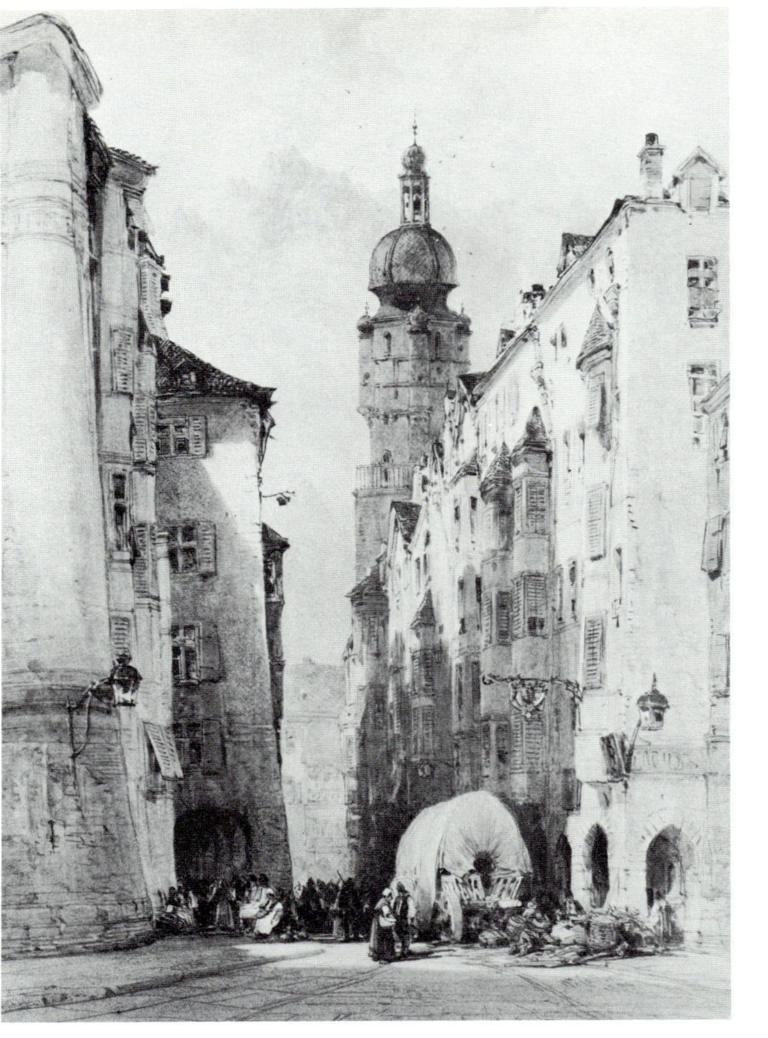

99. 'A Street Scene, Innsbrück, Water-colour
($25\frac{1}{2} \times 18\frac{1}{2}$ in. – 470×648 mm)
Signed: Wm. Callow 1888 (right)
Photograph: Sotheby Parke Bernet and Company

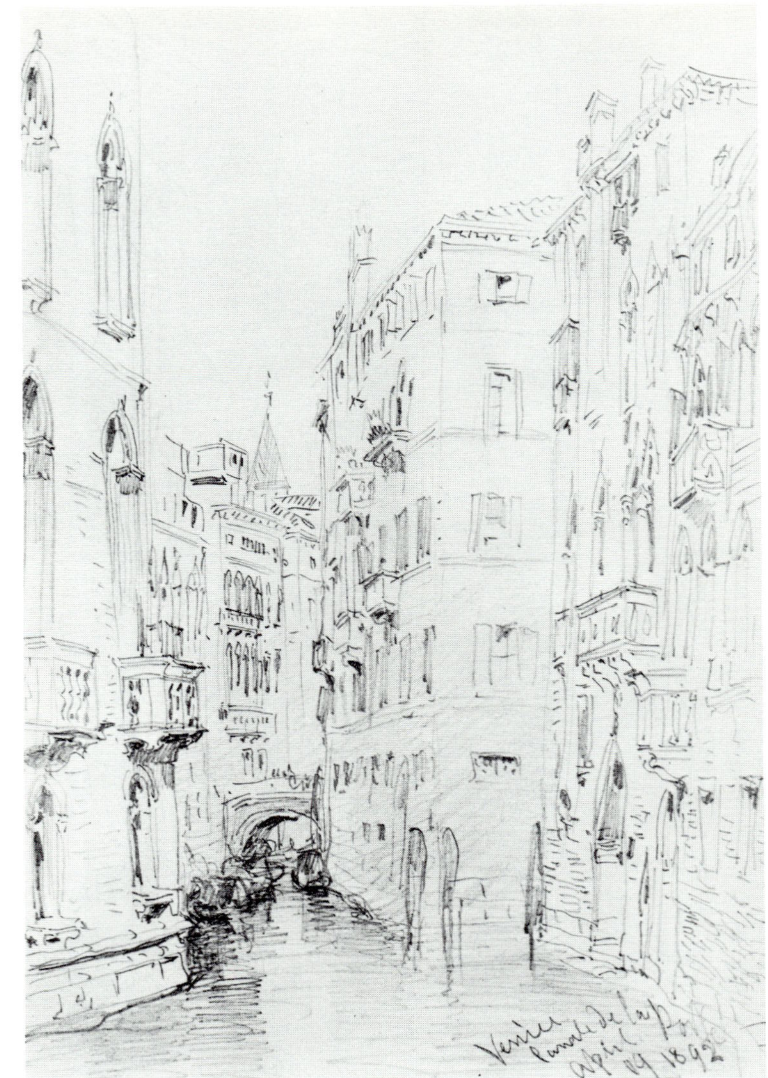

100. 'View of the Canale della Porta, Venice' Pencil on pale grey paper ($9\frac{9}{10} \times 7$ in. – 252×177 mm)
Inscribed in pencil: *Venice, Canale della Porta, April 19 1892*
One of Callow's last drawings of Venice
Reproduced by permission of the Syndics of the Fitzwilliam Museum, Cambridge

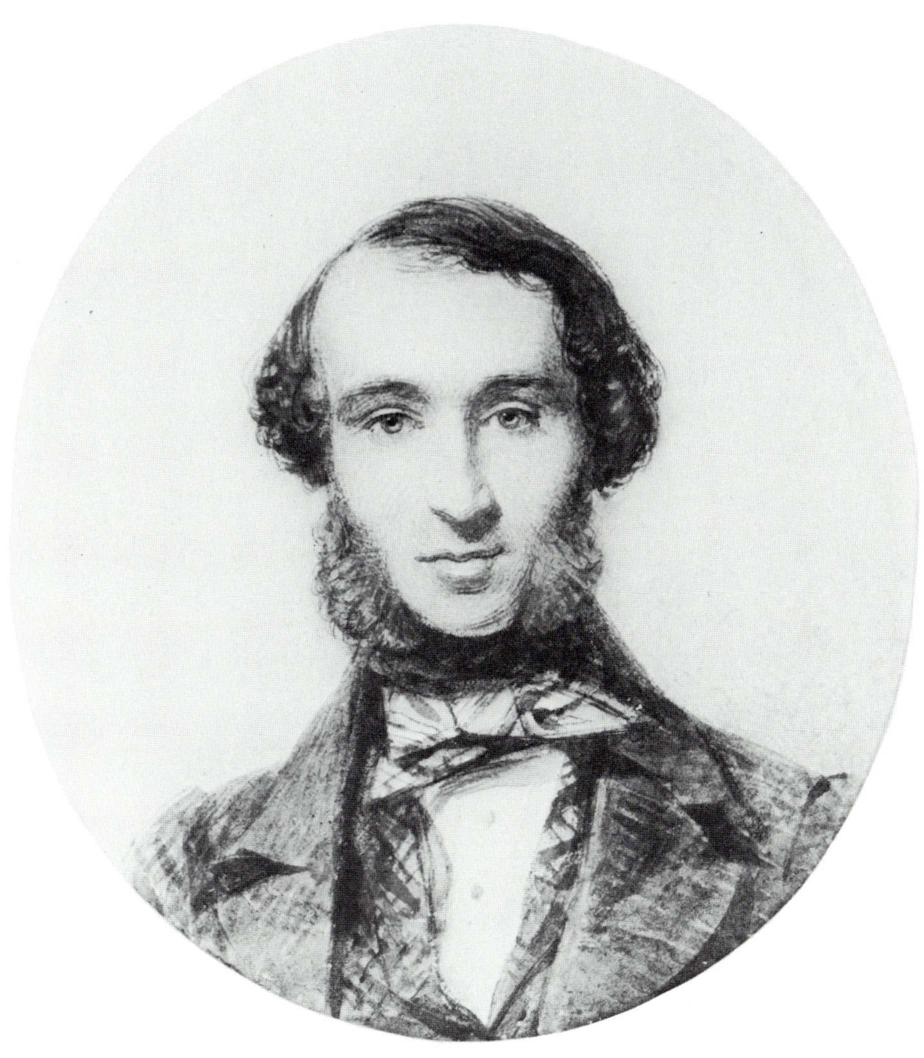

101. 'William Callow as a Young Man' Water-colour portrait (*see* text, page 158)
Collection: National Portrait Gallery, London

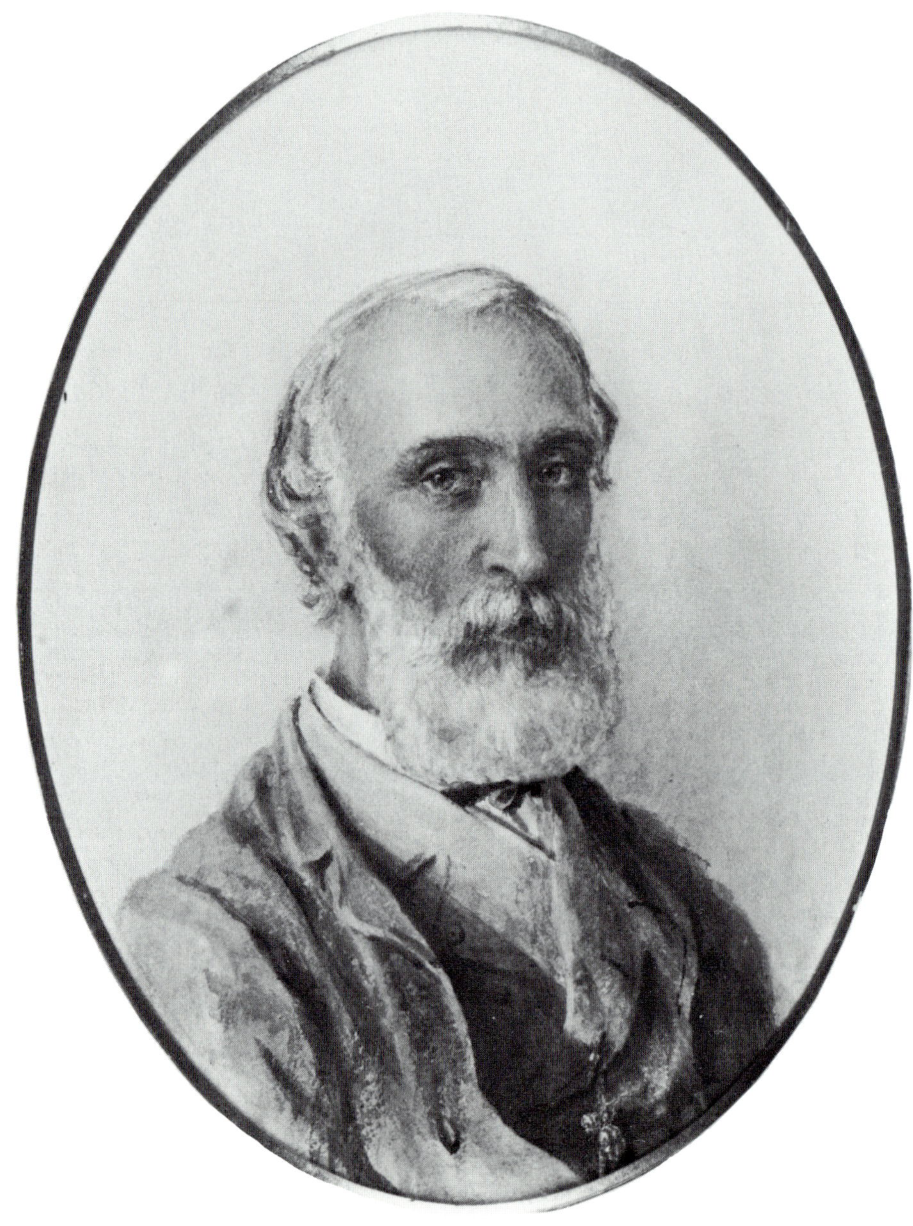

102. 'William Callow' Water-colour (6¼ × 4½ in. – 159 × 114 mm) – regarded as probably a self-portrait
In possession of the Callow family

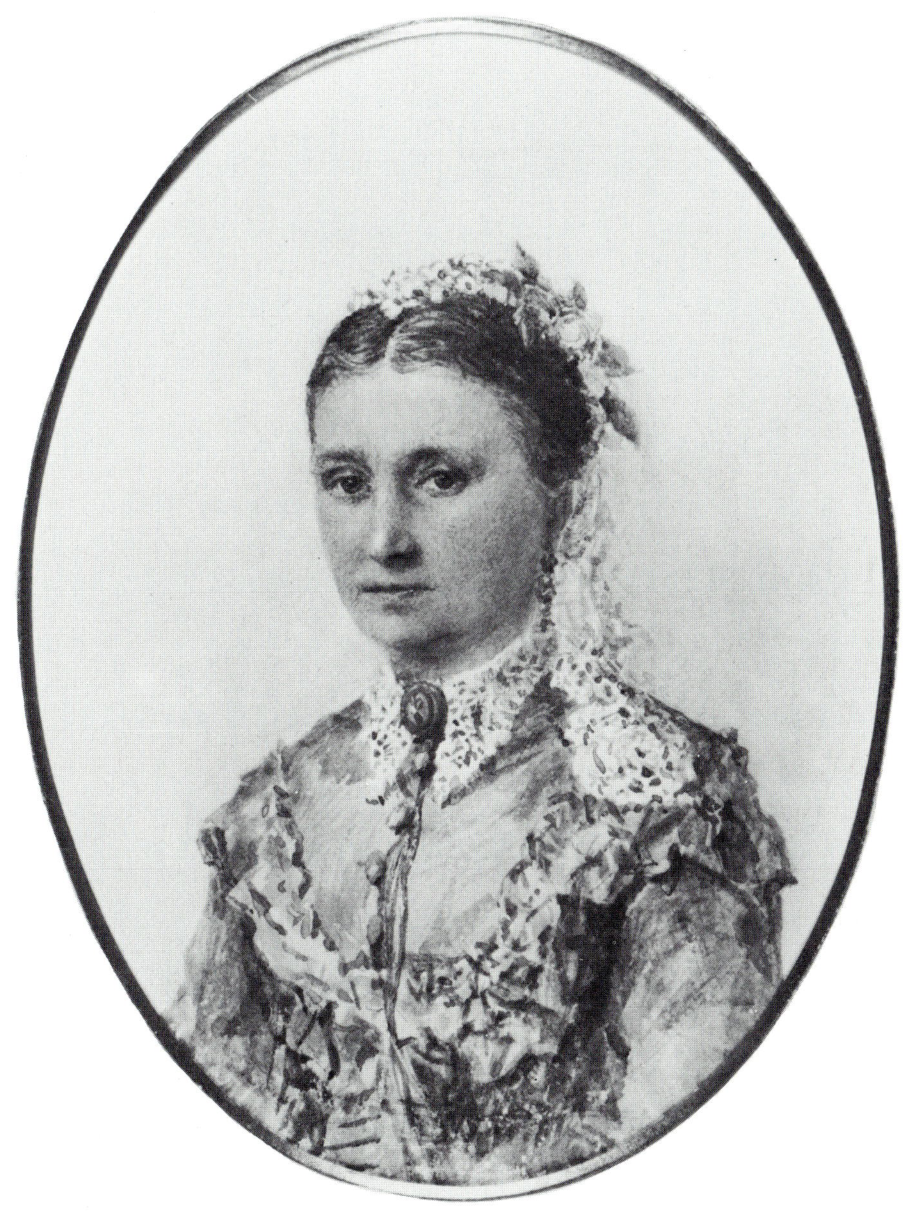

103. 'Harriet Anne Callow' Water-colour. Pair to opposite ($6\frac{1}{4} \times 4\frac{1}{2}$ in. – 159 × 114 mm)
In possession of the Callow family

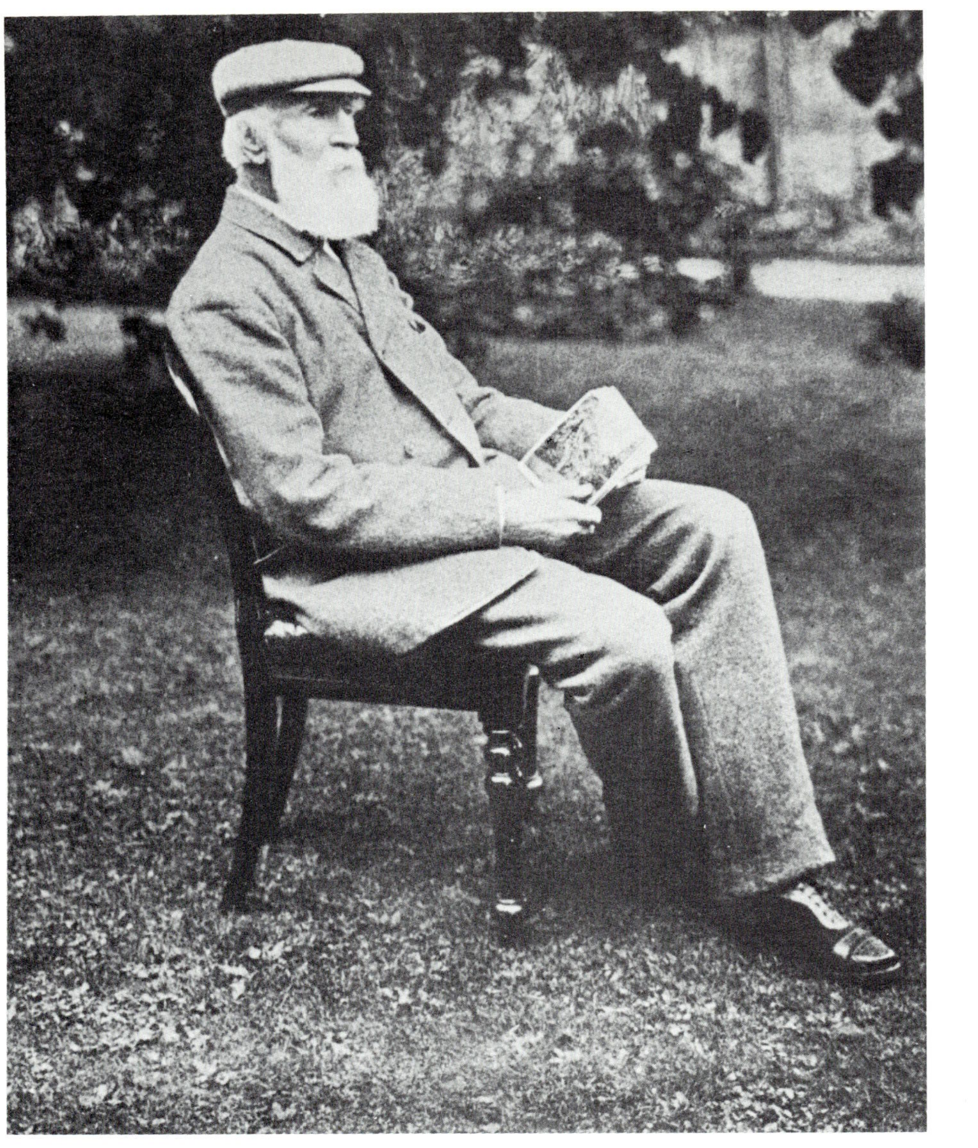

104. William Callow at the age of 86
Reproduced from *William Callow*, edited by H. M. Cundall, 1908

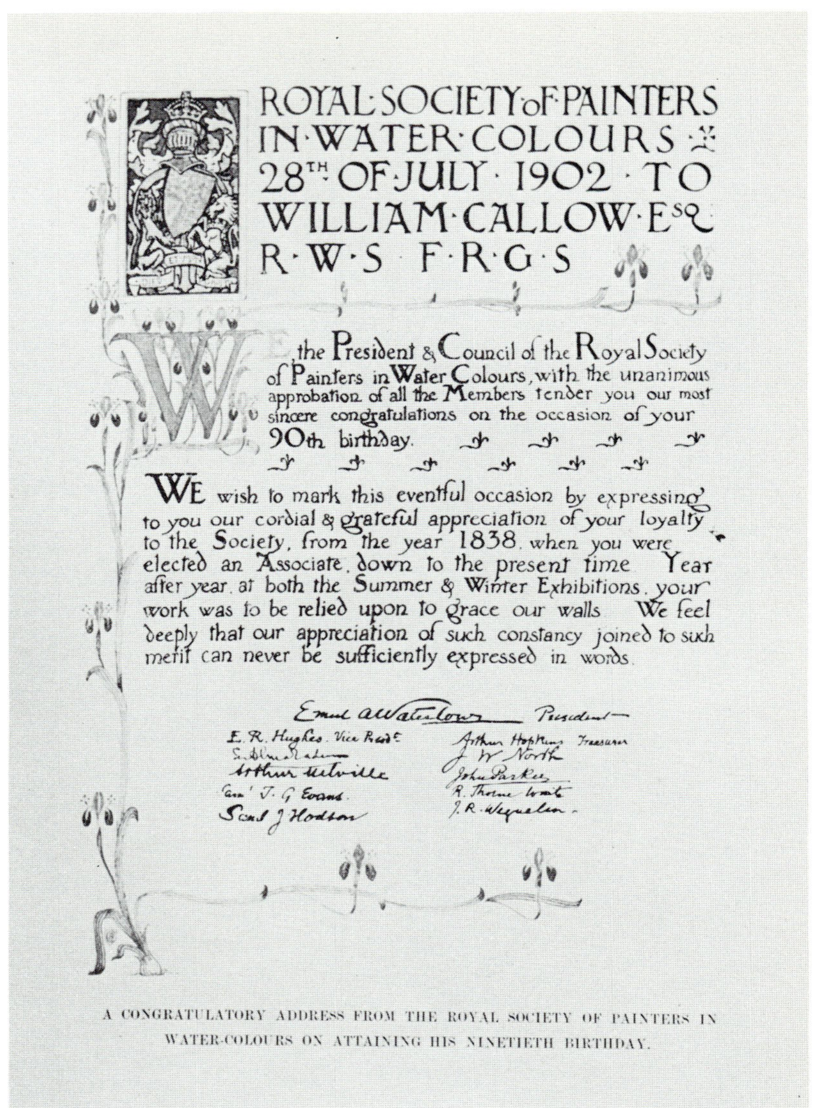

ROYAL·SOCIETY·OF·PAINTERS
IN·WATER·COLOURS
28TH OF JULY 1902 · TO
WILLIAM·CALLOW·ESQ
R·W·S F·R·G·S

WE, the President & Council of the Royal Society of Painters in Water Colours, with the unanimous approbation of all the Members tender you our most sincere congratulations on the occasion of your 90th birthday.

WE wish to mark this eventful occasion by expressing to you our cordial & grateful appreciation of your loyalty to the Society, from the year 1838 when you were elected an Associate, down to the present time. Year after year, at both the Summer & Winter Exhibitions, your work was to be relied upon to grace our walls. We feel deeply that our appreciation of such constancy joined to such merit can never be sufficiently expressed in words.

Ernest A. Waterlow President
E. R. Hughes Vice Presᵗ
Arthur Melville
J. G. Evans
Arthur Hopkins Treasurer
J. W. North
John Parker
R. Thorne Waite
J. R. Weguelin

A CONGRATULATORY ADDRESS FROM THE ROYAL SOCIETY OF PAINTERS IN WATER-COLOURS ON ATTAINING HIS NINETIETH BIRTHDAY.

105. Reproduced from *William Callow*, edited by H. M. Cundall, 1908

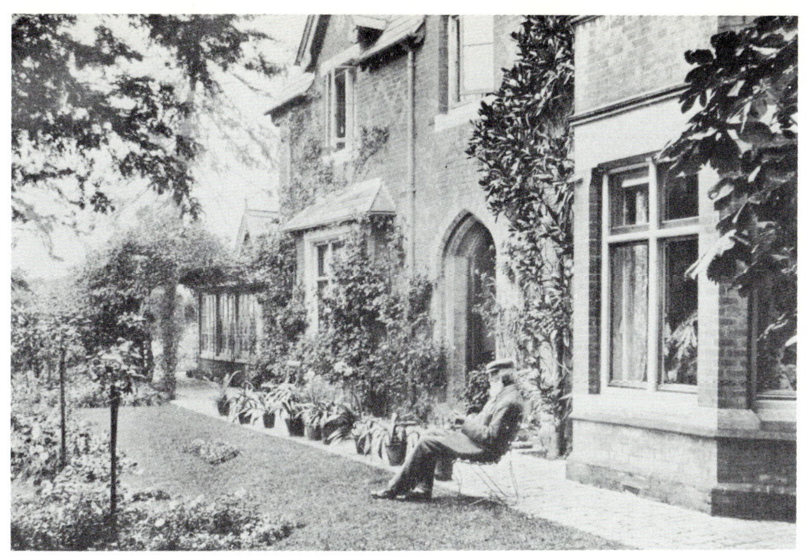

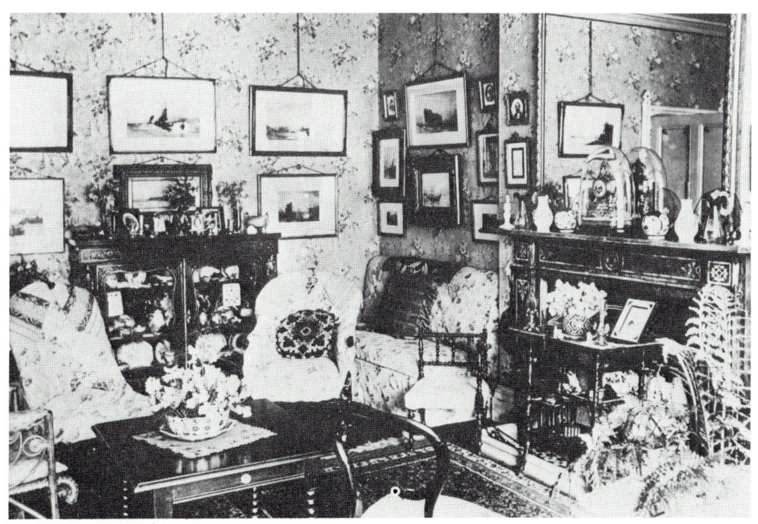

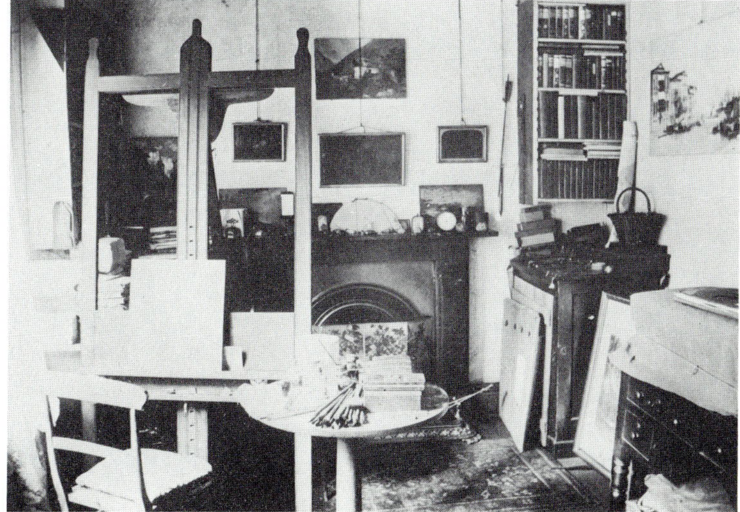

106. *(Top)* The Firs, Great Missenden: home of William Callow from 1861 to 1908
Reproduced from *William Callow*, edited by H. M. Cundall, 1908

107. *(Middle)* Sitting-room in The Firs, Great Missenden – note the portrait of Callow as a young man (left of mirror)
Photograph in possession of the Callow family

108. *(Lower)* Studio in The Firs, Great Missenden
Photograph in possession of the Callow family

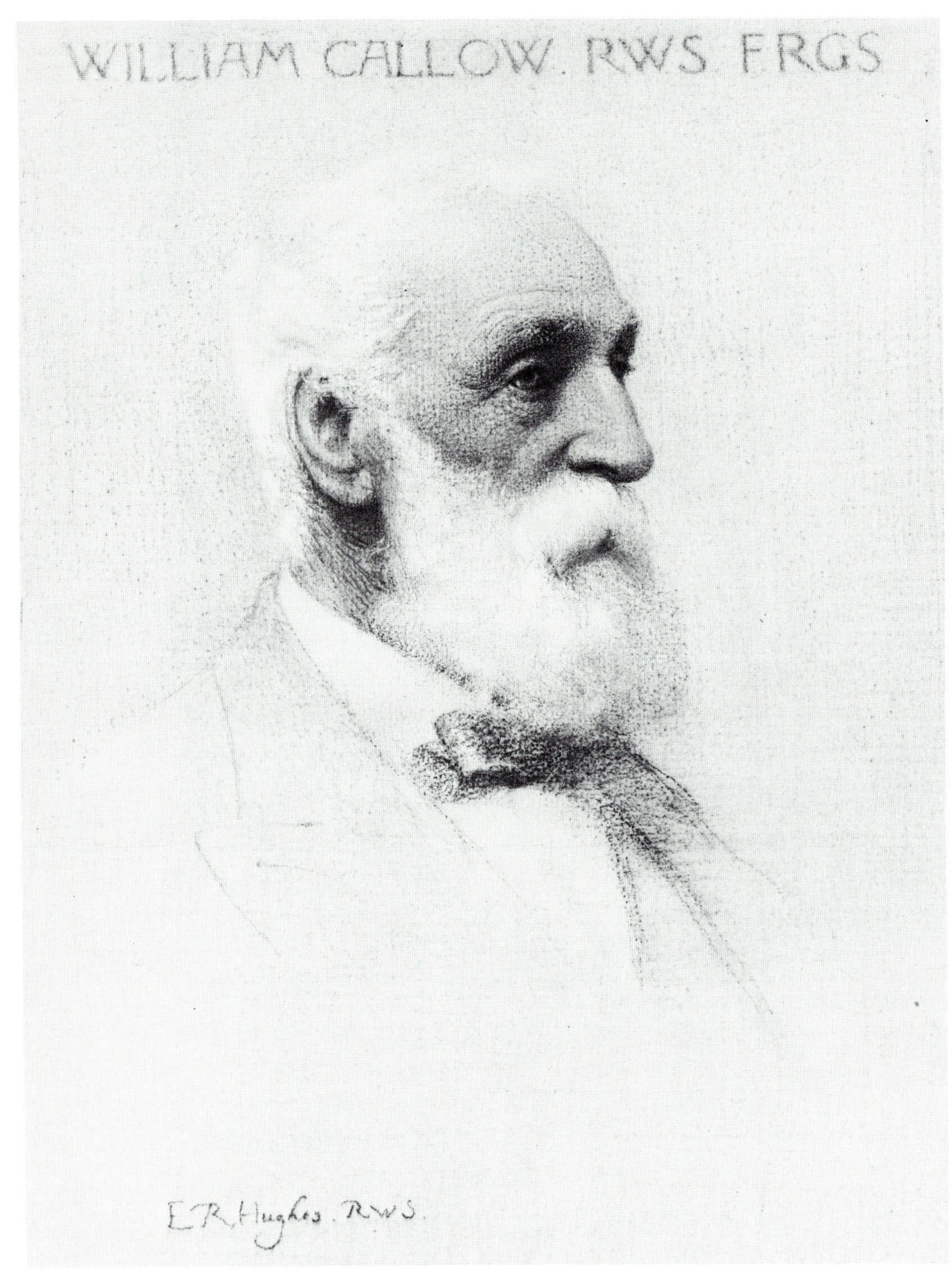

109. William Callow. Pastel. By Edward Robert Hughes, R.W.S.
Collection: National Portrait Gallery, London

in age and the fact that Callow was hardly out of official mourning for Harriet. The honeymoon was spent in Paris and Switzerland. Mary Louisa Callow, 44 years younger than William Callow, seems to have proved an excellent wife, devoted to her husband and extremely proud of his work.

Callow was nearly 72 years old when he executed 'Entrance to the Port of Marseilles', signed and dated 1884 (*illustration no. 96*). A fine example of late work, this was exhibited with the Royal Society of Painters in Water-colours in 1884 and is very similar to a work with the same title, which Callow had included with his first exhibits in 1838. The earlier water-colour was illustrated in *Christie's Catalogue*, 9 November 1971. The basic composition of the later work closely resembles the 1838 version, but Callow has treated this with a skill and enthusiasm, which renders it very much more than a mere copy. He has moved a central boat in the earlier work across to the right (at a different angle) and replaced this with the lively paddle steamer, which he had probably recently observed, while on his second honeymoon. Other details suggest that the topography of the later work gives an authentic view of Marseilles at the time, e.g. some alterations to the top of the lighthouse tower (left) have been added in the 1884 version. The sky has less incident, but, in the general arrangement of detail, the composition is an improvement. A deft manipulation of line and wash results in a water-colour of depth and atmosphere – an example that must refute generalisations as to the quality of the later work of Callow It is essential that water-colours of this period should be examined objectively, without regard to date.

'Market Place, Malines' (*illustration no. 97*), also 1884, is virtually a repeat of several previous versions of this theme, one of which (on a smaller paper – $10\frac{1}{4} \times 14$ in. – 260×355 mm) has the title 'Malines, Maison de Conseil' and is dated 'Sept 17.41, (photograph in the Witt Library). In the illustration example the awning, market stalls, horse and cart (probably modelled in one of the illustrated studies) and the trailing curtain are additions, the two nuns are from the earlier example, but now face out of the picture, instead of exactly opposite. These additions have introduced some extraneous fuss, typical of later versions of earlier work, but the mellow colour tones of the composition have harmony and balance, with the softly blended washes of the sky acting as a foil for the dominant lines of the buildings. The hand of Callow was far from failing, but his work could now be very variable.

In 1887, the Royal Society of Painters in Water-colours presented Queen Victoria with an album of 75 drawings to mark the fiftieth year of her reign. 'Stolzenfels on the Lahn' (*illustration no. 98*) was included in this Jubilee Gift. During the course of that year the whole set of drawings was on display at the Bethnal Green Museum with other Jubilee Gifts and subsequently went to Vienna for exhibition. Callow may have felt that a German Schloss would be a suitable choice of view, but his treatment of the theme is inclined to be tense and fidgety; yet 'Innsbruck', signed and dated 1888 (*illustration no. 99*), depicts a subject with all the freedom of many works executed 30 years previously.

Between 1884 and 1892, William Callow did not go abroad, although his travels included visits to Kent, Devon and Cornwall, the Lake District, Yorkshire and East Anglia. Sketches in possession of the Callow family show that William and Louisa must have spent the first three months of 1888 in Ramsgate. On 3 January 1888, Callow was sketching boats at Ramsgate and a sea-front scene at Broadstairs on 6 January. 'Low Water, Ramsgate', dated 9 January, is inscribed 'quite a summer day' and is of fishing boats, beached at an angle. The treatment is less crisp than from the hand of the younger Callow, but the details of the shipping are still acutely observed. The last Ramsgate sketch is dated 2 March 1888 and inscribed 'sunset'. In the following year they were in Devon and Cornwall. 'Torquay from our Hotel' is dated 'Sept 8, 1889'. 'Dartmouth Castle', 'Sept 9/89', recalls that Callow had first sketched there over 47 years before. He had now reached the age of 77, but was still very energetic, although the sketches give an impression of having been done from pleasant habit rather than with any intention of using them as working references. The Callows continued on into Cornwall, visiting Penzance, Newlyn and Marazion. One particular sketch has the rather touching inscription 'Land's End with Louie' – words that suggest a quiet happiness. A fascinating glimpse of the life of William and Louisa at home in The Firs can be seen in the photograph (*illustration no. 107*), showing the ordered paraphernalia of their cosy sitting-room. The crowded display of pictures on the facing wall appears to include a Charles Bentley; a portrait of Callow as a young man hangs to the right of the mirror, and slightly more to the lower left is the water-colour with a figure added by the Crown Princess of Prussia. Literally hundreds of works by Callow must have been painted in the studio at The Firs (*illustration no. 108*).

In 1892, at the age of 80, Callow felt that he wanted to see Italy once again:

> So, early in April, I started off with my wife on my last foreign tour to bid farewell to the many picturesque old towns which had raised so much enthusiasm in me more than half a century ago. We crossed from Dover to Calais and travelled all night direct to Basle. On the next day I went to the market place and made some sketches of the picturesque fruit and flower stalls with umbrellas over them. From Basle we proceeded to Lucerne, Milan, and Verona, stopping at each place to make some sketches. Finally we arrived at Venice and put up at our old quarters, Hotel Europa, facing the Grand Canal, where I had first stayed in 1840 and on each subsequent visit. On the evening of our arrival the hotel was serenaded by a party of singers in a gondola lit up by Chinese lanterns. Their singing was charming, and as they rowed away, followed by hundreds of other gondolas, the music became fainter and fainter until lost in the distance – a fairy scene only to be witnessed in Venice. After a fortnight of perfect enjoyment, intermingled with the pleasures of sketching, spending our days chiefly in a gondola [*illustration no. 100*] and visiting the Lido and the glorious shores of the Adriatic, we reluctantly left Venice, for myself at least for the last time....

William and Louisa Callow afterwards visited Bologna, Naples and Ancona. At Naples they stayed in an hotel overlooking the Bay. 'At night the scene, with Vesuvius on one side and Posillipo on the other, and the Bay flooded with moonlight was indescribably lovely.' The tour included Pompeii, Capri, Rome, Florence and Genoa, 'where we witnessed more cruelty to horses than in any other town in Italy and our appeals on behalf of the dumb animals were in vain'. While in Paris on the return journey, Callow visited an 'unattractive' exhibition at the Paris Salon. It was 58 years since Callow's 'Vue du point de Richmond' had appeared there, with his first exhibits at the Salon.

The work of William Callow does not usually present much difficulty as to signature. The sequence of illustrations in this book demonstrate a general chronological indication of typical signings.

Earlier work has the neat lettering as in *illustration no. 6*. The more characteristic flourish of the middle and later period is clearly indicated in many of the illustrations (e.g. *nos. 34 and 98*). He frequently used 'Wm' as the form of his first name. Monograms can be present at any date, but the thick, rather clumsily elaborate letters (as in *nos. 12 and 14*), which often read 'C.W.', are very much associated with a period about 1836. After this, the treatment of initials is much more delicate and crisp. Finished exhibition water-colours are usually signed, although this may not be immediately apparent, due to fading and changes in pigment. A sepia signature painted across the lines of dark paving stones or steps, planks of wood, etc., can become very much absorbed into such backgrounds. A total absense of signature or inscription on a work attributed to Callow suggests that it may be a demonstration piece, executed during the course of a lesson – or that it could be the work of Harriet Callow. In the latter case, indications of her style will almost certainly be present.

However, one undoubted complication with regard to the signature of William Callow has to be mentioned. Mary Louis Callow is thought to have persuaded Callow, in his old age, when his sight was even then failing, to sign more of his earlier work, particularly some of the slighter pieces. It can be accepted that Callow did this, but chiefly about the mid-1880s, when his signature was quite strong and reliable (usually in the Wm Callow form), but what must also be accepted is that it was Mrs Callow who later added the name of her husband to certain works, although her motives were not those of deliberate deception. She was a woman from a simple background who would not realise the implications of her actions. Any work on which a signature or inscription had been strengthened (often in ink over pencil) can be taken as having been subject to the misguided attempts of Mrs Callow to give better identification to her husbands' work. Unfortunately, she was not always correct in her reading of an original date and sometimes altered these to give an impossible result. It has to be realised that she was often handling work that had been executed many years before she was born. Items with a provenance that shows them to have been purchased in 1927 from Mrs Callow by Augustus Walker are liable to these additions and attempts at improvement, but are none the less genuine. An experienced fine art dealer should be able to discern such examples. A few attempts at a signature exist, giving a weak impression of the earlier style. These examples from the hand of Mary Louisa Callow have been attributed to the artist's failing sight, but the signature of Callow never retrogressed to that extent, but retained the essential flourish of the most characteristic style until the end of his life, albeit slightly less firm (*see* 'Piazza delle Erbe, Verona', 1903 – Whitworth Art Gallery). A more unfortunate connotation of the additions of Mrs Callow is the fact that she was not always able to distinguish the work of her husband from that of others of a similar style, whose drawings had been in his possession at the time of his death; the writer has knowledge of two such water-colour drawings, marked with the name of W. Callow. However, there is no cause for any real anxiety as to the genuineness of the majority of work appearing under the name of Callow. Mis-attributions from the collection of Mrs Callow are very limited and some have already been identified. It should be stressed that the many water-colour sketches that have the characteristic sepia signature, often with the 'Wm' form, adjacent to a pencilled inscription, with the appearance of this being a later addition, are perfectly correct signatures from the hand of Callow.

On his ninetieth birthday, William Callow was presented with an illuminated congratulatory address (*illustration no. 105*) from the President and Members of the Council of the Royal Society of Painters in Water-colours. If one compares the lettering with that of the pastel portrait (*illustration no. 109*) by Edward Robert Hughes, R.W.S. (1851–1914), it is evident that the illumination must have been the work of this artist, who was probably also responsible for organising the gesture. E. R. Hughes frequently visited Callow, referring to him affectionately as 'The Maestro'. The pastel portrait was a gift from Hughes to Mrs Callow, who was later to mention it, in a letter to the National Portrait Gallery (5 March 1929), as 'a speaking likeness which perhaps only Mr Hughes who knew my husband so well could have done'. A further portrait (in water-colours) was to be commissioned by Mary Louisa from E. R. Hughes, but he died before completing it and the work was finished by his uncle, Arthur Hughes (1832–1915), who had been one of the original followers of the Pre-Raphaelite Movement. This water-colour portrait was bequeathed by Mrs Callow to a niece of Callow, from whose daughter the work was eventually donated to the Royal Society of Painters in Water-colours. Water-colours by Callow of 'The Interior of St Mary's Church, Richmond, Yorkshire' (illustrated facing p. 108 – *Cundall*, plate in Witt Library files) and 'Market Place' are also in the collection of the R.W.S., which includes two volumes of *Sketches in England*, 1848–51, and *Sketches in France and Italy*, 1844–79.

The essentially Art Nouveau style of the birthday presentation is an apt link with the manner of the Water-colour Society at the turn of the century. Sir E. A. Waterlow was a painter in this style, so totally different from that of Copley Fielding, who had been President when Callow was first elected as an Associate. After 28 July 1902, it became the established tradition for members of the Society to visit the 'Grand Old Man' of water-colours on his birthday and also on New Year's Day.

In 1904, the Royal Society of Painters in Water-colours presented King Edward VII and Queen Alexandra with a collection of 59 water-colours, in order to commemorate their coronation. Wiliam Callow was represented by 'Camp St Angelo, Venice'. Obviously, every one of the other 58 works were from a completely different generation. Callow was now the only living exponent of a previous style and, as such, his life and work were attracting renewed interest. He had not only outlived his contemporaries, but also many younger innovators, including Burne-Jones and Birket Foster.

About mid-1906, it was suggested that H. M. Cundall should assist Callow with the writing of his autobiography. Louisa Callow read out all his old diaries to her husband and also carefully wrote down, practically verbatim, many anecdotes as told by Callow. Cundall collated this material into a straightforward, readable narrative, but one that is totally without footnotes or background information. As an autobiographical piece it cannot pretend to make an objective assessment of the work of William Callow. Most of the illustrations from this work (including 22 colour plates) can be seen in the Callow files at the Witt Library, Courtauld Institute of Art. James Callow, one of the two sons of John Callow, A.W.S., was asked to write some form of preface, but, as this proved to be a rather involved history of the ancestry of the Callow family, only the more immediate references were used, without actually acknowledging their source. James Callow was immensely proud of his uncle and wrote:

> High principle, noble bearing, unfliching courage, honour of the most uncompromising kind – these coupled with the gentler graces – amongst which is the gift of a versatile power of conversation – have been distinguishing features in his life: Devoted to his art, he has consistently set before himself a remarkably high ideal . . . but, alas! failing eyesight has deprived him of the power of depicting scenes which he has visited – and of which he has made elaborate sketches. He is even yet a remarkable man and no one would guess that he was born as far back as 1812. Possessed of a remarkably strong physique, he still walks – unaided by a stick, which he vehemently rejects – his five or more miles daily. His powers of memory are still unimpaired, and but for a deafness of the right ear he would still be able to sustain a conversation with the same vivacity of years long since gone by. . . . He can recall for the benefit of his guests almost every incident connected with his itineraries. In his most exquisitely beautiful and artistic home he is thoroughly at peace. Life to him is joyous and beautiful and he declares so happy has his life been that he could cheerfully enter upon it over again were the chance afforded him.

William Callow dictated a dedication for the autobiography: 'To my dear wife Louie, in recognition of her devotion and loving care of me during our twenty-four years of happy married life.' There can be little doubt that this second marriage had been successful, even if the wording of the dedication does suggest a father/daughter relationship, which must have been inevitable. It is interesting to note that in the autobiography Callow recalls his first wife as an excellent pianist, vocalist, linguist, etc., but never mentions her accomplishment as an artist, although it is obvious that this was an interest that they shared – and the real talent of Harriet is evident to anyone who has examined her work. The general portrayal of Harriet Callow is understated, apart from a constant impression of a woman who was never really well. This may be partly due to the circumstances in which the book was compiled, with the devoted Louie taking dictation and assisting H. M. Cundall with the editing. Harriet Callow, of higher social standing and sharing with her husband a talent for art, may well have been a source of unease to the second Mrs Callow. This would explain the reason why she appears to have ignored the water-colour miniature of Callow in later life (*illustration no. 102*) when asked immediately after his death, if a portrait existed. As this was one of a pair with a portrait of Harriet Callow (*illustration no. 103*) in matching frames, adorned with lover's knots, one can forgive the attitude of Mary Louisa. These small portraits were inherited by James Callow, under the terms of her will, although not specifically named, and have come down to his descendants as the work of Callow himself.

At the time of his retirement from teaching in 1882, it seems reasonable to estimate that Callow probably had a personal fortune of at least £30,000, but it has to be remembered that he was to live for a further 27 years. Over this period, his income from painting would be a fraction of what it had been at the height of his career. However, Callow always lived in comfortable circumstances at The Firs, where he employed several servants and a gardener – and continued to be known for his local generosity. Callow can never have been in any kind of financial difficulty, but about 1906, as a result of interest in the art world, he decided to turn out his portfolios and placed some earlier drawings on the market. These sold extremely well and led to the retrospective exhibition of 1907.

This was held at the Leicester Galleries (Ernest Brown and Phillips), Leicester Square, London, from October to November 1907.

> For the first time in an artistic career, extending over a period of about 70 years, the veteran painter, Mr William Callow, has been induced to hold a 'one man' exhibition ... between 60 and 70 of his water-colour drawings were displayed to the evident satisfaction of his numerous friends and admirers. For just 70 years he had been a member of the Old Water-colour Society, during which time he has sent to its exhibitions over 14 hundred drawings, some of which were again seen at the Leicester Galleries. Mr Callow has faithfully upheld the best tradition of the old British school of water-colour paintings and, as one of its last exponents, his work is always interesting to the student. [*The Studio*, p. 142, 1907.]

The Leicester Galleries exhibition was staged as being representative of work executed by Callow over the whole of his career, but in fact the catalogue shows a fairly high proportion of later work. Many of the most vital portfolio drawings would have been sold in 1906. The exhibition aroused considerable interest and was well reviewed:

> Its strength and charm, combined with an exceptional knowledge of technique, would make it remarkable whatever the age or period of the painter ... nonetheless, as a personal preference we find most interest in some of the early work, in which there is a broadness and ease of effect, joined to an economy of means, such as are less striking in the more ambitious and finished drawings. For example, the 'Grand Canal, Venice' (44) which is full of light and a seascape (39) which is a sketch that is full of air, are extremely suggestive and strong. In a later manner is a beautifully finished 'Nuremberg' and several mellow landscapes of English subjects, which have a rare charm of calm and peacefulness. A very large proportion of the subjects are of those picturesque corners of European cities, from Rouen to Rome, and from Nuremberg to Venice, which used to

be the shrines of the artist before picture postcards were invented. None is without dignity and nearly all have distinction.... [*Daily Graphic*, 1907.]

Callow himself almost certainly never fully realised the commercial value of a pencil drawing or simple sketch. 'Near Huddersfield', dated 1862 (*illustration no. 77*), fresh, lively and beautifully spontaneous, was shown two years before his death, when his sight had failed to the extent that he needed aid in selecting exhibits. In his heyday, Callow would not have considered such an example as a suitable exhibition piece. It was Mary Louisa Callow who appears to have had some grasp of the potential of such items.

Callow visited the Leicester Galleries exhibition on 26 October 1907. It was fitting that his last journey to London was made in order to be present at this culminating event in his career. William Callow, who had lived in five reigns and for over 50 years in Great Missenden, was now the oldest living British artist. He was still taking his daily five-mile walk and must surely have become a centenarian, but for an influenza infection followed by complications which he contracted less than four months after the exhibition.

William Callow died on 20 February 1908. The local obituary was long and detailed:

> ... he had an intense longing to live, his life having been throughout one of great happiness and simplicity, seeing beauty in everything and rejoicing in making others happy. His sweet resignation on hearing that his case was so serious was most touching: he bade farewell to those around him, thanking them for their kind attention to him and especially his valued friend of 45 years standing, Dr. J. F. Churchill.... [*Bucks Free Press*, 6 March 1908.]

The eulogistic style of this obituary may sound over-sentimental in terms of what would be published today, but there is an obvious tone of esteem and regret.

> His death cast quite a gloom over the neighbourhood, where he was greatly loved and revered; his nobility of character and charming personality endeared him to all who had the privilege of knowing him. By his poorer neighbours he will be sadly missed. Of his private generosity none will ever know, but he was generous to a fault, especially in cases of suffering....

These quotations present a much-shortened version of a very long tribute.

Sir E. A. Waterlow and many members of the Royal Society of Painters in Water-colours attended the funeral, and distinguished names (including Sir Lawrence Alma-Tameda) sent condolences, but a wreath from H. W. Higgin, who was the gardener, 'in remembrance of a kind master and friend' has equal significance in the story of William Callow with one 'from his old friend and pupil, Lady Anthony de Rothschild, the Dowager Marchioness of Headfort'. William Callow was buried in Great Missenden Churchyard on 25 February 1908. Mary Louisa Callow later had a marble memorial tablet placed in memory of her husband on the south interior wall of the Church of St Peter and St Paul, Great Missenden. A long obituary in *The Times* (24 February 1908) pointed out that Callow had been born as long ago as the year of Napoleon's Moscow expedition. After an outline of his life and career, this obituary comments on the quality of the portfolio drawings, so recently on the market:

> Fresh and sincere in character and beautifully preserved, they at once attracted attention, for here we had what we seldom see in the auction rooms, genuine 'Old English' drawings of the old school in brilliant and unfaded condition. Once more Callow became the fashion ... to cause intense gratification to the venerable artist whose intellect remained unclouded to the last, and who naturally rejoiced to see the public of the 20th century giving such cordial recognition to the work of his youth and middle age.

In 1906, the German periodical *Kunstchronik* had observed:

> The oldest member of the Water-colour Society, Mr William Callow, represents the old school with 'Foscari Palace, Venice', but to some extent his other exhibits form a connecting link with the modern style ...

It was a significant comment. The 1906 Callow exhibits were selected from a span of work over the previous 60 years, but his technique, based on sound methods and not influenced by extremes of art fashion, was one that had to be capable of a reflection in the work of later generations. The career of William Callow is firmly woven into the nineteenth-century British water-colour tradition, displaying qualities of integrity, craftsmanship and gentle charm which have ensured the continued recognition of this artist in our own time. Just as the personality of the man made him so well liked and respected in a very diverse circle, so has the quiet authority of his style become established, not only in the history of the period, but also in the appreciation of a wide range of collectors, for whom the work of this important Victorian water-colourist must always hold interest and value.

Appendix

Some Details of Events in the 30 Years Following the Death of William Callow

PROBATE DETAILS show that William Callow left estate valued at £60, but this can only have been a nominal sum. Certain legal records are not directly available, but it would seem that some kind of formal transfer of capital and property to Mary Louisa Callow was effected in 1886, including the deeds of The Firs. After the death of her husband, Mrs Callow was to continue living in their house for a further 29 years. During this time, she must have had a comfortable income, although she sold Callow drawings at regular intervals over that period.

In 1916, an article on William Callow by T. Martin Wood was published in *The Studio* (Vol. LXVII, no. 275, February 1916). The piece covered a wide area of familiar ground (and included some slight inaccuracies), but the very publication of such an article, only eight years after the death of Callow, confirms his acknowledged position as an important influence in British water-colour painting. 'Callow's water-colours', the article said, 'will always stand out from the later water-colour painting of his time, because he outlived those who practised the system in which he was educated and sustained tradition in spite of the incoming tide of the modern style.'

'A View of an Old Town ($9\frac{3}{4} \times 13\frac{3}{4}$ in. – 247×349 mm) by Callow (dated 1886) was Lot 1 in a sale of 48 works from the private collection of Sir E. A. Waterlow at Christie's on 6 February 1920. This work realised 25 guineas, a respectable price for a nineteenth-century water-colour at that period.

The major sale of works by Callow, in the first two decades after his death, was to Augustus Walker of Walker's Galleries, who acquired some 300 drawings and sketches from Mary Louisa Callow in 1927 (*see* catalogue details, page 242). These were published in *Walker's Quarterly*, April 1927, which also included a short appreciation of William Callow by Frank L. Emanuel, a man of decidedly excitable opinion, with regard to Modern Art, for which he had a choleric dislike. He extolled the merits of Callow, at the expense of the moderns, and concluded:

> ... I feel absolutely certain that those of our landscapists of today who will do the fine work that will live are those carrying on the tradition of the healthy school of British painting typified by Callow, and not those who imitate the work of a group of foreign decadents, who were sodden with absinthe and diseased in mind and body....

If Emanuel had only realised it, such extreme polarisation of opinion, not uncommon at that time, was almost certainly counter-productive and acted against the interests of the work of Callow and similar artists.

The portrait of Callow as a young man was donated to the National Portrait Gallery in 1929. This portrait had been noticed by H. H. Hake, Director of the National Portrait Gallery, during his visit to The Firs, in order to consider the E. R. Hughes pastel as a possible acquisition. A memorandum written by Hake, 18 March 1929, includes the note: 'I also saw hanging on the wall of the drawing-room, a slight sketch, head $\frac{1}{8}$th life-size, of William Callow done as a young man in Paris.' Mrs Callow acceded to his request that this might be donated to the National Portrait Gallery in a letter to Hake, in which she wrote: 'Yes, the small miniature done in Paris may be kept.'[1] In both cases, the wording of these references presents a certain ambiguity. The work is catalogued as by an unknown artist, but one cannot ignore the possibility that it might be a self-portrait. In 1929, Mrs Callow was 72 and rather frail. In her original letter (offering the pastel as a bequest under the terms of her will) she made no mention of the miniature, although she stated that she would be prepared to donate the Arthur Hughes water-colour at once (this she did not consider was such a good likeness as the pastel). The fact that she was subsequently prepared to part with a rare portrait of Callow as a young man does suggest that this did not hold for her a special sentimental attachment. William Callow had left Paris 16 years before she was born and the portrait was of a Callow quite outside her memory of the man to whom she had been married. Several possibilities are presented. By the time that Hake showed an interest in this miniature, Callow had been dead for 21 years and Mary Louisa had undoubtedly become a little confused in some of her recollections, e.g. she seems to have been under the mistaken impression that it was Sir Charles Holmes of the National Gallery who had interviewed Callow in 1907 as to his water-colour methods, instead of Roger Fry. She may well have forgotten that the miniature was a self-portait or (by her use of the expression 'done in Paris') been misinterpreted by Hake. The style of this work has definite hints of that of Callow (note the treatment of the clothes). The full-face representation is not likely to have been elected by an experienced portraitist (or by a painter who was familiar with the usual method of self-portraiture, i.e. employing two mirrors, placed at an angle). It could, however, have been painted from a direct mirror image by an artist who was used to working in reverse – a facility that Callow would have from his work as an engraver. There is no question of the miniature having been painted from a photograph, because the dates of Callow's time in Paris make this impossible. But, whatever theory one accepts as to the hand that painted this likeness, the work has about it a feeling of being a true and personal statement.

Mary Louisa Callow died at the age of 80 on 8 October 1937. Probate records show that she left an estate of over 15 thousand pounds (£15,536–14–3), an obvious proof that some financial arrangement had been made in her favour during the lifetime of Callow. Her sister, Bertha Jefferay, who was later to donate an album of sketches to the Buckinghamshire County Museum, was then also living at The

[1] Extracts from correspondence published by permission of the National Portrait Gallery.

Firs, which is not mentioned in the will, but would appear to have been already transferred to her name. An album of letters both to her husband and to herself was compiled by Mary Louisa, with a slightly over enthusiastic use of scissors and paste, reducing certain items to mere autographs, but showing that (in addition to some already mentioned in this book) correspondents had included such names as Walter Crane, Rackham, Tenniel, Goodall, Poynter, Leighton, Conan Doyle, Baden-Powell and many others of note. This album has only recently been traced, but has now returned to The Firs, having been purchased by the present owners, Mr and Mrs J. L. Wybrew, who also made available two separate letters in their possession.

Most other items of family interest were bequeathed to James Callow, including '... all family portraits, the framed writings of Queen Victoria in the Drawing Room ...' etc., but the diaries of William Callow were not included.

As acknowledged, some of the information and illustrations in this book are reproduced by kind permission of the Callow family, direct descendants of James Callow.

Catalogue of William Callow's Work

Catalogue of Work by William Callow in Public Collections

Victoria and Albert Museum, South Kensington, London SW7 2RL

Reference

661 A-E — **Souvenirs of Rosenau**
The birthplace of H.R.H. the Prince Consort, husband of Queen Victoria. Sketches (5) made in August 1863, during the visit by Callow to Germany (*see* text, page 106). Various sizes

1476–1869 — **Brig at Anchor and Boats alongside**
Watercolour (6⅝ × 9⅝ in. – 167 × 243 mm)
Signed: Callow
Townshend Bequest

1495–1869 — **On the Thames**
Water-colour (7¼ × 10⅛ in. – 184 × 257 mm)
Signed: W. Callow
Townshend Bequest

2988–1876 — **Coast Scene**
Water-colour (8⅝ × 14 in. – 229 × 354 mm)
Signed and dated: William Callow 1869
William Smith Bequest

3021–1876 — **Old Houses, Berncastel, on the Moselle** (*illustration no. 51*)
Water-colour (19¾ × 13¼ in. – 502 × 336 mm)
Signed and dated: W. Callow 1847

3060–1876 — **Market Place, Frankfort** (*illustration no. 78*)
Water-colour (13 × 19 in. – 333 × 483 mm)
Signed and dated: Wm. Callow 1863
William Smith Bequest
Exhibited: Society of Painters in Water-colours, 1863
An etching after this work is in the Department of Prints and Drawings – i.e. 'The Market Place 1863'. Etching by E. M. Wilson, 1906. R.C.A.L. 953–1916

1792–1900 — **Montrichard on the Cher** (Loir-et-Cher) – (*illustration no. 23*)
Water-colour (9⅛ × 12½ in. – 232 × 317 mm)
Signed and dated: W. Callow 1839
Exhibited: 'British Water-colours from the Victoria and Albert Museum', International Exhibitions Foundation, USA, 1966-7, No. 9
Ashbee Bequest

F 52 — **Leaning Towers, Bologna** (*illustration no. 84*)
Water-colour (16 × 12⅝ in. – 406 × 321 mm)
Signed and dated: Wm. Callow 1864

Exhibited: Society of Painters in Water-colours, 1864
Reproduced: *Building News*, January 3rd, 1913 (in colour); *The Connoisseur*, January 1925, facing p. 10; *Catalogue of Water-colour Paintings in the Victoria and Albert Museum*, 1927, Fig. 114
Forster Bequest

D 1839–1907 **Easby Abbey, Yorkshire**
Water-colour ($12\frac{1}{2} \times 19\frac{1}{2}$ in. – 317 × 496 mm)
Signed: Wm. Callow
Inscribed in pencil: Easby Abbey, Sept 20th 1853
Reproduced in *The Studio*, Vol. 67, 1916, p. 10 (*see* Appendix)
Illustration in the Witt Library, Courtauld Institute of Art

D 1840–1907 **The Town Hall, Bruges**
Water-colour ($13\frac{1}{8} \times 18\frac{7}{8}$ in. – 333 × 479 mm)
Signed and dated 1891
Exhibited: William Callow exhibition – Leicester Galleries, October–November 1907

P 2–1909 **View on the Serpentine, Hyde Park**
Water-colour ($9\frac{7}{8} \times 14\frac{1}{8}$ in. – 250 × 358 mm)
Signed and dated: Wm. Callow 1876 (but this is probably a mistake for 1846)
Donated by Mrs Mary Louisa Callow

P 3–1909 **The Serpentine, Kensington Gardens**
Water-colour ($10\frac{1}{8} \times 14\frac{1}{8}$ in. – 257 × 358 mm)
Signed: Wm. Callow
Inscribed in pencil and dated: On the Serpentine June 1877 (this date appears to have been inscribed by M. L. Callow at a later date and should probably read 1847)
Donated by Mrs Mary Louisa Callow

P 4–1909 **West End of the Serpentine, Kensington Gardens**
Water-colour ($10\frac{1}{8} \times 14\frac{1}{8}$ in. – 257 × 358 mm)
Signed: Wm. Callow.
Inscribed in pencil and dated: on the Serpentine June 1877 (probably a mistake for 1847)
Donated by Mrs Mary Louisa Callow

P 5–1909 **The Waterfall in Hyde Park**
Water-colour ($10\frac{1}{4} \times 14\frac{1}{2}$ in. – 261 × 368 mm)
Signed: Wm. Callow.
Inscribed in pencil with title and dated 1842
Reproduced: *The Studio*, Vol. 67, 1916, p. 9 (*see* Appendix)
Illustration in the Witt Library, Courtauld Institute of Art
Donated by Mrs Mary Louisa Callow

P 6–1909 **View in Hyde Park**
Water-colour ($10\frac{3}{8} \times 14\frac{1}{2}$ in. – 264 × 368 mm)
Signed: Wm. Callow
Inscribed in pencil: Hyde Park
Donated by Mrs Mary Louisa Callow

P 7–1909 **View in Kensington Gardens, showing the 'Temple' Cottage** (*illustration no. 34*)
Water-colour ($10\frac{1}{4} \times 14\frac{3}{8}$ in. – 261×365 mm)
Signed: Wm. Callow. Inscribed and dated: Kensington Gardens, June 42
Reproduced in *The Studio*, Vol. 67, 1916, p. 9
Donated by Mrs Mary Louisa Callow

P 8–1909 **View in Regent's Park**
Water-colour ($10\frac{5}{8} \times 14\frac{1}{8}$ in. – 270×358 mm)
Inscribed and dated in pencil: Regent's Park Sketch 1842
Donated by Mrs Mary Louisa Callow

P 9–1909 **View in the Botanic Gardens, Regent's Park**
Water-colour ($8\frac{3}{8} \times 12\frac{1}{4}$ in. – 213×311 mm)
Title inscribed in pencil, dated: June 1857
Reproduced: *The Studio*. Vol. 67, 1916, p. 10 (*see* Appendix)
Donated by Mrs Mary Louisa Callow

P 10–1909 **View in the Botanic Gardens, Regent's Park**
Water-colour ($8\frac{3}{8} \times 12\frac{1}{4}$ in. – 213×311 mm)
Signed: Wm. Callow
Inscribed in pencil with title and dated: May 1857
Donated by Mrs Mary Louisa Callow

P 11–1909 **View on the Serpentine, Hyde Park**
Water-colour ($10\frac{1}{4} \times 14\frac{1}{2}$ in. – 259×368 mm)
Signed: Wm. Callow.
Inscribed in pencil with title and dated: On the Serpentine, July 7 1841
Donated by M. L. Callow

P 12–1909 **Entrance to Hyde Park at Hyde Park Corner** (*illustration no. 35*)
Water-colour ($10\frac{1}{4} \times 14\frac{1}{2}$ in. – 259×368 mm)
Signed: Wm. Callow
Inscribed in pencil and dated: Hyde Park 1842
Exhibited: International Exhibitions Foundation, USA, 1966–7; Thomas Shotter Boys, Centenary Exhibition, Nottingham University, 1974
Donated by M. L. Callow

P 13–1909 **West End of the Serpentine, Kensington Gardens**
Water-colour ($10\frac{1}{2} \times 14\frac{1}{4}$ in. – 267×361 mm)
Signed: Wm. Callow
Inscribed in pencil and dated: End of Serpentine 1842
Donated by Mrs Mary Louisa Callow

P 71–1919 **The Keep at Kenilworth**
Water-colour ($13 \times 9\frac{1}{2}$ in. – 330×242 mm)
Signed: W. Callow
Inscribed in pencil with title and dated: July 30 1856
Bernard H. Webb Bequest

E 3953 – Worcester: The Cathedral seen from the River
Water-colour (9¾ × 13⅞ in. – 248 × 352 mm)
Signed: Wm. Callow
Inscribed in pencil and dated: Worcester 1848
Bernard H. Webb Bequest

E 3954 – 1919 **Arundel Castle**
Water-colour (9⅞ × 13⅞ in. – 251 × 352 mm)
Signed: Wm. Callow
Bernard H. Webb Bequest

P 31 – 1934 **Distant View of Paris**
Water-colour (6⅛ × 9⅝ in. – 156 × 245 mm)
Signed: W. Callow
Bequeathed by Edith, Lady Powell

P 36 – 1939 **The Rue de Rivoli, near the Tuileries, Paris** (*illustration no. 6*)
Water-colour (8⅞ × 6¼ in. – 225 × 158 mm)
Signed and dated: W. Callow 1831
Preparatory drawings for this work are included in the volume of sketches: E. 880, 881 – 1937.
Exhibited: Carnavelet Museum, Paris ('Paris Romantique'), 1957; Thomas Shotter Boys Centenary Exhibition, Nottingham University, 1974

P 9 – 1953 **San Giorgio, Venice**
Water-colour (8¾ × 13⅞ in. – 222 × 352 mm)
Signed and dated: Wm. Callow 1883(?)
Inscribed on the back no. 8 St Giorgio
Bequeathed in memory of Alexander Allan Paton, C.B., by his sister, Mary Paton

P 47 – 1955 **All Hallows Church, Worcester**
Water-colour (7 × 10¼ in. – 178 × 261 mm)
Signed: W. Callow
Inscribed with title and dated: Sep 1.48
Bequeathed by Lewis Downing Pither

P 48 – 1955 **Goodrich Castle, Herefordshire**
Water-colour (7 × 10½ in. – 177 × 266 mm)
Signed: W. Callow
Inscribed with title and dated 1848
Bequeathed by Lewis Downing Pither

P 35 – 1960 **South East Aspect of the 1862 Exhibition Building, looking along Cromwell Road, with a Corner of the South Kensington Museum Gardens visible at the right**
Water-colour (13¼ × 20¼ in. – 333 × 506 mm)
Signed (indistinctly): W. Callow

P 8 – 1968 **Wimbledon Common**
Water-colour on sugar paper (7 × 19 in. – 178 × 493 mm)
Signed: W. Callow
Inscribed: Wimbledon, May 7.51
Given by the National Art Collections Fund from the Herbert Powell Bequest

P 8–1968 **Malines, Maison de Conseil**
Water-colour on sugar paper (7 × 19 in. – 178 × 493 mm)
Signed: Wm. Callow

Album: Sketches
(196) dated 1829–40, made in Paris and its environs or during walking tours in Normandy, Touraine, the Pyrénées, the south of France, Switzerland and Germany
Pencil, wash and water-colour. E 847 – 1041 and E 876A – 1937

John Callow

Hastings, from the rocks at low water
Pencil

Tenby, from Monkestone Bay
Pencil

Cottages, landscapes etc.
23 pencil drawings

Landscapes (2) – pencil, tinted with water-colour

Venice – pencil

Lake and mountain scenery (2) – pencil

Landscapes (2) – pencil

Falmouth: Pendennis Castle, with shipping
Pencil

Running into Falmouth: Shipping
Pencil

Mounts Bay, Cornwall, bringing to for a pilot
Pencil

The Mumbles, with shipping
Pencil

Coast scenes, with shipping – pencil

Coast scenes and shipping (6) – pencil

Studies of trees (5) – pencil

A Hilly Landscape
Pencil and water-colour ($6\frac{7}{8} \times 9\frac{1}{2}$ in. – 174 × 241 mm)
Signed in pencil, J. Callow. E 3196 – 1922

Bamborough Castle
Water-colour
Inscribed in pencil: J.C., Bamborough Castle/from the West/John Callow, July 31/71

THE TATE GALLERY, Millbank, London SW1P 4RG

Reference
2435 **Richmond Castle, Yorkshire** (*illustration no. 76*)
Water-colour
Signed: Wm. Callow
Inscribed: Richmond Castle, Oct. 3, 1853 (appears to read 1848)

2436 **Grand Canal, Venice**
Water-colour and pencil
Signed: W. Callow
Inscribed: Venice, Gd Canal, May 4/1880
Both works presented to the gallery by the artist's widow in 1909

Twenty-six sketches of Continental scenes
Bought from Mary Louisa Callow in 1912

1 St Michael's Church and Belfry Tower, Ghent (1844) (10⅛ × 14½ in. – 257 × 368 mm)
2 St Paul's Church, Antwerp (1844) (10⅛ × 14¼ in. – 257 × 361 mm)
3 Citadel, Namur (1844) (10⅛ in. × 14¼ in. – 257 × 361 mm)
4 Wharf and Groote Kerk, Rotterdam (1845) (10⅜ × 14¼ in. – 263 × 361 mm)
5 Vegetable Market, Ghent (1846) (10⅜ × 14⅜ in. – 263 × 365 mm)
6 Frankfort (1846) (10⅜ × 14⅜ in. – 263 × 365 mm)
7 Frankfort (1846) (10⅜ × 14⅜ in. – 263 × 365 mm)
8 Market Place and St Sebald's, Nuremberg (1846) (10⅜ × 14⅜ in. – 263 × 365 mm)
9 Frauenkirche, Nuremberg (1846) (10⅜ × 14⅜ in. – 263 × 365 mm)
10 Maximilianstrasse, Augsberg (10⅜ × 14⅜ in. – 263 × 365 mm)
11 Innsbrück (1846) (10⅜ × 14⅜ in. – 263 × 365 mm)
12 Botzen (1846) (10⅜ × 14⅜ in. – 263 × 365 mm)
13 Place St Pharaïlde, Ghent (1850) (10⅜ × 14⅜ in. – 263 × 365 mm)
14 Palais de Justice, Malines (1850) (10⅜ × 14¼ in. – 263 × 361 mm)
15 Rathaus, Hanover (1852) (10 × 13¾ in. – 254 × 349 mm)
16 Market Place, Leipzig (1852) (10 × 13¾ in. – 254 × 349 mm)
17 Royal Palace, Dresden (1852) (10 × 13¾ in. – 254 × 349 mm)
18 Rathaus, Gotha (1852) (10 × 13¾ in. – 254 × 349 mm)
19 Rathaus, Eisenach (10 × 13¾ in. – 254 × 349 mm)
20 Moselle Quai (1860) (10⅜ × 14⅜ in. – 263 × 365 mm)
21 Cochem, Moselle (1860) (10⅜ × 14⅜ in. – 263 × 365 mm)
22 Fountain at Coburg (1863) (9¾ × 13⅝ in. – 247 × 346 mm)
23 Grand Place and Market, Coburg (1863) (9⅞ × 13¾ in. – 250 × 349 mm)
24 Old Houses, Giessen (1871) (9¾ × 13⅝ in. – 247 × 346 mm)
25 Feinkirche, Prague (1874) (9¾ × 13¾ in. – 247 × 349 mm)
26 Old Streets, Prague (1874) (9¾ × 13⅝ in. – 247 × 346 mm)

THE BRITISH MUSEUM, DEPARTMENT OF PRINTS AND DRAWINGS, London WC1B 3DG

The folder of water-colours and pencil drawings by William Callow in the collection includes the following:

An Avenue
Signed and inscribed July 14. Purchased from the Florence Fund

St Winifred, Holywell
Inscribed 'Oct 17, 1866' in pencil and signed in water-colours. Purchased from the Florence Fund

Cochem
Dated 1844. Inscribed in pencil and signed in water-colour. Presented by Miss E. P. McGhee. This water-colour is probably as mentioned in the *Athenaeum*, 3 May 1845 – 'Mr W. Callow has been on the Moselle; his "Cochem" is dim and smoky in tone, but otherwise a clever drawing'

Small coastal view with cliffs, unsigned. From the collection of F. J. Nettleford. (Also coloured reproduction in the print folder, entitled **Fishing Boats off the Headland**)

Large pencil drawing, inscribed **Corfu de Gardi, Grand Place Lille** – Sept 6, 1880. Purchased from the Florence Fund
Two very small pencil drawings, inscribed **Goodrich Castle** and **Abergavenny after my sketch** – presented by Mrs Ball

In the print folder:

Two small black and white engravings of Venice

Bay of Naples (*illustration no. 59*)

Sepia engravings of **Whale fishing,** engraved by Sigismund Himely, published Paris

Sepia engraving of **Whiting fishing,** engraved by Sigismund Himely, published in Paris (*see* text, page 18)

Coloured reproduction of **Evreux** (see Southampton Art Gallery)

Coloured reproduction of **Fishing Boats off the Headland**
Black and white engravings from the *Picturesque Annual* series, (*see* text, pages 66–7)

Versailles from the Heights of Satory – engraved J. Saddler

The Garden of Versailles – engraved S. Bradshaw

The Palace of Versailles from the Paris Avenue – engraved S. Fisher

The Lake and Hamlet of Trianon – engraved S. Fisher

The Basin of Neptune, Versailles – engraved W. Watkins

The Canal of Trianon – engraved E. Radclyffe

National Maritime Museum, Greenwich, London SE10 9NF

A Fishing Boat at Naples
Water-colour ($9\frac{1}{8} \times 14$ in. – 231×355 mm)
Signed: Wm. Callow
Inscribed: 'Drawing purchased by Prince Albert in 1841' and 'Bateau pêcheur 17 October 1840'

A Stern View of Two Fishing Boats on the Beach at Lowestoft (*illustration no. 26*)
Water-colour ($14\frac{1}{8} \times 10\frac{1}{8}$ in. – 358×257 mm)
Signed: Wm. Callow
Inscribed: On the beach/Lowestoft Sept. 17.39. (last figure appears to have been strengthened at a later date)

University of London, Courtauld Institute Galleries, Woburn Square, London WC1H 0AA

Inventory no. 6 **Salerno**
Water-colour over pencil ($6\frac{5}{8} \times 13\frac{7}{8}$ in. – 168×354 mm)
Signed, lower left: W. Callow
Inscribed, bottom right: Salerno, May 12/79
William Spooner Collection – Spooner Bequest, 1967

Inventory no. 107 **St Valéry en Caux** (*illustration no. 30*)
Pencil and water-colour and touches of white body-colour on very light grey paper
Inscribed in pencil, in the artist's hand, bottom right: St Valéry en Caux/ Sept 25.41
William Spooner Collection – Spooner Bequest, 1967

Witt no. 4297 **Berncastel on the Moselle**
Pencil and water-colour (20 × 13$\frac{1}{8}$ in. – 508 × 333 mm)
Signed in brush, bottom left: Wm. Callow
Inscribed in pencil in artist's hand: Berncastel, Moselle/Oct. 15.44
Collection: Sir Robert Witt – Witt Bequest, 1952

THE WALLACE COLLECTION, Manchester Square, London W1M 6BN

Reference
P 746 **Entering the Harbour** (*illustration no. 36*)
Water-colour on paper (9$\frac{1}{4}$ × 12$\frac{1}{2}$ in. – 230 × 320 mm)
Signed and dated, lower right: W. Callow 1842
Exhibited: Bethnal Green, 1874–5 (No. 684) as 'French Fishing Boats' (this title was on the old mount)

THE CITY OF ABERDEEN ART GALLERY, Schoolhill, Aberdeen AB9 1FQ

Reference
21.9.4 **Oberwesel on the Rhine**
Water-colour (20 × 29$\frac{3}{4}$ in. – 508 × 755 mm)
Signed: Wm. Callow 1853
Exhibited: Aberdeen 1873 (No. 401)
This water-colour is very similar to 'Oberwesel on the Rhine and the Castle of Schönburg' in the Whitworth Art Gallery (*see illustration no. 33*). The Aberdeen drawing is presented from an angle which excludes the buildings and archway on the right of the Whitworth example. Callow exhibited the above title with the Society of Painters in Water-colours in 1854.

THE NATIONAL LIBRARY OF WALES, DEPARTMENT OF PRINTS, DRAWINGS AND MAPS, Aberystwyth, Dyfed SY23 3BU

The Ruins of Crickhowell Castle
Water-colour (7$\frac{1}{8}$ × 10$\frac{5}{8}$ in. – 180 × 265 mm)
Signed and dated: W. Callow 1849
Purchase: Richard Hughes-Hallet, October 1973

Usk Castle
Pencil drawing (3$\frac{1}{2}$ × 5$\frac{3}{10}$ in. – 90 × 134 mm)
Not signed, but inscribed: 'Usk Castle, Oct 20' in pencil on drawing bottom right
Purchase: Folio Fine Art Ltd, London W1, March 1968

Usk Church
Pencil drawing (3½ × 5⅕ in. – 90 × 132 mm)
Not signed, but inscribed: 'Usk Castle', Oct 20th, in pencil on drawing, bottom left
Purchase: Folio Fine Art Ltd, London W1, March 1968

The two drawings above must be dated 1848 (*see* 'Abergavenny' Oct. 16th 1848 – Birmingham City Art Gallery)

THE CECIL HIGGINS ART GALLERY (North Bedfordshire Borough Council), Castle Close, Bedford MR40 3NY

Near Huddersfield (*illustration no. 77*)
Water-colour (8 × 19¾ in. – 203 × 501 mm)
Signed: Wm. Callow, bottom right corner
Inscribed, in pencil: Near Huddersfield/1862
Exhibited: Royal Society of Painters in Water-colours, 1908
Collection: Gilbert Davis. Purchased from P. and D. Colnaghi Ltd, February 1953

Ponte Cartro, Rome (*illustration no. 28*)
Pencil and water-colour (10¼ × 14½ in. – 260 × 368 mm)
Signed: Wm. Callow, bottom right corner
Inscribed: Ponte Cartro sur le Tibre, 28/Sept '40 (bottom right)
Purchased from P. and D. Colnaghi Ltd, January 1960

Château de Montélimar (*illustration no. 14*)
Water-colour (5¼ × 9¼ in. – 133 × 234 mm)
Signed with monogram, which reads 'C.W.'
Inscribed on verso in pencil: 'Château de Montélimort' (*sic*) Août 2.36. (*see* journal entry in text, page 62)
Exhibited: October–November 1962, Agnew, Water-colours from the Cecil Higgins Art Gallery, Bedford (No. 55)

Grand Canal, Venice
Water-colour (9⅛ × 12⅝ in. – 231 × 320 mm)
Signed and dated: W. Callow/79, bottom right corner
Lot 72. Christie's – 20.10.70
Collection: Mrs M. Noel

ART GALLERY AND MUSEUMS AND THE ROYAL PAVILION, Brighton

Sketch in Würzburg, Bavaria
A water-colour by Callow, on loan to Brighton from the National Loan Collection's Trust

CITY OF BRISTOL (MUSEUM AND ART GALLERY), Queen's Road, Bristol BS8 1RL

Malines
Water-colour and pencil (10⅞ × 14¾ in. – 276 × 374 mm)
Signed and dated: W. Callow 1854

Porta Delle Lettere, Venice
Water-colour (29¼ × 22 in. – 742 × 558 mm)
Signed and dated: William Callow, 1871

TOWNELEY HALL ART GALLERY AND MUSEUMS (Burnley Borough Council), Burnley, Lancs BB11 3RQ

Entrance to the Port of Marseilles (*illustration no. 96*)
Water-colour (21½ × 32½ in. – 546 × 825 mm)
Signed: William Callow 1884
Purchased in 1933 for £62 from R. Haworth, Blackburn
Exhibited: The Whitworth Institute, Manchester (1912), No. 218

MUSEUM AND ART GALLERY (BOLTON METROPOLITAN BOROUGH), Civic Centre, Bolton

Malvern
Pencil and water-colour (10¼ × 14¼ in. – 260 × 361 mm)
Inscribed, dated and signed: Sept 12.1848. W. Callow

Lochinver
Pencil and water-colour (12½ × 20½ in. – 317 × 520 mm)
Inscribed, dated and signed: Lochinver, Sept 3. 1861. W. Callow

Gravedona, Lake of Como
Water-colour (16¾ × 25⅛ in. – 425 × 638 mm)
Signed and dated: William Callow 1895

A Farmer's Cart outside an Inn
Water-colour (12¼ × 18 in. – 311 × 457 mm)

A Cathedral Town on a River
Pencil and water-colour (11 × 20 in. – 279 × 508 mm)
Attributed to Callow

THE BOWES MUSEUM (Durham County Council), Barnard Castle, Co. Durham

The Meeting of the Waters (*illustration no. 88*)
(the confluence of the Rivers Tees and Greta)
Water-colour (9 × 13¼ in. – 228 × 336 mm)
Signed and dated: W. Callow Sept.20. 1872

BUCKINGHAMSHIRE COUNTY MUSEUM (Buckinghamshire County Council), Church Street, Aylesbury, Bucks HP20 2QP

Landscape at Great Missenden
Water-colour (11⅗ × 8⅗ in. – 295 × 218 mm)
Signed: W. Callow
Purchased: Sotheby's 1965

Two unidentified landscapes
($12\frac{1}{5} \times 8$ in. – 310×202 mm) and ($11\frac{4}{5} \times 8\frac{1}{5}$ in. – 301×206 mm)
Source unknown
Also *bound volume of water-colour sketches* of the Great Missenden area, including work by both William and Harriet Callow (1855–77)
Donated in 1945 by Miss Bertha Jefferay (sister of Mrs. M. L. Callow)

ULSTER MUSEUM, Botanic Gardens, Belfast BT9 5AB

Reference

1003 **Oberwesel on the Rhine**
Pencil and water-colour, touches of body-colour ($12\frac{3}{4} \times 18\frac{3}{4}$ in. – 327×480 mm)
Signed: Wm. Callow (right) and dated 1859
Formerly catalogued as 'Scene on the Rhine'
Purchased: Malcolm Mercer, Belfast, 1956

1187 **Bellaggio, Lake Como, from Cadenabbia**
Pencil and water-colour on white paper ($13 \times 8\frac{3}{8}$ in. – 214×330 mm)
Signed, bottom right: Wm. Callow
Purchased from Rodman's, Belfast, 1935

MUSEUM AND ART GALLERY, BRIDPORT, Dorset DT6 3NR

Castle and Bridge
Water-colour ($5\frac{1}{2} \times 9\frac{1}{2}$ in. – 140×240 mm)

BLACKBURN MUSEUM AND ART GALLERY, Library Street, Blackburn

Reference

510 **The Belfry at Ghent**
($13\frac{3}{5} \times 19\frac{7}{10}$ in. – 350×500 mm)
Signed: Wm. Callow

509 **Bodiam Castle, Sussex**
($9\frac{7}{10} \times 13\frac{3}{5}$ in. – 245×345 mm)
Signed: Wm. Callow
Bequeathed by E. L. Hartley, July 1954

124 **Castle of Schönburg, from Oberwesel**
($25\frac{2}{5} \times 18\frac{3}{10}$ in. – 645×465 mm)
Signed and dated: Wm. Callow 1894
Exhibited: Royal Society of Painters in Water-colours, 1894
Purchased from R. Haworth, Blackburn, 1910

511 **Dunkirk**
($14\frac{1}{5} \times 10$ in. – 360×255 mm)
Signed: Wm. Callow
Bequeathed by E. L. Hartley, July 1954

512 **Honfleur**
(9 × 12⅕ in. – 230 × 310 mm)
Signed: Wm. Callow

803 **Market Place**
(10¾ × 15½ in. – 273 × 393 mm)
Signed: Wm. Callow
Bequeathed by Sarah Jane Duckworth, Wilpshire*

513 **The State Barge** (after Turner)
Not signed or dated (4¾ × 6½ in. – 120 × 165 mm)
Bequeathed by E. L. Hartley, July 1954

514 **Venice** (after Turner)
(4½ × 6½ in. – 114 × 165 mm)
Not signed or dated
Bequeathed by E. L. Hartley, 1954

VICTORIA ART GALLERY (Bath City Council), Bridge Street, Bath BA1 2HP

Acc. No. 08.2 **Landscape and Cattle**
Oils (24 × 30 in. – 609 × 762 mm)
Signed: W. Callow
Bequeathed by Alderman Major C. D. Brickmann
On long loan to the Tidworth Military Hospital

CARTWRIGHT HALL (Bradford Metropolitan District), Lister Park, Bradford BD9 4NS

Reference Acc. No.

3–37 **Richmond, Yorkshire**
Water-colour (9¾ × 13¾ in. – 247 × 349 mm)
Signed, bottom right: W. Callow
Purchased from F. R. Meatyard, 32 Museum Street, London WC1, 1937

27–22 **Seascape**
Water-colour (7⅝ × 10¼ in. – 193 × 260 mm)
Purchased from Matthews and Brooke, 1922

2–19 **View of Dartmouth**
Pencil drawing on light blue paper (10¼ × 14¼ in. – 260 × 361 mm)
Inscribed, bottom centre: Dartmouth, July 20 '42
Presented by Frederick A. Rawnsley, Esq., 1919

3–19 **View of Dartmouth**
Pencil drawing on light blue paper (10¼ × 14¼ in. – 260 × 361 mm)
Inscribed in faint pencil, bottom right: Dartmouth, July 22/1842
Presented by Frederick A. Rawnsley, Esq., 1919
Nos. 2–19 and 3–19 are related to the convalescent trip of 1842 and are linked with 'Torquay' – Walker Art Gallery

*An area north of Blackburn

28–22 **Lake Scene with Castle**
Water-colour (7 × $10\frac{5}{8}$ in. – 177 × 269 mm)
Purchased from Matthews and Brooke, 1922

2–37 **Old Houses, Nantes** (*illustration no. 67*)
Water-colour (10 × 14 in. – 254 × 355 mm)
Signed, dated and titled, bottom left: William Callow, August 22nd 1856, Maison du . . . Nantes.
Purchased from F. R. Meatyard

City of Birmingham Museums and Art Gallery, Birmingham B3 3DH

Inventory No.

37/13 **Via dell'Independenza, with the Palazzo Comunale, Bologna**
Water-colour ($8\frac{1}{2}$ × 14 in. – 215 × 355 mm)
Signed: Wm. Callow
Bequeathed by J. Tertius Collins Esq., in 1913
Note: This work was formerly catalogued as 'A Street in Verona' and was shown as such in the exhibitions listed, but has recently been identified by Clovis Whitfield as the above location in Bologna.
Exhibited: 1) Norwich Castle Museum in 1956
2) 'The English Eye' II – The Midland Federation of Museums and Art Galleries (No. 7), 1958
3) Washington and New York, 1962
4) 'The Victorian Vision of Italy' (No. 81) – Leicester Museum and Art Gallery, 1968
5) 'English Artists in Italy' – Victoria and Albert Museum, 1968. Handbook for this exhibition (reference p. 33)

204/14 **Como**
Pencil on pale grey paper, squared ($9\frac{1}{2}$ × 14 in. – 241 × 355 mm)
Signed: W.C. in monogram and inscribed 'Como, 18 Août, 1840'
Presented by Messrs Ernest Brown and Philips (The Leicester Galleries) in 1914
Exhibited: 'The English Eye' II – The Midland Federation of Museums and Art Galleries (No. 6), 1958
'English Artists in Italy' – Victoria and Albert Museum, 1968 (No. 138)

205/14 **Durham**
Pencil on pale blue-grey paper, squared ($9\frac{1}{2}$ × $14\frac{1}{8}$ in. – 241 × 358 mm)
Inscribed: Durham, Sept 20.1843
Presented by Messrs Ernest Brown and Philips in 1914
Photograph: Witt Library, Courtauld Institute of Art

151/19 **Portsmouth**
Water-colour ($16\frac{7}{8}$ × 22 in. – 428 × 558 mm)
Signed: W. Callow
Presented by Mrs Arthur T. Keen in memory of her husband

712′20 **Gravedona, Lake of Como**
Pencil on pale grey paper (9⅜ × 13⅓ in. – 238 × 338 mm)
Inscribed: Gravedona, Como/W.C./16 Août.1840
Presented by Wilfred L. Phillips Esq., in 1920
Exhibited: 'The English Eye' I – The Midlands Federation of Museums and Art Galleries (No. 8) 1958
Original study for the *colour plate*, which follows this pencil drawing in almost exact detail, with the exception of the foreground introductions. The boat (left) is included, but not the figures, fishing baskets, etc. The sea is calmer and the composition does not have the rowing boat (right). The clock is five minutes faster than in the finished water-colour drawing! (Photograph: Witt Library, Courtauld Institute of Art, No. 738/50/5)

54′53 **Tours**
Water-colour and pencil on grey paper (5⅜ × 9 in. – 136 × 228 mm)
Signed: W.C. (monogram) and inscribed 'Tours, Juin 18.36'
Bequeathed by J. Leslie Wright Esq., in 1954
Exhibited: 'Masters of British Water-colour' – Royal Academy, 1949
Photograph: Witt Library, Courtauld Institute of Art
Illustration no. 22 is based on this drawing, which presents a slightly nearer view. The foreground boat in the illustrated work has been developed from the moored craft, which appear to the left of this drawing

55′53 **Père Lachaise Cemetery**
Water-colour (7⅞ × 11⅛ in. – 200 × 283 mm)
Signed and dated: W. Callow 1905
Bequeathed by J. Leslie Wright in 1954
Exhibited: 'Masters of British Water-colour' – Royal Academy, 1949
Photograph: Witt Library, Courtauld Institute of Art

56′53 **Montpellier, South of France**
Water-colour (7¼ × 10 in. – 184 × 254 mm)
Signed: W. Callow
Bequeathed by J. Leslie Wright Esq., in 1954
Exhibited: 'Masters of British Water-colour' – Royal Academy, 1949

57′53 **Abergavenny** (*illustration no. 53*)
Water-colour (10½ × 14⅜ in. – 267 × 365 mm)
Signed: W. Callow, and inscribed 'Oct.16.1848'
Bequeathed by J. Leslie Wright Esq., in 1954
Exhibited: 'Masters of British Water-colour' – Royal Academy, 1949; Wales and the Wye Valley, April–May 1970

51′53 **The Piazzetta, Venice**
Water-colour (13 × 18¾ in. – 330 × 476 mm)
Signed and dated 1877
Bequeathed by J. Leslie Wright Esq., in 1954
Exhibited: 1) 'Masters of British Water-colour' – Royal Academy, 1949
2) Washington and New York, 1962
3) Midland Art Centre, Cannonhill, 1968

53'53 **Rhine Landscape**
Water-colour ($6\frac{5}{8} \times 10\frac{1}{8}$ in. – 168×257 mm)
Inscribed on verso: W.C. 229
Bequeathed by J. Leslie Wright Esq., in 1954
Exhibited: 'Masters of British Water-colour' – Royal Academy, 1949

52'53 **Bordeaux** (*illustration no. 12*)
Water-colour on grey paper ($5\frac{3}{8} \times 9\frac{1}{8}$ in. – 136×231 mm)
Signed: W.C. (Monogram) and inscribed 'Bordeaux Juillet/36'
Bequeathed by J. Leslie Wright Esq., in 1954
Exhibited: 'Masters of British Water-colour' – Royal Academy, 1949

67'31 **Wyn Haven, Rotterdam** (*illustration no. 41*)
Water-colour ($10\frac{1}{8} \times 14\frac{1}{8}$ in. – 257×359 mm)
Signed: W. Callow and inscribed 'Wyn Haven, Rotterdam, Sept 4/45'
Bequeathed by J. R. Holliday Esq., in 1927

151'31 **Edinburgh from Salisbury Crags**
Water-colour ($14\frac{1}{2} \times 21\frac{3}{8}$ in. – 368×543 mm)
Signed and dated: W. Callow 1843 and inscribed with title
Presented by an anonymous donor
Exhibited: Fine Art Society, London, 1931 (No. 93)
Probably as exhibited with the Royal Society of Painters in Water-colours in 1905

65'42 **The Phalz on the Rhine**
Water-colour (35×24 in. – 889×610 mm)
Signed and dated: W. Callow 1847
Presented by Mrs K. M. Fielding in memory of Miss M. A. W. Hudson

John Callow **Colliers on the Beach, Mount's Bay**
Signed and dated: John Callow, 1872
Water-colour ($9\frac{3}{4} \times 11\frac{1}{2}$ in. – 248×292 mm)
Bequeathed by Lady Anderson in 1944
Exhibited: 'The Sea' (No. 4) – Midland Federation of Museums and Art Galleries, 1957

HERBERT ART GALLERY AND MUSEUM (City of Coventry), Jordan Well, Coventry

Reference

6/61 **Eagle Tower, Warwick Castle**
Water-colour on paper ($12 \times 9\frac{1}{10}$ in. – 305×230 mm)
Signed, bottom left: W. Callow
From Palsar Gallery, Stratford, 1961

7/61 **Caesar's Tower and the Old Bridge, Warwick Castle**
Water-colour on paper ($12 \times 9\frac{1}{10}$ in. – 305×230 mm)
Signed, bottom left: W. Callow
From Palsar Gallery, Stratford, 1961

40/64 **View of the River at Stoneleigh Park**
Water-colour on paper ($9\frac{1}{10} \times 12\frac{2}{5}$ in. – 230×315 mm)
Signed twice, indistinctly inscribed and dated: April 11th 1859
From Sotheby's, 1965

1/66 **Fir Trees at Offchurch, near Leamington** (*illustration no. 60*)
Water-colour on paper ($17\frac{3}{10} \times 9\frac{3}{10}$ in. – 325×235 mm)
Signed, bottom right: W. Callow
Inscribed, bottom right: Offchurch, August 16th 1852
From J. Manning 1966

GROSVENOR MUSEUM, 27 Grosvenor Street, Chester CH1 2DD

Shoemakers' Row, Northgate Street, Chester (*illustration no. 64*)
Water-colour ($15\frac{1}{5} \times 24$ in. – 385×610 mm)
Signed and dated 1854

THE FITZWILLIAM MUSEUM, Cambridge CB2 1RB

Reference

1175 **Tournon on the Rhône**
Pencil and water-colour on grey paper ($7\frac{1}{4} \times 10\frac{5}{8}$ in. – 184×270 mm)
Signed in water-colour, lower left, in monogram: W.C.
Inscribed in pencil, lower right: Tournon Rhône/Août 5
(NB. The work must be dated 1836)
Given by Augustus Walker Esq., 1926

1265 **Church of St Eustache, Paris**
Pencil and water-colour with body-colour on paper, laid down ($6\frac{15}{16} \times 5$ in. – 176×127 mm)
Inscribed, lower right (not in the artist's hand): St Eustache, Paris
Bequeathed by J. R. Holliday Esq., 1927

1548 **St Germain l'Auxerios, Paris**
Pencil and water-colour on paper laid down ($5 \times 6\frac{15}{16}$ in. – 127×176 mm)
Inscribed in ink, lower right: Paris. The inscription has been inked over in another hand (*see* text – M. L. Callow, pages 151–2)
Bequeathed by J. R. Holliday Esq., 1927. Received 1931

1549 **S. Giovanni e Paolo, Venice**
Pencil and water-colour on paper laid down ($4\frac{15}{16} \times 6\frac{15}{16}$ in. – 126×176 mm)
Signed with initials 'W.C.' in water-colour, lower left
Bequeathed by J. R. Holliday Esq., 1927. Received 1931.

1550 **Si Pietro, Como**
Pencil and water-colour on paper laid down ($7 \times 4\frac{15}{16}$ in. – 178×126 mm)
Signed in water-colour, lower right: W. Callow
Inscribed in ink over water-colour, lower left: Si Pietro, Como
Bequeathed by J. R. Holliday Esq., 1927. Received in 1931

2351 — **Chester**
Pencil and water-colour on paper ($8\frac{3}{4} \times 12\frac{9}{16}$ in. 222×319 mm)
Given by E. Evelyn Barron Esq., Peterhouse College, 1939

PD 19–1947 — **Rouen** (*illustration no. 24*)
Water-colour on paper ($7\frac{1}{16} \times 9\frac{13}{16}$ in. – 180×250 mm)
Signed in water-colour, lower right: W. Callow
Given by the Friends of the Fitzwilliam Museum, April 1947
Callow visited Rouen in 1830, 1835, 1836 and obtained a Bronze Medal at the Rouen exhibition in 1839. His last visit appears to have been in 1854

PD 23–1947 — **On the Seine at Rouen**
Water-colour on paper ($9\frac{3}{8} \times 12\frac{13}{16}$ in. – 238×326 mm)
Signed in water-colour, lower right (on plank across river): W. Callow
Inscribed verso: Bordeaux on the Garonne
Bequeathed by D. A. Winstanley, Vice Master of Trinity College, Cambridge, April 1947

PD 51–1958 — **The Gardens of Versailles**
Water-colour, heightened with white, on paper laid down ($6 \times 9\frac{3}{16}$ in. – 152×234 mm)
Bought from the Biffen Fund, April 1958

PD 9–1972 — **View of the Canale della Porta, Venice** (*illustration no. 100*)
Pencil on pale grey paper ($9\frac{15}{16} \times 6\frac{15}{16}$ in. – 252×177 mm)
Inscribed in pencil, lower right: Venice/Canale de la Porta April/19. 1892
Bequeathed by Professor G. F. Webb, 1971. Received by museum, 1972

City of Canterbury Royal Museum and Art Gallery, High Street, Canterbury, Kent CT1 2JF

Trongate, Glasgow (*illustration no. 87*)
Water-colour ($18\frac{9}{10} \times 25\frac{3}{5}$ in. – 480×650 mm) (height first)
Signed and dated: William Callow 1870

Cooper Art Gallery (South Yorkshire County Council), Barnsley, Yorkshire

John Callow — **On the Mersey**
Oil on canvas (24×42 in. – 610×1067 mm)

National Gallery of Ireland, Merrion Square West, Dublin 2

Reference Cat. No.

2035 — **The Doge's Palace, Venice** (*illustration no. 90*)
Water-colour on paper ($11\frac{3}{10} \times 19\frac{9}{10}$ in. – 286×505 mm)
Signed and dated: William Callow 1874
Presented by the artist in 1879

2036 — **View of Durham**
Water-colour on paper ($18\frac{3}{10} \times 25\frac{1}{2}$ in. – 466×640 mm)
Signed and dated: Wm Callow 1857
Smith Bequest, 1877

2037 **Landscape with View of Cathedral**
Water-colour on paper ($5\frac{9}{10} \times 10\frac{9}{10}$ in. – 151 × 276 mm)
Smith Bequest, 1877

DUDLEY ART GALLERY (Dudley Metropolitan Borough), 3 St James's Road, Dudley, West Midlands DY1 1HU

Venice
Water-colour with touches of body-colour ($12\frac{3}{4} \times 18\frac{3}{4}$ in. – 324 × 476 mm)
Signed: Wm. Callow (lower right)
A scene on the Grand Canal, near the Rialto Bridge, facing the buildings shown on the left of *illustration no. 48*
Purchased by the Brierley Hill Library from the Fine Art Society in 1950

Smoking Salmon on the Severn
(Private Collection) was No. 11 in the exhibition 'David Cox and his Contemporaries' – Dudley Art Gallery, 1–29 May 1976

THE TOWNER ART GALLERY, Borough Lane, Eastbourne, Sussex BN20 8BB

Convent of Blackfriars
Water-colour ($10 \times 13\frac{3}{5}$ in. – 255 × 345 mm)

St Mary's, Eastbourne
($9\frac{9}{10} \times 14\frac{1}{5}$ in. – 250 × 360 mm)
Unsigned

Old Shoreham
Water-colour ($7\frac{3}{10} \times 15\frac{3}{4}$ in. – 185 × 400 mm)
Signed: Wm. Callow 1873

NATIONAL GALLERY OF SCOTLAND, The Mound, Edinburgh EH2 2EL

Reference:

D 4801Q **Canal in Venice**
Water-colour ($17\frac{1}{4} \times 10\frac{1}{4}$ in. – 438 × 260 mm)
Signed and dated: Porte (?) Venice, August 15/46. Wm. Callow

D 4624 **Marly from St Germain**
Water-colour ($4\frac{3}{4} \times 8\frac{3}{8}$ in. – 120 × 212 mm)
See also water-colour drawing with this title, dated August 24/33, in the Henry E. Huntington Collection

John Callow D(NG)470 **Ships of the Line under Sail**
Water-colour ($10 \times 14\frac{1}{8}$ in. – 254 × 359 mm)
This was formerly attributed to William Callow

ROYAL ALBERT MEMORIAL MUSEUM, Queen Street, Exeter EX4 3RX

Beilstein on the Moselle (*illustration no. 82*)
Water-colour with some body-colour ($11\frac{1}{10} \times 30\frac{1}{10}$ in. – 283×764 mm)
Signed and dated: William Callow 1864 (bottom left)
The title printed on the mount reads 'Bulstein on the Moselle', but this must be a framing error and has been masked in the illustration. The titles 'Beilstein on the Moselle' were exhibited with the Society of Painters in Water-colours in 1864/5
Cat. No. 31, Purchased 1955 via the Sir Harry Veitch Bequest Trust Fund. Acc. No. 20/1955
Exhibited: 'Marine Painting', Victoria Art Gallery, Bath, 1970

FOLKESTONE MUSEUM AND ART GALLERY (Kent County Council), Grace Hill, Folkestone, Kent

Reference Acc. No.

637/63/15 **Old Houses at Hythe**
Pencil drawing ($10\frac{1}{4} \times 14$ in. – 260×355 mm)
Inscribed: Old House at Hythe, August 21st 50

637/63/14 **Lympne Castle, Kent**
Pencil drawing ($10\frac{1}{4} \times 14$ in. – 260×355 mm)
Inscribed: Lympne Castle, August 29.1850

637/62/12/13 **Dover from the Sea**
Pencil drawing ($29\frac{1}{4} \times 11$ in. – 743×279 mm)
Inscribed: Sketch for a drawing painted for Mr. Prinsep and presented to Jamsetjee Jezeboy/. August 18. 1843. Dover
In 1843, Callow exhibited 'Port of Havre' with the Society of Painters in Water-colours. It was purchased by a W. Prinsep as a gift for the distinguished Indian, Dwarkaneth Tagore (grandfather of the poet, Rabindranath Tagore), as it represented the place from which he had first embarked for England. Prinsep then commissioned Callow to paint a view of Dover, as being the place where Tagore first set foot on England. Both water-colours were sent to Tagore in India. The Folkestone drawing shows a detailed view of the harbour and would appear to have been given by Callow to a friend of either Tagore or Prinsep

GLASGOW ART GALLERY AND MUSEUM (City of Glasgow Council), Kelvingrove, Glasgow G3 8AG

Reference Reg. No.

22–29 **The Choir, Canterbury**
Dated 1847

57–14a **Near Sidmouth, Devon**

70–9 **Bridge near Inkermann, Crimea**

70–9a — **Market Street, Hanover**
On buff paper, with pencil grid superimposed for copying
Dated 1852
This is the preliminary drawing for a work auctioned at Christie's, 14 March 1967, with the title 'A Street in a German Town', also auctioned in 1974 as 'French Street Scene'

John Callow — **Dover**
Water-colour ($7\frac{3}{8} \times 10\frac{7}{8}$ in. – 187 × 276 mm)
Unsigned
Shows the beach with grounded dinghy; beyond are the harbour and cliffs, looking westwards

St Helens Museum and Art Gallery (Metropolitan Borough of St Helens), Central Library, Victoria Square, St Helens WA10 1DY

Inveraray Castle (*illustration no. 56*)
Water-colour ($21\frac{1}{4} \times 29\frac{1}{4}$ in. – 540 × 743 mm)
Exhibited: No. 4, Society of Painters in Water-colours, 1850 (see text)
Guy and Margery Pilkington Collection – this collection also includes 'Snowdon towards Portmadoc' by Copley Fielding and 'A French Town' by Thomas Shotter Boys

John Callow — **Waiting for the Tide**
Oil
Bequeathed by Alderman J. Foote, J.P., 1921

Hereford City Museums, Broad Street, Hereford HR4 9AU

Reference Acc. No.

4653 — **Ross, Street Scene**
Pencil drawing ($10\frac{1}{4} \times 6\frac{3}{4}$ in. – 260 × 171 mm)

401 — **Town Hall, Hereford**
Pencil drawing ($10\frac{1}{4} \times 14\frac{1}{4}$ in. – 260 × 362 mm)

3786 — **Place du Bourg, Bruges**
Pencil drawing ($15\frac{1}{4} \times 10\frac{1}{2}$ in. – 387 × 267 mm)
Inscribed: Place du Bourg, Bruges, Feb 17.1850

4653 — **Ross, Market Hall**
Pencil drawing ($7\frac{1}{4} \times 10\frac{1}{4}$ in. – 184 × 260 mm)

4598 — **Flint Castle**
Water-colour ($7 \times 10\frac{1}{4}$ in. – 178 × 260 mm)

6432 — **Wilton Castle**
Water-colour ($7 \times 12\frac{1}{2}$ in. – 178 × 317 mm)

4859 — **Early Morning, going to Market**
Water-colour ($9\frac{3}{4} \times 13\frac{3}{4}$ in. – 248 × 349 mm)

Gray Art Gallery and Museum (Borough of Hartlepool), Clarence Road, Hartlepool, Cleveland

John Callow
Reference

71/20 **A Breezy Day off the Isle of Man**
Oil on canvas (35 × 59 in. – 889 × 1499 mm)
Signed: J. Callow 1867
Donated: Sir William Gray, 1920

12/29 **Seaton Carew 1869**
Water-colour (20 × $4\frac{1}{2}$ in. – 508 × 114 mm)
Inscribed (bottom left): John Callow, Seaton Carew, looking towards Hartlepool, Aug. 13/69
Purchased in 1929

Kirklees Metropolitan Council Libraries and Museums, Princess Alexandra Walk, Huddersfield HD1 2SU

Arran from Bute
Water-colour (18 × 36 in. – 457 × 914 mm)
Signed: Wm. Callow

Valley of the East Lynn, North Devon
Water-colour (25 × 36 in. – 635 × 914 mm)
Inscribed: July 7/47

Late Evening, Murano
Water-colour ($10\frac{9}{10}$ × 15 in. – 275 × 380 mm)
Signed and dated: Wm. Callow 1888

Sidmouth, Devon
Water-colour ($9\frac{9}{10}$ × 14 in. – 250 × 355 mm)
Signed: Wm Callow; and inscribed: Oct 12. 1854
Photographed for the Paul Mellon Foundation

Old Barn
Water-colour ($5\frac{9}{10}$ × 9 in. – 150 × 230 mm)
Signed: W. Callow

River Scene
Water-colour ($6\frac{3}{10}$ × 2 × $9\frac{4}{5}$ in. – 160 × 50 × 250 mm)
Signed: Wm. Callow

The Kirklees collection includes collections at Batley, Bagshaw Museum and Dewsbury Art Gallery, as well as the Huddersfield Art Gallery

City Art Gallery and Temple Newsam House, Leeds

Sèvres (*illustration no. 25*)
Water-colour ($9\frac{3}{10}$ × $12\frac{3}{5}$ in. – 237 × 317 mm)
Purchased in 1946

Ehrenbreitstein and Koblenz from the Heights of Pfaffendorf (*illustration no. 27*)
Water-colour ($18\frac{3}{5} \times 25\frac{3}{10}$ in. – 472×644 mm)
Signed and dated 1839
Bought from T. Agnew, 1961
Exhibited: Society of Painters in Water-colours, 1839

Dover Cliffs
Water-colour ($10\frac{2}{5} \times 14\frac{3}{5}$ in. – 264×370 mm)
Signed and dated 1845
Donated by Miss Elaine Barran in 1926

The collection also includes ten pencil drawings, attributed to Callow, source unknown, inventoried in 1973. These are of very general subjects, not specifically topographical (i.e. thatched cottages, a windmill, house with chickens in the foreground, etc.). Photographic reproductions of these drawings are included in the Callow files, Witt Library, Courtauld Institute of Art

John Callow

A Mountain Landscape
Pencil and water-colour ($7\frac{2}{5} \times 10$ in. – 187×255 mm)
Bequeathed by Sidney Kitson in 1938

THE LEICESTERSHIRE MUSEUM AND ART GALLERY (Leicestershire County Council), 96 New Walk, Leicester LE1 6TD

Fishing Boats at Dover (*illustration no. 43*)
Water-colour ($7 \times 10\frac{1}{16}$ in. – 178×260 mm)
Purchased from a private collection in Leicestershire in 1936

WALKER ART GALLERY (Merseyside County Council), William Brown Street, Liverpool L31 8EL

Torquay (*illustration no. 37*)
Water-colour on paper ($10\frac{1}{10} \times 14\frac{1}{10}$ in. – 256×358 mm)
Signed: W. Callow (centre lower edge)
Inscribed: Torquay, Sept 24.43 (*see* text)
Presented by Henry S. Young, from the collection of Harold E. Young, 1932 (Inventory No. 69)
Lent to Walton Hospital, Liverpool, 1948–57
Exhibited: 'Victorian Water-colours' – Walker Art Gallery, December–February 1974–75

Note:
Exhibit only

San Fedele and the Piazza San Fedele, Como
Water-colour, pen and ink
Signed: W. Callow
Was included in the 'Exhibition of English Water-colours in the Collection of C. F. J. Beausire' – Walker Art Gallery, 1970
A chromolithograph of this work was listed in Geo. Rowney's catalogue, 1864

UNIVERSITY OF LIVERPOOL, SENATE HOUSE, Abercromby Square, Liverpool, L69 3BX

Chartres, the Guillaume Gate (*colour plate*)
Water-colour ($8\frac{9}{10} \times 12\frac{1}{4}$ in. – 228 × 311 mm)
Signed and dated 1838
Sir Sydney Jones Collection
Inventory No. 237

WILLIAMSON ART GALLERY (Metropolitan Borough of Wirral), Slatey Road, Birkenhead, Merseyside

Reference

1 **The Rialto, Venice** (*illustration no. 48*)
Oil (29 × 44 in. – 737 × 1117 mm)
Unsigned, a not uncommon feature of the work of Callow in oils.
Purchased in 1928

2 **Pont de Grenelle, Seine**
Water-colour (5 × 11 in. – 127 × 279 mm)
Signed
Purchased in 1932

3 **St Malo, France**
Water-colour ($10\frac{1}{2} \times 7\frac{3}{4}$ in. – 267 × 197 mm)
Donated in 1936

4 **Paris from the Seine**
Water-colour ($13\frac{1}{2} \times 19\frac{1}{2}$ in. – 343 × 495 mm)
Signed and dated 1849
Purchased in 1928

5 **Richmond Castle**
Water-colour (42 × 32 in. – 1067 × 813 mm)
Donated in 1950

WARWICK DISTRICT COUNCIL ART GALLERY AND MUSEUM, Avenue Road, Leamington Spa CV31 3PP

Landscape
Water-colour ($10\frac{1}{2} \times 6\frac{3}{4}$ in. – 267 × 171 mm)
Bequested by Capt. Mark Field, 1953

John Callow **St Michael's Mount**
Water-colour ($18\frac{1}{4} \times 11\frac{3}{4}$ in. – 464 × 298 mm)
Bequested by Capt. Mark Field, 1953

USHER GALLERY, Lindum Road, Lincoln LN2 1NN

Reference

U.G. 145 **Lincoln Cathedral from the High Street** (*colour plate*)
Water-colour ($13\frac{9}{10} \times 20\frac{1}{10}$ in. – 353 × 510 mm)
Signed and dated 1853

Presented by J. Cyril Collingham, 1933
Exhibited: 'Plate and Pictures in the Diocese' – 19 July to 31 August 1939; 'The Cathedral in Art' – 8 July to 20 August 1972

U.G. 1842 — **High Street, Lincoln**
Pencil drawing (9¾ × 14¼ in. – 248 × 362 mm)
Signed and dated, lower right: Oct 1st 1851
Purchased in 1946

U.G. 2423 — **Stone Bow, Lincoln** (*illustration no. 57*)
(10 × 14⅜ in. – 255 × 365 mm)
Signed and dated: Sept 30th 1851
Purchased in 1960
Pencil drawing for 'Stonebow on the Guildhall, Lincoln' in the Mayor's Parlour (Lincoln District Council), Lincoln (*illustration no. 58*)

THE WHITWORTH ART GALLERY, University of Manchester, Whitworth Park, Manchester M15 6ER

Reference

D.6 1951 (1990) — **Bacharach on the Rhine, Germany**
Water-colour and white body-colour over pencil (10⅝ × 14⅝ in. – 271 × 372 mm)
Presented by the executors of F. B. Dunkerley in 1951
It is possible that this drawing was exhibited with the Royal Society of Painters in Water-colours as 'Old Houses, Bacharach on the Rhine' (1899). The town is just south of Oberwesel

D.2 1904 (430) — **Piazza delle Erbe, Verona**
Water-colour with body-colour over pencil, on cardboard (15½ × 22½ in. – 394 × 570 mm)
Signed and dated: William Callow/1903
Inscribed on back: No. 2/Piazza d'Erbe, Verona
Purchased in 1904
Exhibited: Royal Society of Painters in Water-colours in 1904; Huddersfield Art Gallery, 'Two Hundred Years of British Painting', 1946 (No. 13)

D.5 1952 (2000) — **Poitiers, France**
Water-colour and pencil, heightened with white body-colour (7 × 10¾ in. – 178 × 273 mm)
Signed with monogram – thick lettering, discontinued shortly after this date
Inscribed and dated: Cath et Eglise de Montierneuf/à Poitiers Juin 24.36
Presented by Miss Margaret Pilkington, 1952 (purchased from Walker's Galleries)
Exhibited: Agnew, 1954 (No. 12); Whitworth Art Gallery, 1973 (No. 49)
The view, taken from the south-west, across the river, shows the Cathedral of St Pierre on the extreme left, the Church of Montierneuf in the distance and the Church of Ste Radegonde in centre

D.6 1898 (429) — **Oberwesel on the Rhine and the Castle of Schönburg, Germany** (*illustration no. 33*)
Water-colour and body-colour with slight surface scratching (19⅛ × 25¾ in. – 485 × 655 mm)

Signed and dated: W. Callow 1841
Inscribed on back: Oberwesel on the Rhine/and Castle of Schomberg [*sic*]. The inscriptions on several other versions of this subject also appear to read 'Schomberg', but the correct spelling is Schönburg. This work was probably exhibited with the Old Water-colour Society in 1841 as 'Oberwesel on the Rhine' (situated between Coblenz and Mainz)
Purchased in 1898 (from T. Agnew)
Exhibited: Macclesfield, 1950 (No. 4); Worthing, 1956 (No. 7)

D.23 1970 **On the Rhine**
Water-colour over pencil ($6\frac{3}{4} \times 9\frac{3}{4}$ in. – 171×248 mm)
Signed and dated: W. Callow 1860
Bequeathed by Hector J. Towlson in 1969

Astley Cheetham Art Gallery (Tameside Metropolitan Borough), Trinity Street, Stalybridge, Greater Manchester

Grande Place, Lille (*illustration no. 62*)
Water-colour ($25 \times 35\frac{4}{10}$ in. – 635×900 mm)
Signed: Wm. Callow 1852

Verona (*illustration no. 74*)
Water-colour
Signed: Wm. Callow 1858

Both works purchased through the National Art Collections Fund

City Art Gallery, Mosley Street, Manchester M2 3JL

Reference

1903.12 **The Wartburg** (the place of Luther's captivity in 1521)
Oil on panel ($14 \times 11\frac{9}{10}$ in. – 355×301 mm)
Inscriptions: signed twice (bottom left of centre) and (bottom right centre) – W. Callow/1855
Purchased from Shepherd Bros, 1903
Exhibition of Victorian Paintings, Mappin Art Gallery, Sheffield, 1968

1917.24 **Quillebœuf on the Seine** (*illustration no. 10*)
Water-colour (14×20 in. – 356×508 mm)
Signed: Wm. Callow
Collections: Mrs M. L. Callow, bought from Agnew's, April 28, 1908, from whom bought by James T. Blair, 30 March 1908 (£35)
His bequest, 1917

1946.6 **Dinant on the Meuse**
Water-colour ($13\frac{9}{10} \times 21$ in. – 352×533 mm)
Unsigned
Bequeathed by Miss Anna Maria Philips, daughter of R. N. Philips, M.P. (1815–1890)
Manchester, 1946

NEWPORT MUSEUM AND ART GALLERY (Borough of Newport), John Frost Square, Newport, Gwent NPT 1PA

Bruges
Water-colour (18 × 25 in. – 457 × 635 mm)
Signed: Wm. Callow (no date)
Purchased in 1945 from Frost and Reed, Bristol

Grand Canal, Venice
Water-colour (20 × 29½ in. – 508 × 749 mm)
Signed and dated: William Callow 1895
Local donation in 1914

Tintern Abbey, West Window
Water-colour (16 × 12½ in. – 406 × 317 mm)
Signed and dated: Wm. Callow 1901
Purchased from local auctioneers in 1953

CASTLE MUSEUM (City of Nottingham), Nottingham NG1 6EL

Tours (*illustration no. 22*)
Water-colour (9¼ × 13 in. – 235 × 330 mm)
Signed and dated 1839
Donated by A. E. Anderson

Quai du l'Horloge
Water-colour (12½ × 29¼ in. – 317 × 743 mm)
Formerly attributed to Thomas Shotter Boys

CASTLE MUSEUM, Norwich NR1 3JU

Hadleigh Castle (*illustration no. 83*)
Pencil and water-colour (6⅞ × 10½ in. – 175 × 267 mm)
Inscribed and dated, lower left: Hadleigh Castle/Sept 18/64
Purchased in 1974

LAING ART GALLERY (Tyne and Wear County Council), Higham Place, Newcastle upon Tyne NE1 8AG

Reference

09 – 37 **Palazzo Falier, Venice** (*colour plate*)
(formerly known as 'A Continental Street Scene')
Water-colour (10½ × 14 in. – 267 × 356 mm)
Signed and dated, lower left: Wm. Callow 1847
Bequeathed by John Lambe in 1909

32 – 32 **Landscape with Ruins**
Water-colour (6¼ × 9½ in. – 159 × 241 mm)
Signed, lower left: W. Callow
Donated by William Albert White in 1923
Photo: Courtauld Institute neg. no. 592/62/13

27–111 **Berwick-on-Tweed**
Water-colour over pencil, with scratching-out and some slight touches of body-colour (11 × 30 in. – 279 × 762 mm)
Signed and dated, lower left: William Callow/1871
Donated by Lord Joicey in 1927
Photo: Courtauld Institute neg. no. 593/4/23

45–14 **Alnwick Castle**
Water-colour over pencil ($14\frac{7}{8} \times 21\frac{7}{8}$ in. – 378 × 556 mm)
Signed, inscribed and dated, lower left: Wm. Callow/Alnwick Castle Sept 27
Purchased from Walker's Galleries, London, in 1945
Photo: Courtauld Institute neg. no. 593/2/11

Ashmolean Museum of Art and Archeology, Beaumont Street, Oxford

Tintern Abbey from the West
Water-colour over pencil ($9\frac{3}{4} \times 13\frac{3}{4}$ in. – 248 × 349 mm)
Signed: W. Callow, and inscribed: Tintern Abbey from the West. Oct 21.48
Presented by Mr M. V. Paterson in 1943 through the National Art Collections Fund

Loch Fyne – Inveraray
Water-colour with body-colour (11 × 30 in. – 279 × 761 mm)
Signed, bottom left: William Callow/1861. The title is inscribed on the verso
Presented by Mr M. V. Paterson through the National Art Collections Fund in 1943
Exhibited: 1) Bermondsey Settlement
2) Leicester Galleries – 1907 Callow exhibition (No. 14)
3) Fine Art Society, May 1939 (No. 54)
There is a photographic reproduction of this water-colour in the Witt Library, Courtauld Institute

Distant View of St Peter's, Rome, across the Ponte Sisto
Water-colour over pencil ($6\frac{3}{4} \times 14$ in. – 171 × 355 mm)
Signed: W. Callow; and inscribed: P. Sisto P. Janiculensis, Roma/May 18. 1876 – and with a colour note 'yellow reflection – delicate blue light'
Purchased 1940

A Farm House near Margate
Water-colour over pencil ($10\frac{1}{5} \times 14$ in. – 259 × 355 mm)
Inscribed: Near Margate/June 22, 1849 (lower right corner)
Collection: Sir Bruce Ingram
Virtue-Tebbs Bequest Purchase, 1963
Exhibited: Ashmolean Museum – Exhibition of English drawings purchased from the collection of the late Sir Bruce Ingram – October–November 1963 (No. 13)

Hurstmonceaux Castle
Water-colour over pencil ($13\frac{3}{4} \times 9\frac{3}{4}$ in. – 349 × 247 mm)
Signed: W. Callow; and inscribed: Hurstmonceux Castle/October 31. 1851
Collection: H. C. Lawrence; B. Ingram

Virtue-Tebbs Bequest Purchase, 1963
Exhibited: Ashmolean Museum – Exhibition of English drawings purchased from the collection of the late Sir Bruce Ingram – October–November 1963 (No. 14)

A Romantic Landscape with Two Shepherds and their Flock
Water-colour, with some gum and body-colours ($5\frac{3}{10} \times 7\frac{4}{5}$ in. – 134 × 198 mm)
Signed and dated: W. Callow 1832 (lower margin)
Very early and somewhat uncharacteristic work, resembling the late Shoreham style of Samuel Palmer (1805–1881) and the romantic pastorals of F. O. Finch (1802–1862)
Collection: Sir Bruce Ingram.
Virtue-Tebbs Bequest Purchase, 1963
Exhibited: Ashmolean Museum – Exhibition of English drawings from the collection of the late Sir Bruce Ingram – October–November 1963 (No. 12)

River Landscape in Wales
Water-colour and some pen and ink, over pencil ($12\frac{4}{5} \times 17\frac{3}{10}$ in. – 326 × 440 mm)
Verso: Unfinished version of the same composition
Presented by Mr F. J. Varley through the National Art Collections Fund

Mountainous River Landscape in Wales
Water-colour and body-colour, some pen and ink, over pencil ($12\frac{9}{10} \times 18\frac{2}{5}$ in. – 328 × 467 mm)
Presented by Mr F. J. Varley, 1939, through the National Art Collections Fund

John Callow **Shipping after a Storm**
Water-colour ($12\frac{1}{5} \times 17\frac{9}{10}$ in. – 310 × 455 mm)
Collection: Sir John Crampton
Bequeathed by Miss G. A. P. Boyle, 1867

City of Plymouth Museum and Art Gallery, Drake Circus, Plymouth PL4 8AJ

The Citadel, Plymouth
Water-colour
Signed and dated 1863
Exhibited: 'Painters of Plymouth', 1971 (No. 27)
Pencil drawings: 1) Drake's Island 1884
2) Cattewater, Mount Batten on right, Citadel on left, Plymouth

John Callow **Emigrant Ships leaving the Cattewater**
Exhibited No. 26, 'Painters of Plymouth', 1971 (illustrated in catalogue for this exhibition)

Harris Museum and Art Gallery (Borough of Preston), Market Square, Preston PR1 2PP

Robin Hood's Bay, Yorkshire
Pencil drawing ($10\frac{1}{2} \times 14\frac{1}{2}$ in. – 267 × 368 mm)
1851

Grand Canal, Venice
Pencil drawing ($19\frac{1}{8} \times 12\frac{1}{8}$ in. – 486×308 mm)
1880

Fish Market, Basle
Pencil drawing (10×7 in. – 254×178 mm)
1892

Netley Abbey
Pencil drawing ($10\frac{1}{4} \times 7\frac{1}{4}$ in. – 260×184 mm)
1843

Florence
Pencil drawing (14×10 in. – 356×254 mm)
1876

A Study (landscape)
Water-colour ($9\frac{3}{4} \times 13\frac{7}{8}$ in. – 248×352 mm)

John Callow

Hold Fast as you can! (sea-piece)
Water-colour ($6\frac{1}{2} \times 9\frac{3}{8}$ in. – 165×238 mm)

THE LADY LEVER ART GALLERY, Port Sunlight, Wirral, Merseyside L62 5EQ

The Market Place, Malines (*Illustration no. 97*)
Water-colour ($20 \times 29\frac{1}{2}$ in. – 508×749 mm)
Signed: William Callow 1884 (right foreground)

The Market Square, Frankfort
Water-colour (7×10 in. – 178×254 mm)
Formerly attributed to Holland

ROCHDALE ART GALLERY (Metropolitan Borough of Rochdale), Esplanade, Rochdale

Val di Servor
Water-colour on paper ($9\frac{5}{8} \times 14$ in. – 245×356 mm)
Signed: William Callow (centre left)

READING BOROUGH COUNCIL MUSEUM AND ART GALLERY, Blagrave Street, Reading RG1 1QL

Reference Acc. No.

252.31

A Port Scene
Water-colour on paper ($16\frac{9}{10} \times 26\frac{1}{10}$ in. – 428×662 mm)
Signed and dated: Wm. Callow/1878 (bottom right)
W. I. Palmer Bequest
The frame bears an old label which suggests that the picture was lent to Bristol Art Gallery in May 1909 and was exhibit No. 149
The composition shows shipping in a harbour with part of a town in the middle distance, some rather composite buildings in the near right foreground and

a rowing boat to the left which appears to be almost a reverse of the one shown in 'Quillebœuf' (*illustration no. 10*), suggesting that Callow may have been working from tracings made from the 1835 sketches of Honfleur, Quillebœuf, etc., when he later executed this water-colour

BRIAN O'MALLEY CENTRAL LIBRARY AND ARTS CENTRE (Rotherham Borough Council), Rotherham S65 1JH

John Callow

Seascape – Brittany (*illustration no. 50*)
Oils ($33\frac{9}{10} \times 5\frac{3}{10}$ in. – 860 × 1350 mm)
Gift of Mr Edward Nightingale, 1908

ATKINSON ART GALLERY (Metropolitan Borough of Sefton), Lord Street, Southport PR8 1DH

On the Rhine (*illustration no. 95*)
Water-colour on paper $12\frac{4}{5} \times 18\frac{1}{2}$ in. – 325 × 470 mm)
Signed: Wm. Callow 1878
Exhibited: Society of Painters in Water-colours, 1879
Purchased in 1939

CITY OF STOKE-ON-TRENT MUSEUM AND ART GALLERY, Unity House, Hanley, Stoke-on-Trent ST1 4HY

Reference Acc. No.

257/37

Landscape with Church
Water-colour ($14\frac{1}{4} \times 10$ in. – 362 × 254 mm)
Purchased from the Squire Gallery in 1937

391/40

Lille (*illustration no. 61*)
Pencil drawing (10 × 14 in. – 254 × 356 mm)
Inscribed and dated: 1850
Purchased from the Squire Gallery in 1940

31/53

Canale del Olio, Venice
Pencil drawing ($6\frac{3}{4} \times 9\frac{1}{2}$ in. – 171 × 241 mm)
Inscribed: Canal del Olio May 14.77
See the Art Gallery of South Australia, Adelaide, for reference to a pencil drawing with the same title, dated five days later
Purchased from R. Abbott, Barnes, 1953

116/1960

Glacier du Rhône and the Garlingstock Pass of Furka, Switzerland (*illustration no. 55*)
Water-colour ($29\frac{1}{4} \times 22\frac{1}{4}$ in. – 743 × 565 mm)
Signed and dated: 1849
Presented by Dr W. D. Wilkins, 1960

SUNDERLAND MUSEUM (Tyne and Wear County Council), Borough Road, Sunderland SR1 1PP

Place de l'Hôtel de Ville, Antwerp
Pencil ($14\frac{1}{2} \times 10$ in. – 368×254 mm)
Inscribed: Place de l'Hôtel de Ville, Anvers Jesuit Church
Purchased 1955

CLIVE HOUSE MUSEUM (Shrewsbury and Atcham Borough Council), College Hill, Shrewsbury, SY1 1LZ

Reference No. 0.168 **Old Houses, Pride Hill, Shrewsbury** (*illustration no. 54*)
Water-colour ($10\frac{3}{10} \times 7\frac{3}{5}$ in. – 261×194 mm)
Signed: W. Callow. Almost certainly dated 1848
Reproduced in the catalogue of F. R. Meatyard, London, 1937 (8 guineas)

0.170 **Butcher Row, Shrewsbury**
Water-colour ($15\frac{1}{2} \times 24\frac{1}{2}$ in. – 394×622 mm)
Signed: W. Callow 1857
Purchased 1966
An exhibit with the title 'Double Butcher Row, Shrewsbury' appeared with the Society of Painters in Water-colours in 1857

BEECROFT ART GALLERY (Southend-on-Sea Borough Council), Station Road, Westcliff-on-Sea

Southend
Water-colour ($3\frac{1}{2} \times 10\frac{1}{2}$ in. – 89×267 mm)
Signed and inscribed: '64

Landscape
Water-colour ($6\frac{1}{4} \times 9\frac{1}{4}$ in. – 159×235 mm)
Signed

Attributed to Callow – **Turin Market Place**
Water-colour ($8\frac{1}{2} \times 12\frac{3}{4}$ in. – 216×324 mm)

John Callow **Merchantman entering the Thames**
Oils ($29\frac{1}{2} \times 49\frac{1}{2}$ in. – 749×1257 mm)

CITY OF SOUTHAMPTON ART GALLERY (Southampton Corporation), Civic Centre, Southampton

Reference Acc. No.
112 **Heidelberg** (*illustration no. 21*)
Water-colour ($9\frac{3}{5} \times 13\frac{3}{10}$ in. – 244×337 mm)
Signed: Wm Callow (bottom left)
Inscribed: Heidelberg Sept 20.38 (reads 30)
Presented by Arthur W. W. Brown Esq., 1937

113 **Old Houses near Worcester** (*illustration no. 52*)
Water-colour ($9\frac{1}{2} \times 13\frac{1}{2}$ in. – 241×342 mm)
Signed, bottom right: Wm Callow

Inscribed: Near Worcester 1848
Presented by Arthur W. W. Brown Esq., 1937
Exhibited: Society of Painters in Water-colours in 1907

1344 **Evreux**
Water-colour ($20\frac{3}{10} \times 28\frac{1}{2}$ in. – 515×724 mm)
Signed: Wm Callow
Presented by F. J. Nettlefold, 1948. There is an illustration of this work in the British Museum

GRAVES ART GALLERY (City of Sheffield Metropolitan District), Surrey Street, Sheffield S1 1XZ

Shipping entering Dover Harbour
Water-colour ($13\frac{5}{8} \times 20\frac{1}{4}$ in. – 346×514 mm)
Graves Gift to the Gallery

Venice
Water-colour ($13 \times 18\frac{1}{4}$ in. – 330×464 mm)
Signed, but illegibly dated
Presented to the Gallery

A Continental Street Scene
Water-colour ($8\frac{1}{4} \times 12\frac{1}{4}$ in. – 210×311 mm)
Graves Gift to the Gallery

A Street in Bruges (attributed to Callow)
Oil on canvas ($11\frac{3}{4} \times 9\frac{3}{4}$ in. – 298×248 mm)
Mappin Bequest
Formerly thought to be by Bonington, but the latter never visited Bruges. The painting shows many characteristics of the work of Callow

John Callow **Coast Scene**
Water-colour ($9\frac{3}{8} \times 13\frac{5}{8}$ in. – 238×346 mm)
Signed and dated: John Callow '63
Graves Gift to the Gallery

WAR MEMORIAL ART GALLERY (Metropolitan Borough of Stockport), Wellington Road South, Stockport SK1 3XE

A Town Square in France, with fine architectural detail, three figures
Water-colour ($10\frac{1}{4} \times 7\frac{3}{4}$ in. – 260×197 mm)

THE GLYNN VIVIAN ART GALLERY AND MUSEUM (City of Swansea), Alexandra Road, Swansea SA1 5DZ

Swansea Bay
Water-colour ($7\frac{1}{4} \times 22\frac{1}{2}$ in. – 184×571 mm)
Signed: W. Callow (in pencil, bottom right)
Inscribed: August 10th. 61

John Callow **Ship Ashore**
Water-colour ($7\frac{3}{4} \times 11\frac{1}{2}$ in. – 197×292 mm)
Signed: John Callow

WARRINGTON MUSEUM AND ART GALLERY (Warrington Borough Council), Bold Street, Warrington WA1 1JG

View of Abergavenny
Water-colour ($22\frac{7}{8} \times 15\frac{3}{8}$ in. – 581×391 mm)
Signed and dated: W. Callow 1848
Exhibited: Society of Painters in Water-colours in 1849

CITY OF WORCESTER MUSEUM AND ART GALLERY, Foregate Street, Worcester WR1 1DT

Worcester
Water-colour ($20 \times 28\frac{3}{4}$ in. – 508×730 mm)
By bequest of the Rev. and Mrs C. J. Sale of Holt Rectory, 1918

Worcester from the River
Water-colour ($9\frac{3}{8} \times 13\frac{1}{2}$ in. – 238×343 mm)
Signed and dated 1848
Purchased from the Manning Gallery in 1971

Eastgate Street, Chester
Water-colour ($20\frac{3}{4} \times 29\frac{1}{2}$ in. – 527×749 mm)
Signed and dated 1854
By bequest of the Rev. and Mrs C. J. Sale of Holt Rectory, 1918

THE ROYAL COLLECTION, ROYAL LIBRARY, WINDSOR CASTLE

Fishing Boats at Sea (*illustration no. 8*)
Water-colour ($7\frac{1}{8} \times 10\frac{1}{4}$ in. – 181×260 mm)
Signed: W. Callow 1833
Reproduced: P. A. Anson, *British Sea Fishermen* (1944, p. 8)

The French Coast with Fishing Boats
Water-colour, with touches of white body-colour ($9\frac{1}{8} \times 12\frac{1}{2}$ in. – 232×317 mm)
Signed: W. Callow

A French River Scene with Barges
Water-colour, touches of white ($9 \times 12\frac{1}{2}$ in. – 232×317 mm)
Signed W. Callow
The subject is south-west of Paris, on the Seine

Chatsworth, the Garden Front (*illustration no. 39*)
Water-colour ($7\frac{7}{8} \times 12\frac{1}{2}$ in. – 200×317 mm)
Signed: W. Callow 1843
From Queen Victoria's Souvenir Albums, Vol. II, No. V, p. 11 (a)

The Great Conservatory, Chatsworth (*illustration no. 40*)
Water-colour ($7\frac{7}{8} \times 12\frac{3}{8}$ in. – 200×314 mm)
Signed: W. Callow 1843
Queen Victoria and the Prince Consort visited the Duke of Devonshire, 1–3 December 1843. 'The Conservatory is out and out the finest thing imaginable of its kind' (letter of 4 December 1843, from Queen Victoria to the King of the Belgians – *see* text, page 80). From Queen Victoria's Souvenir Albums, Vol. II, No. V, p. 11 (b)

View of the Rosenau
Water-colour ($6\frac{3}{4} \times 9\frac{3}{4}$ in. – 171×248 mm)
Signed: W. Callow
From Queen Victoria's Souvenir Album 'Views of Saxe Coburg and Gotha', Vol. II, Souvenir Album VII, p. 24 (b)

Rosenau: View from the East Terrace
Water-colour ($9\frac{3}{8} \times 6\frac{7}{8}$ in. – 238×175 mm)
Signed: W. Callow
From Queen Victoria's Souvenir Album 'Views of Saxe Coburg and Gotha', Vol. II, Souvenir Album VII, p. 27 (d)

Coburg and Fortress from Weicherrent
Water-colour ($6\frac{7}{8} \times 9\frac{3}{4}$ in. – 175 mm $\times$ 248 mm)
Signed: W. Callow
From Queen Victoria's Souvenir Album 'Views of Saxe Coburg and Gotha', Vol. II, Souvenir Album VIII, p. 3 (c)

Distant View of Schloss Reinhardsbrunn from the Altsberg
Water-colour ($6\frac{7}{8} \times 9\frac{5}{8}$ in. – 175 mm $\times$ 244 mm)
Signed: W. Callow
From Queen Victoria's Souvenir Album 'Views of Saxe Coburg and Gotha', Vol. II, Souvenir Album VII, p. 47 (b)

The Garden of the Rosenau looking towards the Lauterberg Ruins
Water-colour ($9\frac{3}{8} \times 6\frac{7}{8}$ in. – 238×175 mm)
Signed: W. Callow
From Queen Victoria's Souvenir Album 'Views of Saxe Coburg and Gotha', Vol. II, Souvenir Album VII, p. 27 (a)

Entrance to the Rosenau
Water-colour ($9\frac{3}{8} \times 6\frac{7}{8}$ in. – 238×175 mm)
Signed: W. Callow
From Queen Victoria's Souvenir Album 'Views of Saxe Coburg and Gotha', Vol. II, Souvenir Album VII, p. 27 (b)

Views of the Palace and Grounds of the Schloss Reinhardsbrunn
Water-colour ($8\frac{5}{8} \times 12\frac{3}{4}$ in. – 219×324 mm) (*illustration no. 80*)
Signed: W. Callow 1863 (indistinct)
From the collection of HM Queen Mary. Transferred from Marlborough House, 1959
Reinhardsbrunn was one of the subjects, near Coburg, which Queen Victoria suggested that Callow should sketch during the 1863 visit

Laucha Valley, Reinhardsbrunn
Water-colour ($7 \times 9\frac{1}{2}$ in. – 178×241 mm)
Not signed. Attributed to Callow owing to a similarity of treatment (in the handling of distance) to other drawings by Callow in the Saxe Coburg and Gotha albums
From Queen Victoria's Souvenir Album 'Views of Saxe Coburg and Gotha', Vol. I (index p. 152), Souvenir Album VII, p. 41 (a)

The Kleine Palais, Gotha
Water-colour ($7 \times 9\frac{3}{4}$ in. – 178×248 mm)
Signed
From Queen Victoria's Souvenir Album VII, p. 59 (a)

A Castle in a Mountainous Landscape, a Stream in the Foreground, with Women washing Clothes
Water-colour, touches of white (7×10 in. – 178×254 mm)
Signed: W. Callow

View of Stolzenfels on the Lahn (*illustration no. 98*)
Water-colour ($7\frac{3}{8} \times 10\frac{3}{4}$ in. – 187×273 mm)
Signed: W. Callow, R.W.S. 1887
Included in an album of 75 water-colour drawings presented to Queen Victoria by the R.W.S. to mark her Jubilee in 1887 (*see* text, page 149)

THE ART GALLERY OF SOUTH AUSTRALIA, North Terrace, Adelaide, South Australia 5000

Reference Acc. No.

0.1600 **The Rathaus, on the Platz at Lucerne**
Water-colour on paper ($29\frac{3}{8} \times 22\frac{3}{8}$ in. – 746×568 mm)
Signed and dated 1848
Exhibited: No. 130, Society of Painters in Water-colours, 1848 ('... daylight-looking and truthful' – *Athenaeum*, 13 May 1848, p. 491)

0.1899 **Sorrento Harbour**
Water-colour ($14\frac{5}{8} \times 19\frac{3}{4}$ in. – 371×502 mm)
Signed and dated 1877

4910 D17 **Mercato Vecchio, Florence, 1879**
Pencil and black chalk on grey green paper ($6\frac{7}{10} \times 9\frac{7}{10}$ in. – 170×245 mm)
Inscribed: Mercato Vecchio, Florence May 27.79 (lower left)
Elder Bequest, 1949

4910 D16 **Canale del Olio, Venice, 1877**
Pencil on grey green paper ($6\frac{7}{10} \times 9\frac{7}{10}$ in. – 170×245 mm)
Inscribed: Canale del Olio, May 19.77 (lower left)
Elder Bequest, 1949

7111 D14 **The Fondaco di Turchi on the Grand Canal, Venice**
Pencil on tracing paper ($6\frac{9}{10} \times 23\frac{3}{5}$ in. – 175×600 mm)
Inscribed: Fondaco di Turchi (lower centre)
Gift of Mrs C. K. Callow, 1971

Exhibition: 'William Callow and Thomas Shotter Boys' – Art Gallery of South Australia, 1971. In addition to the above drawing (and the four other listed items) further examples from the collection of the Callow family were also displayed, including 'Bridge of Sighs' (*illustration no. 47*) and 'Fishing Boats at Scheveningen' (*illustration no. 42*)

The Art Gallery of Greater Victoria, British Columbia, Canada

Bolton Abbey
Water-colour with touches of body colour ($8\frac{9}{10} \times 13\frac{3}{5}$ in. – 225 × 345 mm)
Exhibited: 'Nineteenth Century English Water-colours and Drawings' – Collections of the Art Gallery of Greater Victoria/No. 3. Ex. No. 2; 'British Water-colours in the Collection of Mr and Mrs Paul Mellon' – exhibition at the Art Gallery of Greater Victoria – 28 Sept.–17 Oct. 1971, included 'Le Pont Neuf, Paris' by William Callow

The National Gallery of Canada, Ottawa, Ontario, Canada

Bayonne
Water-colour ($6\frac{1}{2} \times 9\frac{2}{5}$ in. – 165 × 239 mm). Not signed or dated
Provenance: Mrs M. L. Callow, bought from P. and D. Colnaghi, 1952
Exhibited: T. Agnew and Son, '79th Annual Exhibition of Water-colour Drawings' – January–March 1952

Marseilles
Graphite and water-colour on paper, laid down ($5\frac{13}{16} \times 9\frac{1}{16}$ in. – 198 × 230 mm)
Signed, lower left: Monogram, with brush
Inscribed, lower right: Marseilles, Juil 28. The year 1836 appears very faintly below on the mounting paper, with the whole date, July 28, 1836, repeated on the mount in another hand (Mrs Callow)
Provenance: Bought from Walker's Galleries Ltd, 1947, where it was exhibited in October 1947 – '43rd Annual Exhibition of Early English Water-colours. (No. 21)

Versailles (*illustration no. 17*)
Water-colour on Whatman paper ($9\frac{1}{10} \times 12\frac{3}{5}$ in. – 230 × 320 mm)
Signed and dated, lower right: W. Callow 1837
Provenance: Mrs M. L. Callow, bought from P. and D. Colnaghi, 1952
Exhibitions: T. Agnew and Sons – 79th Annual Exhibition of Water-colour drawings, Jan.–March 1952; Ottawa – National Gallery of Canada, 1952 – 'Victorian Artists in England'; Colnaghi, London, 1969 – 'European Drawings from the National Gallery of Canada'. No. 72 (reproduced p. 79 of catalogue); Paris, Musée du Louvre, November 20–February 2, 1970 – Raphael à Picasso, Dessins de la Galerie Nationale du Canada (No. 77)

View of Richmond, Yorkshire
Graphite on light blue paper, faded to grey ($10\frac{1}{4} \times 14\frac{9}{16}$ in. – 260 × 270 mm)
Inscribed and dated in pencil, lower right: Richmond, 1853
Bought from P. and D. Colnaghi in 1948
National Gallery of Canada Annual Report 1948–9, p. 16

MUSÉE NATIONAL DU CHÂTEAU DE VERSAILLES (Ministère de la Culture et de l'Environnement), Versailles, France

Versailles from the Heights of Satory
Engraved print, identical to a plate with this title in 'Les Fastes de Versailles' – H. M. Fortoul. *See* text and also catalogue notes for the original drawing which is in the Rhode Island School of Design

The Château and Orangerie viewed from the Swiss Lake (*illustration no. 18*)
Water-colour and pen
Signed and dated 1837

MUSÉE NATIONAL DU CHÂTEAU DE COMPIÈGNE, Place du Palais, 60200 Compiègne, France

Inventory No. 35282 Vue de l'entrée du port du Havre
Water-colour ($24\frac{4}{5} \times 35\frac{2}{5}$ in. – 630×900 mm)
On loan from the Musée de Louvre, Paris

FOUNDATION CUSTODIA L'INSTITUT NÉERLANDAIS, 121 Rue de Lille, 75 Paris VIIe, France

L'Hôtel de Ville de Leipzig (*illustration no. 65*)
Signé et daté à plume en bas à gauche: William Callow/1854
Aquarelle ($28\frac{9}{10} \times 22\frac{4}{5}$ in. – 735×579 mm)
Exp.: Londres, Royal [*sic*] Water-colour Society, 1854 – 49th Exhibition of the Society of Painters in Water-colours. No. 120

L'Escalier de l'Orangerie à Versailles
Annôté par l'artiste en bas, à gauche, à la plume: à Versailles Août 18.1832
Au verso à la mine de plomb: 26 et Versailles. William Callow
Aquarelle sur esquisse à la pierre noire ($5 \times 7\frac{4}{5}$ in. – 127×199 mm)
Provenance: Mme Nothman (vente, Londres, Sotheby, 2 Decembre 1959. No. 61), Thomas Agnew and Sons – Mme L. H. Beattie, 1960, Thomas Agnew and Sons, Londres, inv. no. 1972 – T67
Exp.: Londres, Thomas Agnew and Sons, 1960, Annual Exhibition, No. 107

MUSÉE DES BEAUX-ARTS DE NANCY, Place Stanlislas, 5400, Nancy, France

Entrée du Port de Livourne
Water-colour
Signed and dated: W. Callow, 1844

KUNSTSAMMLUNGEN DER VESTE COBURG, 8630, Coburg, Veste, Germany

Reference Z 4219 Das Mausoleum in Coburg*
($7 \times 9\frac{9}{10}$ in. – 177×251 mm)
Bez. u. li: W. Callow, und re. Mausoleum Coburg Augt 24/1863

* 'Das Mausoleum in Coburg' is dated on the day that Callow was received by Queen Victoria at Rosenau. Some of the other sketches in the Coburg collection were probably included in those shown to the Queen on that occasion

Z 4560 **Ehrenburg Coburg**
($10 \times 14\frac{1}{10}$ in. – 254×358 mm)
Bez. u. li: Ehrenburg Coburg Augt 17th 1863. u. mitte: W.C.

Z 4561 **Rosenau, Gesamtansicht**
($10 \times 14\frac{1}{10}$ in. – 254×357 mm)
Bez. u. li: Rosenau Augt 11. 1863. re. u.: W.C.

Z 4562 **Rosenau, Giebelseite**
Bez. u. li.: Rosenau, Augt. 12/1863
Ohne Signatur

Z 4563 **Schloss Callenberg mit Garten**
($10 \times 14\frac{1}{10}$ in. – 254×358 mm)
Bez. u. li: The Garden Callenberg. Aug 14. 1863, re. u.: W.C.

Henry E. Huntington Library and Art Gallery, San Marino, California, USA

Bayonne
Water-colour ($6\frac{3}{4} \times 4\frac{1}{2}$ in. – 171×114 mm)
Inscribed on verso: Bayonne Août 30. 1833
Bought by Mrs Hope from the artist's widow – purchased from Mrs Hope for the collection of Gilbert Davis (1949)

From the Belvedere
Water-colour ($14\frac{1}{4} \times 15\frac{1}{4}$ in. – 362×387 mm)
Inscribed and dated, lower left: From the Belvedere [*sic*]/Sept 3. 1863
Formerly thought to be an Italian view, but now identified as being executed during the first visit to Potsdam (*see* text, page 107)
From the collection of the artist's widow. Bought from the Squire Gallery for the collection of Gilbert Davis (1947)

Beech, Inveraray
Water-colour (10×14 in. – 254×356 mm)
Signed lower right: Wm. Callow
Inscribed in pencil, lower right: Beech/Inveraray/Jul 22.49
From the collection of the artist's widow. Bought from the Squire Gallery for the collection of Gilbert Davis (1948)

Bologna
Water-colour (10×7 in. – 254×178 mm)
Signed, lower left: W. Callow
Inscribed (in pencil in the artist's hand): The Piazza, Maggiore, Bologna, May 2/77
Bought from Thomas Agnew and Sons, 9 February 1948

Capel Curig (Carnarvonshire, Wales)
Water-colour ($10\frac{3}{4} \times 7\frac{1}{2}$ in. – 273×190 mm)
On verso, in the artist's hand: Passing by Capel Curig, Oct 12th 1858
Bought from the Squire Gallery for the collection of Gilbert Davis (1948)

Dieppe (the Castle)
Pencil (11 × 8 in. – 279 × 203 mm)
Signed, lower left: W. Callow
Inscribed, lower right: Dieppe June 4
Bought from P. and D. Colnaghi, for the collection of Gilbert Davis (1948)
Another drawing in this series is watermarked '1834'

Fishing Vessels entering Dieppe Harbour
Water-colour (18 × 12 in. – 457 × 305 mm)
Signed, lower right: Wm. Callow/1898
Bought at Christie's for the collection of Gilbert Davis (17 Dec. 1948)

Dieppe (from above the town)
Pencil (11 × 8 in. – 279 × 203 mm)
Signed, lower left: W. Callow
Inscribed, lower right: Dieppe June 4
Bought from P. and D. Colnaghi for the collection of Gilbert Davis (1948)

Dieppe – La Fontaine du Grand Cou
Pencil (11 × 8 in. – 279 × 203 mm)
Signed, lower left: W. Callow
Titled, lower right
Bought from P. and D. Colnaghi for the collection of Gilbert Davis (1948)
Another drawing in this series is watermarked '1834'

Dieppe (on the Quays)
Pencil (11 × 8 in. – 279 × 203 mm)
Signed, lower left: W. Callow
Inscribed, lower right: Dieppe/June 4
Bought from P. and D. Colnaghi for the collection of Gilbert Davis (1948)

A Street in Dieppe
Pencil (11 × 8 in. – 279 × 203 mm)
Signed, lower left: W. Callow
Inscribed, lower right: Dieppe June 5th
Bought from P. and D. Colnaghi for the collection of Gilbert Davis (1948)
Paper watermarked 1834

Drachenfels
Water-colour ($10\frac{3}{16} \times 14\frac{1}{8}$ in. – 259 × 359 mm)
Signed and dated 1838
Gift of C. H. Collins Baker

Ecouen
Water-colour ($4 \times 5\frac{1}{4}$ in. – 102 × 133 mm)
Inscribed on verso: Ecouen août 20th 1833
Bought by Mrs Hope from the artist's widow. Bought from Mrs Hope by Gilbert Davis (1949)

Sunset, Paris
Water-colour ($7\frac{3}{4} \times 5\frac{1}{4}$ in. – 197 × 133 mm)
Inscribed: Rue St George, Paris 1832

Lit.: Reproduced Pl. XIV – 'The Old Water-colour Society Club – 28th Annual Vol. 1950'
Bought by Mrs Hope from the artist's widow, bought from Mrs Hope for the collection of Gilbert Davis (1949)
This simple water-colour sketch is essentially a response to colour, very freely treated with swift flat strokes and dabs of the brush, the trees in the manner of some sketches by Boys, the foreground and skyline shown in a very basic, but atmospheric manner – plate in the Callow files, Witt Library, Courtauld Institute of Art

Cattewater, Plymouth
Pencil (14¼ × 10¼ in. – 362 × 260 mm)
Titled and dated: Sept 12/42
Bought from L. Chamberlain by Gilbert Davis 1948)

Pyrénées
Water-colour (9 × 5½ in. – 229 × 240 mm)
Signed with monogram (lower right)
Inscribed, lower left: Entrée des Ht. Pyrénées–Juillet 11 (see journal entry for 11 July 1836)
Bought from Walker's Galleries by Gilbert Davis (1951)

Castle St Angelo, Rome
Water-colour (14½ × 10¼ in. – 368 × 260 mm)
Signed, lower right: W. Callow
Inscribed in pencil: Château St. Ange. Roma/27 Sept 40
Bought from Leggatt Bros, for the collection of Gilbert Davis (1948)

Sorrento
Water-colour (14 × 6¾ in. – 356 × 171 mm)
Signed, lower left: W. Callow
Inscribed, lower right: Sorrento/May 6. 1876
Bought from the Squire Gallery by Gilbert Davis (1948)

Both Banks, St Ouen
Water-colour (9 × 5¼ in. – 229 × 133 mm)
Inscribed, lower left: St Ouen. Juillet 17/34
Bought from Thos. Agnew and Sons for the collection of Gilbert Davis (1950)

Hampstead Heath (*illustration no. 1*)
Water-colour (5½ × 3½ in. – 140 × 89 mm)
From a scrap-book bought by Mrs Hope from the artist's widow. Inscribed below the drawing in the artist's adult hand: Hampstead Heath – my first sketch in colours – W. Callow about 1825
Bought from Mrs Hope by Gilbert Davis (1949),

Hastings
Water-colour (8¾ × 6¼ in. – 222 × 159 mm)
Bought from the Squire Gallery by Gilbert Davis (1948)

Houses in a Landscape
Water-colour (10⅛ × 6⅝ in. – 257 × 168 mm)
Gift of C. H. Collins Baker

Old Palace, Kew
Water-colour (10¼ × 6¾ in. – 260 × 171 mm)
Bought from P. and D. Colnaghi by Gilbert Davis (1947)

Lake Scene
Water-colour (7¼ × 10 in. – 184 × 254 mm)
Signed, lower right: Wm. Callow
Bought from the Squire Gallery by Gilbert Davis (1948)

Malvern Wells
Water-colour (13¼ × 9¼ in. – 337 × 235 mm)
Signed, lower right: W. Callow
Inscribed, lower right: Malvern Wells, August 30/1848
Bought from T. Agnew and Sons by Gilbert Davis (1948)

Montagne
Water-colour (9 × 5¼ in. – 229 × 133 mm)
Monogram signature, lower right
Bought from Walker's Galleries by Gilbert Davis (1951)

Oberwesel
Water-colour (14 × 10¼ in. – 356 × 260 mm)
Signed, lower right: Wm. Callow
Inscribed in pencil (partly illegible): Oberwesel Oct 7
Bought from Thos. Agnew and Sons by Gilbert Davis (1947)

Tain et Tournon
Water-colour (10¾ × 4¾ in. – 273 × 121 mm)
Signed with initials, lower right
Inscribed in pencil in the artist's hand: Tain et Tournon Août 5 (*see* Journal entry, 5 August 1836)
Bought from Walker's Galleries by Gilbert Davis (1949)

Brig – Toulon
Water-colour (9 × 5¼ in. – 229 × 133 mm)
Signed with initials, lower left
Inscribed: Toulon port Juill 27 (*see* Journal entry, 27 July 1836)
Bought from Walker's Galleries by Gilbert Davis (1951)

Hulk – Toulon
Water-colour (9 × 5¼ in. – 229 × 133 mm)
Signed with initials, lower right
Inscribed: Toulon Juil 27.36 (see Journal entry, 27 July 1836)
Bought from Walker's Galleries by Gilbert Davis (1951)

Warship – Toulon
Water-colour (9 × 5¼ in. – 229 × 133 mm)
Signed with initials, lower right
Inscribed: à Toulon/Juill 27.1836
Bought from Walker's Galleries by Gilbert Davis (1951)

Rosenau
Water-colour (7×10 in. – 178×254 mm)
Signed, lower right: W. Callow
Inscribed: Rosenau Aug 12/63
Bought from the Squire Gallery by Gilbert Davis 1948)

Royaumont
Water-colour ($4\frac{3}{4} \times 7$ in. – 121×178 mm)
Signed with initials, lower right: W.C.
Inscribed: dans le parc à Royaumont Août 22. 1833 (*see* text, page 14)
Bought by Mrs Hope from the artist's widow. Bought from Mrs Hope by Gilbert Davis (1949)

Cloisters, Royaumont (*illustration no. 9*)
Water-colour ($6\frac{1}{4} \times 7\frac{3}{4}$ in. – 159×197 mm)
Inscribed in verso: Cloitres à la tour de Royaumont Août 21 1833 premier
Bought by Mrs Hope from the artist's widow. Bought from Mrs Hope for the collection of Gilbert Davis (1949)

The Lake, Royaumont
Water-colour ($9\frac{1}{2} \times 5\frac{3}{4}$ in. – 241×146 mm)
1833
Bought from Walker's Galleries for the collection of Gilbert Davis (1949)

St Germain
Water-colour ($12\frac{3}{4} \times 4\frac{1}{2}$ in. – 324×114 mm)
Inscribed in pencil on drawing: Marly from St Germain Août 24/33
Inscribed on verso in ink: St Germain Août 24 1833
Bought from Mrs Hope for the collection of Gilbert Davis (1949)

St Ouen, Seine
Water-colour ($9\frac{1}{2} \times 5$ in. – 241×127 mm)
Titled in pencil, also pencil notes on drawing
Bought from Walker's Galleries by Gilbert Davis (1949)

Tree Study
Water-colour ($13\frac{3}{4} \times 10$ in. – 349×254 mm)
Signed, lower right: Wm. Callow
Inscribed on the drawing: Valley of the East Lynn (sic), Lynmouth, Sept 6.47
Bought from the Squire Gallery by Gilbert Davis (1948)

Belfry at Tournai
Pencil ($10\frac{1}{2} \times 14\frac{1}{2}$ in. – 267×368 mm)
Titled and dated Sept 10. 1850 (Belfry on the Grand Place, built 1187. Restored and embellished with a steeple – 1852)
Bought from P. and D. Colnaghi by Gilbert Davis (1948)

Versailles, from the Lake
Water-colour (9×5 in. – 229×127 mm)
Bought from the Squire Gallery by Gilbert Davis (1952)

Yarmouth Beach
Water-colour ($10 \times 6\frac{3}{4}$ in. – 254×171 mm)
Signed, lower left: W. Callow
Inscribed with initials on verso
Bought from the Bury Art Gallery by Gilbert Davis (1950)

Cloister, Westminster Abbey
Water-colour ($11\frac{3}{4} \times 16\frac{1}{2}$ in. – 298×419 mm)
Signed, lower left, in water-colour: Wm. Callow
Inscribed below in pencil: Cloister/Westminster/1846
Bought from the Fine Art Society by Gilbert Davis (1948)

The Metropolitan Museum of Art, Fifth Avenue at 82nd Street, New York, NY 10028, USA

Acc. No. 48.149.24 **Caesar's Tower, Warwick Castle**
Water-colour and pencil on paper ($14\frac{1}{4} \times 10\frac{1}{4}$ in. – 362×260 mm)
Not signed. Attributed to William Callow in 1964. The inscription would appear to be in the handwriting of Callow, but the general treatment of the work has a marked resemblance to that of Harriet Callow. (*See illustration no. 46 fig. D*)
Exhibited: English Landscape Artists – Metropolitan Museum of Art, June 26–Sept. 6 1971

The St Louis Art Museum, St Louis, Missouri 63131, USA

Reference 13.68 **Harbour Scene with Hunter**
Pencil drawing on blue paper ($8\frac{1}{8} \times 12\frac{9}{16}$ in. – 207×320 mm)
Signed: Wm. C/Dec 1866 (lower right)
Formerly in the Swetzoff Gallery, Boston, Massachussetts

Museum of Fine Arts, Boston, Massachusetts, USA

Reference 67.78 **The Cloisters, Westminster Abbey**
($10\frac{7}{8} \times 7\frac{3}{8}$ in. – 276×187 mm)
Signed and inscribed: Cloister/Wst Abbey/1877 (lower left, in pencil)
Verso in pencil: Title, signature and RWS

49.1910 **Market Place at Rouen**
($13\frac{3}{8} \times 21$ in. – 340×533 mm)
Signed: W. Callow (lower left, very faint)

Fogg Art Museum, Harvard University, Cambridge, Massachusetts 02138, USA

Reference Acc. No.
1968.55 **Battleships and Longboats at Sea**
Graphite on pale grey/blue paper. No watermark: woven paper ($8\frac{1}{10} \times 12\frac{3}{5}$ in. – 206×320 mm)
Signed, lower left: W. C. Dec. 1866

This drawing and 1968.56 are from a sketchbook of 12 seascapes all on the same paper (*see* St Louis Museum)
Gift in memory of H. Swetzoff from his friends

1968.56 **Ships in Rocky Cove**
Graphite on pale grey/blue paper. No watermark; woven paper ($8\frac{1}{10} \times 12\frac{3}{5}$ in. – 206×320 mm)
Signed, lower left: W.C. July 1866
Gift in memory of H. Swetzoff from his friends

1975.32 **Abergavenny** (formerly catalogued as 'A Town in a Valley')
Water-colour over graphite ($9\frac{1}{2} \times 13\frac{1}{2}$ in. – 240×342 mm)
Signed at lower right in brown wash: W. Callow
Inscribed and dated at lower right: Abergavenny 1848
Gift of Mr George C. Homans, Mrs Henry L. Mason and Mrs Carl J. Gilbert
See City of Birmingham Museum for very similar work (*illustration no. 53*)

YALE CENTER FOR BRITISH ART, Box 2120, Yale Station, New Haven, Connecticut, USA

Reference 64/8/7/6 **Rheinfels and St Goar**

64/12/31/3 **Versailles, 1833**

64/9/9/9 **The Luxor, Paris, 1833**
'In December of this year the boat containing the Luxor, having been towed from Egypt to Havre and up the Seine to Paris, was moored close to the Place de la Concorde . . . I made a sketch of the boat containing the obelisk on the spot' – *Cundall*, p. 23

64/12/31/4 **Garden Stair, Haddon Hall, 1848**

B 1975.4.1470 **Plymouth Dockyard, after the Fire**

B 1975.4.1471 **Le Pont Neuf**
See Art Gallery of Greater Victoria, Canada, page 198

63/5/27/9 **The Citadel and Cattewater, Plymouth**
Pencil sketch
Inscribed: Sep. 13. 1842

63/5/27/10 **Shipbuilding, 1841**

63/5/27/11 **The Rhine at Assmannshausen**
Water-colour ($12\frac{1}{8} \times 17\frac{1}{2}$ in. – 308×444 mm)
Wide view, treated with broad washes of colour
Formerly in the collection of Martin Hardie

B 1975.4.106 **Madonna with Rabbit**
Water-colour ($4\frac{1}{2} \times 6\frac{1}{2}$ in. – 114×165 mm)
After Titian. 'I also used to study at the Louvre whenever I could spare the time, and made numerous copies of the paintings by Rubens, Titian, Ostade, Salvator Rosa and many others. They are still in my possession' – *Cundall*, p. 30

B 1975.4.107 **Landscape with Sheep**
Water-colour ($5 \times 9\frac{1}{2}$ in. – 127×241 mm)
After Rubens

B 1975.4.1052 **Margate**

B 1975.4.1053 **Castle on a Cliff with a Stormy Sky**

B 1975.4.1054 **The Rialto**
Water-colour ($4\frac{1}{4} \times 10\frac{1}{4}$ in. – 108×260 mm)
Signed: Wm. Callow
Inscribed: Augt 18. 1846
Very similar treatment to the 'Bridge of Sighs' (*see illustration no. 47*)

B 1975.3.189 **The Ferry, Glenelg**
(but later identified as 'Wallenstadt from Wesen')

B 1975.3.1106 **Blois on the Loire, 1856**

B 1975.3.1107 **Château d'Ecouen**

B 1975.3.1108 **View of Paris from Charenton**

B 1975.3.1109 **Notre Dame, Paris, 1835**

B 1975.3.1110 **The Seine at St Cloud**

B 1975.3.1111 a & b 2 vignettes on one page

B 1975.3.1112 & 1113 2 vignettes on one mount

MUSEUM OF ART, RHODE ISLAND SCHOOL OF DESIGN, Providence, Rhode Island 02903, USA

Reference 103 **Watermill at St Ouen** (*illustration no. 7*)
Water-colour and indian ink over pencil ($6\frac{3}{10} \times 9\frac{1}{2}$ in. – 160×240 mm)
Inscribed in pencil, lower right: St Ouen, near Paris. Also inscribed in ink on verso, partially visible through the backing, at upper centre, repeated at top right: Moulin de la – yre (illegible) July 3/1831/William Callow
Collection: Mrs M. L. Callow, bought by Walker's Galleries in 1927. Purchased by donor from Colnaghi in 1960
Exhibited: Walker's Galleries, 1927; Newport Art Association, 1961; George Washington University Library, Washington DC – 'English Water-colours and Drawings of the Eighteenth and Nineteenth Centuries' – exhibition travelled by the Smithsonian Institution, 1962–4
Anonymous gift

104 **Montpellier**
Water-colour and chinese white over pencil on blue grey paper ($5\frac{3}{10} \times 9\frac{1}{10}$ in. – 133×230 mm)
Initialled in ink, lower right: monogram with 'c' encircling the 'W'. Inscribed in ink, lower right: Montpellier, Juil 22/1836. 1836 traced over in another hand (*see* M. L. Callow, text, page 178)
Anonymous gift

105 **Versailles from the Heights of Satory**
Water-colour and brown ink ($7\frac{3}{8} \times 11\frac{1}{5}$ in. – 194 × 284 mm)
Signed in pencil, outlined in ink, lower right: W. Callow (date appears to read 1851, but this is impossible. '39' is pencilled underneath the last two digits)
The work is very similar to the illustrated example from the Musée du Château de Versailles, but a slightly more distant view
Collection: Bonham's Auction, May 1964, and Fine Art Society, from whom purchased by donor in 1965
Engraved: J. Saddler for H. M. Fortoul, 'Les Fastes De Versailles', published by Delloye, Paris, 1839. Engraved by Leitch Ritchie for Charles Heath's '*Picturesque Annual for 1839 – Versailles*', published in London, 1839
Anonymous gift

JOHANNESBURG ART GALLERY (JOHANNESBURGSE KUNSMUSEUM), SOUTH AFRICA

The collection includes 30 drawings by William Callow, dated between 1844 and 1874. These were presented anonymously in 1917 to General Jan Smuts, who subsequently donated them to the gallery

Note: Space does not permit the listing of all examples of work by William Callow in collections abroad

*Complete List of Exhibits by William Callow with the Society of Painters in Water-colours, 1838–1908**

1838

Entrance to the Port of Marseilles
Castle and Village of Montrejeau, near Bagnères de Bigorre, Pyrénées
The Town of Vienne, on the Rhône
The Town of Avignon, on the Rhône
Montpellier from the Aqueduct, South of France
Fort St Jean and Part of the Bay, Marseilles
The Old Bridge at Avignon, on the Rhône
View of the Vignemale from Lac du Gaube, Upper Pyrénées

1839

The Town of Schaffhausen, Switzerland
Distant View of Heidelberg, with Rhine River
Mayence on the Rhine
The Town of Lucerne, on the Lake of the Quatre Cantons
Lake of Geneva from the Church of St Martin, Vevey
Ehrenbreitstein and Coblenz from the heights of Pfaffendorf
On the Rhine at Rhense – Castle of Marksburg in the Distance
Rheinfels and St Goar from Castle Katz, on the Rhine

1840

Interior of the Port of Havre
View of Lyons from near the Junction of the Rhône and Soane
Lowestoft Fishing Boats
Tain and Tournon, on the Rhône
Castle and Town of Heidelberg from the Terrace
Rheinfels and St Goar from St Goarhausen, Rhine
The Allée Blanche from Col de la Seigne, Savoy
Lowestoft – Fishing Boats preparing to launch

1841

Oberwesel, on the Rhine
Piazza Falcone from the Villa Reale, Naples
Naples from Porta del Carmine
Gravedona, on the Lake Como
The Rialto, Venice
Maecenas' Villa and Cascatella of Tivoli
Neapolitan Fishing Boat – Sunrise
Venice from the Riva degli Schiavoni

1842

View of Como
Naples from the Sea – Sunrise
View from the Churchyard at Thun, Switzerland
On the Grand Canal, Venice
Château of Dieppe, Coast of Normandy
In the Bay of Naples
Granville, Coast of Normandy
Lake of Wallenstatt, from Weser, Switzerland

1843

Fishing Boat off Dieppe
Citadel at Plymouth – Mount Batten and Cattewater in the Distance
Verona from the Old Bridge
Hospital of the Grimsel and Lake of Klensee, Switzerland
Distant View of Exeter
Street in Bologna, looking towards the Piazza
Torquay, looking over Torbay
On the Grand Canal, Venice, from the Dogana

* Royal Society of Painters in Water-colours from 1881

1844

Durham
Santa Salute and Dogana, Venice
Jedburgh Abbey, Scotland
Entrance to the Port of Tréport, Coast of Normandy
Wetterhorn and Upper Glacier, Grindelwald, Switzerland
Street in Bologna
Ehrenbreitstein, on the Rhine
Edinburgh from Salisbury Crags

1845

Cochem, on the Moselle
Lake of Geneva from Vevey – Morning
Old Houses at Trarbach, on the Moselle
Houses of the Francs Bateliers and Church of St Nicholas on the Canal of Ghent
Vico – Bay of Naples
Street in Calais
The Piazza Falcone, etc., from the Quai St Lucia at Naples
Entrance to the Port of Havre

1846

Street in Rotterdam, with the Church of St Lawrence
Castle and Town of Trarbach, on the Moselle
Dutch Fishing Boat at Dort
Nieder Heimbach, on the Rhine – Bacharach in the Distance
Cathedral of Antwerp from Rue du Port
Rotterdam
The Rialto, Venice
Old Bridge at Avignon, on the Rhône

1847

Amsterdam – Dutch Boats running in – Stiff Breeze
Piazza del Duomo, Trent, in the Tyrol
Casa Grimani, on the Grand Canal, Venice
Bridge of Sighs, Venice, looking towards the Grand Canal
Richmond Castle, Yorkshire
Melrose Abbey from the Banks of the Tweed
Scarborough – Sunrise
The Pfalz with Caub and the Castle of Gutenfels, on the Rhine

1848

Ilfracombe, from Capstone Hill, looking towards Hillsborough
Distant View of Cologne, on the Rhine
Water Mill on the West Lyn, Lynmouth, North Devon
The Neu-Munster, etc., Wurzburg, Bavaria (during the Fair)
Lynmouth from the Sea, North Devon
The Rathaus, on the Platz at Lucerne
Cochem, on the Moselle
Glacier du Rhône and the Garlingstock, Pass of Furca, Switzerland

1849

Distant View of Monmouth
Distant View of Melrose Abbey
The Grönsel Markt, Ghent
View of Ross from the Wye
Llanthony Abbey, Monmouthshire
An Old Street in Frankfort
Goodrich Court – Distant View of the Castle
Lugano, on the Lake of Lugano
Abergavenny from the Monmouth Road
Paris – View of the Tuileries, Pont Royale, etc.
Old House, High Street, Tewkesbury
Maison des Francs Bateliers at Ghent
The Neustadt, Innsbrück
Part of the Ruins of Raglan Castle
West Entrance to Tintern Abbey
Village of Cauterets, Hautes Pyrénées
Riva dei Schiavoni, Venice

1850

Inveraray Castle, the Seat of his Grace the Duke of Argyll
Lucerne, Lake of the Quatre Cantons
Bay of Arran from Lamlash Road looking towards Brodick and Goatfell
Venice – on the Grand Canal – Palazzo Contarini, delle Belle Arti, etc.
The Tolbooth, Glasgow, from the Saltmarket
The Trongate, Glasgow, the Tron Church, etc.
On the Chiesa, Naples
Trent, Valley of the Adige
The Piazzetta, Venice
Old House in the Neustadt, Innsbrück

Weymouth, Dorsetshire – Bill of Portland in the Distance
Tours, on the Loire
View of Inveraray, on Loch Fyne
Street in Calais, looking towards the Grande Place
Old Gateway, Great Malvern, Worcestershire
The Butter Cross, Winchester
Interior of the Bishop's Court, Liège
Dutch Fishing Boats, Amsterdam
Water Mill at Lee, North Devon

1851

Winchester Cathedral from the Quay
The Town and Fortress of Bellinzona, on the Ticino
Tower on the Vrijdags Markt, Ghent
Cauterets, Pyrénées
Durham Cathedral from the River
Castle and Village of Angera from Arona, Lake Maggiore
On the Rokin Canal, Amsterdam
The Weighing House at Amsterdam
Rue St Honoré, Paris, looking towards the Palais Royal
Distant View of Lancaster from the Meadows
The Rialto, Venice, from the Fish Market
The Piazzetta, Venice, looking towards San Giorgio
The Market House, Ross on Wye
Remains of St Mary's Priory, Monmouth
The Blackfriars, Hereford
The Trongate, Glasgow, from the Corner of the High Street
Il Ponte della Paglia Riva dei Schiavoni, Venice
The Pantiles, Tunbridge Wells – Morning
Blois, on the Loire – Evening
Old House at Berncastel, on the Moselle

1852

Palazzo Barbarigo (the Residence of Titian), Venice
Looking into the Grand Place at Lille from the Place du Théâtre
Distant View of Ross on Wye
Grand Entrance to Hurstmonceaux Castle, Sussex
Abergavenny, Monmouthshire – the Holy Mountain in the Distance
Distant View of Naples – Early Morning
Château d'Amboise, on the Loire
The Belfry at Ghent, from the Marché au Grain
The Stone Bow, High Street, Lincoln
Part of the Cathedral, Abbeville
Castle and Village of Mont Richard, on the Cher, Département Loir-et-Cher
Les Halles, Grande Place, Bruges
Place d'Armes, Calais
Riva dei Schiavoni, Venice
Church of the Santa Salute, Venice, from the Belle Arti
Maison des Francs Bateliers, Ghent
Remains of Nether Hall, Essex
Interior of the Port of Havre
The Guildhall, High Street, Exeter
Water Mill at Lee, near Ilfracombe
Chapel of St Jean at Orléans
Chapel of the Holy Blood, Bruges

1853

The Burgstrasse, Hanover
The Rialto, Venice
Church of San Giovanni and San Paolo with the Monument of Colleone
Cathedral of Abbeville from the Grande Place
Mont Blanc from Chamouni.
The Niewe Kerk on the Dam, Amsterdam
The High Street, Lincoln
Interior of the Court of the Wartburg, the Place of Luther's Confinement in 1521
The Market Place, Eisenach
The Hôtel de Ville, Bruges
At Malines, near the Fish Market
The Market Place, Padua
Entrance to the Court of the Ducal Palace, Venice
The Pantiles, Tunbridge Wells
The Hôtel de Ville, Ghent
Interior of the Port of Marseilles
St Mary's Hall, Coventry
Castle of Hammerstein, from Andernach
Frankfort-on-the-Maine
Riva dei Schiavoni, Venice
On the Grand Canal, Venice

1854

Gateway of Battle Abbey, Sussex
Basle, Switzerland, from the Bridge

On the Grand Canal, Venice, looking towards the Foscari Palace
Eastgate Street, Chester – Autumnal Evening
Oberwesel, on the Rhine, with the Castle of Schönberg
Venice
La Place d'Armes, Lille
Dresden from the Gardens of the Japanese Palace
The Rathaus, on the Market Place, Leipzig
Orléans
The Ca' d'Oro de Venise from the Foot of the Rialto
The Castle of Katz from St Goar, on the Rhine
Heidelberg from above the Bridge
Old Houses in Northgate Street, Chester
Tain and Tournon, on the Rhône
From the Ponte della Pieta, Venice
Church of San Pietro, Como
The Breiteweg at Magdeburg
From the Foscari Palace, Venice
Neapolitan Fishing Boats
The Fish Market, Ghent
The Dom Platz, Frankfort

1855

On the Grand Canal, from the Leone Bianco, Venice
Church of St Pierre, Caen
Mayence, on the Rhine
The Dom-Kirche at Würzburg from the Bridge, during the Fair
The Old Feudal Town of Oberwesel, on the Rhine
Castelnuovo from the Molo, Venice
Lutheran Church at Bacharach, on the Rhine
On the Place du Théâtre, Lille
San Giorgio, Venice
Castle of St Angelo, Rome
Canal at Ghent, with the Church of St Nicholas
Crossing the Rialto, Venice
Pallazzo Foscari from the Belle Arti, Venice
The Piazza at Padua
A Street in Verona
The Belfry at Evreux
Corso Francese, Milan
Evening at Sutton Valence
Doune Castle
Eton College – Sunset
Old House at Ghent
The Market Cross at Salisbury
Distant View at Tewkesbury
Tell's Chapel, Lake of the Four Cantons
Foregate Street, outside the Walls, Chester

1856

Huy, on the Meuse
The Santa Salute, Venice
Old Houses on the Rhône at Geneva
The Hôtel de Ville, Brussels
Close Gate and Widows' College, Salisbury
Werner's Chapel from the Inn Yard, Bacharach
The Bear and Billet Inn, Bridge Street, Chester
The Rialto, Venice
Winchester
The Markt Strasse and Rathaus, Hanover
Rue St Pierre, Caen
Trent from the Bank of the Adige
Bellaggio, Lago di Como
The Trongate, Glasgow
Ancien Port de la Ville, Bruges
Goodrich Court, on the Wye
Arundel Castle, Sussex
Durham
The Contarini Palace, Venice
Canal Scene, Lucerne
Ancient Manor House near the Abbey Gate, Malvern, now removed
Portslade, near Brighton
The Ca' d'Oro, Venice

1857

Double Butcher Row, Shrewsbury
A Buckinghamshire Lane – Sunset
On the Grand Canal, Venice
St Sauveur, Caen
Venice
Schloss Elz
Hôtel de Ville, Lille
The Castle at Rheinfels
Rue de la Grosse Horloge, Rouen – Morning
Exeter from the Meadows
Il Ponte Rotto, Rome
Naples
San Giorgio, Venice
Lynmouth, Devon

Quai de Rosaire, Bruges
On the Bridge at Basle
On the Rhine at Cologne
Piazza dei Signori, Verona
Venice from the Dogana
Ehrenbreitstein
Conisboro' Castle, Yorkshire
On the Lago Maggiore

1858

The Piazzetta, Venice
Antwerp – St Paul's
Stirling Castle from the Meadows
Old House on the Quay at Malines
San Giorgio, Venice
Thun – Early Morning
On the Old Walls of Bacharach
The Leaning Towers of Bologna
The Water Gate, Honfleur
St Margaret's Church, Gotha
Venice
The Kaufhaus, Coblenz
Rouen, from the Banks of the Seine
The Cathedral, Chartres – Sunrise
Verona – The Piazza delle Erbe
Geneva
The Keep, Castle Rising, Norfolk
On the Adige, Verona
The Rialto, Venice
Brighton Beach
Above Schaffhausen
Castle and Town of Beaucaire, on the Rhône

1859

Saumur, on the Loire
Piazza Grande, Bologna
Bolton Abbey – Sunset
Pass of St Gothard
Castle and Town of Richmond, Yorkshire
Ducal Palace, Venice – Early Morning
Hôtel de Ville, Antwerp
Old Bridge at Nuremberg
Place au Change, Nantes
Ruins of St Benet's Abbey, near Norwich
Rue de la Grosse Horloge, Rouen
On the Adige, Verona
Temple of Vesta, Tivoli
Stolzenfels, on the Rhine
Grand Canal, Venice
Frankfort-on-the-Maine

1860

Ehrenbreitstein
Brunswick
Place St Pharaïlde, Ghent
Market Day at Richmond, Yorkshire
Venice from the Rialto – Morning
Monmouth Castle
Tivoli with Villa d'Este and the Cascatelle
The Wartburg – The Scene of Luther's Imprisonment
Autumn Afternoon (from Nature)
Il Ponte Rotto, on the Tiber, Rome
Venice from the Dogana
Hôtel de Ville, Calais
Goodrich Court and Castle, on the Wye
A Summer's Evening on the Avon, at Evesham
The Dogana, Venice

1861

Mont St Michel, Normandy
Dom Gasse, Würzburg – Fair Time
Robin Hood's Bay, Yorkshire Coast

'I looked down on boats, and barks; on masts, sails, flags; on groups of busy sailors working at the cargoes of the vessels; on wide quays strewn with bales, casks, merchandize of many kinds; on great ships, lying near at hand in stately indolence; on islands crowned with gorgeous domes and turrets, and where golden crosses glittered in the light, a-top of wondrous churches springing from the sea, going down upon the margin of the green sea, rolling on before the door and filling all the streets I came upon a place of such surpassing beauty and such grandeur that all the rest was poor and faded in comparison with its absorbing loveliness. It was a great Piazza, as I thought, anchored like the rest in the deep ocean.' – An Italian Dream, by Charles Dickens

The Rhine at St Goar
The Moselle at Coblenz
Cochem, on the Moselle
Riva dei Schiavoni, Venice
Street in Innsbrück
Gravedona – Lake Como
Martigny
The Church of St Michael, Ghent
Distant View of Lincoln
On the Inn, Innsbrück

On the Terrace at Heidelberg
Basle
Looking towards the Rialto, Venice

1862

Summer

On the Tiber, Rome
Water Mill at Lee, North Devon
Hastings
The Culag Burn, Loch Inver
Castle of Katz, on the Rhine
Venice
Beaugency, on the Loire
Mill near Antwerp
On the Old Walls at Bacharach
Castel Gandolfo
San Giorgio, Venice
A Street in Evreux, Normandy
Place St Pierre, Caen
Hôtel de Ville, Courtrai
Rheinfels and Village of St Goar
Highland Bothies – Entrance of Glenfinlas
Santa Maria della Salute

Winter

Fall of East Lyn, Lynmouth
The Grey Friars, Coventry
Campsie Glen
Place à Tours
Malvern Wells
Port of Whitby
Sidmouth
On the Shore, Lynmouth
Near Loch Inver, Sutherlandshire
From Lamlash Road, Arran
Maison des Nantais, Nantes
Wimbledon Common
Holy Loch, Argyllshire
Cottage at Malvern
The Torrs, Ilfracombe
From Sandsend, Whitby
Fall of Kirkaig, Sutherlandshire
Glen Rosa, Arran
The Castle Rock, Lynton
The Torrs, Ilfracombe
Glydock, South Wales

1863

Summer

Midday at Haddon
Cologne from the River
Place St Pharaïlde, Ghent
Sunset at Gotha
The Ca' d'Oro, Venice
The Campagna, with Porta San Giovanni, Rome
Falls of the Rhine, Schaffhausen
From the Chiesa, Naples
Market Place, Frankfort
Rheinstein and Assmannshausen
At Antwerp
Heidelberg
Remains of the Palace of the Dukes of Burgundy, Malines
Arona, Lake Maggiore
Canal Reale
Vico, Bay of Naples
Riva dei Schiavoni

Winter

St Nicholas's Priory, Great Yarmouth
Canal Scene, Rotterdam
Salmon Trap on the East Lyn, Lynmouth
A Study near Missenden
Venice
Sidmouth, South Devon
Lynmouth Bridge, North Devon
Rue St Honoré, Paris
Bridge of Sighs, Venice
Uncle Tom's Cabin, Folkestone Beach

1864

Summer

Morning on Lago Maggiore
Market Place at Frankfort
The Moselle Bridge at Coblenz
Beilstein, on the Moselle
Leaning Towers at Bologna
Grand Canal, Venice
Water Gate, Norwich
Old Houses at Pride Hill, Shrewsbury
Distant View of Namur
Stolzenfels and Lahnstein, on the Rhine
The Alien Priory, near Eastbourne
Palazzo Barbarigo, Venice
Cologne
At Unterseen, Switzerland
Old Gate at Rotterdam
The Rialto, Venice
Market Morning at Coburg

Winter

Three Sketches, Abroad
Old Priory at Great Yarmouth
Interior of Richmond Church, Yorkshire, before its Restoration
Two Studies
Two Sketches in the Botanic Gardens, Regent's Park
Three Sketches
Neue Münster, Würzburg
Four Scraps
Three Scotch Views
Souvenirs of Rosenau, Birthplace of H.R.H. the late Prince Consort

1865

Summer

Beilstein, on the Moselle
Château de Montélimar, Rhône
On the Grand Canal, Venice
Fishing Boats at Naples – Early Morning
The Citadel, Würzburg, Bavaria
Castle and Village of Lahneck
Inveraray with the Hill of Duniquoich
Bacharach, on the Rhine
Garden Scene at Versailles
Looking towards Sutton Valence
The Judengasse, Frankfort
Water Mill at Lee, near Ilfracombe
Lochgoilhead, Argyllshire
Old House at Tewkesbury
Pride Hill, Shrewsbury

Winter

Two Sketches of Venice
Isola Bella from Stresa
Three Marine Studies
A Mill and Other Objects
Two Views on the Rhine
Bolton Abbey and Cottage Scene
Three Scotch Studies
Three Sketches on Lago Maggiore
Four Studies

1866

Summer

Entrance to the Gorge of Gondo, Simplon
Lyme Regis, Dorset
Berncastel, on the Moselle – Evening
Venice, looking up the Grand Canal
Lago di Como
Bellagio, Lago di Como
Boppart, on the Rhine
Richmond Hill from Twickenham – Sunrise
Arona, on the Lago Maggiore
Canale della Posta, Venice
On the Piazza delle Erbe, Verona
On the Market Place, Hanover
Entrance to Sutton Pool, Plymouth
Fishing Boat off Lowestoft
Maison des Francs Bateliers, Ghent

Winter

1. Plymouth 2. Amsterdam
Head of Loch Fyne
Study at Glydock, South Wales
1. Brighton 2. Study of Rocks 3. Dover
1. A River Scene 2. Mont Dragon, on the Rhône
1. A Water Mill 2. Rocky Landscape
St Winifred's Well, Holywell, Flintshire
Three Sketches
1. Dieppe 2. Sea-piece 3. A Mill
Four Studies

1867

Summer

Bridge Street, Chester – Morning
Werner's Chapel, Bacharach
Menaggio, Lago di Como
The Courtyard at Heidelberg
Castle and Town of Beaucaire, on the Rhône
Bringing in Fish, Honfleur
By the Venetian Column, Piazza delle Erbe, Verona
The Boompjes, Rotterdam
Street in Rouen
Lac du Petit Trianon, Versailles
Namur – Junction of the Sambre and Meuse
A Water Mill
On the Quay, Frankfort
Entering Port
A Storm at the Mumbles

Winter

Recollections of the Rhine
Mount Edgcumbe and Sandgate
Two Views of the Isle of Wight
Three Marine Studies
Three Sketches of Rhine Scenery
Landscape Study

Four Sketches
Mountain Scenery
Water Mill and Sea-piece
Old Bridge – Morning Effect
Two Landscape Studies
Stormy Weather

1868

Summer

Market Place at Coburg
The Piazza delle Erbe, Verona
On the Riva dei Schiavoni, Venice
Town and Fortifications of Luxembourg
St Pierre, Caen
Rheinfels and St Goar – Summer Rain
Bacharach
Mont Richard, on the Cher
Tintern from the Village
Canale della Posta, Venice
Dutch Boat entering Port
Granville, Coast of Normandy – Waiting for the Tide
Old Mill in Surrey
Orca, Lago Lugano
Grand Canal, Venice
Stormy Weather off Lowestoft

Winter

St Cloud, From Sèvres
Saltwood and Goodrich Castles
Remembrances of the Rhine
Glen Rosa, Isle of Arran
Three Studies, Various
Mountain Scenery
Study at Haddon
Mill Scene and View of Swanage
Four Marine Studies
Coast of Devonshire
Lake Scene – Sunset
The Cliffs, Freshwater

1869

Summer

Coast Scene
Flint Castle – Sunrise
Isola Bella, Lago Maggiore
Church of St James, Antwerp
Richmond, Yorkshire
Piazza Corpus Domini, Turin
Street in Frankfort
Entrance to the Villa Carlotta, Cadenabbia
The Rialto
Namur, on the Sambre
Greenwich
Beilstein, on the Moselle
Sunrise near Rome

Night wanes; the vapours round the mountain curl'd
Melt into morn, and light awakes the world.

Temple of Venus and Rome
Santa Salute, Venice
Port of Fécamp, Normandy

Winter

Study of Trees
Reigate
Two Studies
Twickenham and Eton
Three Studies of Rhine Scenery
Two Sea-pieces
Three Coast Studies
Sunset at Sea
Fishing Boat returning at Sunrise
Sketches of Chester

1870

Summer

Street in Old Trarbach
Dinant, on the Meuse
Canale della Posta, Venice
Fishing Boats at Anchor in the Harbour of Granville
Susa, North Italy
Lausanne, Lake of Geneva
Place de Calende, Rouen
The Market Place, Coburg
The Rialto, Venice – Early Morning
Place du Marché, Tours
Venice
The Chiesa, Naples
The Piazzetta, Venice
Cologne
Boats running into Dieppe
Marksburg, from Rhense, on the Rhine

Winter

Landscape with Mill
Raglan Castle
Old Manor House
1. Torquay 2. Lake of Como

Bacharach am Rhein
Storm and Calm
Study of Sea
1. Peterborough 2. On the Tamar 3. Southampton
1. A Coast Scene 2. Granville 3. Calais
1. Usk 2. Crickhowell

1871

Summer

La Dogana, Venice
St Michel, Foot of Mont Cenis
French Fishing-Boats leaving St Valéry
Canal Scene, Rotterdam
Rue Flamande, Bruges
Above the Falls at Schaffhausen
Hastings – Early Morning
The Old Town of Trarbach, on the Moselle
Naples from Castellamare
King Edward Tavern, Chester
The Vrijdags Markt, Ghent
Posta della Lettere, Venice
The Marché au Lion, Lisieux, Normandy
Mont Richard, on the Cher – Summer Afternoon
Cochem, on the Moselle

Winter

Rain and Sunshine
Frankfort
Trarbach, on the Moselle
Water Mill at Lee, North Devon
Tintern Abbey
The Thames near Gravesend
Bolton Abbey
Bodiam Castle, Sussex
Bacharach am Rhein

1872

Summer

Street in Limburg, on the Lahn
On the Rokin, Amsterdam
Fair Time on the Grande Place, Bruges
At Quillebœuf, on the Seine – Sunrise
The Four Towers, etc., Ems
Tête de Flandres, opposite Antwerp
Canale del Fonteco, Venice
Scarborough from the Sands – Misty Morning
Cathedral, etc., Limburg, on the Lahn – Summer Afternoon
Old Buildings at Boppart, on the Rhine
Looking into the Market Place at Coburg
On the Kool Quai, Antwerp
The Judengasse, Frankfort

Winter

A Windmill
Sunrise and Beach Scene
Torquay
Rouen and Caen
Relics at Brighton
A Water Mill
Landing Fish on Yarmouth Beach
Landscape Studies
Cromer and Dunstanborough
Going to Market
Sunrise and Sunset
Caistor Castle, near Yarmouth

1873

Summer

The Ponte Rotto and Temple of Vesta, Rome
Old Harbour at Folkestone
A Street in Limburg, on the Lahn
Shoreham, Sussex
Botzen, in the Tyrol
The Tour de l'Horloge, Evreux
Old Gateway at Rotterdam
Lugano from the Port
Bacharach am Rhein
The Old Telegraph and Tower, etc., Calais
Conisborough Castle, near Doncaster
The Ca' d'Oro, on the Grand Canal, Venice
Castel d'Ovo, Naples

Winter

Fisherman's Hut – Early Morning
Gypsy Tents
Sunset on the Mountains
Near Sorrento, Naples
A Roadside Inn and Water Mill
Two Studies of Sea
On the Lago Maggiore
Yarmouth Jetty and New Brighton
A Cottage near Malvern
Gathering Rushes
Two Woodland Studies
On the Moselle

1874

Summer

Monmouth Castle
Fishing Boats leaving Honfleur – Early Morning
Riva dei Schiavoni, Venice
Landing Fish at Eastbourne
Old Houses at Berncastel, on the Moselle
Abbeville Cathedral from the Market Place
Berwick-on-the-Tweed from the Castle
Bellagio, Lago di Como
Ehrenbreitstein from the Moselle Bridge
Lisieux, looking towards the Transept of St Pierre
Verona with the Maffei Tower
The 'Golden Hirsch' Apotheke, Giessen

Winter

On the East Lyn, Devonshire
Coast Scene
Barnard Castle, Yorkshire
The Lac de Gaube, Pyrénées
A Water Mill – Early Morning
Cave near Genoa
Bothy, Loch Goyle
Mill on the Scheldt – Moonlight
Lauterbrunnen and Staubbach
Sunset – A Composition

1875

Summer

Rotterdam
Cologne – Autumn Evening
The Grand Canal, Venice
Le Chêvet de St Pierre, Caen
The Castle and Town of Salzburg
Summer Evening on the Wye at Goodrich Castle
Tivoli with the Cascade and Temple of the Sybil
The Holz-Markt, Halberstadt
Albert Dürer's House at Nuremberg
Isola Bella from Stresa, Lago Maggiore
Rheinstein
Waiting for Fish at St Valéry-en-Caux – Sunrise
Coarse Weather at Gorleston Harbour

Winter

On the Rhine
A Water Mill
The Source of the Thames
Clearing the Wreck – Sunset
At Bingen, on the Rhine
Sheep in a Lane
Sunset after a Storm
Wind and Rain
French Fishing Boats
A Waterfall
Dover and Brighton in Former Days
At Killarney – The Weir Bridge and the Castle Crag
Raglan Castle
Study of Sea
A Cottage

1876

Summer

Unter Taschenmacher and Rathaus, Cologne
Entrance to Calais Harbour – Rough Weather
Canale della Posta, Venice
On the Pier at Tréport, Normandy – Early Morning
The Last Glow from the Terrace, Heidelberg
An August Morning at Ems
Weilburg, on the Lahn
The Stadthaus and Markt Platz, Hanover
Nuremberg from a Bridge near the Trödal Markt
Fountain at Marburg, Hesse-Cassel
Grand Canal, Venice, looking towards the Lido – Early Morning
A Rotterdam Canal Scene
Luxembourg – Sunset

Winter

Shanklin Chine, Isle of Wight
Near Pierrefitte (Pyrénées), Cascade of Nantborrant, Switzerland
Cottage near Sidmouth
Beilstein, on the Moselle
Old Houses at Trèves
Two Views in South Devon
Landscape – A Composition
The Coast near Sidmouth
Study of Coast Scenery
Cochem, on the Moselle
An Irish Cabin
Dunkeld
Botzen, in the Tyrol
A Street in Bruges – Morning
A Venetian Canal

1877

Summer

Marburg, Hesse-Cassel
Fishing Boats, waiting for the Tide, Port of Havre – Sunrise
Entrance to the Old Part of Arona, Lago Maggiore
The Peschiera, Genoa
Castle and Town of Runkel, on the Lahn
A Venetian Canal
Loading Oranges and Lemons at Sorrento, from the Marina
The Mercato Ruava, Florence
Chancel of St Sauveur, Caen
Gateway of St Martin's Abbey, Tours
On the Dom-Platz at Ratisbon
Honfleur – Calm, Early Morning
The Ponte Vecchio, Florence

Winter

Rheinfels and Wolfsberg, on the Moselle
Il Diavoletto and L'Abondanza, Florence
A Swiss Valley
Mountain Gorge near Pierrefitte
Two Studies of Sea
Ullswater and Sea Coast
Riva dei Schiavoni
A Stormy Day in Scotland
Matlock
Mentone
The Wye and Wharf
A Country Lane
A Calm Evening
Fishing-Boats in a Squall
A Street Scene

1878

Summer

Ruined Mill near Dolce Acqua, Italy
Fishing Boats at Fécamp, Normandy – Early Morning
Il Mercato Vecchio, Florence
Casa Cavallino, Grand Canal, Venice
The Old Bridge and Tower at Nuremberg
Sunrise on the Seine at Rouen
Ponte del Canonico, Venice
Entrance to the Old Convent of San Gregorio, Venice
Castle of Stolzenfels, on the Rhine
Teatro Marcello, Rome
Dieppe
Market Place at Botzen, in the Tyrol
Canal di Barrettaria, Venice
Place St Pharaïlde, Ghent
In the Judengasse, Frankfort

Winter

On the Moselle
Winchester from the Meadows
Riva dei Schiavoni, Venice
Autumn on the Trent
Mussel Gathering at Lee, North Devon
Bellaggio, on Lake Como, and Isola Bella
East Cowes; and Dunoon, on the Clyde
Souvenirs of Loch Etive
In the Gloaming
A Devonshire Cottage
A Street in Trèves
Old Gateway on the Rhine
River and Coast

1879

Summer

On the Road to Rocca Bruna – Monaco in the Distance
Canale della Posta, Venice
Palazzo Cicogna, Venice
Fishing Boats off Tréport
Town Hall and Market Place, Padua – Early Morning
At the Foot of the Leaning Towers, Bologna
Santa Lucia, Naples
Tour de l'Horloge, Rouen
Port of Granville, Normandy
On the Rhine
Castellamare, on the Quay
San Pietro di Banchi, Genoa

1879–80

Winter

Sunrise and Sunset – Guisachan
Dover and Sandgate
A Street in Rouen
Scarborough from Filey Brigg
Venice at Sunset
On the Moselle
Night coming on – A Study
A Trout Stream
A Belgian Market Place
Old Inn at Langenschwalbach

Distant View of Sherborne, Dorset
Reigate from the Common

1880

Summer

The Old Port of Dartmouth
The Market Place, Giessen, on the Lahn
Fishing Boats in the Port of Granville
St Barnabas, Venice
Bologna, near the Piazza St Petronia
Lake of Como looking towards Menaggio
A Bit of Antiquity at Blois
On the Ponte Vecchio, Florence
The Mists of Early Morning at Quillebœuf, on the Seine
No. 2
No. 6
No. 3

Winter

Stolzenfels
Carisbrooke Castle
Distant View of the Alps above Geneva
On the Tiber, Rome
The Grande Rue, Dunkirk
Carden, on the Moselle
The Last Gleam of Day
Kirkstall Abbey, Yorkshire – Sunset
Old Roman Houses
Il Ponte Rotto, Rome, in 1841
The Coast of Connemara, Ireland
The Post Office, Venice
Mount's Bay, Cornwall

1881

Summer

An Oriel in Haddon Hall, Derbyshire
Piazza dei Signori, Verona
Town and Castle of Dolce Acqua near Bordighera
A Canal through the Island of Murano
Behind the Church of the Frari, Venice
The Tour de Charlemagne, Rue de l'Echelle, Tours
On the Canal dell' Olio, Venice
In the Merceria, Venice
St Helier, Jersey, from Elizabeth Castle
The Great Church of St Lawrence
The Dom Strasse, Würzburg, Bavaria
A Country Lane
Roman Column in the Main Street of Siena
Dinant, on the Meuse

Winter

Study of Coast Scenery
Grasmere, Cumberland
Rue Flamande, Bruges
A Garden Study
Mill at St Ouen, on the Seine
Scarborough from the Sands
Windsor from the Meadows
Old Houses in Bridge Street, Chester
On the Rocks in the Greta at Rokeby
Town and Castle of Blois, on the Loire
The Town of Carden, on the Moselle
Shanklin Chine

1882

Summer

A Spring Day at Florence – from San Miniato
Fossgate Street, York
Landing Fish at St Valéry-en-Caux, Normandy
Tour de Mauconseil, Vienne (on the Rhône)
Ponte St Mosé, Venice
The Belfry at Bruges
The Weighing House, Amsterdam
La Porta Romana, Siena
Near the Rialto, looking towards the Palazzo Foscari, Venice
Piazza del Sopra Muro, Perugia
French Steamer entering Folkestone Harbour in November
The Palazzo Moro, Venice

Winter

Easby Abbey, Richmond, Yorkshire
Declining Day

The clouds that wrapt the setting sun
When Autumn's softest gleams are ending,
Where all bright hues together run
In sweet confusion blending.

The Fish Market, Folkestone
Albert Dürer's House at Nuremberg
Waiting for the Boat
Giessen, on the Lahn
A Water Mill – Early Morning
Two Sea Studies
Distant View of Lyme Regis, Dorset

Cæsar's Tower, Warwick
Dunkeld
Old House at Frankfort

1883

Summer

Casa Cavallo, Venice
Castelnuovo from the Old Port, Naples
Canale della Posta, Venice
Carnarvon Castle – Early Morning
Fishing Boats off Dieppe
Castle and Town of Heidelberg from the Banks of the Neckar
Porta St Andrea, Genoa
A Street in Bologna
Canale Barrattaria, Venice
Greenwich Hospital
A Street in Rouen
The Market-Place, Abbeville

Winter

Two Sea Views
Off the Yorkshire Coast near Whitby
St Giorgio, Venice
Windmill on the Trent
Study of Sea
Street in Trèves
Boppart, on the Rhine
Bellaggio, on the Lake of Como
Village of Rhense, on the Rhine
Bolton Abbey; Eggleston Abbey, Yorkshire
Water Mill

1884

Summer

St Peter's Mancroft and Fish Market, Norwich
The Piazza delle Erbe at Verona
Entrance to the Port of Marseilles
From the Bridge of St Angelo, Venice
Near the Mumbles after a Storm
Roman Columns at San Lorenzo, Milan
On the Market Place at Malines
Il Paradiso, Venice
Folkestone Pier – Fishing Boats going out
Church of St Sauveur, Caen, Normandy
St Peter's Street, York

Winter

Old Bridge at Cæsar's Tower, Warwick Castle
The Castle of Rheinfels from the North
Waterfall – Glen Etive
Palazzo Barberigo, Grand Canal, Venice
Hastings Boat coming Ashore in Rough Weather
The Devonshire Coast – Ilfracombe
Filey Brigg – Yorkshire Coast
Market Place, Courtrai
French Fishing Boats in Harbour – Sunrise
Old Houses at Berne
Schooner making for Port

1885

Summer

Canal Barataria, Venice, near the Post Office
Hastings Boat off to the Fishing Grounds
The Drachenfels from Rolandseck, on the Rhine
Looking up the Lake of Geneva from Vevey
Fortress of Passau, on the Danube
On the Quay near the Fish Market, Folkestone Harbour
Fondamento Barbarigo, Venice
The Rialto, Venice
A Relic of Venetian Architecture in Padua
Distant View of Kirkstall Abbey, Yorkshire
A Corner in Trarbach, on the Moselle
House of the Francs Bateliers, Ghent

Winter

After the Storm
Before the Storm
The Harbour, Torquay – Early Morning
The San Salute, Grand Hotel, Venice
On the Market Place at Malines
A Sunny Spot in a Garden
Campsie Glen, Scotland
Dover – Entrance to the Harbour
Westminster Abbey looking into Henry VII Chapel
London from Holly Lodge, Highgate
Warwick from the Meadows
Ilfracombe from the Beach near Lantern Hill
Hotel of the Golden Chain, Langenschwalbach

1886

Summer

Looking into the Place des Victoires, Paris
The Old Jetty, Great Yarmouth

Street in Verona, near the Palazzo delle Erbe
Honfleur – Fishing Boats entering the Harbour
Oberlahnstein, on the Rhine, Stolzenfels in the Distance
Palazzo Molino, Canale de la Posta, Venice
Naples from the Chiesa – Early Morning
Palaces on the Grand Canal near the Rialto, Venice
Schloss Elz, near the Moselle
Gate House, Rotterdam
On the Quay at Castellamare
From the Cathedral Porch, Trent, in the Tyrol

Winter

Fondaco de Turchi, Venice
Canale de la Posta, Venice
Old Houses near the Port, Dartmouth
Castle and Town of Angera from Arona, Lago Maggiore
Stonegate, York
Hastings Fishing Boat
Entrance to the Harbour, Dover
Water Mill on the East Lyn, Lynmouth
Heidelberg from the Terrace – Sunset
Mentone from the Public Garden
On the Market Place, Prague

1887

Summer

The Rialto, Venice
The Leaning Towers of Bologna
Canal at Ghent
Castle and Town of Cochem, on the Moselle – Autumn Afternoon
Castle and Town of Lourdes in the Pyrénées
Church of St Pietro di Banchi, Genoa
Venice Canal
Amalfi from the Shore – A Summer's Morning
On the Riva dei Schiavoni, Venice
Dolce Acqua, near Bordighera
Schmeider Gasse, Hanover
Canale dell' Olio, Venice

Winter

Street in Bologna
Market Place, Ratisbon
On the Lago Maggiore
Ischl, Switzerland
Marburg, Cassel
From near the Cathedral, Stonegate, York
Lake of Geneva from St Martin
Reinhardsbrunn (the Seat of H.R.H. the late Prince Consort)
Corfu from One Gun Road
Couldron Snout, Yorkshire, where four Counties meet
Venice
St Pierre, Caen, Normandy
Folkestone
From the East Cliff – Sunset

1888

Summer

The Riva dei Schiavoni, Venice
A Summer Evening, Sidmouth, Devonshire
In the High Street, Southampton
The Market House, Marburg, Hesse-Cassel
Palace of Donna Anna, Naples – Evening
The Banks of the Rhine, Bacharach
The Main Street, Innsbrück, Tyrol
On the Barattina Canal, Venice
Amsterdam
The Market Place, Nuremberg
Gateway at Evesham

Winter

Venice Canal
Dieppe from the Sea
Falls of the Liffey
Bar Gate, Southampton
Torquay – Early Morning, looking across the Bay
On the Great Square, Coburg – Market Day
Isola Bella, Lago Maggiore
Fishing Boats on the Sands, Scheveningen
Walhalla on the Danube
Broadstairs – Breezy Day
Late Evening – Murano
Granville, Normandy

1889

Summer

Tell's Chapel, on the Lake of Lucerne – Sunrise
On the Grand Place, Bologna
From the Grindecca, Venice
Place de l'Herberie, Macon
Fishing Boats awaiting the Tide, Honfleur
Rouen – A Street near the River

Near the Campanile, Venice
Tréport from the Shore, Normandy
Entrance to the Grand Canal, Venice
Near the Market, Ferrara

Winter

Entrance to Glenfinlas
Boppart, on the Rhine
Canal in Venice
Old Bridge at Nuremberg
Hastings Fishing Boats – Early Morning
Entrance Gate, Hurstmonceaux
Fishing Boats in a Storm
Under the Cliffs, Sidmouth, Devon
Beilstein, on the Moselle
Old Houses at Frankfort near the Cathedral

1890

Summer

On the Rokin Canal, Amsterdam
Ehrenbreitstein and Coblenz – Sunrise
On the Grand Canal, Venice, near the Balbi Palace

'There is a glorious city in the sea.' – Rogers's *Italy*

Fortress and Town of Huy, on the Meuse – Early Morning
Grande Rue, Lisieux, Normandy, with Church of St Pierre
Judenstrasse, Frankfort
Venice – Sunset
In the Old Market, Florence
Tréport, Normandy, from the Pier, Château d'Eu in the Distance
Maryleport Street, Bristol – St Peter's Church

Winter

Farmyard, Staffordshire
On the River, near Gravesend
View of Schaffhausen
St Helier, Jersey – Early Morning
Distant View of Naples
A Bit of Wimbledon
Caistor Castle, Norfolk
A Summer Afternoon, near Lord Somers's Park, Reigate
Midnight Sun, North Cape (from a Sketch by the late Robert Elweys, Esq.)
Dartmouth Castle
Inner Courtyard, Weilburg-on-Lahn

1891

Summer

Dieppe from the Sands
Ancient Bridges of Rome from the Ponte Rotto
On the Riva dei Schiavoni, Venice
Tower of St Rumbold, Malines, from the Market Place
Kool Quai, Antwerp
Distant View of Rouen – Early Morning
On the Quai at Frankfort
The Rhine at Cologne

But thou exulting and abounding River
Making their waves a blessing as they flow.
Childe Harold, Byron

Citadel and Town of Namur, on the Meuse – Sunset
Fishing Boats in Ramsgate Harbour

Winter

Stolzenfels from the Lahn
Distant View of Worcester
Cæsar's Tower, Warwick Castle
On the Inn, Passau
The Grande Place, Bruges – Market Day
Gorleston Pier, Norfolk
Distant View of Torquay
Arona, on the Lago Maggiore
Two Sketches
1. St Michael's Mount, Cornwall
2. Mont St Michel, Normandy
Bolton Abbey, Yorkshire – Evening

1892

Summer

Part of Lucerne from the Lake
Belfry, etc., at Bruges
Tower at Rudesheim, on the Rhine
On the Meuse, Dinant – Fair Time
Fishing Boats in Ramsgate Harbour – Sunset
Venice from St Giorgio

Underneath day's azure eyes
Ocean's nursling Venice lies.

Bellaggio, on Lake of Como – Morning
Entrance to the Port, Fécamp, Normandy
Church of St Lawrence and Town Hall, Rotterdam

Canal in Ghent, with the House of the Francs Bateliers
Entrance to the Grand Canal, Venice – Early Morning

Winter

Distant View of Norwich
On the Seine at Quillebœuf–Early Morning
Vevey, on the Lake of Geneva
Barnard Castle
Andernach, on the Rhine
Sea-piece
On the Lake of Como
The Castle, Lausanne
Dutch Boats on the Scheldt at Antwerp

1893

Summer

Blois, on the Loire – A Summer Evening
Canal at Malines
Ancona from the Mole
Naples from the Strada di Posilipo
The Harbour, Genoa
Venice, on the Riva dei Schiavoni
On the Adige, Verona
Venice from Belli Arti

A fairy City of the Heart
Rising like water columns from the sea.
Of joy the sojourn, and of wealth the mart.
Childe Harold, Byron

Cochem, on the Moselle
The Cathedral at Abbeville
The Old Bridge at Avignon

Winter

The Lake, Guisachan
Ruins of the Teatro Marcellus, Rome
Woodland Scenery
Dolbadarn Castle, Llanberis
Stormy Weather
French Fishing Boats, Granville Harbour
Home from the Fishing
Beauchamp Chapel, Warwick
The Grand Canal, Venice – Early Morning

1894

Summer

Château d'Amboise, on the Loire
Rheinfels and St Goar, on the Rhine
Fortress and Town of Namur at the Junction of the Sambre and Meuse
Castle of Schönburg, on the Rhine, from Oberwesel
View of Rotterdam, and the Church of St Lawrence
Isola Peschiera from Baveno
Riva dei Schiavoni from the Piazzetta, Venice
Ehrenbreitstein
Cross on the Fischmarkt, Lucerne
The Inner Harbour, Ramsgate – Early Morning
On the Old Market Place – Domo d'Ossola

Winter

Palazzo Molino, Venice
Ullswater
Water Mill on the Seine
Venice from the St Georgio
Glen Etive
Canal in Ghent
Coast near Ilfracombe
A Fresh Breeze
Near the Village of Halton, Bucks

1895

Summer

From the Foscari Palace, Grand Canal, Venice – Sunset
On the Beach at Hastings – Sunset
Cathedral at Antwerp
The Grand Bateliers, Ghent – Dutch Boats clearing out with the Tide
Old Houses at Trarbach, on the Moselle, since destroyed by Fire
Gravedona, Head of Lake Como
Castle of Marksburg, on the Rhine
The Grand Canal, Venice, from the Rialto
Mayence, on the Rhine
Berncastel, on the Moselle

Winter

Weston Mill, near Leamington
Coast at Sidmouth, Devon
Bolt Head, looking towards Salcombe
Gateway, Battle Abbey
Canal near the Frari, Venice
Naples – Early Morning
Vietri and Salerno from the Amalfi Road

1896

Summer

Ehrenbreitstein, Distant View of
The Rialto, Venice
Saumur, on the Loire
Lyons from the Junction of the Saone and Rhône.
View of Dieppe from the Sea
The Pfalz with Caub and Gutenfels, on the Rhine
Tour de l'Horloge, Rouen
The Old Weighing House, Amsterdam
Entrance to the Grand Canal, Venice – Sunset

Winter

At Ilfracombe, North Devon
Castle and Town of Mont Richard, on the Cher
Sidmouth, South Devon
The Serpentine, Hyde Park
On the Grand Canal, Venice
Robin Hood's Bay, Yorkshire

1897

Summer

Casa d'Oro, near the Rialto, Venice
The Moselle Quai, Coblenz, with Ehrenbreitstein
Cathedral of Beauvais, from the Market Place
Entrance to the Grand Canal, Venice

White swan of cities, slumbering in thy nest,
So wonderfully built among the reeds
Of the lagoon, that fences thee and feeds,
White water-lily cradled and caressed
By ocean's streams, and from the silt and weeds
Lifting thy golden filaments and seeds
Thy sun-illumined spires, thy crown and crest!
Longfellow

Rouen – Early Morning
Fishing Boats off St Valéry-en-Caux
Entrance to the Harbour, Weymouth
Old Houses at Cochem, on the Moselle
Amongst the Rocks at Marazion, Cornwall

Winter

On the Galway Coast, Ireland
Fishing Boats off the Heve Lights
Coast of Cornwall
Torquay, looking across the Bay
The Abbey Gate, Great Malvern
Street in Rouen

1898

Summer

Fortress and Town of Dinant, on the Meuse
A Summer Day on the Riva dei Schiavoni, Venice
Palaces near the Entrance of the Grand Canal, Venice
Entrance to the Port of Havre
Old Houses by the River at Malines
Old Tower on the Quai, Frankfort
French Fishing Boats off Dieppe
The Old Walls and Towers, Oberwesel, Rhine – Market Day
Portsmouth from the Sea
Summer Evening – Beilstein, on the Moselle

Winter

On the Tiber, near Ponte Rotto, Rome
Campo St Angelo, Venice
Distant View of Mentone
Fishing Boats entering Dieppe Harbour
Schneider Gasse, Hanover
Chapelle St Jean, Orléans
On the Lago Maggiore

1899

Summer

View of the Town and Lake of Lugano
Fishing Boats in a Calm at the Mouth of the Seine
Distant View of Namur, on the Meuse
Ebrenbreitstein from the Moselle Bridge
Old Houses, Bacharach, on the Rhine
Staen Street, Bruges
Notre Dame de Paris, from Bercy
Fishing Boats off St Valéry-en-Caux
Vico, Bay of Naples
Tragetto St Gregorio, Venice

Winter

Street in Abbeville
Place in Ferrara

Porta San Andrea, Genoa
In a Reigate Lane
View from Tête Noir, Switzerland
Fishing Boats at the Mouth of the Seine

1900

Summer

The Harbour, Bellaggio, looking up Lake Como
Durham Cathedral, from the Opposite Bank of the Wear
Dutch Boats running into Ostend – Stormy Weather
Andernach, on the Rhine – Early Morning
Corner of Bacharach, near the Walls, on the Rhine
Piazza de Frutti, Padua
Allée Blanche and Lake Combal, from Col de la Seigne, Switzerland
Rue de la Boucherie, Calais, with the Old Semaphore Tower
Fishing Boats leaving Havre

Winter

Rue de l'Herberie, Mâcon
St Goar, looking across to Goarhausen
Canale de la Posta, Venice
Trarbach, on the Moselle
Lucerne from the Lake
Cathedral, Courtrai, Belgium
Easby Abbey, Yorkshire

1901

Summer

Namur, on the Meuse
Mont Richard, on the Cher, Loir-et-Cher, France
Market Place, Lille
Tintern Abbey (West Window)
Stirling Castle
Fishing Boats at Tréport, Normandy
Wyn Haven, Rotterdam
Venice from the Dogana
Dymchurch, near Hythe

Winter

Entrance to Leicester Hospital, Warwick
Street in Trent near the Cathedral
A Quiet Pool, Offchurch
Dutch Boats – Rough Water
Canale della Posta, Venice
On the Beach, Lowestoft

1902

Summer

On the Market Place, Leipzig
On the Canale della Posta, Venice
Cochem, on the Moselle
On the Adige, Verona
The Rialto, Venice, from the North
Beaugency, on the Loire
Castel Lettere, near Castellamare
French Fishing Boats off Fécamp, Normandy
Interior of the Port of Havre

Winter

Church of St Sauveur, Caen, Normandy
Hastings – Fishing Boats returning
Old Timber Houses, Lisieux, Normandy
At the Back of the Campanile, Venice
Northgate Street, a Bit of Old Chester
Distant View of Inveraray – Rainy Weather
Cottage near Malvern

1903

Summer

Old Houses, dated 1605 and 1617, at Traben, Moselle
Villa d'Este and Villa of Macona, Tivoli
The Castle of Heidelberg from above the Bridge
Old Houses in Watergate Street, Chester
Distant View of Goodrich Court and Castle, on the Wye
Lake of Como from Bellaggio – Sunrise
Fishing Boats entering the Harbour, Fécamp
Rustic Bridge over the East Lyn
Ruins of Marienburg, with the Winding Moselle

Winter

Beauchamp Chapel, Warwick
Home from Fishing
The Avon, Salisbury
Ruins of the Teatro Marcellus, Rome
Woodland Scenery
Dolbadarn, Castle, Llanberis
Stormy Weather
French Fishing Boats, Granville Harbour
The Grand Canal, Venice – Early Morning

1904

Summer

Castle and Town of Richmond, Yorkshire, from Clink Bank
Interior of the Port, Marseille
Mont Blanc, Dôme du Goute from Chamouni
St Valéry-en-Caux, Normandy – Entrance to the Harbour
Piazza delle Erbe, Verona
Dutch Boats at the Quai, Antwerp
Campanile in the Campo St Polo, Venice
The Rhine at Ehrenbreitstein – Early Morning
Landing Fish at Lowestoft
Distant View of Dieppe from the Sea.

Winter

In the Gloaming
Melrose Abbey – Sketched from Nature, 1843
Distant View of Bamboro' Castle – Sketched from Nature, 1843
A Storm on the Yorkshire Coast
Bridge of Sighs from the Canale della Posta, Venice
Sunset after a Storm
Hastings Fishing Boats

1905

Summer

Fishing Boats off the Coast of Normandy, near Granville
Bolton Abbey, Yorkshire
Hauling up a Fishing Boat, Hastings
The Mersey from Birkenhead – Stormy Sunset
Fishing Quarter, Old Hastings – Sunrise
Ruins of Llanthony Abbey – Stormy Weather
From a Sketch at Père Lachaise
Water Mill, Lee, near Ilfracombe
Mercato Vecchio, Florence (since demolished)
Bamboro' Castle, Northumberland
Maison des Francs Bateliers, Ghent

Winter

Sunset Study
Landscape Study
Beech Avenue, Inveraray
Edinburgh from Salisbury Crags – Painted from Nature, 1843
Durham – Painted from Nature, 1843
Trarbach from Traben, on the Moselle – Painted from Nature, 1844
Street in Innsbrück

1906

Summer

On the Beach, Lynmouth, N. Devon
Grey Friars Hospital, Coventry
On the Grand Canal, Venice
Bologna, at the Foot of the Leaning Towers
Distant View of Inveraray Castle
Distant View of Winchester
French Fishing Boats in Harbour – Low Water
Glen Rosa, Isle of Arran

Winter

Rialto – Foscari Palace, Venice
Culag Burn, Lochinver
Street in Tours, Loire
In the Grounds of Madeley Manor, Staffordshire
Richmond, Yorkshire
Abbey Church, Great Malvern
View of Worcester from the River
The Coast, Ilfracombe
Canal, Rotterdam

1907

Summer

Via di Porta Borsari, Verona
San Salute, Venice
Street Corner in Trarbach, 1844
Market Place, Ratisbon, 1853
St Mary's Church, Richmond, before its Restoration
Water Mill on the East Lyn from Below
Water Mill on the East Lyn from Above
Cathedral at Antwerp, 1844
Street in Trarbach, 1844
On the Grand Canal, Venice
Distant View of Abergavenny

Winter

Contarini Palace, Grand Canal, Venice
Rialto, Venice
Dover – White Cliffs of Old England, 1845
Richmond, Yorks, from River Swale, 1843
Rome from the Palatine Hill, 1848

Old Houses at Chester, 1902
Tragetto, St Gregorio, Venice, 1880
St Sauveur, Caen, Normandy, 1902
Distant View of Durham, 1843
Old Houses near Worcester, 1848
Hereford, 1848
Inveraray, Border of the Lake, 1849
Florence, from St Miniato, 1877

1908

Summer

Scarborough, 1842
All Hallows, Worcester, 1848
Verona, 1880
Abbey Church, Great Malvern, 1848
Near Crickhowell, 1848
Cochem, on the Moselle, 1844
Malvern Wells, 1848
Richmond, 1853
Marburg – Buildings dated 1683–1871
Scarborough, 1842
Cottage at Great Malvern, 1902
Old Hall, Gainsborough, 1853
Rotterdam, 1845
Llanthony Abbey, 1848
Palace Pruili, Venice, 1880
Little Malvern, 1848
San Salute, Venice, 1882
Richmond, Yorkshire, 1858
Near Huddersfield, 1862
Worcester, 1848

Winter

Ben Garve, Loch Assynt, 1861
Scarborough, 1842
Bridge of Ross, 1848
St Nicholas, Ghent, 1844
Whitby, Yorks, 1851
Venice, 1840

NB. List first published in the 1908 autobiography

The spelling of place names introduces a slight difficulty into the presentation of catalogue details. The versions of William Callow were not always accurate, particularly in respect of German locations, with further possibility of confusion in all areas owing to his spidery handwriting. If a work was first shown in a catalogue with an incorrect spelling it is probable that this is how it will appear on the original drawing. For the purposes of this book, there has been some editing of errors, but certain versions, Anglicisations etc. have been allowed to stand in order to keep within the spirit of what was first published in a catalogue and might now be expected to be found on the original work.

Catalogue of Work Exhibited by William Callow at the Paris Salon, 1834–1841

Year	*Exhibit Number*	
1834	267	Vue du pont de Richmond, en Angleterre; aquarelle
	268	Vue prise de la terrasse de St Germain; aquarelle
	269	Une marine; aquarelle
	270	Dessins à l'aquarelle, même numéro
1835	299	Marine; aquarelle
	300	Vue prise à Saint-Germain; idem
	301	Paysage; idem
	302	Marines à l'aquarelle, même numéro
1836	278	Vue du Château de Windsor; aquarelle
	279	Vue générale de Londres, prise de Greenwich; aquarelle
	280	Vue de Honfleur; idem
	281	Vue de l'intérieur du port du Havre; idem
	282	Aquarelles, même numéro
1837	261	Vue des château et ville de Montrichard sur la Cher; aquarelle
	262	Vue prise dans le vallon de Canteretz prise du pont (Hautes-Pyrénées); aquarelle
1838	228	Vue prise dans le vallon d'Argèles, Hautes-Pyrénées; aquarelle
	229	*Le grand canal, à Venise; idem
	230	Vues diverses, aquarelles; même numéro
1839		
1840	209	Vue du château de Windsor
	210	Vue de St Goar et du château de Rheinfelts, sur Rhine; idem
	211	Vue de la ville de Lucerne; idem
	212	Vue du lac de Genève prise de l'église St Martin; idem
	213	Vues diverses; idem; même numéro
1841	270	Vue du château et de la ville de Heidelberg; aquarelle
	271	Vue de l'intérieur du port du Havre; aquarelle
	272	Bâteau pêcheur anglais disposé pour être lancé à l'eau; aquarelle

* *Note*: The 1838 exhibits include a scene on the Grand Canal, Venice. As Callow did not make his first visit to Italy until 1840, it seems possible that he may have modelled this exhibit on a work by Bonington

Paintings Exhibited by William Callow at the Royal Academy, 1850–1876

(*Medium:* Oils, unless otherwise stated)

Year	*Exhibit Number*	
1850	26	Old Bridge at Nuremberg
	1032	Fécamp in Normandy; Fishing Boats entering the Harbour (water-colour)
1851	12	Canal Scene at Ghent – Church of St Nicholas
	590	Broclen Toren, on the Lys at Courtrai
1852	136	Porte Guillaume, Chartres
	138	Lucerne
1853	32	Mont Richard on the Cher, France
	34	Part of the Old Walls at Bacharach on the Rhine
1854	26	The Wartburg; the Place of Luther's Captivity in 1521
	922	Riva dei Schiavoni, Venice (water-colour)
	1288	Porta della Carta, Venice
1855	34	Near the Cathedral, Frankfort
	615	Bridge Street, Chester
1856	389	Rotterdam
1857	964	The Piazza at Padua
1860	343	The Piazza at Padua (water-colour)
1862	168	Place at Ghent, with the Birthplace of Charles V
1864	213	Derby Hall, Chester
1866	19	St Mary's Priory, Monmouth
	332	Lympne Castle, Kent
1867	187	Fordes Hospital, Coventry
1869	350	Near the Market-House, Ross, Herefordshire
1870	397	Market Place at Leipzig
1872	449	A Bit of Antiquity, Chester
1874	362	Street in Frankfort
	683	The Cross at Salisbury, while under Repair
1875	629	Entrance to the Close at Evesham
	1166	A Street in Hanover
1876	1292	Market Place at Frankfort: looking towards the Cathedral

Work Exhibited by William Callow at the British Institution, 1848–1867

(*Medium:* Oils)

Year	*Exhibit Number*		
1848	9	Canal Scene at Ghent, Church of St Nicholas	(19 × 25 in. – 482 × 635 mm)
	83	The Bridge of Sighs, Venice	(26 × 25 in. – 660 × 635 mm)
	98	A Street in Frankfort on the Maine	(25 × 21 in. – 635 × 533 mm)
	139	Old Houses at Trarbach on the Moselle	(33 × 27 in. – 838 × 686 mm)
1849	194	The Ponte della Paglia, Venice	(17 × 24 in. – 432 × 610 mm)
	325	The Kool Quai, Antwerp	(22 × 20 in. – 559 × 508 mm)
1850	375	A Street in Bologna, looking towards the Grand Square	(40 × 34 in. – 1016 × 864 mm)
	441	The Trongate, Glasgow	(27 × 24 in. – 686 × 610 mm)
1851	51	La Piazza d'Erbi, Verona	(36 × 47 in. – 914 × 1194 mm)
	97	The Hôtel de Sens, Paris	(19 × 25 in. – 483 × 635 mm)
	446	At Frankfort	(19 × 22 in. – 483 × 559 mm)
1852	320	Looking up the Street of Innsbrück, from the Golden Roof	(34 × 29 in. – 864 × 737 mm)
	344	Old Houses in Coney Street, York	(20 × 22 in. – 508 × 559 mm)
1853	209	The Town Hall of Courtrai, Belgium	£15.15.0
	231	Mill at Antwerp	£15.15.0
1854	122	Venice	£26.5.0
	228	Venice	£26.5.0
	391	Bacharach	£12.12.0
1855	126	The Kauf-haus on the Mosel-Quay, Coblenz	£15.15.0
	399	Market Day at Richmond, Yorkshire	£15.15.0
1856	19	High Street, Tewkesbury	£15.15.0
	198	The Butter Cross, Salisbury	£15.15.0
1857	11	Tintern Abbey	£15.15.0
	118	Abbeville Cathedral	£15.15.0
1858	88	The Rialto, Venice	
1859	178	Dover Beach in Old Times	£15.15.0
	239	Interior of the Port of Havre	£15.15.0
1860	331	Goethe's House, Dom Platz, Frankfort	£73.10.0
1861	120	Fish Market, Malines	£21.0.0
	343	Rouen Cathedral	£21.0.0
1862	371	Rheinfels and St Goar	£21.0.0
1863	207	Derby Hall, a Relic of Old Chester	£15.15.0

Work Exhibited by William Callow at the British Institution, 1848–1867

Year	*Exhibit Number*		
1864	475	Hanover	£21.0.0
1866	109	Tower at Andernach	£15.15.0
	423	Street in Milan	£15.15.0
1867	157	Lympne Castle	£12.12.0
	418	Havre – Sunset	£12.12.0

Exhibits by William Callow at the Royal Liverpool Academy, 1839–1862

Year	*Exhibit Number*		
1839	488	The Town of Lucerne (Water-colour, without frame)	£42.0.0
	542	The Lake of Geneva (water-colour, without frame)	£44.2.0
1842	470	Château de Dieppe	
	506	Naples from the sea – Sunrise	
	495	Preparing to launch a Lowestoft Fishing Boat	
	509	The Lake of Wallenstatt	
1848	120	The Bridge of Sighs, Venice	
	150	Street in Frankfort on the Main	
1850	147	Old Bridge at Nuremberg	
	206	Street in Bologna, looking towards the Grand Square	
	96	Exterior of the Priory of Blackfriars, Hereford	
1851	118	Frankfort	£12.12.0
	189	Lucerne	£15.15.0
	280	Mill near Antwerp	
1852	110	Old Houses in Coney Street, York	
	161	The Market Place of Verona	
	203	A Nook at Haddon	
1853	35	Street in Innsbrück, looking towards the Golden Roof (catalogue spells this 'Innsprück')	£52.10.0
	84	Market Place, Frankfort	£15.15.0
	279	Ancient Conduit – Lincoln	£18.18.0
1854	144	From the Dogana, Venice	£26.5.0
	179	Riva dei Schiavoni, Venice	£126.0.0
	230	Trarbach-on-the-Moselle	£31.10.0
1855	168	Venice from the Church of St Giorgio	£26.5.0
	169	Venice – Grand Canal from the Foscari Palace	£26.5.0
	181	Interior of the Wartburg, near Eisenant	£18.18.0
1856	106	The Belfry, Calais	£15.15.0
	178	The Piazza, Padua	£21.0.0
	483	The Rialto, Venice	£157.10.0
	614	Street in Verona	£52.10.0
1857	67	Abbeville Cathedral	£15.15.0
	182	Tintern Abbey	£15.15.0

Exhibits by William Callow at the Royal Liverpool Academy, 1839–1862

Year	Exhibit Number		
	344	Canal Scene at Ghent	£21.0.0
	347	The Barbarigo Palace, Venice	£21.0.0
1858	94	Street in Frankfort	£18.18.0
	360	Houses over the Witham, Lincoln	£15.15.0
	792	Rouen Cathedral	£18.18.0
1859	389	Lympne Castle, near Hythe	£15.15.0
	393	Amsterdam	£15.15.0
	540	Rue de la Grosse Horloge, Rouen	£42.0.0
1860	345	The Fish Market at Malines	£21.0.0
	489	Geneva	£18.18.0
	618	The Wartburg – Scene of Luther's Imprisonment	£52.10.0
1861	341	Place at Ghent, with the Birthplace of Charles V	£12.12.0
	1056	Grand Canal with the Foscari Palace, Venice	£15.15.0
1862	419	Bridge of Sighs, Venice	£18.18.0
	462	Goethe's House, Dom Platz, Frankfort	£84.0.0

Manchester Art Treasures Exhibition of 1857

Exhibit Number		
664	Windsor Castle	Lent by R. Freeland Esq.
665	Exeter	Lent by Wm. Leaf Esq.
666	Sketch for Venice	Lent by Wm. Leaf Esq.
667	Reichenbach	Lent by Wm. Leaf Esq.
668	Rue St Pierre, Caen	Lent by W. Callow Esq.
669	*Nieuekerche	Lent by J. Labouchère Esq.

*'Many months since I requested from Mr. Labouchère the loan of a large drawing of Amsterdam, which is one of my more recent and certainly one of my best works ... decidedly superior to some of those on your list ... I am asking that the Amsterdam drawing should be exhibited without fail, even if it should be required to withdraw some of those already selected ...' – extract from a letter, dealing with his Manchester exhibits, written by Callow, 15 April 1857. (Reproduced by permission of J. L. Wybrew.)

Exhibits by William Callow with the Norfolk and Norwich Association for the Promotion of Fine Arts, 1855–1883

(Compiled from catalogues in possession of the Castle Museum, Norwich)

Ford's Hospital, Coventry
Exhibited: No. 86 N. and N.A. for the Promotion of Fine Arts, 1855 (£10.10.0)

Boppart on the Rhine
Exhibited: No. 134 N. and N.A., 1855 (£5.5.0)

The Bishop's Court, Liège
Exhibited: No. 163 N. and N.A. 1855 (£5.5.0)

Old Custom House on the Moselle, Coblenz
Exhibited: No. 107 N. and N.A. 1856 (£10.10.0)

Winchester (water-colour)
Exhibited: No. 311 N. and N.A. 1856 (£7.7.0)

Ancient Manor House, Near the Abbey Gate, Malvern (water-colour)
Exhibited: No. 343 N. and N.A. 1856 (£10.10.0)

Arundel Castle, Sussex (water-colour)
Exhibited: No. 345 N. and N.A. 1856 (£8.8.0)

Bridge Street, Chester
Exhibited: No. 29 N. and N.A. 1860 (£12.12.0)

Teatro Marcello, Rome
Exhibited: No. 42 N. and N.A. 1878 (£26.5.0)

Old Gateway at Rouen
Exhibited: No. 121 N. and N.A. 1878 (£26.5.0)

Matlock (water-colour)
Exhibited: No. 137 N. and N.A. 1878 (£21.0.0)

Mentone (water-colour)
Exhibited: No. 139 N. and N.A. 1878 (£21.0.0)

Scene on the Moselle
Exhibited: No. 473 N. and N.A. 1878 (lent by the Dowager Lady Buxton)

*Portrait of Sir Jeffrey Wyatville (water-colour)
Exhibited: No. 23 N. and N.A. 1883 (lent by Mr M. Wyatt)

*Street in Cairo (water-colour)
Exhibited: No. 46 N. and N.A. 1883 (lent by Mr M. Wyatt)

* Both these exhibits are uncharacteristic of the general œuvre of Callow, who was certainly never in Cairo. However, we know that his father, Robert Callow, had worked on alterations to Windsor Castle under the direction of the architect, Sir Jeffrey Wyatville (who was also an R.A.). M. Wyatt could be related to Wyatville, who had assumed that name, instead of plain Wyatt, in order to give himself an added distinction. The Wyatts, architects and painters, had a long association with Newman Street, including Mathew Coles Wyatt

Exhibits by John Callow with the Norfolk and Norwich Association for the Promotion of Fine Arts, 1855–1870

(Compiled from catalogues in possession of the Castle Museum, Norwich)

Shipping off the Needles, Isle of Wight
Exhibited: No. 99 N. and N.A. 1855 (£10.10.0)

Merchant Barque leaving the Downs
Exhibited: No. 116 N. and N.A. 1855 (£10.10.0)

The Black Midden Rocks
Exhibited: No. 179 N. and N.A. 1868 (£26.5.0)

Entrance to Yarmouth Harbour – Towing out a Brig
Exhibited: No. 183 N. and N.A. 1868 (£18.18.0)

Blackwell Reach, Greenwich Hospital in the Distance
Exhibited: No. 191 N. and N.A. 1868 (£26.5.0)

Merchantmen Signalling for Pilots
Exhibited: No. 241 N. and N.A. 1870 (£42.0.0)

Disabled Ship in Tow – Ilfracombe in the Distance
Exhibited: No. 275 N. and N.A. 1870 (£21.0.0)

Paintings Exhibited by John Callow at the Royal Academy, 1844–1856

(*Medium:* Oils)

Year	*Exhibit Number*	
1844	639	Lowestoft Fishing Boat
	988	Colliers in Ballast
	1026	A Frigate running before the Wind
1854	243	Indiaman off Dover
1855	664	Indiaman beating up Channel
	1309	Wreck in Granville Bay, Jersey; Mont Orgueil Castle in the Distance
1856	589	Distant View of St Michael's Mount, Cornwall

Work Exhibited by John Callow at the British Institution, 1851–1855

(*Medium:* Oils)

Year	*Exhibit Number*		
1851	378	Wreck on the Rocks in St Brelade's Bay, Jersey	(20 × 28 in. – 508 × 711 mm)
	413	On the Thames, breaking up a Brig	(26 × 22 in. – 660 × 559 mm)
1852	525	Entrance to Yarmouth Harbour – towing out a Brig	(21 × 33 in. – 533 × 838 mm)
1853	333	Breaking up a Wreck	£12.12.0
	408	Hurst Castle on the Solent – Steamer towing out a Brig	£12.12.0
1854	389	Collier discharging near Penzance	£12.12.0
1855	315	Merchant Barque laying to off Dover	£42.0.0
	344	The Mew Stone, Plymouth	£15.15.0

Catalogue of Exhibition of Water-colours by William Callow – The Leicester Galleries (Ernest Brown and Phillips), Leicester Square, London. October–November 1907

1 On the Quai, Malines (1898)
2 Dunster Castle (1847) (*Cundall*, plate facing p. 144)
3 Sketch in Potsdam Palace (the joint work of Her Imperial Majesty the late Empress Frederick of Germany and William Callow) – in possession of the Callow family (*Cundall*, plate facing p. 128)
4 Isola Bella from Stresa (1875)
5 Palazzo Molino, Canale della Porta, Venice (1894)
6 Riva dei Schiavone, Venice (1846)
7 Bruges, Hôtel de Ville (1844)
8 Bamboro' Castle (1843)
9 Riva dei Schiavone, Venice (1894) (*Cundall*, plate facing p. 78)
10 Broadstairs, a Breezy Day (1888)
11 In the Market Place, Leipzig (1902) (Bonham's, 5 July 1978)
12 Glen Rosa, Isle of Arran
13 Market Place, Lisieux, Normandy (1871)
14 Loch Fyne, Inveraray (1861) – *see* Ashmolean, Oxford, page 189
15 The Rialto, Venice (1882)
16 On the East Lyn, Devon (1847)
17 St Valéry-en-Caux (1904)
18 Hastings, Early Morning (1889) (*Cundall*, plate facing p. 22)
19 Palazzo Moro, Venice (1882)
20 On the Thames at Gravesend
21 Teatro Marcello, Rome (1903)
22 Distant View of Kirkstall Abbey (1885)
23 Santa Maria della Salute and Grand Canal, Venice (no date)
24 Berwick on Tweed (1871) – *see* Laing Art Gallery, page 189
25 Dutch Boats running into Ostend (1900)
26 Easby Abbey, Yorkshire (1853) – *see* Victoria and Albert Museum, page 164
27 The Cathedral, Antwerp (1895) (*Cundall*, plate facing p. 94)
28 Gorleston Pier, Norfolk (no date)
29 The Grands Bateliers, Ghent (1895)
30 Salzburg, Germany (1875)
31 The Belfry at Bruges (1882) (*Cundall*, plate facing p. 106)
32 Entrance to the Seine (1899)
33 Bologna (1889)
34 Fishing Boats, Scheveningen
35 Riva dei Schiavone, Venice (1888)
36 Scarborough, Early Morning (1872)
37 Bargate, Southampton (1888) (In the High Street, Southampton – *Cundall*, plate facing p. 30)
38 Dutch Boats on the Scheldt

39 Seascape
40 Old Bridge, Nuremberg (*Cundall*, plate facing p. 96)
41 Distant View of Town and Castle of Heidelberg–*see* Southampton Art Gallery, page 193
42 Fountain at Blois
43 Innsbrück, Tyrol (1888)
44 The Grand Canal, Venice (1846)
45 The Rhine at Cologne (1891)
46 Lake of Lugano (1873)
47 Tour de l'Horloge, Rouen (1895) (*Cundall*, plate facing p. 26)
48 Entrance to Dover Harbour (1886) (*Cundall*, plate facing p. 10)
49 Namur (1901)
50 Gateway at Evesham (1888)
51 Seascape
52 Ghent (1876)
53 Vevey, Lake of Geneva
54 San Giorgio, Venice (1846)
55 London from Holly Lodge, Highgate (1841) (*Cundall*, plate facing p. 86)
56 Roman Columns, San Lorenzo, Milan (1884)
57 On the Grand Canal, Venice (1896)
58 Looking into the Place Victor, Paris (1888)
59 Limburg on the Lahn (1873)
60 Market Place, Malines (1884)–*see* Lady Lever Art Gallery (*illustration no. 97*)
61 Temple of Vesta, Tivoli (1875)
62 Place de l'Herberie, Mâcon (1900)
63 Town Hall, Bruges (1891) ('The Grand Place, Bruges'–*Cundall*, plate facing p. 90)–*see* also Victoria and Albert Museum, page 164
64 Market Place, Nuremberg (1888)
65 Bellaggio (1900)
66 Study of Cottages

Note: A further exhibition of the work of Callow was held at the Leicester Galleries in 1909

Catalogue of William Callow's Sketches Exhibited at Walker's Galleries, New Bond Street, London, in April 1927

ENGLAND

Title	*Year*	*Size*
Alnwick Castle	1843	(21 × 14¾ in. – 533 × 375 mm)
Alnwick Castle	1843	(21 × 14⅜ in. – 533 × 365 mm)
Algarkirk (Lincoln)	*date uncertain*	(13½ × 8⅞ in. – 343 × 225 mm)
St Albans (Gate)	,, ,,	(10 × 13⅞ in. – 254 × 352 mm)
Barnes on the Thames	,, ,,	(12½ × 9 in. – 317 × 229 mm)
Berwick on Tweed	1843	(20 × 13 in. – 508 × 330 mm)
Borrowdale	1872	(13⅝ × 9⅝ in. – 346 × 244 mm)
Bolton Abbey	1858	(13⅝ × 9⅝ in. – 346 × 244 mm)
Botley, Staffs	1842	(14 × 9⅞ in. – 356 × 250 mm)
Boscabel House	1872	(13¼ × 9½ in. – 337 × 241 mm)
Botley, Staffs	1842	(13¾ × 9¾ in. – 349 × 248 mm)
Brighton	1853	(14⅞ × 5¼ in. – 378 × 133 mm)
Borrowdale (The Grange)	1872	(13⅝ × 9¾ in. – 346 × 248 mm)
Borrowdale (The Grange)	1872	(13½ × 9⅝ in. – 343 × 244 mm)
Crickhowell	1848	(13¾ × 7¼ in. – 349 × 184 mm)
Carnarvon Castle	*date uncertain*	(10½ × 14½ in. – 267 × 368 mm)
Caldron Snout (Yorkshire Dales)	1853	(9⅝ × 13¾ in. – 244 × 349 mm)
Chiswick on the Thames	*date uncertain*	(9 × 6⅛ in. – 229 × 156 mm)
Cheshunt, Herts	,, ,,	(10 × 6¾ in. – 254 × 171 mm)
Dover, Boat fishing	(early)	(6⅛ × 8⅜ in. – 156 × 213 mm)
Dover, Boat fishing	(early)	(8¾ × 6¼ in. – 222 × 159 mm)
Dover, Boat fishing	1845	(14⅞ × 5¼ in. – 378 × 133 mm)
Didlington Castle	*date uncertain*	(13¾ × 9¾ in. – 349 × 248 mm)
Easby, Yorks, Interior of Church	1860	(9¾ × 6⅞ in. – 248 × 175 mm)
Folkestone from the Cliffs, Sunset	*date uncertain*	(12¾ × 9⅛ in. – 324 × 232 mm)
Folkestone	1858	(12¾ × 9⅛ in. – 324 × 232 mm)
Flamstead, Cheshire	*date uncertain*	(6¾ × 9¾ in. – 171 × 248 mm)
Fall of the? (illegible)	1853	(13¾ × 9¾ in. – 349 × 248 mm)
Goodrich Castle (Wye)	1848	(14 × 7⅛ in. – 356 × 181 mm)
Goodrich Castle (Wye)	1848	(14 × 7¼ in. – 356 × 184 mm)
Goodrich Castle (Wye)	1848	(10¼ × 6¾ in. – 260 × 171 mm)
Glydock	1849	(14 × 7⅛ in. – 356 × 181 mm)
Hall? (title unknown)	*date uncertain*	(6⅝ × 10¼ in. – 168 × 260 mm)
Haddon Hall	1849	(9 × 5⅛ in. – 229 × 130 mm)
Haddon – Banqueting Hall	1858	(13¾ × 7 in. – 349 × 178 mm)
Halton, Bucks	*date uncertain*	(9½ × 6¼ in. – 241 × 159 mm)
Halton, Bucks	,, ,,	(9⅝ × 6½ in. – 244 × 165 mm)
Halton, Bucks	,, ,,	(9¾ × 6½ in. – 248 × 165 mm)
Hythe, Canal near	,, ,,	(10 × 6½ in. – 254 × 165 mm)
Ilfracombe, Lantern Hill	1847	(14¼ × 9⅝ in. – 362 × 244 mm)

Catalogue of William Callow's Sketches Exhibited at Walker's Galleries

Title	*Year*	*Size*
Ilfracombe	1847	($14\frac{1}{8} \times 9\frac{1}{4}$ in.–359×235 mm)
Ilfracombe, from Hillsborough	1847	($14\frac{1}{4} \times 9\frac{1}{4}$ in. – 362×235 mm)
Keevil, near Bradford	1850	($8\frac{7}{8} \times 5\frac{3}{8}$ in. – 225×137 mm)
East Lyn, Rustic Bridge	1903	($13\frac{5}{8} \times 19\frac{3}{4}$ in. – 346×502 mm)
East Lyn, Valley	1847	($10\frac{1}{8} \times 14\frac{1}{8}$ in. – 257×359 mm)
East Lyn, Valley	1847	($14\frac{1}{4} \times 9\frac{3}{4}$ in. – 362×248 mm)
Leamington – A Quiet Pool	1874	($9\frac{3}{4} \times 13\frac{5}{8}$ in. – 248×346 mm)
Lodore, Derwent Water	1872	($13\frac{5}{8} \times 9\frac{3}{4}$ in. – 346×248 mm)
Lowestoft, on the Beach	1839	($9\frac{7}{8} \times 13\frac{3}{4}$ in. – 250×349 mm)
Lowestoft, Fishing Boats	1839	($13\frac{1}{2} \times 9\frac{7}{8}$ in. – 343×250 mm)
Lowestoft, Fishing Boats	1839	($13\frac{7}{8} \times 10$ in. – 352×254 mm)
Mumbles, Pennard, from Three Cliffs Bay	*date uncertain*	
	1861	($18\frac{3}{4} \times 12\frac{3}{8}$ in. – 476×314 mm)
Mumbles, Lighthouse	1861	($20\frac{3}{8} \times 13\frac{1}{2}$ in. – 518×343 mm)
Mumbles, Storm off the	1881	($17\frac{1}{2} \times 11\frac{3}{4}$ in. – 444×298 mm)
Madeley Manor, Staffs (House and Cattle)	*date uncertain*	
	1843	($13\frac{3}{4} \times 9\frac{7}{8}$ in. – 349×250 mm)
Madeley Manor, Staffs (Sheep and House)	*date uncertain*	
	1843	($13\frac{3}{4} \times 9\frac{7}{8}$ in. – 349×250 mm)
Madeley Manor Staffs (House and Garden)	*date uncertain*	
	1843	($14 \times 9\frac{7}{8}$ in. – 356×250 mm)
Madeley Manor, Staffs (Lake)	1843	($13\frac{7}{8} \times 9$ in. – 352×229 mm)
Madeley Manor, Staffs	1843	($14\frac{1}{4} \times 10$ in. – 362×254 mm)
Madeley Manor, Staffs	1843	($14\frac{1}{4} \times 10$ in. – 362×254 mm)
Madeley Manor, Staffs (Waterfall)	1843	($9\frac{7}{8} \times 13\frac{3}{4}$ in. – 250×349 mm)
Madeley Manor, Staffs	1843	($13\frac{7}{8} \times 9\frac{7}{8}$ in. – 352×250 mm)
Madeley Manor, Staffs	1843	($13\frac{7}{8} \times 9\frac{7}{8}$ in. – 352×250 mm)
Madeley Manor, Staffs (Lake)	1842	($13\frac{3}{4} \times 9\frac{7}{8}$ in. – 349×250 mm)
Madeley Manor, Staffs (Scene from)	1843	($14\frac{1}{4} \times 10$ in. – 362×254 mm)
Malvern (Powick)	1848	($14\frac{1}{4} \times 6\frac{3}{4}$ in. – 362×171 mm)
Middleham Castle	1853	($6\frac{1}{2} \times 10\frac{1}{4}$ in. – 165×260 mm)
Norfolk, St Benets Abbey	*date uncertain*	($10 \times 6\frac{1}{2}$ in. – 254×165 mm)
Oystermouth Castle	1861	($20\frac{1}{2} \times 13\frac{1}{2}$ in. – 521×343 mm)
Oxwich Bay, High Tor	1861	($18\frac{3}{4} \times 12\frac{3}{8}$ in.–476×314 mm)
Offchurch	1852	($9\frac{1}{8} \times 12\frac{5}{8}$ in. – 232×321 mm)
Ryde	*date uncertain*	($10 \times 6\frac{7}{8}$ in. – 254×175 mm)
Reigate Heath	1845	($14\frac{5}{8} \times 7\frac{1}{4}$ in. – 371×184 mm)
Richmond, Yorks	1858	($14 \times 9\frac{7}{8}$ in. – 356×250 mm)
Richmond, Yorks	1853	($18\frac{5}{8} \times 11\frac{7}{8}$ in. – 473×302 mm)
Richmond, Yorks	1853	($18\frac{1}{8} \times 12\frac{1}{2}$ in. – 473×317 mm)
Richmond, Yorks	(*date uncertain*	($18\frac{1}{4} \times 13\frac{3}{8}$ in. – 464×340 mm)
Castle Rising, Norfolk	,, ,,	($19 \times 25\frac{5}{8}$ in. – 483×657 mm)
Swansea Bay	1861	($21\frac{5}{8} \times 7$ in. – 549×178 mm)
Swansea Bay	1861	($21\frac{5}{8} \times 7\frac{1}{4}$ in. – 549×184 mm)
Swanage	1875	($10\frac{3}{4} \times 8\frac{5}{8}$ in. – 273×219 mm)
Sidmouth	1854	($14 \times 9\frac{7}{8}$ in. – 356×250 mm)
Swanage, Studland Church	1875	($10\frac{5}{8} \times 8\frac{1}{2}$ in. – 270×216 mm)
Salcombe	1877	($13\frac{1}{2} \times 9\frac{5}{8}$ in. – 343×244 mm)
Salcombe (near)	1877	($9\frac{1}{2} \times 13\frac{1}{2}$ in. – 241×343 mm)
Sketch	*date uncertain*	($11\frac{7}{8} \times 5\frac{7}{8}$ in. – 302×149 mm)
Southampton, Bargate	,, ,,	($5 \times 6\frac{7}{8}$ in. – 127×175 mm)

Catalogue of William Callow's Sketches Exhibited at Walker's Galleries

Title	*Year*	*Size*
Southend	1864	(10$\frac{1}{2}$ × 3$\frac{1}{2}$ in. – 267 × 89 mm)
South Wraxhall, near Bedford	1851	(8$\frac{7}{8}$ × 5$\frac{1}{2}$ in. – 225 × 140 mm)
Southampton, Near	*date uncertain*	(9$\frac{1}{8}$ × 6$\frac{1}{2}$ in. – 232 × 165 mm)
Shoreham	1873	(15$\frac{1}{2}$ × 7$\frac{1}{8}$ in. – 394 × 181 mm)
Trent, On the	1886	(6$\frac{1}{4}$ × 11$\frac{3}{8}$ in.–159 × 289 mm)
Trent, On the	1886	(8$\frac{3}{4}$ × 10$\frac{1}{4}$ in. – 222 × 260 mm)
Tintern Abbey	1848	(13$\frac{1}{2}$ × 9$\frac{1}{2}$ in. – 343 × 241 mm)
Thames at Bourne	(early)	(8$\frac{3}{4}$ × 6$\frac{3}{8}$ in. – 222 × 162 mm)
Wharfe, On the	1858	(13$\frac{1}{2}$ × 9$\frac{5}{8}$ in. – 343 × 244 mm)
Whitby, Near	1851	(12$\frac{5}{8}$ × 9$\frac{1}{4}$ in. – 321 × 235 mm)
Whitby, Salthrick Bay	1851	(13$\frac{1}{2}$ × 9$\frac{1}{2}$ in. – 343 × 241 mm)
Whitby, from the West	1851	(12$\frac{7}{8}$ × 7 in. – 327 × 178 mm)
Wilton Castle	1848	(13$\frac{1}{2}$ × 7$\frac{3}{8}$ in. – 343 × 187 mm)
Warwick Castle	1852	(12$\frac{7}{8}$ × 9$\frac{3}{8}$ in. – 327 × 238 mm)
Warwick	*date uncertain*	(13$\frac{7}{8}$ × 5 in. – 352 × 127 mm)
Warwick, Beauchamp Chapel	1852	(9$\frac{1}{4}$ × 6$\frac{1}{4}$ in. – 235 × 159 mm)
Wimbledon Common	1851	(19 × 7 in. – 483 × 178 mm)
Wimbledon Common	1851	(19$\frac{1}{4}$ × 9 in. – 489 × 229 mm)
Wimbledon Common	1851	(19 × 7 in. – 483 × 178 mm)
Westminster Cloisters	*date uncertain*	(7$\frac{1}{8}$ × 10$\frac{5}{8}$ in. – 181 × 270 mm)
Wimbledon	,, ,,	(10$\frac{1}{8}$ × 7 in. – 257 × 178 mm)
Worcester Church, Near	,, ,,	(7$\frac{1}{8}$ × 9$\frac{3}{4}$ in. – 181 × 248 mm)
Westminster, Entrance to Henry VII Chapel	,, ,,	(7 × 10$\frac{1}{8}$ in. – 178 × 257 mm)
Windsor	1835	(9$\frac{1}{2}$ × 5$\frac{1}{4}$ in. – 241 × 133 mm)

WALES

Title	Year	Size
Abergavenny	1848	(14$\frac{1}{8}$ × 10 in. – 359 × 254 mm)
Famous Window	*date uncertain*	(5$\frac{1}{4}$ × 7$\frac{5}{8}$ in. – 133 × 194 mm)
Flint	1868	(10 × 7 in. – 254 × 178 mm)
Flint Castle	1868	(10 × 6$\frac{7}{8}$ in. – 254 × 175 mm)

SCOTLAND, IRELAND

Title	Year	Size
Arran	1849	(14 × 7 in. – 356 × 178 mm)
Arran	*date uncertain*	(13$\frac{5}{8}$ × 9$\frac{5}{8}$ in. – 346 × 244 mm)
Assynt Loch	1861	(19 × 12$\frac{3}{8}$ in. – 483 × 314 mm)
Assynt, Near Loch	1861	(20$\frac{1}{2}$ × 13 in. – 521 × 330 mm)
Balgowrie, Bridge of	1857	(13$\frac{5}{8}$ × 9$\frac{5}{8}$ in. – 346 × 244 mm)
Brodick Castle	1849	(14 × 7 in. – 356 × 178 mm)
Brodick Castle	1849	(14 × 10 in. – 356 × 254 mm)
Dunoon	1849	(14 × 7 in. – 356 × 178 mm)
Dalmalley	1849	(14$\frac{1}{8}$ × 8$\frac{3}{4}$ in. – 359 × 222 mm)
Dalmalley	1849	(14$\frac{1}{8}$ × 10$\frac{1}{8}$ in.–359 × 257 mm)
Edinburgh	1842	(20$\frac{1}{2}$ × 14$\frac{1}{4}$ in.–514 × 362 mm)
Ettrick Glen	1878	(9$\frac{1}{2}$ × 5$\frac{1}{4}$ in.–241 × 133 mm)
Fyne, Loch	*date uncertain*	(14 × 7 in.–356 × 178 mm)
Inver Loch	1861	(20$\frac{1}{2}$ × 9 in.–521 × 229 mm)
Inver Loch, Quinag	1861	(18$\frac{3}{4}$ × 10$\frac{1}{8}$ in.–476 × 257 mm)

Title	*Year*	*Size*
Inver Loch	1861	(20½ × 12¾ in. –521 × 324 mm)
Inver Loch, Suelvin	1861	(20½ × 13¼ in.–521 × 337 mm)
Inver Loch, Suelvin	1861	(20½ × 12 in.–521 × 305 mm)
Inveraray Castle	1849	(14 × 7 in.–356 × 178 mm)
Inveraray	1849	(14 × 6⅞ in.–356 × 175 mm)
Inveraray Beech Trees	1849	(14 × 7 in.–356 × 178 mm)
Jedburgh Abbey	1843	(20⅛ × 12⅞ in.–511 × 327 mm)
Kirkaig, Heathery Pool	1861	(18⅞ × 12¼ in.–479 × 311 mm)
Kirkaig, Falls	1861	(13 × 20½ in.–330 × 521 mm)
Melrose	1843	(20 × 12⅞ in.–508 × 327 mm)
Melrose Abbey	1843	(20 × 12⅞ in.–508 × 327 mm)
Glen?	1849	(14 × 7 in.–356 × 178 mm)
Ben Mist?	1849	(14 × 7 in.–356 × 178 mm)
Mapa	1876	(13⅝ × 6½ in.–346 × 165 mm)
Stressa	*date uncertain*	(13⅝ × 5¼ in.–346 × 133 mm)
Ramor Loch, Virginia Cavan	1878	(13⅝ × 8 in.–346 × 203 mm)
Ramor Loch, Virginia Cavan	1878	(13¾ × 8⅞ in.–349 × 235 mm)
Ramor Loch, Virginia Cavan	1878	(13⅝ × 6⅝ in.–346 × 168 mm)
Ramor Loch, Dunancry River	1878	(9⅝ × 10⅝ in.–244 × 270 mm)
(The Lodge, Marquis of Headfort's Seat)	*date uncertain*	

FRANCE

Title	*Year*	*Size*
Aix	1836	(8⅞ × 5¼ in.–225 × 133 mm)
Angoulême	1836	(8⅞ × 5⅜ in.–225 × 137 mm)
Angoulême	1836	(10¾ × 9 in.–273 × 229 mm)
Avignon	1836	(10⅝ × 6⅛ in.–270 × 156 mm)
Château Eronne	1833	(7¾ × 9⅜ in.–197 × 238 mm)
Bonneval	1836	(9 × 5⅛ in.–229 × 130 mm)
Beaugency, Loire	1836	(9 × 5⅜ in.–229 × 137 mm)
Blois, Loire	1836	(10¾ × 4¾ in.–273 × 121 mm)
Blois, Loire	1836	(13 × 5 in.–330 × 127 mm)
Bordeaux, Palais Gallière	*date incertain*	(6⅞ × 4⅞ in.–175 × 124 mm)
Bordeaux on the Garonne	,, ,,	(9⅛ × 6⅞ in.–232 × 175 mm)
Chartres, Port Guillaume	,, ,,	(6¾ × 4⅞ in.–171 × 124 mm)
Seine, On the	,, ,,	(9½ × 5⅛ in.–241 × 130 mm)
Seine, On the	,, ,,	(9½ × 7 in.–241 × 178 mm)
Seine, Charenton	(early)	(9⅛ × 6¾ in.–232 × 171 mm)
Seine, Paris	*date uncertain*	(9¼ × 4⅞ in.–235 × 124 mm)
Seine, Mont Valériên	1834	(9⅜ × 4⅜ in.–238 × 111 mm)
Seine, Bercy	1834	(9½ × 6 in.–241 × 152 mm)
Seine, à Bercy	*date uncertain*	(9⅛ × 5¾ in.–232 × 146 mm)
Seine, St Ouen	1834	(9¼ × 5½ in.–235 × 140 mm)
Seine, St Ouen	1834	(9⅝ × 5⅛ in.–247 × 130 mm)
Seine, St Ouen	1831	(9⅛ × 6⅛ in.–232 × 156 mm)
Seine, near Montmartre	1832	(9⅜ × 6½ in.–238 × 165 mm)
Loire, Watermill	*date uncertain*	(13⅝ × 9⅝ in.–346 × 247 mm)
Lyon, Saône	1836	(10¾ × 4⅝ in.–273 × 117 mm)
Marseilles, Port	1836	(10⅜ × 8¾ in.–264 × 222 mm)
Marseilles, Port Entrance	1836	(10½ × 7 in.–267 × 178 mm)

Catalogue of William Callow's Sketches Exhibited at Walker's Galleries

Title	*Year*	*Size*
Marseilles	1836	(8⅞ × 5⅛ in.–225 × 130 mm)
Marseilles	1836	(9⅛ × 5¼ in.–232 × 133 mm)
Martigny (Switz.)	1838	(10 × 7 in.–254 × 178 mm)
	1836	(9 × 5¼ in.–229 × 133 mm)
Mont Dragon and Château	1836	(8⅞ × 5⅛ in.–225 × 130 mm)
Mont Richard and Château	1836	(10⅝ × 9 in.–270 × 229 mm)
Montpellier	1836	(8⅞ × 5 in.–225 × 127 mm)
Mont Richard	1836	(6⅞ × 5¾ in.–175 × 146 mm)
Orléans	1836	(8⅞ × 5 in.–225 × 127 mm)
Paris, from the Champs Elysées	1836	(13½ × 8¼ in.–343 × 210 mm)
Paris, Rainy Weather	(early)	(9⅛ × 7 in.–232 × 178 mm)
Paris, Notre Dame	1835	(9⅝ × 6⅝ in.–247 × 168 mm)
Poitiers	1836	(10½ × 6⅞ in.–267 × 175 mm)
Pyrénées, Entrance	1836	(9¼ × 5½ in.–235 × 140 mm)
Pyrénées, Château de Lourdes	1836	(8⅞ × 5 in.–225 × 127 mm)
Pyrénées, Hautes	1836	(10¾ × 9 in.–273 × 229 mm)
Pyrénées, Château Vidalos	*date uncertain*	(10⅜ × 7⅜ in.–264 × 187 mm)
Paris, Père Lachaise	,, ,,	(9½ × 6¾ in.–241 × 171 mm)
Paris, Père Lachaise	,, ,,	(9¼ × 5⅞ in.–235 × 149 mm)
Paris, St Cloud	1839	(6¾ × 10 in.–171 × 254 mm)
Rouen	*date uncertain*	(7 × 9⅛ in.–178 × 232 mm)
Royaumont, Le Parc	,, ,,	(9¼ × 5⅜ in.–235 × 137 mm)
Saumur	1836	(10½ × 7¼ in.–267 × 184 mm)
Saumur	1836	(9 × 5¾ in.–229 × 146 mm)
St Marie Port (Garonne)	1836	(8⅞ × 4⅝ in.–225 × 117 mm)
St Valéry les Caux	1841	(14⅜ × 10 in.–365 × 254 mm)
San Remo	1877	(9¾ × 6⅝ in.–248 × 168 mm)
Seine Watermill	*date uncertain*	(13⅝ × 7¼ in.–346 × 184 mm)
Seine at St Cloud	,, ,,	(9¼ × 3¾ in.–235 × 95 mm)
Seine, Mont Vacours	1834	(9¼ × 3¾ in.–235 × 95 mm)
Seine, Mont Valent	1834	(9¼ × 4⅛ in.–235 × 105 mm)
Seine, in Caudebec	*date uncertain*	(13 × 4⅝ in.–330 × 117 mm)
Seine, from St Germain	1833	(12½ × 4¾ in.–317 × 121 mm)
Toulon	1836	(9 × 5¼ in.–229 × 133 mm)
Toulon	1836	(10½ × 7¼ in.–267 × 184 mm)
Toulon	1836	(8⅞ × 5⅛ in.–225 × 130 mm)
Toulon	1836	(9 × 5¼ in.–229 × 133 mm)
Toulouse	1836	(8⅞ × 5½ in.–225 × 140 mm)
Toulouse	1836	(9⅛ × 4⅞ in.–232 × 124 mm)
Tournon	*date uncertain*	(10⅜ × 7 in.–264 × 178 mm)
Tournon, et Tain	1836	(10⅝ × 4⅝ in.–270 × 117 mm)
Paris, from Charenton	1834	(12¾ × 4½ in.–324 × 114 mm)
Paris	(early)	(8⅛ × 4⅞ in.–206 × 124 mm)
Paris, Versailles	*date uncertain*	(9⅛ × 3¼ in.–232 × 83 mm)
Paris, Hôtel de Sens	,, ,,	(6⅞ × 4⅞ in.–149 × 124 mm)
Paris, Versailles	,, ,,	(8¾ × 4¾ in.–222 × 121 mm)
Paris, Versailles	,, ,,	(8⅞ × 5¾ in.–225 × 146 mm)
Paris, Versailles	1832	(7⅞ × 5 in.–200 × 127 mm)
Paris, Marly, from St Germain	1833	(8⅜ × 4¾ in.–213 × 121 mm)

ITALY

Rome

Title	*Year*	*Size*
Campagna di Roma, Porta Giovanni	1840	(14⅛ × 10 in.–359 × 254 mm)
The Forum, Arc de Constantine	1840	(14⅛ × 10 in.–359 × 254 mm)
Ponte Cartro, Tiber	1840	(14⅛ × 10 in.–359 × 254 mm)
Temple of Venus	1840	(14⅛ × 10 in.–359 × 254 mm)
Château d'Ange	1840	(14⅛ × 10 in.–359 × 254 mm)
On the Tiber	1841	(14¼ × 10 in.–362 × 254 mm)
Temple of Mars	1876	(9¾ × 13¾ in.–248 × 349 mm)
Portico of Octavia	1876	(13¾ × 9⅝ in.–349 × 247 mm)
Temple of Minerva	1876	(13¾ × 6½ in.–349 × 165 mm)
Pont St Bartolomeo	1876	(13¾ × 6½ in.–349 × 165 mm)
Goldsmith Arch	1876	(9⅝ × 13¾ in.–247 × 349 mm)
Ponte Molle	1879	(13½ × 9⅝ in.–343 × 247 mm)

Naples

The Chiesa	1876	(13¾ × 6½ in.–349 × 165 mm)
Bay of Naples	1840	(14 × 9¾ in.–356 × 248 mm)
Castel Nuovo	1840	(14 × 10 in.–356 × 254 mm)
Piazza Falcone	1840	(14 × 9¾ in.–356 × 248 mm)
Distant View from Castlemare	1840	(14 × 9¾ in.–356 × 248 mm)
Vico, Bay of Naples	1840	(14 × 9¾ in.–356 × 248 mm)
Vico, Bay of Naples	1840	(14 × 9¾ in.–356 × 248 mm)
Castellamare	1876	(13¾ × 6½ in.–349 × 165 mm)
Vesuvius	*date uncertain*	(9¾ × 6¾ in.–248 × 171 mm)
Avato, Arc de Triomph	1838	(10 × 13¾ in.–254 × 349 mm)
Arona, Lago Maggiore	1840	(14 × 9½ in.–356 × 241 mm)
Albano, Castel Gandolfo	1879	(13⅝ × 6⅜ in.–346 × 162 mm)
Florence, Ponte Vecchio	1876	(13¾ × 6½ in.–349 × 165 mm)
Terni, Cascade	1840	(10 × 14¼ in.–254 × 362 mm)
Gaeta, Moladi	1840	(14 × 9¾ in.–356 × 248 mm)
Marino	1840	(14 × 9¾ in.–356 × 248 mm)
Menaggio	1905	(13½ × 9½ in.–343 × 241 mm)
Metu, from Sorrento	1876	(13⅛ × 6½ in.–333 × 165 mm)
Sorrento	1876	(13⅝ × 6½ in.–346 × 165 mm)
Sorrento, Marino	1876	(13¾ × 9⅝ in.–349 × 244 mm)
Sorrento	1876	(13¾ × 9¾ in.–349 × 248 mm)
Salerno	1879	(13½ × 6⅜ in.–343 × 162 mm)
Salerno, Vitri	1879	(13½ × 6⅜ in.–343 × 162 mm)
Spoleto	1840	(14⅛ × 10 in.–359 × 254 mm)
San Remo	1877	(9½ × 6⅝ in.–241 × 168 mm)
Tivoli, Château d'Este	1840	(14¼ × 10 in.–362 × 254 mm)
Tivoli, Temple of Vesta	1840	(14¼ × 10 in.–362 × 254 mm)
Tivoli, la Grotte de Sybilles	1840	(9¾ × 13¾ in.–248 × 349 mm)
Verona	1840	(14¼ × 10 in.–362 × 254 mm)
Venice	1846	(10¼ × 14⅛ in.–260 × 359 mm)
Castel Gandolfo	1840	(14¼ × 9¾ in.–362 × 248 mm)
Castel Gandolfo	1840	(14¼ × 9¾ in.–362 × 248 mm)

GERMANY

Title	*Year*	*Size*
Cochem Moselle	1844	(20×13 in.–508×330 mm)
Alberga	1877	($6\frac{5}{8} \times 9\frac{5}{8}$ in.–168×244 mm)
Berncastel	1844	($20 \times 13\frac{1}{2}$ in.–508×343 mm)
Bingen, Rhine	1838	($11 \times 8\frac{1}{4}$ in.–279×210 mm)
Bingen, Rhine	1838	($11 \times 7\frac{7}{8}$ in.–279×200 mm)
Baden-Baden	1838	($13\frac{3}{4} \times 9\frac{3}{4}$ in.–349×248 mm)
Baden-Baden	1838	($9\frac{3}{4} \times 13\frac{3}{4}$ in.–248×349 mm)
Baden-Baden, Vieux Château	1838	($13\frac{3}{4} \times 9\frac{3}{4}$ in.–349×248 mm)
Baden-Baden	1838	($13\frac{3}{4} \times 9\frac{3}{4}$ in.–349×248 mm)
Coblenz	1838	($10\frac{7}{8} \times 8\frac{1}{4}$ in.–276×210 mm)
Drachenfels	1838	($13\frac{3}{4} \times 9\frac{3}{4}$ in.–349×248 mm)
Elz Schloss	1844	($20 \times 13\frac{1}{4}$ in.–508×337 mm)
Heimbach, Rhina	1838	($13\frac{3}{4} \times 9\frac{3}{4}$ in.–349×248 mm)
Heidelberg	1838	($13\frac{3}{4} \times 9\frac{3}{4}$ in.–349×248 mm)
Heidelberg	1838	($13\frac{3}{4} \times 9\frac{3}{4}$ in.–349×248 mm)
Holzenfels	1838	($13\frac{3}{4} \times 9\frac{3}{4}$ in.–349×248 mm)
Heidelberg	1874	($13\frac{1}{2} \times 9\frac{1}{2}$ in.–343×241 mm)
Ischel	*date uncertain*	($13\frac{5}{8} \times 9\frac{1}{2}$ in.–346×241 mm)
Limburg	1871	($13\frac{1}{2} \times 9\frac{1}{2}$ in.–343×241 mm)
Marburg	1838	($13\frac{3}{4} \times 9\frac{3}{4}$ in.–349×248 mm)
Marburg	1838	($13\frac{3}{4} \times 9\frac{3}{4}$ in.–349×248 mm)
Marburg, Cassel	1871	($13\frac{1}{2} \times 6\frac{3}{8}$ in.–343×162 mm)
Marienburg and Moselle	1844	($19\frac{3}{4} \times 12\frac{3}{4}$ in.–502×324 mm)
Runkel	1871	($13\frac{1}{2} \times 9\frac{1}{2}$ in.–343×241 mm)
Runkel	1871	($13\frac{1}{2} \times 9\frac{3}{4}$ in.–343×248 mm)
Reichenbach	1838	($10 \times 14\frac{1}{4}$ in.–254×362 mm)
Rhine, Ehrenfels	1838	($10\frac{3}{4} \times 8\frac{1}{2}$ in.–273×216 mm)
Rhine, St Goar	1838	($10\frac{7}{8} \times 8\frac{1}{4}$ in.–276×210 mm)
Rhine, Chute Schaffhausen	1838	(14×10 in.–356×254 mm)
Rhine, Schaffhausen	1838	($14 \times 9\frac{3}{4}$ in.–356×248 mm)
Rhine, Louèche (Switz.)	1838	($10\frac{3}{4} \times 8\frac{1}{2}$ in.–273×216 mm)
Salzburg	1874	($13\frac{1}{2} \times 9\frac{1}{4}$ in.–343×235 mm)
Salzburg	1874	($13\frac{1}{2} \times 9\frac{1}{4}$ in.–343×235 mm)
Salzburg	1874	($13\frac{1}{2} \times 9\frac{1}{4}$ in.–343×235 mm)
Schaffhausen	1838	($14 \times 9\frac{1}{2}$ in.–356×241 mm)
Weilburg, Schloss	1871	($13\frac{1}{2} \times 9\frac{5}{8}$ in.–343×244 mm)
Wallenstadt, Wesen	*date uncertain*	($14 \times 9\frac{3}{4}$ in.–356×248 mm)
Würtzburg	1874	($13\frac{1}{2} \times 9\frac{1}{2}$ in.–343×241 mm)

VARIOUS CONTINENTAL LOCATIONS

Danube, Castle Steffelberg	1874	($13\frac{1}{2} \times 9\frac{1}{2}$ in.–343×241 mm)
Huy	1844	(14×10 in.–356×254 mm)
Palais de France, Bruges	1844	($20\frac{1}{2} \times 14\frac{1}{4}$ in.–521×362 mm)
Breuner	1838	($10 \times 6\frac{7}{8}$ in.–254×175 mm)
Val d'Aosta	1838	($10 \times 6\frac{5}{8}$ in.–254×168 mm)
Glacier du Bois, Chamouni	1838	(14×10 in.–356×254 mm)
Andermatt	1838	(14×10 in.–356×254 mm)

Catalogue of William Callow's Sketches Exhibited at Walker's Galleries

Title	*Year*	*Size*
Nant Borrant	1838	(14 × 10 in.–356 × 254 mm)
Distant Alps	*date uncertain*	(14 × 10 in.–356 × 254 mm)
St Michel	1865	(13⅜ × 9½ in–340 × 241 mm)
Switzerland, Val	1838	(14 × 10 in.–356 × 254 mm)
Thun	1838	(14 × 10 in.–356 × 254 mm)
Glacier	1838	(14 × 10 in.–356 × 254 mm)
Col de la Seigne	1838	(14 × 10 in.–356 × 254 mm)
Bay, from Breuner	1838	(14 × 9⅞ in.–356 × 251 mm)
Sèvres	1838	(14 × 10 in.–356 × 254 mm)
Lac de Lucerne	1838	(14 × 10 in.–356 × 254 mm)
Spenbbach, Switz.	1838	(14 × 10 in.–356 × 254 mm)
Grimsel Pass	1838	(14 × 10 in.–356 × 254 mm)
Lac de Genève	1838	(14 × 10 in.–356 × 254 mm)
Geneva	1840	(14 × 10 in.–356 × 254 mm)
Basle	1846	(14 × 10 in.–356 × 254 mm)
Château Val d'Aosta	1838	(10 × 7 in.–254 × 178 mm)
Mont Blanc	*date uncertain*	
Flüelen Platz	1838	(10 × 7 in.–254 × 178 mm)
Kant Gutenfels Platz	1838	(11 × 8¾ in.–279 × 222 mm)
Sans Souci	1874	(6⅝ × 9⅝ in.–168 × 244 mm)
Potsdam	1874	(9⅝ × 6¼ in.–244 × 159 mm)
Bruges	*date uncertain*	(6⅞ × 5 in.–175 × 127 mm)
Rouen	1836	(9⅞ × 6¾ in.–251 × 171 mm)
Rouen, Distant View	1836	(9⅞ × 6½ in.–251 × 165 mm)
Rouen, Cathedral	*date uncertain*	(6⅞ × 9¾ in.–175 × 248 mm)
The Luxor, France	1833	(9⅛ × 12⅝ in.–232 × 321 mm)
Bruges	*date uncertain*	(12 × 8⅛ in.–305 × 206 mm)

Walker's Galleries added a footnote, pointing out that some of these exhibits had already been sold to public and private collections. The general catalogue of work indicates the whereabouts of many of the former acquisitions

Selected Bibliography

BOOKS

Clifford, D., *Collecting English Water-colours*, John Baker Ltd, Revised edition 1976

Cundall, H. M., *William Callow, R.W.S., F.R.G.S.* A. and C. Black, 1908

Dubuisson A. and Hughes, C. E., *Richard Parkes Bonington*, John Lane, The Bodley Head, 1924

Hardie, Martin, *Water-colour Painting in Britain* (*The Victorian Period*), Batsford, 1968

Huish, Marcus B., *British Water-colour Art*, A. and C. Black, 1904

Maas, J., *Victorian Painters*, Barrie and Jenkins, 1969

Mallalieu, H. L., *Dictionary of British Water-colour Artists up to 1920*, Antique Collectors' Club, Woodbridge, 1976

Reynolds, Graham, *A Concise History of Water-colours*, Thames and Hudson, 1971

Roget, J. L., *A History of the Old Water-colour Society*, Longman, 1891

Roundell, James, *Thomas Shotter Boys*, Octopus Books, 1974

Sir Leslie Stephen and Sir Sidney Lee (Editors), *Dictionary of National Biography* (*Second Supplement, Volume I*), Smith and Elder, 1908–9

Thieme and Becker, *Allgemeines Künsterlexikon*, Seemann, Leipzig, 1968

Thomas, Denis and Bennett, Ian, *Price Guide to English Water-colours*, Antique Collectors' Club, Woodbridge, 1971

Wood, C., *Dictionary of Victorian Painters*, Antique Collectors' Club, Woodbridge, Revised edition 1978

JOURNALS

The Art Journal, published by J. F. Vertue and Co. Ltd, London

Athenaeum, published by John Francis Ltd, London

Index

Index

Numerals in *italics* refer to the illustration numbers

Note. The Catalogue sections are not indexed